WITHDRAWN

THE

TERRITORY OF FLORIDA:

OR

SKETCHES OF THE TOPOGRAPHY,

CIVIL AND NATURAL HISTORY,

OF

THE COUNTRY, THE CLIMATE, AND THE INDIAN TRIBES,

FROM

THE FIRST DISCOVERY TO THE PRESENT TIME,

WITH A MAP, VIEWS, &C.

———————

BY JOHN LEE WILLIAMS.

———————

THE

TERRITORY OF FLORIDA:

OR

SKETCHES OF THE TOPOGRAPHY,

CIVIL AND NATURAL HISTORY,

OF

THE COUNTRY, THE CLIMATE, AND THE INDIAN TRIBES,

FROM

THE FIRST DISCOVERY TO THE PRESENT TIME,

BY JOHN LEE WILLIAMS.

A FACSIMILE REPRODUCTION
of the 1837 EDITION
with
INTRODUCTION
by HERBERT J. DOHERTY, JR.

FLORIDIANA FACSIMILE & REPRINT SERIES

GAINESVILLE, 1962
University of Florida Press

1962 FACSIMILE REPRODUCTION OF THE 1837 EDITION
WITH PREFACE, INTRODUCTION, AND NOTES ADDED.

Library of Congress Catalogue Card No. 62-14789

LITHOPRINTED BY DOUGLAS PRINTING COMPANY, INC.
BOUND BY UNIVERSAL-DIXIE BINDERY, INC.
JACKSONVILLE, FLORIDA

EDITORIAL PREFACE.

THE SECOND VOLUME in the University of Florida Press Floridiana Series was written by a man who "employed every interval of leisure, and every opportunity, that business or accident has presented, to collect such facts, as would enable me to point out its [Florida's] geographical peculiarities, its native productions and its civil and natural history." John Lee Williams was a colorful personality and his *Territory of Florida* was for almost thirty-five years the only history of Florida in print. It was published sixteen years after the United States had acquired the colony of Florida from Spain in 1821, and during these years of American ownership Williams was a witness to many federal acts in Florida: the creation of the territorial government, the beginnings of a democratic form of rule, the institution of civil liberties, the clearing of titles to land, the sale of land to settlers at reasonable prices, and the development of internal improvements. The United States had not solved the Indian problem, and in 1837 was at war with the Seminoles in the attempt to move these Indians to the Trans-Mississippi region and free Florida from what the white farmers considered the "Indian scourge."

Williams began his account with the discovery of Florida and traced its history to the summer of 1837. As Professor Doherty has stated in his introduction, *The Territory of Florida* is replete with errors of fact, but the volume does have enduring merit because it is also filled with the observations of a perceptive, intelligent man.

Herbert J. Doherty, Jr., is associate professor of social science and history at the University of Florida and editor of the *Florida Historical Quarterly*. He has written articles on Florida for historical journals, and his knowledge of the development of Florida in the American period is

v

further attested by his books: *The Whigs of Florida, 1845-1854* (Gaines-ville: University of Florida Press, 1959) and *Richard Keith Call: South-ern Unionist* (Gainesville: University of Florida Press, 1961).

The support given this reprint series by the Graduate School of the University of Florida, and the interest of Linton E. Grinter, Dean of the Graduate School, made it possible to index the book.

REMBERT W. PATRICK

University of Florida
March, 1962

General Editor of the
Floridiana Series

INTRODUCTION.

THE *Territory of Florida* by John Lee Williams is not to be read as a literal historical account. Rather, it is itself a piece of history—a document out of our past which sheds light on some aspects of that past. It is a source work. It is of interest to those who find enlightenment in the observations of an intelligent American—a man whose training was largely legal, whose interests were directed toward outdoor activities, but who loved books and writing. This book shows us how such a man—a product of the eighteenth and nineteenth centuries—approached the task of describing to his contemporaries a new territory of the American Union.

This book is more a gazetteer than a history, but insofar as it attempts to be a history it reflects the limitations on the amateur writer of history in early America. Though contemporary writers and newspapermen referred to *The Territory of Florida* as *the* history of Florida, and though it stood as the only generally available history of early Florida for almost thirty-five years, Williams did not have access to as much material on Florida when he wrote the book as the average American today can find in a good-sized public library.[1] Indeed, insofar as Williams drew from the works of William Darby, James G. Forbes, Charles Vignoles, William H. Simmons, Bernard Romans, John and William Bartram, and William Roberts, he was relying on accounts which contained precious little reliable historical information.[2] Far more useful as historical sources were the still unidentified "ancient manuscript in the Spanish language" to which he makes reference, and the work of Garcilaso de la Vega.[3]

Consequently, though Williams' book presented the best account of Florida history that had been done to his time, the greater amount of material available to historians today has shown Williams' history to be inadequate, and in many particulars incorrect. Every Floridian will immediately spot the erroneous date of Ponce de León's first voyage to Florida, but it should be remembered that Williams was merely perpetuating an old error found in many works until the end of the nineteenth century. Though the long and rather illuminating treatments of the De Soto expedition and of the "Patriot" uprisings after 1812 rise above the level of much of the rest of the "history" in this volume, the average reader is advised to use the historical portions of the book with cautious skepticism. The lasting value of this pioneer work lies in its descriptions of territorial Florida and in the insights it gives us into the conditions under which life was lived in ante-bellum Florida. In other words, its greatest value lies in the personal observations of Williams about Florida and his experiences in the territory.

Two types of research went into *The Territory of Florida.* In addition to his use of printed and manuscript sources, Williams spent several years of his life in physical explorations of the geography and natural endowments of Florida. The volume was preceded in 1827 by Williams' *A View of West Florida,* which grew from his explorations of Middle Florida (the district between the Apalachicola and Suwannee rivers) in connection with the location of a new seat of government for Florida.[4] He had promised in this first volume that if it were well received he would do a similar one on East Florida. The success of the early work spurred him on to complete the second volume. For ten years he laboriously collected his information. In his own words: "I have traversed the country in various directions and have coasted the whole shore of the Peninsula, from Pensacola to St. Marys, examining, with minute attention, the various clusters of Keys or Islets, that are grouped on the margin of the coast. I have ascended many of the rivers, explored the lagoons and bays, traced the ancient improvements, scattered ruins and its natural productions, by land and by water."[5] When completed, however, his second book was not limited to East Florida but embraced the entire territory and corrected some errors made in the earlier book. A scholar of Williams' own day, the anthropologist Daniel G. Brinton, observed that this book was "the fruit of years of laborious investigation, of absorbing devotion to one object, often of keen mental and bodily suffering, and will ever remain a witness to the energy and zeal of its writer."[6]

As one might expect, Williams was not a native of Florida. He was born in Salem, Massachusetts, in 1775 but moved with his parents to New York State in his early years. There his parents engaged in farming but, as is not uncommonly the case, the son soon discovered that he had no desire to continue in the parents' way of life. Wanting a better education than his father was able to provide for him, Williams left home after a stormy break with his family. He entered Hamilton-Oneida Academy at Clinton, New York, where he paid his way by tutoring younger students. He was graduated with honor and then studied law, still supporting himself by tutoring until he was able to win admission to the bar. He moved from New York to Virginia and is reported to have engaged in large-scale business speculations (probably in land) "in the West" until his health became impaired.[7]

It was a search for a healthier clime that brought him to Spanish Florida in 1820.[8] It was, however, a Spanish Florida which was in the throes of transfer to the United States. When that transfer was completed in the summer of 1821, Williams, then residing at Pensacola, found himself one of the "old" American inhabitants. In the newly acquired community he became a leading member of the bar and was labeled one of the two trustworthy lawyers in Pensacola by Judge Henry M. Brackenridge.[9] By 1823 he was a justice of the peace in Pensacola and was identified with the political faction that centered around Joseph M. White and Judge Brackenridge. In that year an unofficial poll of Escambia County residents was held to recommend to the President of the United States a candidate from the region for appointment to the territorial Legislative Council. In the canvass, Williams received 154 votes—more than any other one of the nine men who received support.[10] The President, however, declined to be guided by the poll.

In 1823 Williams was also appointed, with Dr. William H. Simmons of St. Augustine, to locate the site of a new seat of government for Florida. The practice of alternating Legislative Council meetings between Pensacola and St. Augustine—in effect having two capitals—had proved to be too inconvenient to continue. Acting under legislative mandate, Governor William P. DuVal therefore had appointed the two commissioners to inspect the area between the Ochlockonee and Suwannee rivers and to choose there a capital site midway between the extremities of the populated parts of Florida. Williams sailed from Pensacola in fulfillment of this appointment on September 30, 1823, and after a difficult journey of near-epic proportions he reached St. Marks on October 24.[11] With Dr. Simmons he explored the area between the Ochlockonee and St. Marks rivers. After an abortive attempt to probe the Suwannee River region, Williams and Simmons agreed on the Tallahassee area north of St. Marks for the new capital.[12]

In this difficult expedition, Williams had frequently found himself handicapped by the deficiency of maps and general information about Florida. Some geographical confusion in the journals of his expedition testifies to this deficiency. This lack of information seems to have provided his first impulse to write about Florida. Williams was not too discouraged by the unknown nature of the terrain he traversed, for he was a hardy man who was quite at home in the woods. At this time he was described as "tall and thin, though strong and muscular from out-of-door exercise; his face, framed by the long hair that fell to his shoulders, showed strength of will; his eyes were keen and piercing." By his own account, the illness that had brought him to Florida had been overcome within six months of his arrival.[13]

Though he had been endorsed for appointment as a member of the Legislative Council and later for appointment as a district attorney, Williams was not much drawn to politics. He was for years a justice of the peace, but he seems to have held no other public office except the post of alderman in Pensacola in 1825.[14] One of the few recorded political controversies in which he became embroiled occurred in Pensacola during 1823 and 1824. William F. Steele, the contentious and apparently incompetent district attorney of West Florida, became involved in disputes with the White-Brackenridge faction. Williams testified against Steele and otherwise supported those seeking to remove the district attorney from his job. In retaliation, Williams suffered prosecution by Steele on charges of perjury and assault. The controversy finally was brought to a conclusion with the removal of Steele by President James Monroe.[15]

By the late 1820's Williams had moved his field of operations to Middle Florida, though whether or not he actually moved his residence there is not clear. At least he was practicing law in the courts of Middle Florida by 1828.[16] By 1830 Williams had moved to the east coast and established himself in St. Augustine.[17] There he practiced law, dabbled in business, was an adherent of the Presbyterian Church, and apparently continued his association with the political friends of Joseph M. White. In 1831 he acted as a director of the "Planters and Citizens Company," formed to build a canal joining the Matanzas and Halifax rivers. In 1833 Governor DuVal made him a justice of the peace for St. Johns County.[18]

There is no evidence that Williams saw active service in the second Seminole War (1835-1842). His age alone would have been an argument against presuming that he did. Indeed, legend has it that he moved in peace among the Indians during that struggle. Yet documents show that in 1832 he was assistant adjutant general of the Second Brigade of Florida Militia, commanded by Joseph M. Hernandez.[19]

By the middle of 1834 Williams had decided upon another move, this time to the St. Johns River village of Picolata. About twenty miles west of St. Augustine, and connected with that city by a stage line, Picolata was astride what was at that time a rather important route tying St. Augustine to the outside world. The mails, and a considerable amount of commercial traffic, came from the North to Jacksonville, thence by river steamer to Picolata, and then overland by stage to the ancient city. About a mile north of the steamboat landing at this river village, Williams made his final home on the banks of the majestic stream.[20] There he lived "not in a splendid villa, surrounded with the appliances of luxury and wealth—but in an humble retreat, with the Florida pine-barren for his lawns, and the wild blossoms of nature for his parterre."[21]

Governor John H. Eaton in 1835 renewed Williams' appointment as a justice of the peace—an appointment that was again renewed in 1837 by Governor Richard K. Call—but his main preoccupation was now the completion of his painfully compiled work, *The Territory of Florida*.[22] It was published in 1837 in New York by A. T. Goodrich. Only a thousand copies of the first edition were printed and they rapidly sold out.[23] The great popularity of the work undoubtedly stemmed from the high degree of curiosity about Florida which resulted from the raging second Seminole War. Even among the army officers in Florida the book was sought as a source of information. Samuel Forry of Berlin, Pennsylvania, an army surgeon who had seen the book advertised in the New York newspapers, wrote a fellow officer requesting a copy of it if it should be on sale at his friend's post. Of Williams, Forry wrote, "Capt.

Galt represents him as a man of good intentions, mediocre talents, but an intimate knowledge of the country—he is a brokendown gentleman, residing at Picolata. . . ."[24] Despite the widespread popularity of his book, Williams calculated in 1854 that his profit from it amounted to only about $200.

One of the most trenchant criticisms of Williams' *Territory of Florida* ever written was that by Daniel G. Brinton in 1859. Brinton wrote that the book was "a mere compilation, collected without criticism, and arranged without judgment; an entire ignorance of other languages, and the paucity of materials in our own, incapacitated Williams from achieving anything more. Nor can he claim to be much of a naturalist, for the frequent typographical errors in the botanical names proclaim him largely debtor to others in this department. His style is eminently dry and difficult to labor through. . . . Yet with all its faults—and they are neither few nor slight—this is the most complete work ever published concerning the territory of Florida. . . ."[26]

In Picolata, Williams settled into a quiet country life after the publication of this book. He was visited occasionally by friends, wandering literary figures, and travelers. Probably his correspondence and writing occupied most of his time. He was reportedly revising his "History," as the *Territory* was called, and he perhaps corresponded with such acquaintances as Washington Irving, Samuel Goodrich ("Peter Parley"), and John James Audubon. He allegedly had traveled through parts of Florida with Audubon, assisting him by virtue of his knowledge of the country and conditions.[27] In his later years Williams was less and less active. In 1838 and 1839 he loaned his name to the antistatehood movement which sought to separate East from West Florida, but he seems to have given no other support to the cause. He turned his Picolata residence into a garden spot; when he was not gardening or writing, the dulcet notes of his flute could be heard through the pine barrens.[28] In 1851 he appeared briefly in the public prints to defend the Picolata postmaster against charges of tampering with the mails.[29] In 1854 he made a rare visit to Jacksonville, which evoked a lyrical sketch of him by the Jacksonville *Florida Republican*. He was described as possessing "that benignity of countenance which, when naturally belonging to youth, becomes more striking and winning in age." His spartan mode of life was noted and the editor discreetly wondered if there might not be as well "a scantiness in his literary materials." Brusquely, he suggested that publishers who deluged newspapers with books might easily divert some of them to Williams.[30]

In 1856 the Historical Society of Florida, a forerunner of the present Florida Historical Society, was organized at St. Augustine. It was only natural that John Lee Williams should be a charter member, although this was the last year of his life.[31] In his little house by the side of the great river Williams died suddenly on the seventh day of November, 1856.[32] Two days later Daniel G. Brinton arrived to visit him. Brinton's words speak eloquently of Williams' last days:

It had long been my desire to visit and converse with him about the early days of the state, and with this object, on the 9th of November, 1856, I stopped at the little town of Picolati [sic], near which he lived. A sad surprise awaited me; he had died on the 7th of the month and had been buried the day before my arrival. I walked through the woods to his house. It was a rotten, ruinous, frame tenement on the banks of the St. Johns, about half a mile below the town, fronted by a row of noble live oaks and surrounded by the forest. Here the old man—he was over eighty at the time of his death—had lived for twenty years almost entirely alone, and much of the time in abject poverty. A trader happened to be with him during his last illness, who told me some incidents of his history. His mind retained its vigor to the last, and within a week of his death he was actively employed in various literary avocations, among which was the preparation of an improved edition of his History, which he had very nearly completed. At the very moment the paralytic stroke, from which he died, seized him, he had the pen in his hand writing a novel, the scene of which was laid in China! His disposition was uncommonly amiable and engaging, and so much was he beloved by the Indians, that throughout the horrible atrocities of the Seminole war, when all the planters had fled or been butchered, when neither sex nor age was a protection, when Picolati was burned and St. Augustine threatened, he continued to live unharmed in his old house, though a companion was shot dead on the threshold. What the savage respected and loved, the civilized man thought weakness and despised; this very goodness of heart made him the object of innumerable petty impositions from the low whites, his neighbors. In the words of my informant, "he was too good for the people of these parts." During his lonely old age he solaced himself with botany and horticulture, priding himself on keeping the best garden in the vicinity. "Come, and I will show you his grave," said the trader, and added with a touch of feeling I hardly expected, "he left no directions about it, so I made it in the spot he used to love the best of all." He took me to the south-eastern corner of the neat garden plot. A heap of fresh earth with rough, round, pine sticks at head and foot, marked the spot. It was a solemn and impressive moment. The lengthening shadows of the forest crept over us, the wind moaned in the pines and whistled drearily through the sere grass, and the ripples of the river broke monotonously on the shore. All trace of the grave will soon be obliterated, the very spot forgotten, and the garden lie a waste, but the results of his long and toilsome life "in books recorded" will live when the marbles and monumental brasses of many of his cotemporaries shall be no more.[33]

Here, then, is the major contribution of John Lee Williams to Floridiana.

HERBERT J. DOHERTY, JR.

NOTES

1. A full-scale history of Florida did not appear until George R. Fairbanks, *History of Florida from Its Discovery by Ponce de Leon in 1512 to the Close of the Florida War in 1842* (Philadelphia: J. B. Lippincott; Jacksonville: Columbus Drew. 1871).

2. Darby, *Memoir on the Geography and Natural and Civil History of Florida* . . . (Philadelphia: T. H. Palmer, 1821); Forbes, *Sketches, Historical and Topographical, of the Floridas* . . . (New York: C. S. Van Winkle, 1821); Vignoles, *The History of the Floridas* . . . (Brooklyn: G. L. Birch, 1824); Simmons, *Notices of East Florida* . . . (Charleston: A. E. Miller, 1822); Romans, *A Concise Natural History of East and West-Florida* . . . (New York: Printed for the Author, 1775); John Bartram, *"Journal," An Account of East Florida* . . . (London: W. Nicoll, 1766); William Bartram, *Travels through North and South Carolina, Georgia, East & West Florida* . . . (Philadelphia: James and Johnson, 1791); Roberts, *An Account of the First Discovery and Natural History of Florida* . . . (London: T. Jefferys, 1763).

3. See "Preface," iii; Garcilaso de la Vega, *La Florida del Ynca, historia del adelantado Hernando de Soto* (Lisbon: Pedro Crasbeeck, 1670).

4. *A View of West Florida, Embracing Its Geography, Topography, &c., with an Appendix Treating of Its Antiquities, Land Titles, and Canals, and Containing a Map Exhibiting a Chart of the Coast, a Plan of Pensacola, and the Entrance of the Harbour* (Philadelphia: H. S. Tanner, 1827).

5. "Preface," iii.

6. *Notes on the Floridian Peninsula, Its Literary History, Indian Tribes and Antiquities* (Philadelphia: Joseph Sabin, 1859), p. 70.

7. Jacksonville *Florida Republican*, August 31, 1854; Caroline Mays Brevard, *A History of Florida From the Treaty of 1763 to Our Own Times*, ed. James

Alexander Robertson (2 vols.; DeLand: Florida State Historical Society, 1925), I, 78n.

8. *Florida Republican,* August 31, 1854; see also p. 303 below.

9. Clarence E. Carter (ed.), *The Territorial Papers of the United States* (25 vols.: Washington: Government Printing Office, 1934-60), XXII, 877.

10. *Ibid.,* 803, 884.

11. "Journal of John Lee Williams," *Florida Historical Quarterly,* I (April, July, 1908), No. 1, pp. 37-44; No. 2, pp. 18-29; see also Carter, XXII, 855n; Brevard, I, 77.

12. "Journal of John Lee Williams," No. 2, pp. 24-27.

13. Brevard, I. 78n; Brinton, *Floridian Peninsula,* p. 69; p. 303 below.

14. Carter, XXII, 884-85; "Some Officials of the City Government of Pensacola," *Florida Historical Quarterly,* III (January, 1925), 31.

15. Carter, XXII, 863n, 874, 898-99, 910-12, 973, 977-78; XXIII, 214n.

16. Samuel Pasco, "Jefferson County, Florida, 1827-1910," *Florida Historical Quarterly,* VII (October, 1928), 145.

17. Carter, XXIV, 402.

18. *Ibid.,* 592-93, 601, 682, 816.

19. *Ibid.,* 697.

20. St. Augustine *Ancient City,* July 26, August 2, 1851; *Florida Republican,* August 31, 1854; Daniel G. Brinton, *A Guidebook of Florida and the South, for Tourists, Invalids and Emigrants, with a Map of the St. John River* (Philadelphia: George MacLean; Jacksonville: Columbus Drew, 1869), p. 70.

21. *Florida Republican,* August 31, 1854.

22. Carter, XXV, 105, 376.

23. *Florida Republican,* August 31, 1854.

24. Samuel Forry (Ft. King, Fla.) to Lt. J. W. Phelps (Ft. Heileman, Fla.), September 15, 1837, in *Florida Historical Quarterly,* VI (April, 1928), 215-16.

25. *Florida Republican,* August 31, 1854.

26. *Floridian Peninsula,* p. 70.

27. *Ibid.,* p. 72; Brevard, I, 78n.

28. Carter, XXV, 474, 633; Brevard, I, 78n.

29. *Ancient City,* August 2, 1851.

30. *Florida Republican,* August 31, 1854.

31. Julien C. Yonge, "Minutes of Organization in 1856 and List of Members," *Florida Historical Quarterly,* III (July, 1924), 8. In view of Williams advanced age, it seems rather unlikely that he was physically present at the organization of the Society in St. Augustine.

32. *Florida Republican,* November 19, 1856.

33. *Floridian Peninsula,* pp. 71-72. The unpublished manuscripts which Brinton refers to apparently have been lost. At any rate, their whereabouts is unknown today. In reference to the reputed revision of the "History," Ray E. Held says in his "Spanish Florida in American Historiography, 1821-1921" (University of Florida Ph.D. Thesis, 1955), p. 39, "If it would have shown as much improvement over the 1837 publication as the latter had shown over its predecessor, it is especially unfortunate that the work was not finished and published."

THE

TERRITORY OF FLORIDA:

OR

SKETCHES OF THE TOPOGRAPHY,

CIVIL AND NATURAL HISTORY,

OF

THE COUNTRY, THE CLIMATE, AND THE INDIAN TRIBES,

FROM

THE FIRST DISCOVERY TO THE PRESENT TIME,

WITH A MAP, VIEWS, &C.

BY JOHN LEE WILLIAMS.

OSEOLA.

THE

TERRITORY OF FLORIDA:

OR

SKETCHES OF THE TOPOGRAPHY,

CIVIL AND NATURAL HISTORY,

OF

THE COUNTRY, THE CLIMATE, AND THE INDIAN TRIBES,

FROM

THE FIRST DISCOVERY TO THE PRESENT TIME,

WITH A MAP, VIEWS, &C.

BY JOHN LEE WILLIAMS.

NEW-YORK:

A. T. GOODRICH.

1837.

Mahlon Day, Printer.

PREFACE.

—

IN the preface to my View of West Florida, published in 1827; I inti-
mated an intention of publishing, at some future period, a similar view of
East Florida. To be, also, accompanied with a Map of the country.
Since that time I have employed every interval of leisure, and every opportunity, that business or accident has presented, to collect such facts, as
would enable me to point out its geographical peculiarities, its native productions and its civil and natural history. I have traversed the country in
various directions and have coasted the whole shore of the Peninsula, from
Pensacola to St. Marys, examining, with minute attention, the various
clusters of Keys or Islets, that are grouped on the margin of the coast. I
have ascended many of the rivers, explored the lagoons and bays, traced the
ancient improvements, scattered ruins and its natural productions, by land
and by water. In addition to my own observations, I have availed myself
of the knowledge collected by others. I am under obligations to the writ-
ings of Garcelasso de la Vega, Romans, Roberts, Stork, the elder and
younger Bartram, Darby, Forbes, Vignolles and Simmons, for various and
extensive information, and I was lately favored with a rare and ancient
manuscript in the Spanish language, in which the early history of Florida
was condensed, with a regular succession of dates and events. On the subject of the ancient aborigines of the south, this manuscript has been of
great use to me ; on that of the missions established in the interior of the
country for the dissemination of the Catholic religion, and for subjecting
to the crown of Spain the powerful tribes which, at that time, swarmed over
these extensive and beautiful regions, this information is in my estimation
invaluable. We can now fully account for the piles of ruins, the extensive
moats, the deep ditches, the numerous roads, the broad avenues, and the

wide spreading fields, that even now, show signs of former cultivation.
For a perusal of this manuscript I am indebted to the politeness of Mr.
Tria one of the Aldermen of this city.   And for its translation, I am under equal obligations to my lamented friend, the late Thomas Murphy Esq.
Mr. Alvarez, Keeper of the Archives, has also carefully examined the
protocols in his office, and thus enabled me to correct or establish many
dates and facts of this history.   Still I have to regret that the work is very
imperfect.   Not one half of the Territory has been yet surveyed.   But
a small portion is yet inhabited.   The outline south of Tampa Bay and
Indian River, I have been unable to fill up.   The interior of this part of the
Territory is wholly unexplored by white men, and the descriptions of the
Indian inhabitants is at best imperfect.   Such as it is, I have compared it
with the statements of the elder Bartram and of Col. Gadsden, who
crossed a corner of it near the head savannas of St. John's river.   When I
explored the coast, my force was not sufficient to ascend the large rivers
that enter the Gulf of Mexico, and the great lakes that are believed to
supply these rivers, are wholly unknown.

From the eastern coast to the everglades, the distance is short ; I entered
the borders of these.   To explore them effectually the winter season must be
improved.   A boat must be had large enough to carry fuel as well as provisions and lodgings, for the eye can discover no timber, but rests on a boundless
range of grass meadows, interspersed with Lagoons and Lakes, and swarm-
ing with gnats and musquetoes.   The traditions of the Indians state that
there are many lovely Islets of timbered land interspersed over these wild
and watery regions ; it may be true, but it is at least uncertain.   It is stated
in the manuscript of Mr. Tria, that at the time the English took possession of
Florida, the catholic Yemmassees fled beyond the marshes, to islands inac-
cessable to white men.   It also states that a Spanish Gov. of Florida sent
persons to inhabited islands in the great Myacco Lake to seek for pearls
that were found in muscles.   It is greatly to be hoped that our government
will cause this part of the Territory to be carefully explored.   We should
not be indifferent to a knowledge of our own territories, at the same time
that we send exploring vessels to examine the waters of the south seas.
In the natural history of Florida, I have come very far short of my original
intentions.   Want of leisure and books were both felt as obstacles to the in-

vestigation of a field so boundless, but they were not the only ones. It was suggested to me by some friends whose opinions I have been accustomed to respect, that the subjects of natural history are not generally interesting to the mass of readers, and that it might be more expedient to devote to these a separate work.

Among various improvements of the Map, I have inserted a complete outline of St. Andrews bay. This extensive sheet of water had never been examined by any of the surveyors of our coast or of the public lands, and the sketches on all our charts and maps, represent anything, but a correct delineation of one of the finest harbors on the Gulf of Mexico. The Wakasasse Bay embraces the Fresh Water Keys, a group so extensive, that I have been unable to do more than to point to their location. Gauld here skipped over thirty miles of the coast, and modern surveyors have followed his example, probably because this bay is shut in, by an extensive reef, through which a navigable channel was not discovered. I however have much reason to believe that such a channel does exist, although I have not been so fortunate as to discover it. The Wakasasse river enters the east side of this Bay.

The mouth of the Ouithlacouche river and the Anclote Keys, are correctly laid on Patten's Chart, published in 1828. They are placed too far south on most of the Charts. On this Chart also, the Bay of Espiritu Santo is restored to its proper size and shape. It has been shamefully misrepresented on most of the former charts, and even on the recent Maps of Florida, professing to be correct.

Cape Roman or Puerta Longa, I discovered, to be the extreme point of a large Island, fifteen miles in length. The Caximba* sound, which separates it from the main, is nine miles long and affords six feet water through. The width could not be discovered, it being full of extensive islands. To my great surprise, I have found here several well cultivated plantations, long hid from the civilized world. Sharks River, which occupies so conspicuous a place in most of our maps, I have omitted, simply because I could not find it. From Racoon point about twelve miles above the cape, I examined the coast with much attention, but discovered only one small stream, called Dry river. It is connected with some lagoons, and

* Pronounced Kahamba.

they have another outlet behind an island, about six miles north. It is possible that such a river does exist farther north. No improvement can ever be made in Gauld's survey of the Florida Keys. And the Atlantic coast is generally correct. The whole face of the country east of the St. John's river is more particularly, and I trust more correctly exhibited on mine, than on any former map. Still perfect correctness cannot be expected, until the country is surveyed.

I present the work to the public, as the best I have been able to render, and I trust that the leading facts and outlines will be found generally correct. The style and manner has occupied less attention than the subject deserves, but had the author abilities, he has not had leisure to improve them.

HISTORY OF FLORIDA.

THE name "Florida" was at one period, applied to all that tract of country, which extends from Canada to the Rio del Norte. This extent has, in a course of two hundred years, been curtailed by various political arrangements, until it was finally settled, by the treaty with Spain, in 1795. Roberts, in his natural history, states, that this name was given by Ponce de Leon, in consequence of his having discovered the country, on Easter day, in the year 1512. Without disputing with De Leon, the credit of naming the country, we must certainly deny that he was the original discoverer; as it is known, that Sebastian Cabot coasted the whole of its eastern shore, in 1498.

By the treaty with Spain, in 1795, the Perdido was constituted the western limit of Florida. On the north, the 31° of north latitude was extended, from the Perdido to the Chattahooche river, the boundary, thence descended that river to the forks of Appalachicola; it thence proceeded eastward, to the head of St. Mary; thence down that river to its mouth. On the east, it is bounded by the Atlantic Ocean; and by the Gulf of Mexico, on the south. Its length, from east to west, is about 385 miles: and its width, from north to south, varies from 50 to 250 miles, forming an area, of 57,000 square miles, and 37,000,000 acres of land. Its present population is 34,725 souls.

The face of the country is uneven, but not mountainous. Numerous rivers intersect it, from north to south and some in all directions; several of them, especially the St. Marys, St. Johns, and Appalachicola, afford excellent navigation for coasting vessels. The whole extent of the sea coast, is indented with bays and lagoons, and the interior of the country is diversified with beautiful lakes and ponds, abounding in fish and fowl, of various kinds, and of the most delicate flavor. No part of the United States affords greater facilities for internal and external commerce. A large portion of the country, is covered with pine forests; the trees of which, standing at a considerable distance, from each other, without brush or underwood, affords an opportunity for the grass and flowers to spread luxuriantly, over the surface of the earth, during the whole year. The borders of water courses, however, are usually skirted by hammocks, of hard timber, entangled with grape and other flowering vines.

Notwithstanding so large a portion of Florida is of that quality, usually termed " pine barrens," and much of it extremely poor, still there are many extensive tracts of table land, hammock and swamp, of the richest soil, finely adapted to the culture of sugar, rice, cotton, corn, tobacco and fruits. A considerable quantity of the pine land, is equally rich, and the barrens, themselves, afford extensive ranges of grazing land, usually intersected with streams of pure water. Many parts of the Territory abounds in yellow pine and live oak timber. Our sea coast is generally healthy, in many parts remarkably so. The interior is not behind the coast, in this respect, unless it be, near extensive marshes. The seasons are mild, the mercury rarely arising to 90° in summer, or desending to 30° above zero in winter.

The southern coast of Florida, between Perdido and cape St. Blas, a distance of a hundred and forty miles, is formed of pure white sand, principally silicious, but mixed with calcareous particles of broken sea shells. Between cape St. Blas and Appalache Bay, the sand becomes of a yellow brown color, and extensive salt marshes alternate with the sand hills. From the Appalache river to the Suwanne, a distance of 80 miles, a soft calcareous rock forms the sea coast : it is uniformly covered with coarse grass and rushes, which extends from the woody coast, several miles into the sea. The same limestone forms the base of the peninsula and of the Florida Keys ; but in the Appalache Bay it is sheltered from the storms, and is very shoal, so that, at low tide, the sea appears like a green meadow five or six miles from the coast. South of the Suwanne, the shore and keys present a bare rock with small trees of cabbage and cedar growing in the crevices, until we pass the Anclote Keys ; the sea then beats heavily on the shore, and makes a rough coast, as far south as Isle Roman. The pine barrens here, usually extend to the rocky shore.

About the 27th degree, the coral insect begins to cover the calcareous rock, with his various and beautiful habitations. The first that we discovered near shore, is at Sarrazota sound or bay ; they become more general, farther south. The Florida Keys are wholly covered with them. From Appalache river, to Cape Sable, the reef extends very far from the shore. Opposite Wakasasse Bay, it is near twelve miles distant. It is broken at Tampa Bay and at Charlotte Harbor, and it closes with the land, at the middle curve of Cape Sable. The coral formation is prominent as far as the Soldier Keys. Key Biscayne is sandy, as is the coast north of it, as far as Jupiter Inlet. From thence the Coquina formation lines the coast, as high as Anastasia Island, in front of St. Augustine ; here it ceases, and not a rock of this formation is north of this Inlet. Coralines are discovered in Indian river, and even as high as Halifax river, but in no proportion to those on the western coast. North of St. Augustine, the whole coast is formed of white silicious sand, as far as the St. Marys.

Between the Perdido Bay and the Escambia River, the interior country presents an exterior surface of fine silicious sand, on a substratum of clay. This clay presents various colors, as red, white, yellow and blue. The strata are often 30 feet thick, and are worked into excellent bricks. Iron sand-stone, of a dark brown color, is sometimes found here, especially near the Escambia River ; most of it appears to have been melted ; it is hard and answers well for rough walls. This tract of country is generally poor. It affords some good pine timber, and good grazing in wet seasons. Bricks are the most valuable productions ; they form a considerable article of commerce.

The peninsula, extending near 30 miles, between St. Rosa Sound and Pensacola Bay, is from two to five miles wide. It has a poor sandy soil, in some places chequered by small hammocks, pleasantly situated for country seats. It is in some places subtended by peat, and at others with soft iron sand stone.

On the north side of Pensacola Bay, Black Water River descends through a valley of fine timbered land. Near the head of the stream there are good hammock and pine tracts. Between this river and the Escambia, the Pine Level affords some excellent farms.

North of the Chactawhatche Bay, a high ridge of land divides the water courses, which fall southwardly into the bay, and northwardly into Shoal and Titi creeks ; both tributaries of Yellow Water River. This ridge terminates, near the sources of Allaqua river, Uche and Shoal Creeks, in groups of high peaks.

A pleasant country extends from the Allaqua to the Uche Valley. It forms the eastern part of Walton county. The Allaqua passes over a soapstone formation. The Uche creek drains the only limestone country, west of the Chactawhatche River. North of the Uche creek, burrstone is found, extending, in detached masses, far into Alabama and Georgia. It seems a congeries of small tellina shells, quite entire, cemented together with a strong alluminous matter, nearly as hard as chalcedony. It is quite porous and has been manufactured into excellent mill-stones. It is of a light brown color, its break conchoidal, has an earthy appearance, and rings like marble.

Ponds and lime sinks are numerous between the Chactawhatche and Chipola rivers. Large springs, forming navigable streams, frequently

2

burst from this formation. The waters, although perfectly transparent, are highly impregnated with lime, and are considered as rather unhealthy. Approaching the Chipola, the limestone acquires greater firmness, loses the shelly structure and clayey concrete ; it often swells into hills, or high platforms, covered with grass ; but from want of soil, trees cannot take root. At other places, the rocks diverge in broken fragments, and are interspersed with dogwood, plumb and hydrangie bushes. The land, in this district of country, is excellent and already supports a dense population. But they do not extend more than twenty miles from the Alabama line ; towards the coast, the pine barrens again predominate. The Econfina river bursts from the limestone formation and traverses a valley of fine land, to the Bay of St. Andrews.

The limestone of Florida, is a deposition, but little harder than chalk, of a bluish cast, amorphous, with nodules of hornestone. It hardens when exposed to the air ; lies in different strata, and ascends to the ridge of the peninsula. The different strata are separated by clay or sand. Chrystalized limestone is found in Hamilton county near the Suwanne river, and on the Econfina, in Washington county.

On the east side of the Appalachicola, there are very high rocky banks, but after passing them, there are few indications of stone, until we approach Leon county. Here a ledge of rocks surrounds the Appalache Bay, at four to six miles distance, forming falls and rapids in all the streams, passing into the bay, except Oscilla, which finds a passage beneath it. A higher stratum pervades the hills of Tallahasse ; it is of a light yellow, enclosing both shells and bones, but when calcined forms a very good mild lime. The silex contained in the limestone formation, is usually of a light grey color, does not form kidney shaped masses, but spreads through the mass, in cones, full of holes, which are filled with calcareous matter ; when this is washed out by the water, the residue forms very rough flinty reefs. The hornstone is quite opaque, breaks with a conchoidal fracture, and gives fire freely with steel. But it is void of that greasy feel, usual to the kidney shaped masses. The rock formation is very productive of grass. This vegetable constantly springs up from it, through salt or fresh water, even to the depth of twenty feet. Oysters grow to the rocks in great masses, and are hard to separate from them. Through Gadsden and Leon counties, the limestone is covered with yellow or red clay, from 20 to 100 feet deep ; the red clay here, terminates an extensive formation, which extends along the east side of the Apalachian mountains, through Georgia and the Carolinas. It is always rich in vegetable productions, and lies in graceful undulations ; in its natural state, covered with black oaks, cane brakes and vines. The soil in this part of the Territory, is usually a brown loam, very rich and productive ; the pines usually mark those lands latest cultivated ; these are extensive and strongly marked with ancient ditches, foundations, wells &c. The springs are numerous and pure, rising above the limestone, but they scarcely ever attain the size of mill streams, ere they are precipitated into the caverns of the earth, to join the subterraneous torrents which occasionally burst out in navigable rivers. Lakes, ponds, and sinks are also common. Some of the former can scarcely be excelled in beauty. The waters of most of them are transparent and cool, abound in fish, and evidently appear to be connected with the rivers beneath the surface of the earth. They are, however, usually tinctured with lime.

East of the Wakasasse Bay, the coast bends rapidly to the southeast. In this angle, the coast is flat and filled with a large cluster of islands, called the Fresh Water Keys. The Wakasasse River empties its waters behind them, through a low marshy coast. The country then rises into rich hammocks, and extends over a series of sandy ridges, occasionally broken by masses of limestone, to the Allachua country. This is a Seminole name given to a rich tract of land thirty or forty miles in extent but wholly undefined as it regards boundary. The name has been applied to a county of great extent ; which, however, embraces the original Allachua. This part of the country is curiously diversified with savannas, lakes, ridges of hammock, and plains of pine barren. The soil is equally various, in one part covered with a rich black loam, in another sand mixed with limestone, sandstone, or flint. In some places for a great extent, not even a pebble can be found. Some of the savannas, the Allachua in particular, are 15 miles in length, covered with tall grass ; adjoining a ridge of sand hills will remind one of the sea coast, and the hammocks present groves of live oak, exactly similar to the shores of the Gulf, which are however twenty-five to thirty miles distant. On the whole, the Allachua is a fine country of land, and will support a dense population ; the titles to the land here are generally settled. There are considerable tracts of good land on both sides of the Santaffe river, which empties into the eastern side of the Suwanne. But from that stream to the Georgia line, the lands are poor, rolling, pine barren ; this kind of land extends eastward, to the heads of St. Marys and Nassau rivers.

South of the Allachua, the lands towards Fort King, are diversified with pine groves and hammocks of an excellent quality. That towards the sea coast, falls off in gentle swells of pine land.

South of Fort King, the Big swamp, Long swamp and Wahoo swamp, present large bodies of first rate sugar lands. On every part of the country, watered by the Ouithlacouche, the lands are diversified with rich hammocks, dense swamps, good pine flats, wet savannas and extensive grassy

ponds.   South of the Ouithlacouche and near the sea coast, is a very extensive tract of rich swamp land, eight or ten miles in length, and from three
to four in breadth.   The country, from Fort Couper to Chicuchatty, is a
high healthy country and much of it covered with a rich soil.

Between Chicuchatty and Fort Alabama, there are considerable ridges
of sand hills ; but on the head waters of Hillsboro river, are many beautiful
and rich hammocks.   East of the great Bay of Tampa, the country is
usually covered with pine.   Some of the lands, that have a substratum of
clay, will produce excellent crops, and there are occasionally small hammocks about the water courses.   The Indians cultivate excellent lands, in
the neighborhood of Hitchepucksasse.   But in general, from the bay to
Peace river, the country is flat and rather poor, even as far south as Char-
lotta Bay.

So far as Peace and Macaco rivers have been explored, they rise in good
strong land.   Below Apopkachee Lake, the Indian towns had become, before
the war, quite populous ; some of them contained, from one to two hundred
houses.

But from this lake to the Apopka on the Ocklawaha the country runs
into ridges of sandy pine barrens, and this is the character of all the region
about the head waters of the Ocklawaha.   Some of the ridges break off,
abruptly, into high peaks.

Between the Allachua country and the St. Johns river the surface is generally covered with pine timber.   From the heads of Santaffe and Black
Creek to the Orange Lake Creek there is a ridge of high sand hills broken
by numerous ponds and Lakes, among them are many tracts of good land
that formerly sheltered small Indian villages.   Such were the Ettini and
Santaffe hammocks.

East of this ridge the country is flat pine land diversified with streams of
good water, and is altogether most excellent for grazing.   The east side of
the St. John's, is very similar to the west, except that the grass is
not so abundant and of course less valuable for raising stocks of
cattle.   Hogs on the contrary, thrive better on the east than on the west
of the St. John's.

There is little difference in either soil or productions from the St. Marys
to Musquito.   The sea coast is covered with palmettoes.   Two or three
miles from the sea shore, there is a strip, from one to four miles wide, covered
with excellent land, bordering on the lagoons, that stretch parrallel with the
shore.   West of that are flat pine lands.

South of Musquito, and of Volusia on the St. John's, the country changes rapidly.   Vast grass meadows, and savannas, diversified with clusters of
cabbage-palms, and live oaks, are separated by strips of pine land and ham-

mocks of wild orange, and verges fast towards a tropical complexion, which increases as you approach Cape Florida.

The Peninsula, which extends southwardly between the Atlantic and the Gulf, is yet imperfectly explored. In soil and productions, it varies, considerably from the northern part of the Territory. This difference is more remarkable after passing the 27th degree of latitude. The shores and Islands of the south are uniformly covered with mangrove bushes ; these as we approach the cape, become forests of tall trees. This timber extends as far into the country as the salt water.

The back country presents a singular alternation of savannas, hammocks, lagoons and grass ponds, called altogether the Everglades. These extend into the heart of the country, for two hundred miles north of Cape Sable. They are drained on the north by the noble river St. John's, and on the west by Macaco or Charlotte river. A great number of small streams drain it on the east and west ; among the former are the St. Sebastians, St. Lucia, Potomac, Rattones, and Miame, and among the latter the Gallivan, Swallow river and St. Marys. Sharks river, if it exists at all, must enter the Gulf much farther north than it is located, on Vignoles' and Tanners' maps, as we have critically examined the coast, from cape Sable, ten or twelve miles north, where no such river is found. There is a curious contrast between the calm and gentle swells of the Gulf of Mexico, and the furious surf that eternally lashes the Atlantic coast. In the Gulf, the tide rises only two and a half feet, but on the Atlantic, it rises more than six feet. In the Gulf on the western side of the peninsula, the soundings range from seven to fourteen fathoms, at twenty miles from the coast. On the Atlantic, the same distance from the shore, in many places, soundings are lost. The eddies of the Gulf stream, throw upon the eastern coast, such a quantity of broken shells, called coquina, that, from St. Augustine to Key Largo, the mouths of all the rivers are dammed up, and their waters thrown back on the country. Such are the waters of Indian river, as well as Hillsborough, Halifax and Matanzas. These are shut out from the sea, by banks of shells and sand, from fifteen to thirty feet high. The waters thus barred out from the ocean, unite laterally, and form extensive lagoons, peculiarly calculated for inland navigation. At this time, fourteen miles of canal would open an inland navigation from Jupiter Inlet, to the river St. Marys, a distance of three hundred miles. When the waters of these Lagoons are greatly swelled, by rains in the upper country, they burst their shelly barriers and open a deep channel into the ocean, through which the waters are soon drained, and the waves again commence a natural dam, to close the inlet. Jupiter Inlet has several times been opened and closed, and the Matanzas, about ten years since, underwent the same operation. As soon as the shells are cast on the shore, the rains dissolve the calcareous matter, chrystalization commences, between the fragments, and the rudiments of a rock are formed. The Coquina formation has probably commenced within a few hundred years. It extends from Anastatia Island, south, beyond Indian River, but is scarcely ever six miles wide, and generally not more than two. We think the formation began at the south ; the rocks there appear much older than they do here. Very small quantities of shell are thrown on the coast, at Cape Canaveral, while here, they are extremely abundant. The strata are horizontal, and of various thickness. They have been quarried to the depth of twenty feet, but we have not been able to learn how much farther they descend into the earth. The houses of St. Augustine and the extensive old fort Marian, are built of this stone.

CLIMATE.

The climate of Florida is various, embracing six degrees of latitude and as many of longitude. We necessarily feel a great difference of temperature between the north and the south, as well as between the east and the west. The mean temperature of St. Augustine is about $68\frac{1}{2}°$. It is a little higher in Pensacola ; at that place it is also colder in the winter. Frost is felt at some seasons, in every part of Florida, though not usually below latitude $27°$. During eighteen years that we have resided in Florida, the greatest heat has been $96°$ of Farenheit, in the shade. Three or four times it has arisen to this height, and on the sixth April, 1828, it was as low as 30. At that time ice was made an inch thick at six mile creek, and cut off the crops of corn and cotton as far south as Tomoko, while at St. Augustine and Duns Lake, the marks of frost were scarcely discoverable. In usual seasons, the mercury rises to about $90°$ in the hottest days of midsummer, and falls to 43 during the coldest days of winter. In West Florida, the north west winds are felt, much more powerfully, than in East Florida. Its effect on fruit trees is extremely obvious. The sweet orange cannot be depended on at Pensacola, while at St. Augustine it, in usual seasons, affords the staple of commerce. The land and sea breezes alternate with much greater regularity in West than East Florida. The Peninsula of East Florida projects so far to the east, as to divide the current of the trade wind ; one portion of it passes up the coast and forms the charming seabreeze that fans us so constantly, each day of summer, except it be kept in check, by the north east wind. In west Florida, the struggle is between the north west wind and the trade wind. During winter, our north east winds are chilly, damp and often rough ; but they are never charged with frost, which is often the case with the north west.

DISEASES AND HEALTH.

The health of Florida has been justly proverbial, still there are parts of the Territory that have ever proved unhealthy, and the healthiest parts have, at times, been visited with epidemics, of a very fatal character. In the year 1765, a regiment of soldiers were sent from England to Pensacola, during a very hot summer ; on their arrival they were confined, during day and night, within the walls of the fort, at Barrancas, which excluded the sea breezes ; they soon became infected with a malignant fever, which proved very fatal to the common soldiers, while that part of the troops which continued on board the vessels, enjoyed perfect health.

In 1821, St. Augustine was visited with the yellow fever. It broke out in several old buildings situated in the back part of the city, which had for a long time been closed up, their owners having retired to Havanna. On the cession of the country to the United States, a sudden increase of population occasioned these houses to be thrown open and rented to strangers. One of them was hired late in October to several American Officers, three of them fell immediate victims to the fatal disease. In some instances the sickness commenced in vessels lying in the harbor, which had brought fruit from Cuba. One of these had on the voyage lost the Captain and most of the crew, by sickness. Some early cases of fever were traced to other vessels. In most cases however, the sickness seemed to originate in the place of its operation. Since this period, St. Augustine has been distinguished as one of the most healthy spots, in the United States.

In 1822, Pensacola was again visited by the yellow fever. The court of General, then Gov. Jackson was fixed there ; the place was full of strangers, and there was no efficient police. The streets and lots were exceedingly filthy, especially near the bay. At this time, a cargo of spoiled codfish arrived from Cuba, and was distributed among the huckster shops. From this moment, the pestilence spread like wild-fire, sweeping whole families, and often whole streets in one general destruction, which ended only, with a total removal of the whole population, or rather the recent population, for none of the old inhabitants were afflicted with the pestilence.

Key West was distressed by a similar visitation in 1824. The fever was particularly fatal to the young Officers of the fleet under Commodore Porter. In 1829, the same place was nearly depopulated by the same fever.

Key West is surrounded by the sea, and exposed to breezes from every quarter of the compass. A portion of the Island is covered with salt ponds. While the tide ebbs and flows freely into these, no injury could result. When that is not the case, they ought to be opened. At certain seasons of the year, seaweeds, in great abundance, are cast on the shore, and usually

smell very badly, but they soon decay and are washed away by the tide.
There appears no reason why this Island should be permanently unhealthy.
Indian Key is peculiarly healthy, and it is worthy of remark, that musqui-
toes disappear in a great measure from these Islands when cultivated.

The Tomoko settlement, in East Florida, St. Marks, in Middle Florida,
Fort Gadsden on the Apalachicola river and the western bank of the
Chipola, have often been visited by malignant fevers. All these places are
surrounded by low and rich lands, and the latter situation is covered by a
very dense population. It is believed that the health of all these places
will improve, as the country around becomes more extensively cultivated.

Tallahassee, the seat of our Territorial government, is a new town settled
in 1824. It has been usually healthy, except the years 1831 and 1832;
during these seasons fevers prevailed over the Middle District generally.
Since those periods, the inhabitants have in common seasons enjoyed excellent health.

Tampa Bay, where nearly three hundred troops have been stationed, for seven or eight years, has proved peculiarly salubrious. Not one
death has occurred by fevers of any kind. Indeed there have been very
few deaths from any cause.

When a new country is first improved, and the surface of the earth with
all its decaying vegetable matter is exposed to the sun, it is then if ever,
subject to fevers. We cannot with certainty foretell what may be the effect of a crowded population in this climate. But, thus far, our prospect of
health, equals that of any state in the union.

WEATHER.

St. Augustine has become celebrated for restoring tone to the system, in
Pulmonary and Bronchial complaints. And invalids from every part of the
United States resort here, during the winter season to avoid the severity of
the northern frosts, and to enjoy the mildness of our southern breezes.

Sea bathing is greatly practiced in west Florida by all classes of citizens,
and is believed to restore more strangers to health, than any other prescrip-
tion. The benefits resulting from it, in East Florida are equally great, in
proportion to its practice. Riding and walking are exercises more practiced, in St. Augustine, than in any other part of the Territory.

From October to June, the weather is usually serene and temperate. A
few very hot days generally occur about the month of June and the beginning of July. In February we often experience a week of cold uncomforta-
ble weather, and rough winds from the North East are frequently felt early
in the Spring. But in usual winters, we see no snow, and frost continues

but for a few days. Flowers decorate our gardens and our wild savannas, during the whole year.

There are however, exceptions to this routine of soft breezes and blooming flowers. In the year 1765, Mr. John Bartram, English botanist, spent the winter months in East Florida. On the 3d of January, being on the St. Johns river, south of lake George, he states the "thermometer was at 26° wind N. W. The ground was frozen an inch thick on the banks : this was the fatal night that destroyed the lime, citron and bananna trees in St. Augustine." In 1774, there was a snow storm, which extended over most of the Territory. The ancient inhabitants still speak of it as an extraordinary white rain. It was said to have done little damage.

During the year 1822, in February, the cold was so intense in West Florida, that all the fruit trees were killed, to the ground ; and several persons, in exposed situations, were chilled to death. This season was comparatively mild in East Florida. On the contrary, East Florida suffered exceedingly, from a violent frost on the 6th of April, 1828. The winter had been unusually mild, there had been no check to vegetation, in trees or plants. On this bitter night, crops of cotton, corn and fruits, were all destroyed. The thermometer, at Six Mile Creek, on the St. Johns River, stood at 27°. This frost did not extend to West Florida.

Severe storms, are usually expected about the equinoxes, though several successive years often intervene without a gale. They rarely penetrate far inland. Although a few vestiges of severe hurricanes are seen, which must have prostrated all the timber on extensive tracts of country, yet none have been experienced, since the Americans have taken possession of Florida. Showers of rain are frequent during the summer ; they are sometimes, but not usually attended by severe lightnings. During the season of 1830, the lightning was unusually fatal.

The average temperature, at Mr. Andrew Ellicot's station, on the Appalachicola river, during the months of August and September 1799, taken at 7 A. M. and 2 P. M. was 77° and 86°. On the 28th August the heat at the same hours was 74° and 96°. It has never been higher in any part of the Territory, so far as our information extends.

During the winter of 1800, at Pensacola, the mean temperature, was at 7 A. M. 44°, at 2 P. M. 54. The coldest days at the same hours was 30° and 51°.

At Amelia Island, the same year, the mean temperature in January, was 44° at 7 o'clock and 61° at two o'clock P. M. In St Augustine, during the years 1825, 6, 7, and 8, the mean temperature was 68½°

The coldest day in 1825 was 30th Dec. . . . 42°

The hottest, 20th Aug. . . . . - 94°

In 1826, the coldest day, 21st Jan.   .   .   .   .   44°
The hottest, 5th July. .   .   .   ,   .   .   92°
In 1827, the coldest day, 6th Feb.   .   .   .   .   43°
The hottest, 16th July   .   .   .   .   .   92°
In 1828, the coldest, 6th April   .   .   .   .   27°
The hottest   .   .   .   .   .   .   95°
1829, the coldest   .   .   .   .   .   32°
The hottest   .   .   .   .   .   .   96°
1830, hottest   .   .   .   .   .   .   96°

The winter of 1830, was so mild that banannas grew in the open gardens, at St. Augustine, without injury, and were in blossom on the 15th May. Corn also, grew, during the whole winter. We had roasting ears in May, and abundance of Irish potatoes, which were planted in December.

During the month of February, 1835, East Florida was visited by a frost, much more severe than any before experienced. A severe north west wind blew ten days in succession, but more violent for about three days ; during this period the mercury sank seven degrees below zero. The St. Johns River was frozen several rods from the shore, and afforded the astonished inhabitants a spectacle as new as it was distressing. All kinds of fruit trees were killed, to the ground ; many of them never started again, even from the roots. The wild groves suffered equally with those cultivated. The orange had become the staple of our commerce ; several millions were exported from the St. Johns and St. Augustine, during each of the last two years. Numerous groves were just planted out, and extensive nurseries could scarcely supply the demand for young trees. Some of the groves had, during the previous autumn, brought to their owners, one, two and three thousand dollars ; and the increasing demand for this fruit, opened in prospect, mines of wealth to the inhabitants,

" Then came a frost, a withering frost."

Some of the orange groves in East Florida were estimated at, from five to ten thousand dollars. They were at once rendered nearly valueless. The Minorcan population, at St. Augustine, had been accustomed to depend on the produce of their little groves of eight or ten trees, to purchase their coffee, sugar and other necessaries from the stores , they were left without resource.

The town of St. Augustine, that heretofore, appeared like a rustic village, their white houses peeping from among the clustered boughs and golden fruit of their favorite tree, beneath whose shade, the foreign invalid cooled his fevered limbs and imbibed health from the fragrant air, how is she fallen ! Dry unsightly poles with ragged bark, stick up around her dwellings, and where the mocking-bird once delighted to build her nest, and tune her lovely song, owls now hoot at night, and sterile winds whistle through the leafless branches. Never was a place more desolate.

With the blessing of usual seasons for two or three years, we shall probably begin again to have some fruit. The young groves are rising from eight to ten feet high, and a few blossoms were this spring discovered on a few trees ; but it will require ten years to restore our groves to the state they were in before the frost destroyed them.

The groves of wild orange are at this time, 1837, in full bearing, south of of Volusia on the St. Johns river, and at Musquito on the coast of the Atlantic.

Peaches, plumbs, and figs, are again in full bearing, and the mulberry, the Multicaulis in particular, are now rapidly increasing, and will soon add a new production to the commerce of Florida.

Most of the tropical fruits, will grow as far north as 27° of latitude ; although in some particular seasons, they will be likely to suffer from the cold. The cocoanut and sugar apple grow wild at Cape Sable and Cape Florida, and even as high as Charlotte Harbor.

The ovino, custard apple, hickok, and huesco plumbs are abundant, on the east bank of Indian River.

BAYS.

Perdido or lost bay, divides Florida from Alabama, on the west. It is a pleasant sheet of water, about 30 miles in length and from two to six miles wide, and swarms with excellent fish. Its banks, in many places, are formed of clay bluffs, proper for bricks. The country around, is healthy and abounds in excellent pine timber. The land however, is generally poor. The western arm, stretching near to Bonsecours, is called La Lance. This bay has a narrow and crooked outlet, the bar shifting, from five to seven feet water.

Pensacola, formerly called Ochusa, took its name from a tribe of Indians, who formerly inhabited the northern bank. It is from twenty-five to thirty miles long and from four to seven broad. It was discovered by Maldonado, one of Ferdinand de Soto's officers, in 1540. It was then called Ochusa by the natives. About eleven miles from the Gulf, it is divided into three parts : the western arm is called Escambia Bay ; this is eleven miles long and four broad, and receives the Escambia River from the north, among numerous, marshy islands. The middle arm is called Yellow Water Bay ; it is nearly the same size as Escambia. It receives the Yellow Water River, from the east, through several mouths. Black Water Bay, an oval sheet of water, seven miles long and two broad, is attached to the N. W. end of Yellow Water Bay. Black Water Bay is full of small islands. It receives from the north Black Water River and Cedar Creek.

East Bay is the third prong, it extends about seven miles into the country, where it tapers off into a small river, very near to St. Rosa's Sound. This is a noble bay, admits the largest class of our Frigates, which can lie in safety, sheltered from all winds. It is connected with St. Rosa Sound on the south east, and through that with the Chactawhatchee Bay and thence into the Gulf, through the Pass L' Este, at the east end of St. Rosa Island. Its entrance, between the fort of Barrancas and the west end of St. Rosa, is about three fourths of a mile wide. It has at the lowest tides 21 feet of water on the bar, and usually 24 to 25. Large vessels coming from the eastward, should keep in seven fathoms until the Lighthouse bears north by west, then run for it across the bar, till the west end of St. Rosa bears east by south, you will then be within the island and may haul up to the east. Vessels coming from the westward may safely run to five fathoms, then take the same course. Vessels drawing no more than 14 feet, may bring the light to bear north three fourths west, then steer for it, till within a half mile, thence E. by N. till sheltered by the island. The ebb tide sets S. W. directly on the Caycos shoal. The flood tide sets across the middle ground.

The Grand Lagoon extends from the entrance of Pensacola Bay, below Barrancas, eight miles westward, and within three fourths of a mile of Perdido Bay, with which it might be connected at a trifling expense. It has an inlet from the Gulf near the west end. Near Barrancas, the entrance of the Lagoon is constantly growing more shoal.

The Big Bayou opens from Pensacola Bay, one and a half miles above Tartar Point. Three miles farther up the bay, Bayou Chico presents an inlet to Camp Clinch. This is a beautiful little sheet of water, and a fine harbor for the small craft attached to the station.

Bayou Texar enters the bay one mile above Pensacola. It is four miles long, but narrow. The Bayou Mulatto enters the bay from the east twenty five miles from the coast.

St. Rosa Sound is about forty miles, from east to west, and from one half, to two and a half miles wide. Vessels drawing five feet may pass through it into Chactawhatchee Bay, and thence, through Pass L' Este, into the Gulf. This Sound is sheltered from the Gulf by St. Rosa Island. On its northern shore are many small hammocks, finely watered, affording charming sites for country seats.

Chactawhatchee Bay bay affords good navigation for vessels drawing six feet water. It extends from east to west, forty miles, and is from seven to fifteen miles wide. It receives the Chactawhatchee River from the north, also the Aliqua and several large and fine creeks. There is much excellent land and abundance of fine live oak on the north east shore of this bay. The eastern shore is low, rich ground, the western high pine barren, with small shell hammocks. The reeds and grass are so high and thick, that the N. E. shore, for eight or nine miles, cannot be approached, except through some water course. This bay is much affected by storms, and many shoal capes extending far into the bay, the navigation is considered dangerous. It communicates with the Gulf, through Pass L' Este, at the south west end, and is connected with Pensacola Bay by St. Rosa Sound. When the wind blows strongly from the south, it raises a heavy surf on the bar of Pass L' Este, and when the tide ebbs against it, a passage should not be attempted. The British established a profitable fishery here. It might at this time be improved to great advantage.

St. Andrews Bay was, until lately, almost unknown. At some future time, it must become a place of importance. It is easy of access, has eighteen feet water on the bar, has good anchorage and is perfectly sheltered from all winds. Its various arms are very capacious, some of them extend thirty miles into the country. The north and eastern divisions extend near to the rich settlements of Chipola, the principal part of the trade, of which, passes through this bay. The main entrance is between Sand Island and Hammock Island. Another channel between Hammock and Crooked Islands is almost as good, but is not so direct to the sea. The main body of the bay extends north twelve miles, and thus far, averages from two to five miles in width. One mile from the sea beach, an arm about one mile wide, runs westward, parallel with the coast, for twenty miles. Ten miles from the sea, another arm branches off to the eastward thirty miles. This arm is in some places ten and in others not more than one mile wide. It approaches within seven miles of the Chipola Inundation. A company has been incorporated to connect the two waters. Should this be carried into effect, St. Andrews will command the trade of Appalachicola River.

The Wapaluxy Bay recedes from St. Andrews, fifteen miles from the sea, on the western side of the north arm. It is a circular basin about twelve miles in diameter, and is from twelve to fourteen feet deep. It is surrounded by low flat pine barren, a creek enters the western border, which interlocks with the pond branch of the Chactawhatchee. Four miles above Wapaluxy, on the north arm, is Little Oyster Point, thus far any vessel may ascend that can cross the bar. From this point to the head of the bay is eight miles, the water gradually shoals to seven feet. Here, at the ware houses of Sewal and Bower, the produce of the interior country is shipped. At this place the Econfina River enters the bay. The sound behind Hammock Island affords shelter for vessels drawing 18 feet water, and is easy of access at either end of the island.

St. Josephs Bay presents a wide entrance from the N. W., affording on the bar, seventeen feet water. A middle ground occupies much of the space, between Cape False and the peninsula. On this, there is from nine to eleven feet. There are two channels nearly equal in depth, the one near to Cape False on the N. W. the other close to the point of the peninsula, on the south side .of the entrance. The bay is from seven to eight miles wide and near twenty in length. The water shoals near four miles from the S. E. end of the bay. Here is a picturesque Island about two miles from the end, covered with live oak, cedar and palms. The N. E. shore is intersected by ponds and lagoons. The southern point of the crooked peninsula stretches far into the sea and forms Cape St. Blas. On the eastern shore of this bay the town of St. Joseph has lately been built. The north end of this peninsula is blown up, into sharp and high sand hills ; behind these, near the south entrance, is a level plain, covered with a forest of tall pines, which may be seen far at sea.

The Appalachicola Bay is formed by the islands of St. Vincents and St. George, enclosing the mouth of the river. It is thirty miles long and eight wide. Vessels drawing fourteen feet water can enter the bay, and with eight feet, can approach the mouth of the river, at the village of that name. The river Appalachicola being the only river that extends far into this part of the country, the Village here must ultimately become a place of considerable importance, unless the connection of the Chipola, with the east arm of St. Andrews, or the new town of St. Joseph shall divert the rich produce of the interior into other channels. The Appalachicola Bay is connected with the Gulf, by the Indian Pass, between St. Vincents Island and the main. This pass is rapidly filling, with oyster shoals ; there is not, at present, more than four feet water on the bar. The main channel is between St. Vincents and St. George islands and on the east side of a round sand bar, called Flag Island, situated in the entrance. From the north end of St. Vincents an extensive oyster bar runs in a circle eastward, nearly enclosing the inlet ; a narrow passage runs near the west end of St. George Island, sweeping round to the north east, making a circle, near to Cat Point, before it crosses over to the mouth of the river. St. George Sound opens a communication, between Appalachicola Bay and the Gulf. It is upwards of twenty miles long and from three to four wide, and, but for an oyster bar, would afford an important inland passage. This bar crosses the sound, from north to south, and has not three feet water at low tide, indeed it is in many places quite bare. But a passage of deep water is said to have been lately found through this bar. Near Cat Point, the oysters are numerous and large. Between St. George and Dog Islands the channel is wide and deep. At the east end of Dog Island there is a fine harbor with eleven feet water. New River enters the sound, exactly north of the west end of Dog Island.

Oclockony Bay is about seven miles long and from one to two miles broad. It has six feet water on the bar, at low tide. The river of the same name enters the west end, but a large branch is divided off to the west which, after skirting James Island, for nearly 20 miles, joins New River and with it enters St. George Sound.

Appalache Bay is that large indentation of the coast, which sweeps round, from South Cape, to Histahatchee Bay, forming a circle, of seventy to eighty miles.. This bay is open to the south and affords no safe harbor to large vessels. The shoals off South Cape break the seas so that merchant vessels drawing from ten to twelve feet may lie in safety off the mouth of the river, and with eight feet, may enter the Spanish Hole, where they are sheltered from all winds. A great reef of rocks project from the shore of the bay from ten to twenty miles, and many round shoals rise in different parts of it. Among these there is usually from ten to twelve feet water, and as there is no heavy seas, except when southern storms arise, the Appalache is usually navigated in safety. It is wholly surrounded on the north and east by green marshes, sprinkled with islets of cedar and live oak; in some places with cabbage-palms, which grow higher on this rocky coast, than in any other part of Florida The port of Magnolia is much frequented, since the establishment of the seat of Government, at Tallahasse, and a new town has lately been laid out, at St. Marks, the old fort of the Spaniards. In this bay, commerce will keep pace with the rapid population of the country. Seven feet water can be carried to Magnolia, sixteen miles from the mouth of the Appalache, on the St. Marks fork of the river. A rail road is now completed, connecting Tallahasse with St. Marks.

The Wakasasse Bay is formed by the delta of the Suwanne River. It is sheltered from the Gulf by Oyster Shoals. The eastern part is filled with the Fresh Water Keys. It has 12 feet water, and is perfectly sheltered; but a navigable entrance has not yet been found, although there are strong reasons to believe that there is one. It may be entered from the Anclote Keys by crafts drawing seven feet.

Anclote Sound is sheltered on the west, by Anclote, Jacs and Sand Keys. There is ten feet water and good anchorage behind the main key. It is easy of access both north and south of the island. It is three miles from the island to the shore. The south end of this sound is on some of the old maps called St. Joseph. From this to Tampa Bay, there is an inland boat channel.

Tampa Bay, called by the Spaniards Espiritu Santo, is the largest bay in the Gulf of Mexico. It lies between 27° 4′ and 28° N. latitude, and between 5° 3′ and 6° W. longitude from Washington. It is forty miles long, and in one place thirty-five wide, and has from eighteen to twenty feet water on the bar. It is easy of access and affords safe anchorage for any number of vessels. It receives Hillsborough River from the north; at the mouth of which is situated Cantonment Brock, a beautiful station, that does honor to the judgment and taste of the veteran General who formed it. On the S. E. fourteen miles from the Cantonment, Manate River enters, through a mouth near a mile in width, and in some places, ten feet deep. Indian and Alafia Rivers enter the bay, between the Hillsborough and Manate. Oyster River enters twenty miles below Manate. The eastern part of this bay, was, by the British called Hillsborough, and the little bay attached to the north side, Tampa. The little Tampa is an elliptical basin about ten miles in diameter, but very shoal. Numerous islands are scattered over this bay, especially on the western part. Among the most pleasant are Egmont, in the mouth of the harbor, Minnies, Long, and Borrd Islands. Fish and turtle are abundant; in the S. W. part in particular, such numerous and extensive shoals of fish are met, as almost to impede a boat in the shoal waters. The Spanish fishermen keep a schooner here, to carry fish and turtle to the Havanna. From fifteen to twenty men are constantly employed in curing them and in conveying them away to market. Sea-fowl are also exceedingly numerous; the beautiful flamingoes, in particular, appear in long files, drawn up on the beach, like bands of soldiers in red uniforms. The country around this extensive bay, is generally poor land, for the most part pine barrens, interspersed with small oak hammocks, and low savannas. On the south of Oyster River, however, there is an extensive hammock of rich land. Similar hammocks extend as far as Sarrazota Bay, with some interruptions.

Sarrazota Bay extends from Tampa, fifteen miles down the coast. It is separated from the Gulf by an island of the same name. It is from three to five miles wide. The north part, adjoining Tampa, is much filled with islands. It may be entered through Long Boat inlet, with eight feet water. This is between Long and Sarrazota Islands. The southward inlet, called Bocca Seca, has only four feet water on the bar. It is connected by a small creek with Palm Sound, but the natives usually haul over their canoes, across a hammock about twenty rods wide. On the east shore of this sound, there are extensive old fields, of rich land. The hammock is covered with live oaks and cane. The shore is rocky and high, the ruins of about fifteen old houses are seen among the grass and weeds. We found in 1828, in the old gardens, among luxuriant weeds, tomatas, lima beans, and many aromatic herbs, perfectly naturalized.

Palm Sound extends seven miles behind Palm Island. It is about one fourth of a mile wide, but navigable only for small boats. Palm Bay extends near ten miles, behind a peninsula connected to the main land on the south. Across this narrow isthmus there is a haulover, of about 100 yards. From the south part of Sarrazota Bay to Charlotte Harbor, the pine country approaches near to the coast, is high rolling land, covered with tall pines, and has pleasant streams of pure water, running into these bays and into the sea. From this to Cleni Inlet, is about twelve miles. As the lagoon extends from this inlet north for several miles, a canal across the pine barren, of eight miles, would complete an inland communication from Tampa, and even from Wakasasse Bays, to Charlotte Bay. This could be easily accomplished, as there are several fine brooks crossing the space, which would supply sufficient water to a canal.

Gasparilla Sound extends from Cleni Inlet to Charlotte Bay, a distance of six miles. It is about two miles wide. Cleni Inlet, between Cleni and Gasparilla Islands, has four feet water. Gasparilla Inlet, between Gasparilla and North Islands, has six feet water on the bar. From Bocca Grande to Carlos Bay may be twenty-five miles. It is full of islands, among which Pine is the largest. It lies eight miles south of Bocca Grande, which is the main channel; it has fourteen feet water on the bar, and is easy of access. Macaco River enters twenty-five miles east of Bocca Grande. It is here two miles wide, and twelve feet deep. Peace River also joins the Macaco near the entrance of the bay. This river extends far to the north-east, is large and deep. Toampa Island lies five miles south of Bocca Grande. It is about a mile long, from east to west, is a rich shell hammock, and produces many tropical fruits, as cocoa nuts, limes, oranges, &c., but is badly cultivated. The proprietor is a stout, healthy, old, white-headed Spaniard, very industrious; carries on fishing to a great extent; keeps two small schooners running to Havanna, with fish and turtle. His village is built on the west end of the island, and consists of from eighteen to twenty palmetto houses, mostly occupied by various branches of his extensive family. There are three other fishing establishments in the bay. Many of the islands in this bay are fertile, but the Spaniards and Indians who occupy them, cultivate very little land. A small quantity of corn, beans and melons satisfy them, as they live principally on fish.

Carlos Bay is connected with Charlotte by Sanybal Sound. The deepest channel is from the Gulf, between Moosa and Caloosa Islands. The bay extends fourteen miles into the country northwardly, and receives the Caloosahatche River from the N. E. The Caloosa Channel has twelve feet water on the bar, but the broad entrance east of Caloosa Island is

4

shoal. Under the east end of the island there is deep water, and a good harbor against all but southerly winds. There is a large fishing establishment up the bay, in sight of Caloosa Island.

The Caximba is a narrow sound that separates Isle Roman from the main. It is nine miles in length, and scarcely half a mile wide in any part. It is full of mangrove islands ; has six feet water on each bar. But where the tides meet the channel is very narrow, crooked, and muddy. Coasting vessels may easily pass through by employing one of the native pilots. There are several plantations near this Sound. That of John Durant, a native of Savannah, Georgia, lies on the south side, about a mile from the western inlet. Another, near the eastern inlet, is owned by a mulatto man. They all employ several native Indian families, to assist in cultivating the ground. The produce of the farms sell at a high price, to the fishing companies, who, in return, furnish them with clothing, powder, lead, &c. Many birds are also caught by the Indians, and sent to the Havanna in neat willow cages. They make bird-lime from the juice of the Gum Elemi, which they call Gumbo-limbo.

Gallivans or Delaware Bay is the nook formed east of Punta Longa or Cape Roman. From the north point of this bay, the Caximba enters and Gallivans River disembogues into the north east side. The north part of the bay, being filled with islands, separated by deep channels, its extent has not been explored. It affords perfect shelter for vessels drawing eight feet water. There is twelve feet sheltered from all winds except the south east.

Richmond Bay is the broad space, between the Florida Keys and Cape Sable. It is open to the west, but sheltered on all other sides. The depth of water is about nine feet. The bottom is rock, with a thin coat of white, soft calcareous mud, like white-wash. There are many channels, which passing between the keys, enter this bay, from various points, these are usually crooked and narrow and always about six feet deep.

Sandwich Gulf extends from Key Largo to Rio Rattones, a distance of more than forty miles, and is generally about six miles wide. It is usually from seven to nine feet deep. There are many inlets into this bay from the Atlantic, the principal of which are Angel-fish, Black Caesars, Saunders, Fowey and White Inlets. All these have about six feet water on their bars.

Among the Florida Keys, there are several small bays and sounds, which afford shelter for vessels bound to and from the Gulf of Mexico. The first is on the east side of Elliott's Key. It has eight feet water and there is an inlet in front of it, through the outward reef.

Before Key Tavernier, there is a harbor, in which, the Wreckers make a general rendezvous ; but the depth or extent of it is not known to us.

New Found Harbor lies west of the Honda Keys and is partially sheltered by the outward reefs. It has twenty feet water, which may be entered across the reef.

The Harbor, on the west end of Key West has 24 feet water and is easy of access, but is exposed to the north and west winds. At the north east end of the island is Spanish Harbor; it is safe for small vessels, drawing eight feet water.

Among the reefs of the Dry Tortugus's, there is said to be an admirable harbor, sufficiently deep and capacious for Vessels of the line. All we know of it is, the report of Commodore Rodgers to our government, which may be seen.

On the eastern coast of the Peninsula, there are no Bays. The rivers and inlets afford harbors for coasting vessels. The first of these, above Cape Florida, is New River, which has six feet water on the bar. Jupiter Inlet is next, it has opened and closed so often, that it is impossible to know the depth of water. It has had five fathoms and at other times not one. This is the most southern entrance to Indian River. Just below Cape Canaveral is the main inlet to this river. It is little frequented and the depth of water on the bar has varied from seven to eleven feet.

Musquito Inlet has nine feet on the bar, at low water. Vessels drawing eight feet may ascend Halifax River eight miles, and with six feet, may reach the Orange Grove twelve miles from the bar. The South Lagoon may be navigated about the same distance. After crossing the bar, the harbor is perfectly safe. The harbor of St Augustine is extremely similar to that of Musquito, and the North and Matanzas rivers are navigable on each side of the city, to about the same distance as the Halifax and Hillsborough. Small vessels and steam boats may enter the Matanzas Inlet and pass through the sound to St. Atgustine.

The St. Johns River has ten feet water on the bar, and is navigable for vessels drawing eight feet, into the lakes George and Dunns, one hundred and fifty miles from the bar. Nassau River may be entered with eight feet.

Fernandina Bay, at the mouth of the river St. Marys can receive vessels drawing twelve feet, and is entered with more safety, than any harbor on the southern coast. It is perfectly safe. During the destructive embargo and non-intercourse of Mr. Jefferson, this port was much frequented by foreign vessels, and became suddenly a place of much importance; but it fell with the non-intercourse law. The surrounding country affords few objects of commercial concern. Should the canal, across the peninsula of Florida, be ever carried into effect, this bay is intended for the Depot of the produce transported across the country. The St. Marys enters this bay, from the' west, navigable for large vessels one hundred miles.   A navigable Lagoon connects it with the river St. Johns, and another with Savannah River, so that the advantages of this bay, in a commercial point of view are very great.

CAPES.

Cape St. Blas is situated in Washington county, in latitude 29° 42′ and longitude 8° 29′ W. from Washington.   It lies at the south end of St. Josephs bay.   Its shoals extend more than twenty miles into the Gulf, in successive ridges.   Vessels drawing ten feet water should keep three miles from this cape in good weather, and in southern swells still farther.   The point is a low sand bank, and the pine forests discovered, are at least three miles north of the point.

Cape St. George, the next in succession, lies in latitude 29° 52′ and longitude 7° 56′ W.   It is in Gadsden county, on the south side of St. George Island, about five miles from the west end.   It is not perceptible more than five miles at sea.

South West Cape is also in Gadsden county in front of Oclockony Bay and is the S. E. end of James Island.   There is no distinct point, but the shoals extend, in succession seven or eight miles, to the S. E.   On this cape, the pine woods extend to the sea.   Vessels bound to St. Marks should keep from five to seven miles S. E. of the cape, before they haul up to the north.

Punta Longa, or Cape Roman, is situated in latitude 26° and longitude 5° 46′ W.   It is the south point of a large island, and projects fifteen miles from the main land, and from a S. W. point a succession of sandy shoals extend fifteen miles farther, in a S. S. W. direction.   Vessels drawing six feet water may avoid this cape, by passing through the Caximba, and by a passage of nine miles, shun a dangerous voyage of sixty miles.

Cape Sable is the most southward point of the peninsula.   It is in laitude 25° 4′ N and 4° 10′ W. longitude.   It is called, on the Spanish charts, Punta Tanche. As the land terminates in three projections, each of which is somewhat circular, it is difficult to designate the exact spot, for the Cape. Each of these projections are high and pleasant shell banks, extending back, in grass fields, called the Caloosa old fields. The reef of rocks, which has baricaded the coast, from Appalache Bay, ends at the south side of the middle projection, and there causes, as the tide ebbs and flows, a very turbulent sea. The rock again projects from the shore, about four miles east of the cape, and leaving Richmond bay, a circular basin, it subtends the whole group of Florida Keys.

Sound Point is a very shoal projection, from the Island of the same name which lies in front of and on the S. E. side of Key Largo. Carysford reef is a corresponding projection of the opposite reef on the east side of Hawks channel. Two thirds of the wrecks that happen on the southern coast, occur here, or within a short distance of this point. The coast is of the roughest reef rock, and covered, to some distance under water, with mangrove bushes. Among these the waves have carried every possible kind of wrecked matter, broken ship timbers, spars, plank, shreds of canvas, cordage, old iron, glasses, crockery, &c. are piled in ruinous confusion, upon the mangroves.

Cape Florida is the S. W. end of Key Biscayene. There is nothing in the situation, to justify the term, but custom has fixed it there. A very excellent lighthouse had been erected at this place and it marked the entrance of Hawks channel, but is now burned down by the Seminoles. It stands in lattitude 25° 38′ and west longitude 3° 13′.

Cape Canaveral is the only remaining projection of any note on this coast. It is situated in front of Indian River, in latitude 28° 15′ north, and west longitude 3° 22. From this cape, a shoal extends east eight miles. About five miles N. E. there is a reef of rocks usually bare; the water is deep around them; small vessels may safely run inside of them, but should keep at least three or four miles from the shore.

ISLANDS.

St. Rosa is a narrow sandy island extending from the mouth of Pensacola Bay, opposite to the Fort of Barrancas, to the Pass L' Este, a distance of 50 miles. It is about half a mile wide, and is conspicuous, for its pure white sand hills, which appear like drifted snow banks. It is very barren; a few crooked live oaks and pitch pines, grow in spots, on the north side of the island; while scrub oaks and yapon bushes, tangled with vines, form impenetrable thickets on the northern sides of the white sand hills. These are excellent shelters for deer, which are numerous. During winter, abundance of water fowl cover the fresh water ponds, which are found among the vallies. There is usually, a heavy surf, breaking on the south shore of the island; during storms, it is tremendous. Several vessels have been wrecked on this shore. A small fort and pilot house formerly stood on the west end of this island; they are now in ruins. But the United States are erecting in their place a formidable fort. Opposite the mouth of St. Andrews Bay, there are three islands; Sand, Hummock, and Crooked islands. The first is near three miles from the shore, and about a mile in circumference. It produces a few bunches of tall grass (ueniola latifolia) and a peculiar sort of sea cress, excellent for sallad; but a great portion of it is bar-

ren. Early in summer, it is wholly covered with the eggs of sea fowl. Be,
tween this island and the shore, there is a narrow channel eight feet deep
the rest of the space is shoal.

Hummock Island commences, a mile S. E. of Sand Island, and extends,
parallel with the coast, about six miles. It is quite narrow and produces
nothing but grass, sea cress and purslain. A ridge of low sand hills skirt
the western side. The main channel, into St. Andrews, runs from the Gulf
directly to the west side of this island, near the centre, then passes along
the island to the north end. Then passes close to the N. E. end of Sand
Island, into the centre of the bay. On Gauld's chart, the west point of St.
Andrews is made to extend to the south end of Hummock Island, and
Crooked Island is alone marked, as separate from the shore. It is not im-
probable, that these two islands have, lately, been separated from the point.
The sound, behind this island, forms an excellent harbor, easy of access,
from either end. There is eighteen feet water on the bar.

Crooked Island lies a mile south of the former. Its north east end approaches near to the main shore, but there is a deep channel between. It is
about as long as the former, but juts out into the Gulf in form of a crescent.
It is narrow at each end, but half a mile wide in the centre, where it is covered with a grove of pine trees. Between the south end of this island and
Cape False there is 8 feet water.

St. Vincent Island bounds Appalachicola Bay, on the west. Its form is
triangular; the north and west sides are each about ten miles long and the
eastern, from five to six. It is thickly covered with timber, lofty pines shade
the sea coast; while the eastern side is diversified with palms, live oaks and
magnolia, scattered over the grassy surface, which give it the appearance of
a fine park, rather than a lonely uninhabited island. A charming stream of
fresh water, enters the bay from the centre of the east side. The north
shore is broken by large marshes and Lagoons.

St. George's Island is about forty miles long, and from one half, to two
miles wide. Its west end is opposite to, and eight miles distance from, the
mouth of the Appalachicola River. For about four miles its direction is E.
by S.; it then bends N. E. The eastern end is about three miles from the
main shore, and about the same distance from Dog Island. Its southern
shore is thrown up in two or three sharp parallel ridges of yellowish brown
sand, in some places forty feet high. The centre is usually covered with
pine forests, among which are small hammocks of live oak and cedar. The
northern shore is indented with bays, marshes and lagoons. This side of
the island seems to be increasing. The east end is much washed by the
seas. It is low and barren.

Dog Island lies in the same direction and about the same distance from the shore, as St. George's, and is similar to it, in surface and productions. It is about seven miles long and one wide. There is an excellent harbor at the north east end, which will admit vessels drawing ten feet water.

James Island lies inland, behind Dog Island. It is formed by a branch of the Oclockony, which leaving the head of that bay runs S. W. and enters New River, four or five miles from the coast. The island thus cut off, is about twenty miles long, and from three to six wide. Alligator Harbor is a small bay in the S. E. point of the island. The land is poor, covered with pines and palmettos, and broken by ponds of water. The east end is covered with extensive marshes. The S. E. point is called South West Cape.

There are several islands of considerable extent, formed by the several outlets of Suwanne River. The soil on them appears to be rich alluvion. They are sprinkled over with cedars, palms, and live oaks. A Mr. Bradley began a settlement on one of them, but left it on account of sickness.

The N. E. part of Wakasasse Bay is filled with islets called the Fresh Water Keys; being situated in front of the estuaries of the Suwanne and Wakasasse Rivers. Many of these are pleasant and rich little spots, and there is plenty of fish and turtle among them. These islets are but imperfectly explored.

Still farther south are the Cedar Keys, an extensive group jutting far into the Gulf. They are very rocky, and separated by innumerable salt creeks. The cedars and other trees on these islets are small and sparse.

Opposite Turtle Mount there are three beautiful oval islands, about a mile apart, and the same distance from the shore. The longest is more than a mile in length, and all of them are well timbered.

Between the Cedar and Anclote Keys the Mangrove Islands are numerous, but usually small. Whenever an islet is separated at some distance from the others it is uniformly selected by some nation or tribe of birds. They load every branch almost to breaking. Gulls, curlews, and cranes often associate on the same key, but the cormorants, pelicans, fish-hawks, man-of-war birds, and eagles, live by themselves, admitting no associates. On approaching these aviaries of nature, the whole tribe rises in mass, and wheel round your head with loud screams, and are in some instances so numerous as to darken the air.

Anclote Key is situated about ten miles from Ouithlacouche River. It is three miles from the coast, about one mile long, of an oval form, and has ten feet water all round it, with good anchorage.

Joe's Key is two miles long, lies half a mile south of Anclote.

Helley's Keys are a range of sandy islands extending in front of Tocobagos, or St. Joseph's Bay. From Tocobagos to Tampa there is a boat channel behind these keys, but at some places it is very shoal at low tide.

Egmont Island lies in the entrance of Tampa Bay. It is merely a sand bank about a mile in length.

Mullet Keys lie north of the channel. There are several of them ; one is two miles long.

Minnies Island is also north of the channel, ten miles from Egmont. On this island there is plenty of fresh water.

Barnaby is a sandy key, south of Egmont.

Long Island closes the entrance of Tampa Bay on the south. It is seven miles long and divides the north part of Sarrazota Bay from the Gulf. Like most other of the islands on the coast, it is covered with mangroves.

Oyster Islands are a group that divide Tampa from Sarrazota Bay. Many of these are high, and rich in fruits and flowers. The hawey, a minute fig, is first seen on these islands ; farther south they are abundant.

Sarrazota Island lies south of Long Island, and is separated from it by Long Boat Inlet. Several small islets are grouped around the south end. These are bounded by Rio Seco, which terminates Sarrazota Bay on the south.

Palm Island is formed by the waters of Sarrazota Bay and Palm Sound. The Indians usually hauled their canoes over the south point of this island to save a long circuit at low water. There is a considerable hammock on this island, of a good quality, especially near the south end. It is several miles in extent.

Cleni is the first island in front of Charlotte Bay. It is a mile long, low and sandy. A narrow inlet separates it from Gasparilla.

Gasparilla is the second island proceeding south. It is six miles long, but narrow ; it has beautiful groves of gum elemi, and clumps of ovino trees. The east side is in many places covered with haweys.

Crooked Island lies on the north side of Bocca Grande, and is separated from Gasparilla by an inlet of the same name.

Round Island is on the south side of Bocca Grande, which is the main entrance to Charlotte Bay.

Capativa extends about seven miles down the coast. It was, with Sany-bal, formerly occupied by a tribe of Muspa Indians.

Sanybal is twelve miles long, and about two miles wide. It has on its margin some narrow hammocks. A Company from New-York, in the winter of 1833, surveyed a town at the S. E. end of the island. One elegant house was built and several smaller ones, but at this time, 1837, it is nearly deserted.

Caloosa is the last of this chain of islands ; it lies partly in front of

Carlos Bay. It is about five miles long, and from one to two wide. It is a beautiful, wild, solitary place ; it is diversified with thick groves of heavy timbered hammocks, and broad grass savannas, sprinkled with flowers, ovino and cotton shrubs, entwined with grape and nickernut vines. The perennial cotton shrub we first discovered on this island.

Pine Island is the largest inside of the bay. It consists principally of high pine land ; it is five miles long and two wide. On its border there are some narrow hammocks. It is situated on the east side of the bay, about ten miles south of Bocca Grande, and has on the north end a considerable fishing establishment.

Toampe is situate five miles south of Bocca Grande, in the heart of the bay. It is one mile long, from east to west, and half a mile wide. It is the seat of the Calde family. Their village consists of near twenty palmetto houses, and stands on the south west point of the Island. This Island is a high shell bank, covered with large timber. A small portion of the land is under cultivation. The inhabitants living principally on fish, turtle, and coonti ; the last, they bring from the main. Here are several cocoanut trees in bearing, orange, lime, papayer, hawey, and hickok plum. They raise cuba corn, peas, mellons, &c. I am told that most of the Islands in this bay, are nearly as fruitful as Toampe. They are innumerable. The Muspa Indians, once a numerous tribe, formerly inhabited these wild haunts.

Isle Roman is separated from the main by the Caximba. It is about thirty miles south east of Carlos. It is near fifteen miles from north to south, and ten to twelve from east to west. The north end is much cut up with creeks and lagoons, but contains some extensive hammocks, and old Indian fields. Three or four good plantations are under cultivation. That occupied by John Durant, a native of Savanna, lies about a mile from the western coast, the white oyster clifts of which, are seen half way through the Caximba. Corn, peas, and mellons, are the principal productions. The interior of the island is pine barren. The south point of the island is the Cape Acies, or Punta Longa, of the Spanish charts, and the Cape Roman of the British ; it terminates in dangerous shoals, which extend fifteen miles into the gulf.

The Caximba islands are extremely numerous, and but little known ; one on the north of the main inlet, must be five or six miles in length. Jewfish island lies about two miles from the western entrance, on the north side of the channel ; it is often visited by fishing parties of Spaniards, who admire the fish. The group extends as far east as the Gallivan river.

Musquito Key lies at the mouth of St. Mary's river. It is three miles in length, and apparently contains good land. Many smaller islands are scattered about it.

Rocky Keys are a considerable cluster of islands, above the mouth of Hujelos river. These islands are, for the most part, formed of curious coralines, some of them have beautiful hammocks on their shores.

Pavilion Key lies inside of the bass bank, and is marked as a point of land on the old charts.

Racoon Island, is also marked as a long point. It is surrounded by a cluster of islets.

The Florida Keys, are altogether an extraordinary archipelago of islands and reefs. They commence in latitude 25° 35′ on the Atlantic side of the peninsula, and from thence, extend in a group which describes the arc of a circle, bending westwardly, two hundred miles. They end in the Tortugas shoals, in latitude 24° 32′ and longitude 6° 10′ west. It has been made a question, whether these keys are fragments of the continent, torn by the abrasion of the tide : or whether they are additions constantly increased, by the labors of the Zoophite. It is not my intention to argue this question, but to state the few observations I have made among them.

Key Biscayno is the most northerly of the group. It is about seventy miles N. E. from Cape Sable. It is seven miles long, and two broad. It produces many mangroves, some hammocks on the north side, and much sand on the south. A lighthouse is located on the west end, where it is called, but without any reason, Cape Florida. The light house is now burned by the Indians. Here is plenty of fresh water. Sandwich Gulf spreads in a sheet six miles wide, on the north, separating it from a rocky coast. Bear Cut on the east, is a mile wide, and six feet deep. Here commences the passage, called on the English charts, Hawks channel ; at this island terminates the silicious sand, so abundant in East Florida. The Fowey rocks lie about two miles S. E. of this island, and form the commencement of the reef, that shuts Hawk channel from the sea. This channel affords safe navigation, for vessels drawing twelve feet : it is never less than fifteen feet deep, and is from four to six miles wide.

Soldier Keys are three small islands, in a row, six miles south of Biscayno.

The Paps are a small cluster of islets, two miles S. E. of the Soldiers.

Castor and Pollux are two small keys, lying west of the Paps, and east of Saunders Cut.

Elliot's Key lies south of Saunders Cut ; it is eight miles long, and three-fourths of a mile wide. It is rocky, but has a rich soil. The eastern side shows to advantage ; is covered with luxuriant grass and herbs, among which the maguy, the queen of plants, raises her pendulous white flowers, high in the air. Scattering ovino and mastic trees, give it the appearance of a plantation, and one is surprised to see no buildings, or animals, in a spot so flourishing. The west side of the island is thickly covered with wood. On the east side of the island there is a safe harbor, of eight feet water. Caesars Creek washes the south end of the island.

Jennings Island is about one mile long, and lies between Caesars and Angelfish creeks.

Largo Keys are a chain of islands, near thirty miles in extent, and in width very unequal, from half a mile to four miles. The south shore is very rocky; most of it is covered with heavy timber, but so entangled with vines, and so infested by musquitoes, that few have proved hardy enough to explore its recesses. In many places, it has both black and red loam to a considerable depth, which might undoubtedly be cultivated to great advantage. It produces a great number of wild fruits and flowers, which flourish most luxuriantly. About half a mile up Taverniers Creek, which enters the island below Sound Point, which is said to extend across to Sandwich Gulf, there is a small plantation commenced by Capt. Walton, planted with fruit trees. Sound Island lies in front of Tavernier Creek; the extreme ends are called North and South Sound Points. Behind these points there are harbors sufficient to shelter the wrecking vessels. Sound Key has no fresh water.

Carysford reef commences opposite the north end of Largo and ends just below N. Sound Point. The S. E. end of Carysford, is dry at low water. A deep inlet passes through the reef here, the current setting towards Key Tavernier. A narrow creek terminates Key Largo, and divides it from Long Island. A light ship is stationed behind Carysford reef, a little to the east of N. Sound Point.

Key Tavernier lies in front of the south end of Largo. It is small and low. It is remarkable only, as the rendezvous of all the wreckers. A small harbor affords shelter for their vessels, and the situation is important only, as it commands a view of Carysford reef, the most dangerous part of the coast. From this spot the wreckers scour the reefs and keys in every direction, sending daily north and south, three or four of their fleet, to the extreme points of the Florida Keys; so that vessels in distress, usually receive offers of assistance within a few hours. Numbers of vessels are thus saved from total loss every season. Doubtless these hardy veterans of the deep, have at some times, imposed on those whom they proposed to benefit. But we happen to know that much ingratitude has also been practised by those who have been saved from ruin by the wreckers. At all events, an excellent court is established at Key West, where all claims of salvage are legally and expeditiously adjusted, and there is no necessity for unfortunate masters of vessels to submit their causes to the arbitration of interested men.

Key Tavernier is succeeded by Key Rodrigues; it lies four or five miles west of and opposite to the channel, between Largo and Long Island ; it is small and of little value. Here terminated the surveys of the celebrated English Engineer, Gauld. His surveys of the coast and Florida Keys, can scarcely ever be improved. It is a great pity that the policy of war should have put a stop to his labors, that were equally valuable to America and England.

New Mattacumbe is four miles long, and about two miles wide. It has a broken rocky surface, but is clothed with a forest of hard woods, vines and plants, some of the latter very beautiful. Many kinds of fruit might be cultivated advantageously at this place. The wells of fresh water on the east end of this island are inexhaustable. They appear to be natural fissures in the madrepore rock, placed there by a Bountiful Providence, to supply the navies that have, time out of mind, frequented these latitudes.

Big Lignum Vitae Key is about one mile long, and half a mile wide, is situated behind the channel that separates Mattacumbe and Long Islands, and about two miles distant. It contains more good land than any other island in this part of the group: part of it is under cultivation, the rest is covered with hard timber.

Indian Key, on some of the old charts called Matanzas, was distinguished, by the destruction of a large crew of Frenchmen by the Caloose Indians. The vessel of the French, was wrecked on the reefs out side of this island, and the crew only escaped shipwreck to be massacred by the savages. It is one mile south of New Matacumbe, and contains about seven acres, the whole a Madrepore rock, in the clefts of which a few mangroves and flowering shrubs originally took root, and afforded roosts for innumerable variegated perewinkles that crawled over the branches.

At this time much of the island is improved as a garden, the rocky surface being covered by a bed of mould drawn up from the channel. Several buildings ornament the island ; a superb Hotel overtops them all, erected by the enterprising proprietor, Mr. Housman. Large stores are supported here principally by the wrecking business. This little island is becoming a fashionable resort for invalids from the north, the climate being healthy and pleasant, and the insects less numerous than in most of the keys.

Indian Key is 75 miles south west from Cape Florida, and 75 north east from Key West.

Old Mattacumbe is five miles long, and two wide. In surface it is similar to New Mattacumbe, but there is a greater quantity of good land on this than on the other island. This island was the last place of refuge of the Muspa and Caloose Indians, who formerly inhabited the eastern shore of the Mexican Gulf.

The space between the Mattacumbe and the continent, is sprinkled over with small islets, called Lignum Vitae Keys.

Viper Key, called on different charts, Bivora and Vivora, is five miles long, and from half to a mile wide. It is of a triangular form, and is much cut up with salt ponds and lagoons. On the shores are several hammocks of hard woods, but so narrow as to be scarcely fit for cultivation. There is a pretty harbor at the east end, sheltered by small keys.

Duck Key is a narrow rocky islet, containing some fine salt ponds. Mr. Howe, from Charleston, made a considerable establishment on the island for the purpose of making salt, but having died some time since, the project has been abandoned. It is about two miles long.

The Vacas or Cow Keys are ten or twelve in number, and extend about fifteen miles in length. Some of them are four miles in length, while others are scarcely half a mile long ; some are covered with tall pines, some with hammock trees, and some almost entirely with grass. On the north side of the group they are generally rocky, and bear many small palmetto trees. There are from ten to fifteen families scattered over them. Knights Key, the south west key of this cluster, has a good house and cleared field, that appears to great advantage from the water. Most of these keys possess good springs and wells of fresh water, and turtle are abundant in the neighborhood.

Sombrero is a crooked little island, covered with fragments of wrecks, with clumps of mangrove bushes. It lies five miles south west from Knights Key, and about the same distance from Cabbage Island, out upon the edge of the reef. Here there is a broad channel extending from the Atlantic, between the keys into Richmond Bay. It is usually ten feet deep.

Cabbage Island is the longest of a considerable cluster of islets, called the Honda Keys. It is two miles long, and two-thirds of a mile wide ; it is covered with tall cabbage trees interspersed with fruits and flowers, and appears rich and pleasant, but we did not explore the interior of the island. The Honda Bay lies in lat. 24° 35' and has from two and a half to five fathoms of water. It is well sheltered and safe from all winds. There is a small, but pleasant settlement on the east side of the harbor, with a well of good water.

This cluster of keys extend fifteen miles west, and about ten in a north direction, over an extensive coraline shoal; they are extremely numerous and separated by innumerable narrow channels. They are generally clothed with a dense vegetation of trees, shrubs, herbs and grass, sprinkled with various kinds of flowers. The trees of the hammocks are overtopped with a kind of vine, whose leaves spread over the limbs like a green carpet ; the seaside grape, different kinds of plumbs, and custard apples are frequently

found in the hammocks.   They are of all sizes, the largest extend ten miles
north and south, and three to four in width, and from this size they are
found not half an acre in extent.   The northern points of this cluster are
covered with tall pines, somewhat sparsely scattered over the surface of the
rocky soil.   Among these islands there are numerous salt ponds and lagoons, to and from which the tide flows and ebbs with great rapidity.

Samba Keys are six in number, or rather one great Key, the surface of
which is cut by the currents into six parts.   They extend about five miles
in each direction; they are however merely the shells of islands of which
the centres want filling up.   The shores are high and look promising, but
they immediately fall back into salt ponds.

Key West is the next island in succession.   It is seven miles long and
two wide.   The east end is divided by a channel through which the tide rapidly flows into an extensive salt pond that covers one third of the island.
The west end of the island however is solid ground, based on a limestone
rock, over which the zoophite has spread a few feet of coralines, and the thick
forests have on the top of both a rich soil.   Only a small part of this is cleared
and cultivated in gardens, where the pine apple bananna plantain and
various other tropical fruits reward the toil of the planter, and the stately
cocoanut raises his tall head abundant in rich fruit and broad expanding
leaves, supplying at once necessity and ornament.   The whole island is on its
surface very stony, though covered with a dense forest of various valuable
trees.   This part of the island has generally a rich soil of red or black loam.

Wells of Fresh water may be obtained in any part of the island by cutting through the limestone rock from six to ten feet deep.   The rock is a
deposite of lime without grit, and so soft that it may be cut with an axe.
Many of the small ponds, at the west end of the island, have been trenched
so that the tide ebbs and flows through them; this has rendered the place
more healthy.   Improvements have been principally confined to the west
end of the island, where the relinquishment of Congress, to three leagues
square, has been located by the proprietors.   This grant will cover all the
good land on the island.   The harbor is at the north west, which is entered
through a channel of four fathoms of water.   The best anchorage is on the
east side, where there are wharves and large ware houses for the accomo-
dation of trade.   There are some coral banks near the mouth of the harbor.   The N. W. winds, at some periods, affect vessels moored here ; they
are safe from all other quarters.   A shoal extends from the south side of the
island ; it is covered with a perfect forest of marine plants, infinitely various
in size and texture.   Southern storms sometimes tear these from the rocky
bottom and drive them in heaps upon the shore, to ferment, and sometimes
to create very unpleasant vapors, and are supposed to affect the health of

the town. Some experiments have been made on the salt ponds, situated in the heart of the island, which have been successful in producing salt, of a good quality. The bottom of these ponds are uniformly of limestone, but they require to be smoothed, in most places, before they can be advantageously raked. A canal has been cut from the north shore into the principal pond. We have heard no reason assigned, except a want of enterprize, why the salt ponds of this key, should not be as productive, as those on the Bahama's. Key West has been greatly benefitted by the trade carried on in wrecked goods, which are usually deposited here for sale. In other respects it is a superior situation for trade, and in time of war its harbor will be of vast importance. It is said to be capable of defence, at a reasonable expense. The original name of the Island was Cayo Huesso. It was for many years occupied by the Calde family, as a fishing establishment. They abandoned it for the island of Toampi, in Charlotte harbor, which they now occupy. The first American settlement made on Key West was in April, 1822.

The West India, squadron commanded by Commodore Porter, was stationed here, from April 1823 to Oct. 1826. And the Mexican squadron under the same commander, was stationed here afterwards. It is at this time inhabited by about fourteen hundred souls.

The Mangrove Islands, or Mule Keys, are small islets, scattered over a coral reef, that extends fifteen miles west of Egmont channel. This reef is about eight miles wide. Most if not all these islets are covered with water at high tides. It is bounded on the west by the grand entrance. It is from four to five miles wide and from seven to ten fathoms deep.

The Marquesas are two small keys about three miles south west of the Entrance Key, and are on the same reef, which extends nearly twenty miles west. On the west end of this reef, the silicious sand again appears in shifting banks.

The Entrance Key lies west of the grand entrance. It is crooked like a half moon. It is five or six miles long and in some places near a mile wide.

The Tortugas Keys are eleven in number, situated on a coral reef, which is about fifteen miles in extent. This reef is about ninety miles west of Cape Sable, sixty five miles west of Key West, and one hundred miles N. W. from Havanna. Of this group, a few of the largest are about three feet above the common tides. Seven of them are covered with mangrove bushes and bastard lignumvitae. The smaller ones are covered with herbs and grass. The S. W. Key, though one of the smallest, is most important to be known, because it ends the chain of Florida Keys. A reef of coral rock extends a quarter of a mile S. W. from it. North of this is a long sandy key. Under the lee of this there is good anchorage, about a quarter of a mile from the shore. The best harbor is near Rush Key; this is sheltered from the sea by a large reef of rocks and a flat shoal, and is quite smooth even in a gale. There is eighteen feet water close to the bank. Three broad channels lead to this harbor, which is capacious enough for a large fleet. The channels among these keys abound with fish and turtle, but they afford neither fresh water nor wood, except small bushes, and are important, only as a harbor.

Five or six miles west of the Tortugas, there is a large bank of coral rock and white patches of sand. These extend three or four miles west and north, and have from six to twelve fathom water. From a vessel they appear very shoal, but are not dangerous.

The Florida Keys are sheltered from the sea by a coral reef that extends near two hundred miles in length, and at a distance of from three to seven miles, forming a channel between it and the keys, usually three fathoms deep. This channel affords a safe passage for coasting vessels in smooth water all the way to the Mangrove Islands, where it ends. From this, which on the English charts is called Hawks Channel, several other channels branch off northwardly through the keys into the Gulf west of Cape Sable. The first has only eight feet water, it enters at Bahia Honda and winds northwardly round the Pine Islands into Richmond Bay. The second passes the west end of Key West and diminishes in depth to twelve feet where it enters into Richmond Bay. Coasting vessels drawing eight or nine feet, usually run through this pass, but strangers should take a pilot at Key West. On the English charts this pass is called Egmont Channel.

Bocca Grande is a pass between the Mangrove and the Marquesas Keys. It is about fifteen miles west of Key West. It is usually three miles wide, and has six or seven feet water. There is a middle ground with patches of coral rock, but they have on them from two and a half to three feet water.

There is a broad channel between the Marquesas and the Tortugas, with fifteen fathoms water; but the eastern side, next the Marquesas, has patches of coral, and banks of quicksand, in some places not more than from five to twelve feet under water.

In all these channels there is good anchorage, and the bottom can be clearly seen from the mast of a vessel in clear weather. The water is always of a light color within the reefs.

The reef ends directly south of the west end of the Marquesas. It is here about three miles wide, with five fathoms water. Proceeding eastwardly it soon becomes narrower, but more shoal. It is here about four miles from the keys. The first key on the reef is about nine miles S. S. W. from Key West. It is called Sand Island, and has a revolving light. Four miles west of this, there is a patch of rocks; about two miles east there is another patch; from this there is from two to three fathoms for about five miles east, but there is four and a half fathoms on the reef, opposite to the west end of Key West. To enter, bring the light on Key West to bear about N. N. W. ; after passing the reef, run west so as to leave the light three-fourths of a mile on the right hand, then run close round the N. W. point of the island into the harbor.

Proceeding eastward on the reef to bring the east end of Key West N. W. about seven miles, there are three small sandy keys called Samboes. The reef here becomes narrow; between the two west keys there is a channel of four fathoms, and between the two eastern ones another channel of three fathoms.

For ten miles east of the Samboes, which are sandy islets, the reef spreads to four miles wide, and is very shoal, having at some seasons bare patches of rock; but opposite Newfound Harbor the reef is about three-fourths of a mile wide. Here was situated Loo Key, but it is washed away; some reefs of rocks, however, remain. About a mile west of these rocks, there is a fair channel of four fathoms water. To the east for three miles there is about sixteen feet water; it then deepens for five miles to three, four, and five fathoms. The reef runs pretty straight past Bahia Honda; it is about three miles from the keys.

Key Sombrero is the easternmost islet on the reef. It is situated six or seven miles S. E. from Bahia Honda, and four miles S. W. from Knight's Key, the western key of the Vaccas group. It is but a patch of rock, covered with a few mangroves and pieces of wreck. From Sombrero to the west end of Old Mattacumbe the reef is broken and irregular in breadth and depth. There are patches of coral rocks, some under and some above water. Seven or eight miles off the east end of Vaccas, there are several bad ones. Off Bivoris there are more, some near the surface, others deeper, off the west end of Old Mattacumbe. At the east end of this key there is a good harbor for coasting vessels. Indian Key is passed close to the east side, where there are convenient wharves constructed. Southwest from this last key about three miles, is the Alligator shoal, where one of our sloops-of-war was wrecked. In this shoal there is only four feet water.

Opposite Key Rodrigues the reef has only about seven feet water, and is three miles from the islands. Eastward of this the coral rocks increase, and the reef is often broken by channels of deep water. There is one, in

particular, off Sound Island, of four fathoms, through which the tide rushes with great velocity, especially in easterly storms.

Opposite to the north end of Key Largo, commences Carysford reef,
which extends to the last mentioned channel. This is the most dangerous
part of the whole reef. More vessels are wrecked here than on the whole
coast besides. The coral rocks are sprinkled over this part of the reef;
many of them entirely above water.

The reef extends nearly to the Soldier Keys, a little south of Biscayno light; it varies in breadth from one to two miles, and is covered with
rocks. During fair weather vessels of any size may sail very near to this
reef along its whole course. In the inside channel they should keep within a mile of the keys, as there are scattering coral rocks near the reef in
many places, and the south side of the channel is most shoal.

So far as I have been able to examine the extraordinary group of islands
and reefs on our southern coast, I have found the soft calcareous rock to
subtend the whole group. It is the same formation that encircles the Gulf
of Mexico as far as the Appalache River, and I believe it to be the foundation of the whole peninsula. But the surface of every reef and island is
covered with strata of zoophites of almost every description. Their labors
are continual, and their work constantly progressing in an infinite variety
of beautiful forms and colors. Two-thirds of the distance between the
Mattacumbe islands and the main, is bare at low water, and presents a
surface bristling with fresh coralines, interspersed with young mangroves,
from three inches to the size of trees. Little islets are rising above the
water, from one rod, to one, two, and three miles apart; some covered
with bushes, others with a heavy growth of timber. Narrow channels,
generally about six feet deep, wind among them in every direction, and
many of these convey the tide through the reefs, from Hawks' Channel
to Richmond Bay. The bottom of all these channels is formed of the soft
limestone; but it is usually covered with a white-wash of dissolved matter,
about a foot thick. When stirred it gives to the water a milky tinge.
These channels are the favorite haunts of the turtle, and almost every
kind that live in the water may be found here. The inhabitants of the
keys are generally adepts in the art of spiking them. One of these sports-
men, who resides on Indian Key, is said to have spiked and secured sixteen
in one day. Fish are not so numerous among the keys as they are about
the 27° of latitude. There are, however, many kinds, and some of them
highly prized; and among which are the Jew-fish, porgy, hog-fish, and
bass. There is also a species of cray-fish, which lives in holes among
the coralines, of two or three pounds weight, which is excellent eating.
It is variegated with beautiful colors, but wants the long claws of the

lobster. Large and beautiful concks are also numerous on some of the flats near Key West, where they are much used for soups. The most superb corals, in white clusters, are found on Long Reef. The delicate purple are principally confined to the Lignum-vitæ Keys.

After passing the Florida Keys, Jupiter or Gomez Island next presents itself. It is twenty-five miles long and from half a mile to two miles wide. The eastern side presents a beach sloping off half a mile to low water mark. The ridge of sand hills is high ; behind this is a space covered with small oaks and palmettoes, while the western side terminates in hammock, and where the island throws projections into Hobe Sound, the hammocks are of such extent that they might form small farms, of excellent land. This side of the island is rocky, near the shore. Four miles from the south end, several fruit trees still remain, that were planted long since ; among these are cocoanuts, oranges, limes and plums. Several old fields indicate former settlements. Several dangerous reefs of rocks lie in front of this island.

St. Lucia Island was formerly connected with Jupiter, and the whole was granted to Don Eusebius Gomez, on account of public services, rendered the goverment of the province. A few years since, the high waters of St. Lucia River, forced a passage through the coast at the place called the Gap, on the old charts, and about four miles south of the black rocks. In 1831 a mile in front of the north end of the island, was torn away by storms. This island is sixteen miles long, and extends from Jupiter, to Indian River inlet ; at the north end it is three miles broad. The surface of this Island is exactly similar to Jupiter. Indian River contains innumerable mangrove Islands, none of which are of much extent except—

Meritts Island. It lies west of Cape Canaverel, and extends thirty miles in length, and is for a considerable distance more than two miles wide. The western side generally presents a surface of high rolling pine land. The south end is a reef of rocks of the Coquina species. Three miles from the south end are fine looking hammocks. On the N. E. side the hammocks are more extensive, and a considerable plantation was began here, by a Mr. Merritt ; some fruit trees, of his planting, still remain. The eastern shore is mostly a low mangrove swamp.

Bissets Island is a low narrow island, situated in the N. W. side of Hillsborough Lagoon. It is eight miles long, but contains very little good land. It is surrounded by hundreds of small islands, which fill the Hillsborough, from New Smyrna, to Ross's old plantation, a distance of fourteen miles. Some of these islets are high and pleasant, bearing palm trees and grass, but most of them are low and covered with mangroves. Dog Island is about two miles wide, and has a good soil. Gallups Island is nearly as large ;

both islands have clusters of low oaks, and cabbage-palms. Hallifax river contains a similar group of small islands.

Anastatia Island, extends from the little bar of Matanzas, to St. Augustine. It is twenty-one miles long, and two broad. It was granted to Jesse Fish by the Spanish Government, except the Kings quarries and the site of the Tower. His heirs are still in possession. It contains a few hundred acres of excellent land, a part of which is improved in a fine orange grove. A lighthouse occupies the place of the old Spanish Tower. The quarries of Coquina stone are extensive ; they have furnished stone for the principal buildings of St. Augustine, as well as the Fort and sea wall, and other buildings ; and plenty still remains for all purposes, public and private.

Fort George Island, extends from the mouth of St. John's River, to Talbot Inlet, about three miles, and it is more than half that width. It is the seat of Zephaniah Kingsley Esqr. It contains a good deal of excellent land, much of which is highly improved.

Talbot Island extends from the Inlet to Nassau River, about four miles. Messrs. Houston and Christopher, are the proprietors, who cultivate valuable plantations on the island.

Amelia Island extends from Nassau to St. Mary's River. It is fifteen miles long and four miles wide. A considerable proportion of the island is good land ; several extensive plantations were formerly cultivated on it. Fernandina, situated at the north-west end, was once the county seat of Nassau County. During the time of non-intercourse and embargo laws, this town rapidly increased to a place of importance ; with those laws, it died a natural death. It may revive when our peninsular canal is carried into effect.

The Two Sisters are two small, but fertile islands, situated on the north side of St. John's River, above Fort George Island.

McDonald's Island is near the new canal, and is about three-fourths of a mile long. There is on it about fifty acres of excellent land.

Tiger Island is situated in the mouth of St. Mary's River, opposite Fernandina. It is more than a mile in length, and of a crooked form. It is mostly marsh, with a few small hammocks.

The marsh in front of St. Mary's extends four or five miles, but it contains no arable land.

Nassau Island lies about eight miles from the mouth of the river ; is five or six miles in extent, but nearly all marsh.

Fleming's Island extends from Doctors' Lake to Black Creek, a distance of twelve miles, on the west side of St. John's River ; the land is excellent and highly cultivated in Sea Island cotton, provisions, and cane.

Murphy's Island is near the east side of the St. John's, directly above Dunn's Creek. It contains about two thousand acres of land ; a part of it is excellent hammock, the rest is pine land and swamp.

Kingsley's, or Drayton's Island is situated at the north end of Lake George. It is three miles long and two wide. A considerable portion of the land is excellent. A small improvement has been kept up, for several years, near the north end. It is beautifully situated opposite the outlet of the lake, and will, at some time, become a delightful plantation.

RIVERS.

The Perdido forms the western boundary line between Alabama and Florida. It rises in Alabama, about thirty miles above the Florida line. It is navigable about seven miles above the bay, to some saw-mills. It is a noble mill stream, and its banks are covered with superior yellow pine timber.

The Connecuh rises in the south-east part of Alabama. Its general course is S. W. till it meets the Escambia River, near the north line of the Territory. It there loses its name in the Escambia, which is a much smaller stream. Here it turns a S. E. course, and enters the north-west end of Escambia Bay, through several deep channels. Its principal tributary streams are the Sepulgas, Murder Creek, and the Big and Little Escambia rivers. The lands on the borders of this river are rich, but are often overflowed, which renders planting on the river bottoms a hazardous employment. In the autumn agues and fevers prevail, on the low grounds.

Where there is clay enough in the soil, to form good embankments, the waters might be leveed off, and the land would be equal to any in the world.

Black Water River is only about fifty miles long, but is navigable for boats, near twenty miles. It is narrow and crooked, but deep, and is a fine mill stream. It empties into a bay of the same name which is attached to Yellow Water Bay. It is full of Islands, and about seven miles long. Above the bay, it receives Cold Water Creek from the west. These waters generally, rise from fine springs on the borders of a good farming country, called the Pine Level.

Yellow Water River rises in Covington county, Alabama. It runs a course of ninety miles and enters the N. E. side of Yellow Water Bay, through several mouths. It receives, in its course, Shoal River, from the S. E. the principal branches of which are Titi and Pond branches. It is navigable for boats forty miles, to Barrows Ferry. The Aliqua River rises in the Knobs of Walton county, and after a course of about twenty-five miles, enters the north side of Chactawhatche Bay. It is navigable to

Vaughns, fifteen miles from its junction with the bay. This river is formed suddenly from large springs, some of them large enough for mills.

Chactawhatche River rises in Pike county, Alabama, and after a southern course, of one hundred and fifty miles, enters the east end of Chactawhatche Bay. It is navigable for boats, about eighty miles. At the north line of Florida, it receives Pea River from the west; the latter is the largest and longest stream. Uche Creek enters, about twenty-five miles from the mouth, and Sandy Creek about forty miles, both from the west ; and Holmes Creek from the east, as well as Big Barren and Pond Creeks. Holmes Creek is navigable to the Big Spring at all times and to Shacklefords landing, fifteen miles higher, at most seasons.

Econfina River rises in Washington county, south and east of Oak Hill, and after a course of thirty miles, enters the north arm of St. Andrews Bay. It is navigable to the Natural Bridge, fifteen miles from its mouth. Below the Natural Bridge, it receives the waters of Hamblys spring, and a number of extraordinary fine springs burst into the west side of this river, for three or four miles. The lands on its banks are generally of a superior quality, and at the same time perfectly healthy. Bear Creek is a navigable branch which enters the Econfina, from the east, four miles from its mouth. This river abounds in trout of a superior quality.

The Wetappo River rises in Washington county, west of the Chipola, and after pursuing a very crooked S. W. course about twenty miles, it turns suddenly to the west, where it receives the S. E. branch, and five miles farther, enters the east end of the east arm of St. Andrews Bay. This river is usually twenty feet deep, but at its entrance into the bay, the water is not more than four feet. The S. E. branch extends within seven miles of the Chipola River, and is deep enough for boats of any description. It is a superior stream for fish, trout in particular. It is through the S. E. branch of this stream, that it is contemplated to connect the waters of the Appalachicola River and St. Andrews Bay.

Appalachicola River is formed by the junction of the Chattahooche and Flint Rivers, about one hundred miles from the Gulf of Mexico.

The Chattahooche River, rises near the corners of the four states, of Tennessee, South Carolina, Georgia and Alabama, and strikes the north line of Florida, at 31st degree of north latitude. About twenty-one miles below this, it is joined by the Flint. The latter river rises in De Kalb county in Georgia, and pursues a course, nearly south, to its junction with the Chattahooche. Vessels drawing eight feet water can ascend to the Forks, a distance of one hundred miles. The Chattahooche is navigable for Steamboats to Columbus. The Flint may be navigated, about forty miles, to Bainbridge. It receives the Chipola thirty-three miles from its mouth. This branch rises in Richmond and Henry counties in Alabama, and is navigable as far as the Natural Bridge, above Marianna. A passage has been broken from the Appalachicola, into the Chipola, just above the situation where the Wetappo approaches the latter river, and by overflowing the natural banks of the Chipola, has formed a lake of considerable extent. The Appalachicola enters the bay, through several mouths, and has thrown into the bay a great extent of marshy delta. The lands on the banks of this river, are generally rich, and the produce conveyed to market down its various channels is already very considerable, and is rapidly increasing.

The Oclockony River rises in Irwin county, Georgia, and pursuing a southwardly course, it enters the bay of the same name, seven miles from the Gulf, and about twenty west of St. Marks. Lieut. Swift reported seven feet water on the bar, at the entrance of Oclockony Bay. Steamboats may probably ascend fifty or sixty miles at most seasons of the year. A branch called Crooked River, breaks off above the bay, and after a course of twenty miles, enters New River, a small stream that reaches the Appalachicola Bay, directly north of the west end of Dog Island. Tugulo, Little River, Robinsons Creek, and Rocky Comfort are branches of this river.

The Appalache River is formed at St. Marks by the junction of the Wakully and St. Marks Rivers ; the Wakully rises from the earth, eleven miles north west from St. Marks. Boats drawing six feet may ascend to the head. The upper part of the river is full of small islands, and even the crooked channels are filled with long grass, so as to impede the navigation. The St. Marks rises in a small pond, nineteen miles N. E. from its junction with the Wakully. Boats drawing four feet, can ascend to its source. Schooners drawing seven feet, ascend to Magnolia, seventeen miles from the Gulf. It is probable that the real source of this river is in Irwin county, Georgia ; that after traversing Mickasukey Lake, it sinks into the earth and ultimately rises at the pond at Brockhaven. Numerous streams direct their course towards its supposed channel, and sink into the earth. Large sinkholes also, and at one place a large stream appears above ground, where this river is supposed to flow. Below St. Marks the navigation is very crooked and much impeded by Oyster bars. Congress in 1829, appropriated a sum of money, to improve the navigation. It is greatly needed, as commerce is rapidly increasing here, and will progress with the population of the Middle District. A lighthouse has lately been erected at the entrance of this river.

The Ocilla River rises in Irwin county, Georgia, and enters the Territory in two branches, about ten miles apart. These unite about fourteen miles below the line. The eastern branch forms the division line between Madison and Jefferson counties. The western branch, from the Georgia line nearly to the place of its junction with the eastern branch, spreads into a wide grassy lake, more than a mile wide. About thirty miles from its mouth it falls over a rocky ledge, and twelve miles from the Gulf, it sinks under ground for three fourths of a mile. From this bridge to the sea, it is navigable for small vessels. It receives from the east a considerable stream, called Foenahalloway. This stream abounds with excellent fish.

The Chattahatchee, or Stony River, takes its course southwardly from Sampala Pond, which, by the Spaniards, was called San Pedro. It runs through a barren country, and falls into the Gulf about fourteen miles east of the Ocilla.

Achenahatche, or Cedar River, rises in numerous lakes, in the eastern part of Madison county, and falls into the Gulf about thirty miles east of the mouth of Suwanne. This river is small, but is the outlet of a rich grazing country.

Histahatche River is formed by the junction of three streams, at the falls, nine miles from the Gulf. It spreads into a round bay before it enters the Gulf. From this to the falls, it is very deep, and its rocky shores are scooped by the waters into numberless grotesque and fanciful shapes. From the bay to the Gulf the passage is shoal. The land about this stream is very rocky, but heavily timbered.

The Suwanne is formed by the junction of the Little Suwanne and Allapahaw Rivers. The Ouithlacouche rises in Doole county, Georgia, and joins it six miles below the Allapahaw. The Little Suwanne rises above the Okefanakow Swamp, in Appleby county, Georgia. The Suwanne makes a very circuitous course to the Gulf, into which it carries an extensive delta. It empties its waters through numerous shallow channels. From the bar, which has no more than five feet water, fifteen feet may be carried as high as the Santaffe, which enters from the east, fifty-five miles from the bar. Above the Santaffe there are several ripples, where the waters are no more than six feet deep. This depth may be carried up to the Ouithlacouche. The bed of this river is uniformly rocky. The Santaffe rises in a long pond, on the ridge of the peninsula. It runs a course of about fifty miles, and receives the outlet of Sampson's Pond, or Alligator Creek, New River and Sanfilaseo, above the bridge, and the Echatuckne below the bridge. The natural bridge covers the stream for about three miles. In high freshes, the subterraneous passage is not sufficiently large to receive all the water, and then a large stream passes over it.

The Wakasasse rises in Allachua county, and running a southwardly course through a long range of ponds, it enters the Wakasasse Bay behind the Fresh Water Keys. This stream passes through a fine grazing country, as the name imports. The remains of several Indian houses are situated about seven miles from the mouth of it. This river is little known. Should the bar be sufficiently deep to admit merchant vessels, a convenient depot for the produce of the Allachua country may be found on its banks.

The Ouithlacouche rises in the Seminole District, on the east side of the military road, south of Lake Ware. Its course is N. W. till it approaches Camp King, it then turns westward and enters the Gulf above St. Clement's Point. This is a narrow and swift stream, and in many places rocky. The bar is shoal; boats, however, may ascend within fourteen miles of Camp King. From the Silver Spring, a navigable water of the Ocklawaha, to this place, is seventeen miles. This is decidedly the place where the waters of the Atlantic and the Gulf can be connected by the shortest cut, and besides, that the land is comparatively level, the height of the table land is here only eighty-seven feet above the tide, while the height on the route by Black Creek and Santaffe, recommended by the Board of Engineers, is $237\frac{1}{2}$ feet. It is matter of regret that the Engineers did not examine this route ; and the more so, as it was particularly pointed out by our delegate in Congress.

Hillsborough River rises a little south of the Ouithlacouche. It has a S. E. course of about 50 miles and enters the north end of Hillsborough Bay. Boats can ascend this river about 20 miles, to the falls. Cantonment Brook is situated at the east side of its mouth.

Manatee river rises in the unexplored country east of Tampa Bay, and is about a mile wide at its entrance. It has ten feet of water to the Falls of Haffia. It is little known beyond, except that several considerable branches extend through the country, the largest of which, spreading northward, was by the English called South Hillsborough. The Manatee enters the bay 15 miles S. E. from Cantonment Brook.

Talackchopko, or Peace River, is the same named Asternal on Vignolles' Map. It rises in the interior from Lake Apopkochee, and pursues a westward course until parallel with Charlotte Bay; it then turns south for about 18 miles and enters the north side of the bay, some miles below the mouth of Macaco River. It was 60 yards wide where Capt. Clark's survey crossed it.

Macaco, or Charlotte River, is supposed to have its source in Myacco Lake, in the heart of the Peninsula. We have not been so fortunate as to find white man or Indian that had ever visited the lake or the river more than fifty or sixty miles above Charlotte Bay. There, it flowed with a rapid current, and the stream was two miles wide and twelve feet deep. The north bank was a wide and deep swamp. The south bank had a narrow strip of high ground, which soon fell off into mangrove swamp.

7

This is the largest river on the western side of the Territory. It is to be regretted that it has never been explored to its source.

Caloosahatchee River enters Carlos Bay; it appears to be a large stream, but has never been explored. A Spanish fishery has been established at its mouth.

Delaware, or Gallivan River, enters the east end of the Caximbas, among numerous islands. It is a bold stream, and vessels drawing eight feet can sail into it. How far it is navigable is unknown. There is a high and pleasant bank on the south side of the river, but it seems to be confined by the mangroves at some distance back. There is a good harbor for coasting vessels in front of this river.

St. Maria and Hujelos, or Swallow River, are separated only by a point. They are small streams and their sources are unknown. The Hujelos is the southern boundary of Hackleys' claim, on the west. This is, by the native Indians, called Chittahatche, or Snake River. They relate that thirty miles up it there are several good islands, covered with oak timber and mastic, but they say that they are prevented from hunting there by the snakes. Except Dry Creek, or Sable Creek as it is sometimes called, there is no river below the Swallow River. This creek throws up at its mouth high banks of sand, and is doubtless very rapid in high freshets. It has an excessive crooked course among the mangroves, which terminates in a drain from the Glades.

Sharks River I could not find, and think that it does not exist. Below the Upper Camachee Field, 15 miles above Cape Sable, the water was very deep, and there appeared much current among a cluster of islands. A stream might enter behind them, but nothing like what is represented on the map for Shark's River.

Miame River is a small stream that issues out of the Glades and enters Sandwich Gulf, behind Cape Florida. It is about six feet deep where it enters the gulf. The tide rises about 4 miles up in a rocky channel. It there forks, and the north branch descends from the Glades in a rapid current over a limestone rock. The height of the Glades above the tide has not been ascertained. The inhabitants here say 40 feet ; I feel confident that it is more than half that height. Fifty feet, if cut through would drain a vast extent of grass meadow, that appears to the eye quite boundless. There may be lagoons of great depth, but they cannot be extensive, as the waters, to appearance, are not more than, from two to four feet deep.

The River of Rats, or Rattones, is extremely similar to the Miame in its course. The tide, however, scarcely affects it, and falls over a plane less inclined than the Miame. A prong of this stream is connected with a branch of New River. Indeed, there is little doubt that all the streams on this coast, up to Indian River, are drains from the Glades, and thus may communicate with each other. Arch Creek is a considerable stream that enters the bay between these two rivers. It waters a rich tract of land.

New River has a longer course than the Miame and Rat Rivers. The Glade here recedes farther from the coast. It has six feet water on the bar, and it may be navigated several miles into the country.

The Potomac leaves the Glades about fifteen miles from the coast and enters Hillsborough Inlet, where it is joined by the waters of Bocca Rattones, which has for several years been closed up. There is six feet water at the mouth of the inlet, which is narrow and rocky. [Since writing the above, Hillsborough Inlet has closed, and Bocca Rattones is again open.]

Jupiter Creek is a sluggish stream, which runs a N. E. course about 15 miles, and enters the south-west end of Hobe Sound.

Middle River is a drain somewhat larger, and pursues a course from west to east of about twenty miles, and enters Hobe near the last creek.

Greenville River enters the sound, a short distance from the last river. Its northern branch is near thirty miles long, and traverses a pine country after leaving the glades.

St. Lucia enters Indian River near the south end, with a broad bold stream, which appears more like an arm of the bay, than a river. It continues thus for ten miles in a westerly direction. Here is a large bend, and its course is from the south ; here it passes through two small lakes. At twenty-two miles from the mouth it suddenly contracts into a narrow and crooked, but deep stream ; which is encumbered with old cypress trees. Romans states, that it passes through the savannas and glades, but rises far back in the high grounds of the peninsula. This is contradicted by Vignolles, who says that it is soon lost in the swamps ; that it is a mere drain from the glades. The waters of this stream have, within a few years past, forced a passage through the coast, at the place marked on the charts, the Gap. Probably, this is not the first time the channel has been opened. The tide passes and re-passes this new inlet, with great rapidity. The bar was not sounded by me. It appeared shoal. In the winter of 1832 this inlet was carefully examined ; recent storms had made great changes in the islands of the coast ;—a full mile had been cut off from the island on the north side of St. Lucia Inlet, and the channel had deepened to eight feet on the bar.

Indian River is a vast lagoon. It was formerly called Ys. The distance from its head branches to Jupiter Narrows is about one hundred miles. It is in some places four miles wide ; in others not fifty yards. In some extensive reaches it would swim a frigate, at others six feet water can scarcely be found across the channel. The depth of water is greatly affected by the seasons. When the southern inlets are closed the waters rise very high, before they have power to force open the closed inlets. The north branch of this river rises in McDougal's Swamp, five miles S. W. from New Smyrna. It inundates the centre of the swamp for about fourteen miles ; it then confines itself to a deep crooked channel, and receives the west branch from the pine woods, about sixteen miles from New Smyrna. It is likely that the western branch has the largest course, as the current is more rapid than that of the north branch. Its course, to the haulover, is about S. E. In passing southwardly it gradually spreads to a width of four miles, and opposite to Cape Canaverel it is more than six miles wide. It becomes very narrow opposite Crane Creek, and widens again at the inlet to four miles. The deepest water is usually on the west side. The eastern side is filled with islands in many places, particularly above and below the inlet, and on the east side of Merritt's Island. It receives from the west many tributary streams. Elbow Creek enters just above the south point of Merritt's Island. It is a large stream. Crane Creek is less, and enters below the south point of the island. Turkey Creek is still less, and enters about three miles south of Crane Creek. These three creeks drain a branch of the glades, that approach within twelves miles of Indian River.

St. Sebastians River rises in the Glades, and pursuing a N. E. course, enters the river eighteen miles below Merritt's Island, and twenty-seven above the Inlet. This is the longest tributary stream of Indian River, except St. Lucia, which has been considered as a branch, until lately, when it forced a passage through the beach, and thus cut off about three miles of Indian River, to the south, where it is connected with Jupiter Narrows. These Narrows are a labyrinth of narrow, deep and crooked channels, that connect the south end of Indian Lagoon, with Hobe Sound. The tide passes swiftly through them ; they are separated by a vast number of mangrove islands. These narrows extend about eight miles. Hobe Sound is a handsome sheet of water, from a quarter to half a mide wide, and extends from the narrows to Jupiter Inlet, about eight miles further. Before St. Lucia River broke the chain, Indian River, and Hobe Sound formed one great Lagoon, near two hundred miles long. This great Lagoon undergoes frequent changes. There is every reason to believe that, at some former period, it discharged a great column of water at Cape Canaverel, which appears like a bank of sand, forced into the Atlantic by a rapid stream. This river being choked up by the Coquina formation, which constantly accumulates on the coast, the waters were driven laterally into the St. Lucia, which in its course became blockaded ; and a great lake collected behind the coast, until the accumulated waters burst new channels into the sea. Jupiter Inlet has opened and closed three times, within seventy years. There is at this time, three inlets. The old Indian Inlet, 40 miles below Cape Canaverel, St. Lucia Inlet, and Jupiter Inlet, all of which are shoal and appear to be closing up. When one or more of these shall close, it is to be expected that the force of the tide will render the others deeper. Should the old inlet and St. Lucia be closed, the navigation of the whole lagoon would be greatly benefitted. For turtle and fish, Indian Lagoon is equal to Tampa Bay.

Hillsborough Lagoon extends from Çape Canaverel to Musquito Inlet, a distance of forty miles. The southern point is in some places six miles wide. It has no tributary streams. The north end, for fourteen miles, is full of mangrove Islands ; and some, that have high ground, covered with palms and other timber. Vessels drawing eight feet, can ascend twelve miles to Turtle mount, and sloops can pass the Cigeras, or Mount Rodney, four miles further. This Lagoon interlocks with Indian Lagoon. A small creek connects the east end of Hillsborough Lagoon, with the waters of Indian River, on the east side of Merritt's Island. At the Haulover, the distance is only half a mile, between the navigable waters of each. It abounds in turtle, and fish of the best quality and size. New Smyrna was situated on the western bank of this lagoon, four miles south of Musquito Bar.

Halifax Lagoon extends from Musquito Bar, northward to Tomoko, a distance of twenty-three miles. It is usually a mile wide, and has many islands and extensive marshes at the south end. Eight feet water may be had as far as Pellican Island, eight miles north of the bar, and sloops have ascended to the Orange Grove, four miles higher. The Bar of Musquito Inlet, is about the same depth as that of St. Augustine, and the harbor is easy of access, and when entered perfectly safe. Halifax and Hillsborough Lagoons, meet at this bar. Several small streams enter the Halifax. Spruce Creek is navigable from 15 to 20 miles, one half that distance, through extensive marshes. The Kings road crosses it over a wooden bridge, ten miles from the lagoon ; the creek is there ten feet deep.

Tomoko Creek enters at the head of the lagoon, on the west side.

Smiths Creek and Haulover Creek, unite before they enter the north end of the lagoon. Haulover Creek rises in the savanna, near the head of Matanzas River, and not half a mile west of the coast. Smiths Creek is a drain from the pine woods, west of the former, and is navigable for boats, sixteen or seventeen miles from the lagoon.

The Matanzas Sound, separates Anastatia Island from the main. From the Bar of St. Augustine, to the Matanzas Bar is 21 miles, and an arm or lagoon extends seven miles further, to Mala Compra, the seat of Gen.

Hernandez. It is, on an average, three fourths of a mile wide, and receives, at the south lagoon, Longs Creek; Pallaciers Creek near the Matanzas bar ; Moses and Moultree Creeks twelve and five miles south of St Augustine, and St. Sebastians, just below the city. Vessels drawing nine feet water, have often loaded at Matanzas Inlet and passed through the sound to St. Augustine,

North River rises in Cabbage Swamp west of Diego Plains, and after a southern course of twenty-five miles, meets the Matanzas at the Inlet of St. Augustine. It has no tributaries except Guano Creek and several pleasant brooks, from the pine woods. It is navigable for schooners twelve miles ; thus far, it is about half a mile wide. Boats drawing five feet ascend to the plains, eight miles farther.

The St. Johns is a noble river, sweeping round a large extent of the Peninsula in a circular form. Its sources, although, probably within twenty miles of the coast, have never been explored. It often spreads from three to five miles, in width ; at other places it is not one fourth of a mile. It is exceedingly crooked, meandering through a beautiful and healthy country. Although, in a straight line, it may not be one hundred and fifty miles from its mouth to its source, yet, in its meanderings, it is more than twice that distance. Vessels drawing eight feet water, enter Lake George and Duns Lake, one hundred and fifty miles from its mouth. At the entrance of this river, there is twelve feet water on the bar. It is here only one mile wide. A lighthouse on the south side of the river, marks the entrance.

From the best information we have been able to collect, the St. Johns. rises nearly opposite to Cape Canaverel, in the extensive grass meadows that extend, east and west, from three to twelve miles, and twenty to thirty north and south, but separated from the waters that run south, into the Everglades, by a very crooked rise of cabbage land, but little elevated above the adjoining meadows. Indeed it is more than probable, that in wet seasons they may be connected.

The head streams are numerous, and although, from three to six feet deep, are so full of grass that a canoe cannot be pushed up them without great labor.

The first open navigable water is a Lake about five miles long and one wide, near fifty miles south of Lake Monroe. About a mile north of this, a large stream enters from the S. E. which appears to rise in a small lake about a mile distant. The river now widens, in the course of three or four miles, to two hundred yards, and has a depth of eight to ten feet. The eastern bank is from eight to ten feet high with small beautiful hammocks, broken through by several tributary streams. The west side an unbroken marsh.

Three small Lakes now embrace the river in the distance of as many miles. The river is then divided among numerous large marshy islands, so that the main channel is hard to be found ; ponds and lagoons of every shape are numerous, and no pine woods to be seen on the west.

In a few miles a Lake opens to the north, perhaps five miles in circuit and averaging six to seven feet deep. The river leaves this Lake near three hundred yards wide and twelve to fifteen feet deep, and continues to meander through grass meadows, marshes, hammocks and clusters of cabbage trees, occasionally increased by tributary streams, the largest of which comes from the south west ; in which direction the pine timber again appears.

Seven miles above Lake Monroe, Lake Peyton joins the river on the west side, at the extremity of a long sharp bend. It extends to the westward fourteen miles in an oval form, becoming narrow towards each end ; the eastern, is indeed scarcely half a mile wide for a considerable distance. In the centre, where the width is perhaps five miles, there is a circular island with a shoal extending to some distance towards the east. The water of the lake is usually six feet deep, except the east end which is no more than three feet. The eastern part of the lake is bordered with cypress swamp. The western part by hammocks covered with cabbage palms, live oaks and other hard timbers. A large Indian old field lies on the south side of the lake near the end. Near it a considerable stream passes into the lake ; this stream rises about a mile from the lake in several large sulphur springs. On the west side of the stream, on the lake shore is a considerable Seminole village.*

Two miles below Peyton Lake, the river embraces a large island, near three miles long and one broad.

The country here, is diversified with grass savannas, swells of pine land, oak hammocks and clumps of palms ; in many places near the river, the grass meadows are rich and beautiful.

Four miles from the island the river enters Lake Monroe over a sand bar on which there is little more than three feet water.

This Lake is of an oval form, seven or eight miles long and three to four wide, towards the south end ; it is narrow at the north end. A very long point of land runs from the S. E. end, more than a mile towards the centre of the lake, dividing it into two deep bays, into the eastern of which the river discharges itself. The depth of water is on an average about eight feet, though deeper towards the N. W. end. The river passes from the lake over a bar of five feet.

* The above lake was discovered in the spring of 1837 by Lt. Peyton, 2d artillery. To whom I am under obligations for this information.

The eastern shore of the lake is thinly shaded with hammock trees, beyond which, grass savannas extend for several miles. Several large medicinal springs rise near the N. E. shore. At the S. E. near the entrance of the river, the bank is formed of concrete shell rock, that might answer for building. On the S. W. side there is a hammock of some extent, covered with loose shells; on this is situate Camp Mellon, established by Col. Fanning about the 5th Feb., and attacked by Philip on the 8th. In this affair the Seminoles were severely handled, and driven off with the loss of several men, after a close engagement of four hours.

Lake Monroe abounds with excellent fish. North of Lake Monroe, the river is usually from thirty to fifty yards wide, from two to three fathoms deep, and very crooked. The banks variegated with meadows of grass, twenty feet high, hammocks of live oak, magnolia, &c. and clumps of cabbage trees, generally rich land, for thirty miles to Berrisford.

Berrisford was the most southern settlement made by the English on this river. It is a high rich hammock on the N. E. side, separated from the river by a pleasant lake, half a mile wide, and two or three long. A large mineral spring rises behind the north point of Berrisford. It is very transparent, five to six fathoms deep, thirty yards broad, abounds in fish, whole companies of which may be seen sailing in every part of the fountain. The column of water thrown up forms a creek thirty yards wide, and six feet deep, which enters the lake near a mile from the head.

For twenty miles the river continues to pass through a country similar to that from lake Monroe. It then passes through the west end of Long Lake, at the entrance of which on the west bank, is a wild orange grove. The east end of this lake is connected with Dexter's Lake by a creek one and a half miles long. Dexter's Lake is a triangular sheet of water, about six miles in circumference. Into the N. E. angle enters Spring Garden Creek. This creek rises in a large spring, five miles east of Dexter's Lake, and at the north end of Spring Garden Plantation, the property of Colonel Rees, of South Carolina. The spring affords water sufficient to manufacture the sugar and mill work of the plantation. It is the first experiment of damming up and raising water on the spring head, and has succeeded perfectly well. Spring Garden Lake, is a shallow water, extending from near the spring, nearly a mile south, bounding the western side of the plantation. The whole course of navigation from this to the St. Johns, is about twenty miles. Long Lake is six miles from east to west, and sufficiently deep for any craft that can pass Lake George.

Six miles brings us to Volusia, a pleasant military post, six miles above Lake George, on the N. E. bank of the river. This place was long occupied as a plantation; the soil is rich shell land, rising into considerable emi-

ST. JOHN'S RIVER & VOLUSIA on the RIGHT BANK.

Sarony & Mc Gowran's Litho. 30, Wall St. NY

nences. Here the old Indian trail crosses the river leading from St Augustine to Chicuchatty. A road is now opened from this to Tampa Bay by Pilacklacah...

The river enters Lake George over a bar of four feet water. This lake is about fifteen miles long, and eight wide. It averages about twelve feet in depth. There are several pleasant and rich tracts of land on its borders, and it contains two large islands near the north end. Drayton's Island, owned by Mr. Z. Kingsley, contains near three thousand acres of land, on which is a considerable plantation. The Silver Spring, a beautiful fountain, rises on the S. W. border of the lake, the outlet of which, is navigable for boats. The Salt Spring rises about five miles from the N. W. shore ; the estuary is navigable for steam boats to the head. A very handsome creek on the eastern side of the lake, has excellent land on its banks.

Seven miles of bold and open water brings us to Little Lake. This is an expansion of the river five or six miles in circumference, with a very crooked channel winding through it.

Mount Royal is a small tract of land on the north shore of the river south of the lake, formerly an English farm.

North of the lake is Mount Tucker, formerly a very extensive plantation, with a high lookout mound, close to the lake shore. On the west side of the river, enters the Ocklawaha, the largest tributary of the St. Johns.

This river rises about sixty miles east of Tampa Bay, near the centre of the peninsula, and after passing through two smaller lakes, enters Lake Eustis, about nine miles south of the road leading from Volusia to Tampa. The north end of Eustis approaches near to the road, its outlet is fordable in dry seasons, but at other times is fifty yards wide, and six to eight feet deep. A bridge was thrown across this place by General Eustis ; it was afterwards destroyed by the Indians. A large lake spreads out below the crossing, but little is known respecting it. Pain's Landing used formerly to be considered the head of navigation, but since the establishment of the Indian Agency at Fort King, boats have come up into Spring Creek, three miles east of that post. Twenty miles below Spring Creek, Orange Creek enters from the west. From thence it passes through vast clusters of Islands, which impede the navigation for about eight miles. It enters the St. Johns opposite Mount Tucker, through very extensive swamps of rich land. The government of the United States have granted $10 000 to improve the navigation of this stream.

Twenty miles below the Ocklawaha, Dunn's Creek enters from the east. This creek is navigable for schooners into Dunn's Lake. From this creek it is eight miles to Palatka, the seat of Doct. Brush, of New-York, where a ferry was kept before the Seminole war, on the road leading from St. Au-

8

gustine to the Allachua country.   Palatka is now destroyed by the savages.
Five miles below this, Rice Creek enters from the west ; it is navigable
about twenty-five miles.   It has its source in the Etteni cluster of ponds,
thirty miles west.

Thus far the river is very narrow, and very crooked ; below this it widens
and becomes much straighter.   In a distance of twenty-five miles to Picolata, it is in some places three miles wide.   At Picolata on the east, and
Bayard on the west, the great road from St. Augustine to Tallahasse
crosses.   This far the tide rises from ten to eighteen inches., A line of
steamboats runs from Savanna to this place.

Six Mile Creek enters from the east, five miles below Picolata, and Black
Creek at twelve miles, on the west side.   This creek has a good navigable
channel, fifteen miles to Garey's Ferry, where a military post is established.

Mandarin is a small village on the east bank of the river, three miles
below the mouth of Julington Creek.   Girts Creek enters from the west,
five miles above Jacksonville, and Trout Creek five miles below.   Pablo
enters from the south three miles above the bar.

There is an inland communication between the St John's and St. Mary's,
navigable for steamboats.

The tide is perceptible in the St. John's more than a hundred miles from its
mouth.   Its waters are of a brown color, tinged by the abundant vegetables
washed in its course.   It abounds in fish, and its alligators have been celebrated by Bartram the younger rather correctly than otherwise.

Nassau River rises about half way between the St. John's and St. Mary's.   Its sources are in large swamps west of the King's Road.   It pursues
a meandering course of about fifty miles, through extensive marshes, and
enters the Atlantic over a bar of six feet at low water.

St Mary's River is the boundary line between Florida and Georgia.   It
rises in Oquafanoke Swamp in Apling County, Georgia, and discharges its
waters into the Atlantic in lat. 30° 40½′ N. between Cumberland and Amelia Islands.   There is thirteen and a half feet of water on the bar at low
tide.   The tide rises six and a half feet.   High tides at full and change of
the moon, at half past six o'clock.   This river is clear and limpid water,
and navigable for large vessels, eighty-five to one hundred miles.   The navigation is safe, the banks almost perpendicular.   It is, however, a very
crooked stream.   The little St. Mary's is a southern branch, that enters the
river about 25 miles above the town, and directly below the plantation of
Z. Kingsley, Esq.

Spanish Creek rises in Little Oquafanoke Swamp, and enters the river
just above Colerain.   Big Creek rises in Allachua County, and is the south-

ern branch of the St. Mary's. Its source is in a large pond. The inland communication between this river and the St. John's, is large enough for the passage of steamboats. Congress has lately expended several thousand dollars for the purpose of improving this communication.

LAKES.

The first lake worthy of notice in the western part of the territory, is McDavid's. It is situate on the north line of Walton County. It is about three miles long and two broad. It is a beautiful sheet of water, abounding in fish and water fowl.

Lake Wimico is near the coast in Washington County. It is seven miles long and three broad. It has a navigable outlet into the Appalachicola River. Its west end is five and a half miles from the St. Joseph's. It is now connected with the St. Joseph's by a rail road.

Hort's Lake is an inundation of the Appalachicola River, covering a large extent of country. The Chipola river passes through it. It has not been well explored.

Iamony Lake is situate in the north part of Leon County, is between eight and nine miles long, and from three to four broad. It discharges its waters into the Ocklockony River.

Lake Jackson is four miles N. W. from Tallahasse. It extends north and south about ten miles, and is in some parts five miles wide.

Mickasooke Lake lies east of Lake Jackson. It is twelve miles from north to south, extending into the State of Georgia. The western part is much the largest, and is in form a triangle. Much of this lake is covered with tall grass, of which cattle are so fond, that they often wade where the water is over their backs to feed on it.

Old Tallahasse Lake is in the S. E. part of La Fayette's Township. It is three miles long from east to west, and about a mile wide. It has long been celebrated for its excellent trout.

Sampala Lake, the San Pedro of the Spaniards, is situate in Madison county, on the north side of the eastern military road. This is a superior water for fish. It has an outlet into Foenahalloway, or Chattahatchee River.

Alligator Lake is situate in the north part of Allachua, now Columbia County, on the south side of the military road. In winter it is three miles long and almost as wide. It receives several creeks, but has no outlet, except a sink hole, which in summer drains the pond nearly dry. It is then an excellent grazing tract. It probably communicates with New River, a north branch of the Santaffe.

Randolph, or as the inhabitants call it, Ocean Lake, is on the north side

of the St. Augustine road, about fifteen miles N. E. of Alligator Lake. It
is one of the heads of the St. Mary's River, and is claimed by Georgia as
the main source of that river. It is said to be six or seven miles long, and
two or three wide.

Pithlachucco Lake is within the Arredondo Grant, in the centre of Allachua County. It is nine miles long and three wide. Its outlet, called
the River Styx, falls into the great sink of Allachua Savanna.

Hogmaster's Lakes are two, closely connected together, extending east
and west about seven miles. They lie south of Mr. Levis' Plantation, in
the heart of the Allachua grant. They are almost covered with grass.

Orange Lake, in the same grant, is eleven miles long and from one to
five miles wide. When this lake is rendered navigable from its head to the
Ocklawaha, and thence into the St. John's River, it will be the depôt of the
produce of the Allachua country.

The Etteni Ponds are a large cluster, of all sizes and shapes, up to four
or five miles in extent. They extend south of the Ockawilla Savanna to
the Orange Lake Creek. The largest of them is the head of Big Cedar
Creek. They derive their name from a tribe of Seminole Indians, whose
towns were situate among them.

Doctor's Lake is rather an arm of the St. John's River. It extends
south-west, towards Little Black Creek, about seven miles, and is from
two to three miles wide, and navigable for schooners.

Dunn's Lake lies between St. John's and Musquito Counties. It is fifteen miles long and four to five wide. It is a beautiful sheet of water,
abounding in fish and water fowl, and is navigable for large schooners.
Dunn's Creek connects it with the St. John's. It receives the Haw
Creeks at the S. E. end. The three creeks unite near the lake, and form
a channel navigable for boats four or five miles.

Lake George is fifteen miles long and eight to nine broad. It is pretty
uniformly twelve feet deep. It receives many pleasant streams, from
the east and two large springs from the west. The salt spring rises five
miles from the lake, and admits boat navigation to the head. The silver
spring rises only a mile from the lake and throws into it, a tribute of transparent water. The river above Lake George expands into several small
lakes. Spring Garden Creek does the same, and the Ocklawaha, more than
either.

Lake Eustis is near the head of the Ocklawaha, and is said to be of an
oval form about five miles on the course of the river, and four miles wide.
On the S. E. side there are high sand hills.

One branch of the Ocklawaha passes through two more large lakes.
The southernmost is Apopka; it is large but little known.

Apokachee or Big Apopka is situated south of Hitchepucsassee, is the head of Talackchapko or Peace River ; it is said to be ten miles long and five or six wide. At the outlet on the S. E. end the Seminoles had several towns containing two hundred houses, which were burned by Col. Goodwin, at the close of General Scott's campaign.

Tokopalika Lake is situated in the centre of the peninsula of East Florida, and is connected with the southern Everglades by a chain of lakes and lagoons. Standing on the N. E. shore, no land can be seen in a southern direction. Gen. Jessup's campaign extended south as far as this lake. Philip's principal towns were in this vicinity, and here he remained unmolested during the whole Seminole war, with the exception of the establishment of fort Mellon on Lake Monroe, supposed to be twelve to fifteen miles east of this Lake.

Lake Monroe is sixty miles from Lake George in a south east direction ; It is seven miles long and from three to four miles wide. It is usually full eight feet deep. It is of an oval form, narrowest at the north west end, and has a long point jutting from the south east end more than a mile towards the centre of the lake, dividing the south end into two deep bays. It abounds in fine fish, and is altogether a healthy and pleasant sheet of water. Fort Mellon is on the S. W. bank. ✳

Lake Ware is situated between the Seminole Agency and Tampa road, and the Ocklawaha river. It is said to be five miles long and three miles wide ; Pilhuena Island, near the south end of this lake, is described as a rich and romantic spot. Its luxuriant orange groves are said, formerly to have over-shadowed a red sprig of Royalty, who appears at least to have possessed some taste in rural scenery.

Fresh Water Lake lies parrallel and near to the southern Atlantic coast. Its north end approaches within ten miles of Hobe Sound. From thence, it extends southwardly, twenty-four miles, and is usually from two to three miles wide. There are several large lakes in this neighborhood, but they have not been explored, by any person, to my knowledge.

The same observations apply to Lake Macaco ; several old maps exhibit waters on the interior of the Peninsula, connecting the principal rivers on both sides. I am inclined to believe, that the peninsula has not been explored, far from either coast, south of Tampa Bay and Indian Lagoon. When Ferdinand de Soto invaded Florida, he found an Indian Chief named Macaco in the neighborhood of Tampa Bay, and his province bore the same name. When I visited Charlotte Bay, in 1828, I found several native Indians, about the Spanish fisheries, who called Charlotte River, by the name of Macaco, but they could not be made to comprehend anything about such a lake. Not one of the writers who have described this country, since the change of flags, has been able to obtain any certain intelligence relating to this part of the peninsula.

ANIMALS.

The Horses of Florida are a breed of hardy ponies, small and easy to support ; they will keep fat on the wild grass and herbage of the country, but they are not heavy enough for the harness. They are excellent travellers in a new and sandy country like ours. The breed is said to have been brought, originally, from Andalusia in Spain. It is thought that a breed of horses, from the English, mixed with the native poney, would unite most of the qualities, desirable in that useful animal.

Mules are not raised here, but they are frequently brought from the neighboring states, and sometimes from Campeachy and Texas. They are principally used for draft. They live longer, and are more easily kept than the English horse.

The native cattle are a large breed with broad horns and close, sleek hair. They are good breeders, but have not been highly valued for their milk. They often become very fat on the wild grass of the country. The marshes on the coast, often give the milk, as well as the beef, a disagreeable flavor and a bad taste. Cattle bred in the interior country, often become sick when brought near the coast for grazing.

Few oxen are used in the yoke, because agriculture is yet in its infancy in the Territory.

Sheep succeed well in the higher parts of the country. The flavor of the mutton is good, and the meat of a tolerable quality.

Goats are raised with ease ; they even seem to succeed best when most neglected. They multiply faster than any other domestic animal, and their increase is a clear profit to the owner.

Of dogs we have every kind. The hound is extremely useful to the early settler on the frontier, and pointers and water-dogs are highly valued on the coast, where fowls are abundant.

Hogs succeed to admiration ; they grow fat where every other animal would starve. They delight in the small shell-fish and marsh roots on the coast, while the mast and black bracken roots, in the country, are equal favorites with them.

Of wild animals, the deer is most important ; they are numerous in almost every part of Florida. They however do not grow so large here, as in the Middle States, and they are still smaller towards the capes of the Peninsula.

Panthers are numerous in many parts of the Territory. In some of the grazing districts they are particularly destructive to calves. They are very shy animals and rarely seen.

Bears are most numerous about the cane-brakes. They destroy abundance of hogs, and are usually very fat.

Wolves are found in all the unsettled parts of the Territory ; but except in purloining a calf occasionally, they are little known. Their attention is usually directed to the sheep, and of these, there are, as yet, very few in the Territory.

Wild cats and foxes are rare. Opossums and racoons extremely numerous. The latter, in particular, about the sea-coasts live on fish and oysters, and become lumps of fat.

Otters and minks are numerous about the water courses. There are two kinds of squirrel ;—the small grey, and the pine squirrel. The latter is a beautiful animal. His body is usually of a rich, glossy, brown color, and his head black, and very often one half of his face white. The Salamander is a land mole, about half the size of a rat. He is peculiar for throwing up rows of small sand hills over the woods, where the ground is easily excavated. He lives oñ the roots of plants. Rats and mice are numerous and troublesome every where. The small ground mole often commits depredations in the gardens, and especially in the orange nurseries.

REPTILES.

A great variety of Tortoises inhabit the territory. The common Land Tortoise, vestudo guacca, is from seven to ten inches long, very thick and clumsy, its head fat, and its tail covered with scales, its shell a dark brown on the back, and pale yellow beneath. It usually lives in deep shady woods, and feeds on insects. The female lays five eggs, and covers them up in sand, leaving them to hatch by the heat of the sun.

The Gopher is much larger than the land tortoise. It frequently weighs from six to twelve pounds. It delights in soft sandy land, where it can push its burrows with little labor. It is usually taken by digging pits, before the mouth of its burrow. Soup and gumboes made of their flesh, are in high estimation. They feed in the evening and morning, on the dewy grass and herbs, but never stray far from their holes. They lay two or three eggs near their habitations, these are quite round, with hard shells, about the size of hens eggs ; they are covered about four inches in sand, and left to hatch by the heat of the sun.

There is a very small tortoise found in Florida, not larger than a dollar. They are curiously striped with yellow, they are quite docile, and placed in a tumbler of water, they make very clever pets. I have not seen the species in any other place.

The Painted Tortoise, testudo picta, is found in our rivers where they become brackish with the tide. They delight to bask in the sun, upon old logs, on limbs that hang over the water, from which they drop at the first appearance of danger. It is somewhat larger than the land tortoise.

The Snapping Tortoise, testudo serpentina, grows to a huge size; our Lakes and Lagoons are well supplied with them. They often bite at the hook, and make very good food.

The Green Tortoise, testudo mydas, is very numerous among the Florida Keys. They are found, more or less, in every part of the Gulf of Mexico, and they also extend up the eastern coast of Florida, in considerable numbers. They grow to a great size. They usually average from ninety to a hundred pounds, but one was caught near the Ouithlacouche river, by Capt. Dagget, of the Dighton, weighing six hundred. Another was brought into Key West, weighing near eight hundred. Their heads are small and round, their feet long and webbed somewhat like fins. They come upon the beach, during the moonlight nights, of the summer season, dig holes in the edge of the grass, near high water mark, and lay from 112 to 130 eggs, and bury them from two to three feet deep in the sand. The turtle hunters often find them at their nests, and turn them on their backs, where they remain safely till they are conveyed away. When pursued on shore, they throw the sand with great violence behind them. They are very social, and herd together in large communities. Many inhabitants of the Keys, live by hunting them. A good turtler, will take from ten to twenty in a day; they not only surprise them by land, but they pursue and strike them at sea. The tortoise spike is one inch and a half long; the point that pierces the shell is only three fourths of an inch square, sharp and highly polished; a grooved shoulder is raised in the centre, to which a cord is tied, a very short socket enters the end of a long straight pole, from which the spike easily slips. Great judgment is requisite in striking the tortoise; if the blow be too heavy, the shell is cracked by the shoulder of the spike, and it will not then adhere, but if correctly entered, the force of the largest tortoise will not disengage the spike. The animal flies like a harpooned whale, but soon looses breath, and is easily towed to the boat. Large nets are also used in deep water, to catch them. By the quantity, tortoises are sold about the keys, at six and a half dollars per hundred weight; at retail, twelve and a half cents per pound, is a common price.

The Hawk-bill, testudo imbrecata, is a rare turtle on our coast. It is occasionally taken among the green ones. It is not highly valued for food. Its shell is highly estimated in commerce, and finds a ready sale among the manufacturers of combs, snuff-boxes, &c.

The soft-shell, testudo feron, inhabits our fresh water lakes; it is covered with a gelatinous gristle, instead of a shell. It is shaped like the green tortoise, and his feet are somewhat webbed. He usually feeds on frogs, but is particularly fond of young ducks. Its flesh is quite equal to that of the green tortoise. It rarely weighs over twenty pounds.

Turtling forms so important a branch of southern industry, that a turtle-crawl is considered an essential appurtenance to a habitation ; as much so, as a barn is to a northern farmer. Turtle is the permanent stock. The crawl is a pen made where the water is about two feet deep, at low tide. Mangrove poles are generally driven into the beach, so near together that the turtle cannot pass between them. The tide thus flows freely about them, and they are daily fed with sea-grass or purslain.

The Alligator, lacerta cinerous, is undoubtedly the ugliest creature living. Floating on the water he resembles a log. On land he looks like a huge snake, with the addition of thick, short legs, and sprawling claws. But it is in his wallow, a large mud hole among the rushes, that the alligator is quite at home, surrounded by a hundred young imps of ugliness, all barking like young puppies, and constantly pursued by the male for food. The female then adds rage to her natural deformity, and often kills her whelps by the strokes of her tail, while fighting in their defence. If any of our readers wish to become acquainted with the chivalric character of the male, let them consult William Bartram's Travels in Florida, page 129. These hideous reptiles are, however, more disgusting than danger-ous. I have often seen people bathe within a few yards of them, with per-fect safety ; nor have they, so far as we have ever heard, attempted to in-jure any person. They often attack dogs and hogs, and have, rarely, at-tempted to seize cattle swimming in the water. During the warm season they spend the night in holes of fresh water near the coast ; but usually retire into the sea or some deep water during the day. Some inhabit the inland lakes and rivers, but salt lagoons are their favorite residence, where fish, turtle, and frogs are plenty ; they are not delicate in their choice of food. They sometimes swallow pine knots for want of better eating. During the warm evenings of summer, it is difficult for strangers to sleep near their haunts, on account of their bellowing. In the southern parts of the Territory, they keep abroad during the winter ; but they are not so nu-merous there, as in the St. John's River, and Appalachicola Bay, which are greatly infested by them. Their nests are truly described by Bartram, nor has he greatly exaggerated their numbers ; but I have never discovered the ferocity that he describes. Their eggs are usually laid in five or seven tiers, one above another, with layers of green vegetables and mud between each ; the whole is then plastered over with mud, and forms a cone four feet high, and as many in thickness. The heat of the fermenting vegeta-bles and the sun's rays hatch the eggs, and the young whelps, about six inches long, crawl, in succession, from a hole near the top of the nest, and instinctively seek their mother in some neighboring wallow. The alligator differs from the crocodile in their teeth ; the fourth pair of the crocodile passes upwards in a groove,—the alligator's perforates the upper jaw. The feet of the crocodile are webbed, those of the alligator are half-webbed. The crocodile does not bellow like the alligator. The flesh of the alligator is said to be wholesome and pleasant food, and is eaten by many people. Their hides make excellent leather.

There is a great hiatus between the alligator and the striped lizard, lacerta scorpio. This reptile is only six or seven inches long, with sides striped alternately with red and brown, and has large red gills. It is a greasy, disgusting thing, and very impudent, intruding itself into the chambers of the new settlers. It is, however, innocent, feeding on flies and other insects.

The Swift, lacerta veloxa, is from five to six inches long, of an ash color, striped and dotted with brown. The tail long, of a deep green, and extremely brittle ; when broken off it is re-produced in a short time.

The Florida Cameleon, lacerta agilis, is less ugly than any of the lizard family. It is very domestic ; delights to run over the vegetables in the gardens, peas in particular. It will often sit on a leaf and puff out its under lip like a bladder, speckled with rubies, looking you all the time in the face with great assurance. It is almost transparent. While living on vegetables it is of a most beautiful green, while those that are found on dark or burnt soils are of a dark brown; some are beautifully speckled with scarlet spots.

The Black Newt, L. terestris, is usually found under rotten timber, and rarely appears abroad.

The Bull Frog, rana accellata, is found in great numbers in some of our grassy ponds, but they are not so large or so numerous as in the Middle States. They live only in pure water, and feed on young ducks and cray-fish. They, in their turn, become the prey of the alligator, who will, in the course of a few weeks, clear a considerable pond of them.

The common Brown Frog, rana temporaria, is more numerous than any other of the species. The female lays thousands of eggs at a litter; these produce the little brown frogs, that we see after a shower, all of a size, crawling in multitudes over the ground.

The Green Frog, R. esculenta, is sometimes seen in the northern parts of Florida, but they are rare. About the month of May the female spawns, and the male attends to regale her with an unusual croaking noise. This kind of frog is in some countries highly valued, as a wholesome and delicious food.

The Little Tree-Frog, hyale, is of a fine pale green color. They usually live among the branches of trees, and feed on moths, worms, &c. They are rarely seen, on account of their similarity of color to the herbage they inhabit. Like the green lizard, this reptile assumes the color of the objects it inhabits. They are very musical reptiles, and rejoice at the fall of rain.

The House Frog, hyale domestica, is usually concealed under the roof, or in some hole, from which it can easily approach the open air. He is also very musical; in damp weather and during settled rains joins his notes with those of the tree frog and cricket, in a general serenade.

The Garden Frog, H. hortularius, imitates to perfection the barking of a puppy. His note is so loud as to become very disagreeable.

The Rattlesnake, crotillus horridus, is cccasionally found in the islands and dry hammocks of Florida. The pine woods are so frequently burnt over that most of the reptile tribes are destroyed; some few get into the gopher holes and shelter themselves from the flames. The low parts of the Territory are too wet for them, and the south is too hot. There are, perhaps, less snakes in Florida, than in any State or Territory of the same extent in the Union. I have spent nineteen years in this Territory, and visited almost every part of it, and during that time I have not seen so many poisonous snakes as I have discovered in half a day in the western part of Pennsylvania.

The Copperhead has been discovered only in the western part of the Territory, and there very rarely.

The Moccassin is the most numerous snake in the Territory. It inhabits still waters. About the mouths of some rivers they bask on logs and limbs of trees, and often drop into boats passing under them. Their bite, although not so terrible as that of the rattlesnake, is yet very poisonous.

The Viper, coluber berus, has been seen in some parts, but is very rare.

The Ground Rattlesnake is about 12 inches long. It is frequently seen coiled in a circle, flat like a piece of ferretting ; in this situation it lies on a fence rail, or log, and has been seized by children, as a plaything. Its bite often produces a lingering illness, though not frequently mortal.

The Black Snake, constrictor, is considerably numerous. One kind lives among the titi bushes, that cover streams running through the pine barrens. They often grow large and catch many chickens. They are not poisonous. A less kind inhabits the water ; these are numerous in some places.

The Coachwhip is the largest and most numerous kind of snakes in Florida. They exactly resemble a thread-covered whip, with a black handle. The body is remarkably slender, of an ashy grey color. They are quite innocent.

The Pine Snake is long and slender also, and chequered with black, on a

light ground, the cheques are scarcely a twelth of an inch square.   It is innocent.

The King snake wears a coat of brilliant hues.   Black, brown, yellow
and white colors shine in mixed rings of an inch in length.   He is about
four feet long, somewhat stouter than the pine snake, and has the credit of
destroying the rattle snake, wherever he can find him.

The Bull Snake is of the size and color of the rattle snake, but is not
poisonous ; his shape is more slender, he is sometimes called the Gopher
snake.

The Garter, Riband, Green and Grass snakes are occasionally seen, but
there are few of either kind.

INSECTS.

The Insects of Florida are numerous as her vegetable productions, and
were it not for the birds that destroy them, they would render the country a
wilderness.   Yet so careless are the inhabitants of their interests, that ten
persons are found to destroy the innocent warblers, for one that attempts to
destroy the pestiferous insects.   Those most common, are—

The Beetle.—Scarabeus.

Night-walker.—Melalonthe. He flies about in the night and eats off the
leaves of plants.

Stagg Beetle.—Lucanus.

Bacon Bug.—Dermestes.

Lady-bird.—Coccenilla. This insect feeds on the aphides, or tree-lice and
is very useful to gardens.

Wevil.—curculia. A most destructive insect, in this climate, destroying every kind of grain ; indian corn in particular, is so much injured by it,
in a few weeks, as to render it useless.   It is common to leave the corn un-
husked, to guard, in some degree, against the evil.

Metal Bug.—cicindela. Appears clothed in copper highly burnished.

Cochineal.—C. cacti. The larvae of this insect resides, during the winter, under a white web, on the leaf of the prickly pear, or the articulation of
the nopal, where it leaves its eggs to hatch in the spring and to feed on the
flower of the plant.   Both larvae and imago are filled with the purple
dye.

Dermestes cardaneus.   A small oval spotted bug.

D.——— domesticus.   The little bug that turns wood to a white pow-
                der, called powder-post.

D.——— ferugenia.   Feeds on rose buds.

D.——— carrabeus.   Feeds on the tender leaves of trees.

D.——— cassida.   A smaller spider.

D.——— farfidela. Produces the Earwig.

Ptinus pulsator. Ticks his everlasting note on the old paper, in Florida, as well as every other place. He is, by superstitious people called the death watch.

P.—— fur. The book-worm.

P.—— campyrus. The fire-fly.

The above are insects with shelly wings of the class caleoptra. The following have wings of a softer texture, of the class hemeptera.

Cockroach.—Bletta. A most infamous stinking bug, very numerous and very mischievous, eating papers, wafers &c. ; no place can be guarded against them. Some grow to two inches in length. They are brown, but after moulting, their new covering is almost white. The natives dissolve them in spirits to cure wounds and spasms.

Grass-hopper. Locust.—gryllus. The former are plenty, the latter rather scarce. A large chocolate colored grasshopper is found in Florida, three inches long, often very numerous, on the marsh grass. They are very sluggish, scarcely removing to avoid death. They seem born for no purpose but to propagate their species and to die.

Katydid.—cicady. This insect lays her eggs near the edge of the orange leaf, the edge of one lopping over the other like scales. The leaf of the tree is their food.

C.—spumonia lays her eggs on the stalk of some plant, and encloses them in a bunch of froth. This froth is by some called snake spittle.

Vine-fretter.—aphis puceron. Is very destructive to vines, rose bushes, cabbages &c. There is said to be one hundred and fifty species. On every species of plant they vary in form and color. They derive their whole nourishment, from the juice of the plant they inhabit. Fortunately they have many enemies ; the caterpillar will devour one hundred pucerons in an hour.

Gall Bug.—chermes. An insect similar in appearance to the puceron, but the chermes enter the twig, or leaf, and raise an excrescence about it which we call gall-nut.

Thrips are minute insects, of various forms, that live on the flowers of plants.

Bed Bug.—betulanius. Found in houses,where there is a want of industry and neatness, very rare in Florida.

Ant.—formica. These insects, the little red ant, in particular, are terrible pests. They penetrate the earth and every thing that exists on the face of it. They do not raise hills of sand, as at the north, but they undermine trees and plants, destroy furniture and crawl into every kind of food. There are few varieties.

Butterfly—lepidaptera. Innumerable. While in this state of existence, they are not only innocent, but afford much pleasure by their brilliant colors and graceful undulations. But in the erucæ, or caterpillar state they are infinitely mischievous. In some instances, they have destroyed whole crops of cotton in a few days. The most common species of the butterflies in Florida are,

Peacock —papillio io. This butterfly produces the eruca gossippium ; most destructive to the cotton plant.

Tortoise-shell,   P. urtical.   Feeds on the asclepias.

Blue,   P. eimon.

Yellow,   P. flava.

White,   P. alba,

Citron Moth,   P. extreus.

The eruca often covers the limbs of the orange, stripping the branches.

Tobacco Moth,   P. faciola.

Very destructive to the tobacco.

Hawk Moth,   P. iris.

Eyed Sphynx,   S. ascellatus.

Death Head,   S. atropos.

This insect gives rise to many foolish superstitions.

Clothes Moth,   Phalena sargatella.

Very destructive to clothes, furs, skins, &c.

Cabbage Moth.—P. oleracia. This insect will in a few days time, make riddles of every cabbage in a garden. They must be carefully watched every morning in the summer, and destroyed as fast as they appear.

Musquito Hawk.—Libellula. Called by some the dragon fly, is bred in the water, but hovers about moist places, and lives principally on musquitoes.

Bay Fly.—Ephemera. This fly is the innocent tenant of a day, but very numerous at some seasons.

Rustic Fly.—E. vulgata. Similar to the above.

River Fly.—Rombica, Spring Fly.—Phygarea. Both these species, in the larvae state, enclose themselves in a silken web, to which they attach sand, sticks and bits of shells, by way of fortification. They confine themselves to fresh water.

The Hymenopterea, or stinging insects, are very numerous.

Wasp.—Vespa. Are of several kinds. The large black wasp builds his mud dwellings, under the roofs or ceilings of houses. The small black wasp constructs a comb, like the honey bee, and hangs it to a limb. The yellow jacket burrows in the ground, as in the northern states.

Honey Bee.—Aphis. The honey bees found wild in Florida, are smaller than those which are domesticated in the northern states, their honey is very white and pure, and when made from the orange flower, the aroma of the blossom is distinctly perceptible, and much admired. The ants, moths and spiders, wage eternal war with this favorite insect, and it requires constant attention, to guard them from their enemies. The trouble is however well repaid, and the raising of them ought to be encouraged.

Humble Bee.—A. bombyleous. This common insect is very often robbed of his small store of honey, by the bears.

Gall Fly.—Cynips. This insect produces on the lonicena and some other shrubs, excresences of a very extraordinary shape and size.

Saw Fly.—Tenthredo. Pine timber, cut in the summer, is pierced full of holes by this living auger. In order to guard against his ravages, timber should be cut in the winter and pealed ; when thus exposed to the sun, the albumen becomes too hard for his operations.

Ichneumon.—Manifestator. A harmless insect and useful in destroying caterpillars.

Two winged insects of the Deptra class, are very numerous, at certain seasons.

House Fly.—Musca domesticus. Not so bad in Florida, as in the middle states.

Gad Fly.—M. astres. Extremely numerous and vindictive.

Horse Fly.—M. equi. Of these there are five kinds—1st. the large black, called thunder bug, an inch long ; 2nd. small black ; 3d. the small brown, very numerous near the sea-coast ; 4th. the green fly with a black head, a perfect savage ; 5th. the slender green fly seen only in the morning and evening.

Horse Guard, a species of large Hornet that burrows in the sand ; destroys the flies.

Gnat.—Culex. Four kinds—1st. the Gallinipper, with speckled legs, near half an inch long ; 2nd. Musquito, which infest the low mangrove swamps, on the southern end of the peninsula, and the low and wet ground, in every part of the Territory, are more or less infested by them ; and in some places, the hammocks and pine woods swarm with them. The whole territory affords no object so unpleasant to strangers, as this little troublesome insect. But even in their worst haunts, an extensive cultivation of the land, nearly exterminates them. 3d. Sand Fly ; this insect continues but a short period, and is confined to the coast ; 4th. the Mite Gnat, is common to every part of America, and we have our share of them.

Insects without wings, or Aptera.

Red Cotton Bug.—Baccareum. An insect that pierces the capsule of the cotton, enters the seed and deposits its egg. The seed emits an oil from the hole that stains the floss of the cotton, of a yellow brown color. Sometimes the capsule dies, but more frequently survives in a sickly state

Mite Red Bug.—Londicorreus. Is too small to be observed by the naked eye. It resides on old rotten wood and moss. They crawl over a person in myriads, insinuating themselves under the skin, and raising large burning blotches, which produce an inveterate itching. The best remedy is immediately to bathe in salt water or spirits.

Sea Tick.—Sanguineus. Are confined to a few locations.

Wood Tick.—Ovino. These are frequent in all the unsettled parts of the territory.

Cheese Mite.—Siro. Itch Mite.—Exulcerons. Very rare in Florida.

Spider.—Aranea. There are many kinds.

Silk Spider.—A. Flavia. About the size of a pigeons egg. He extends strong lines of yellow silk, to a great distance, from tree to tree. It is so strong that small birds have been caught and held by it.

Giant Spider.—Gigantea. Covers four inches of ground, with its sprawling hairy legs. His bite is poisonous, but not mortal; the inflammation usually subsides in a few hours.

Crab Spider.—A. cancer. This unusual insect is found near the sea-coast. The orange tree is his favorite residence. He bears a shell similar to a crab, dark mottled brown on the back, and yellow underneath. Each side is armed with three red spikes.

House Spider.	A. labarinthicus.	
Water.	A. fimbreata.	All these kinds are innocent,
Black.	A. halorisiea.	and not numerous.
Wanderer.	A. viatica.	
Field.	A. graminia.	

Flea. pulex. Abundant in the new settlements in dry hammock lands. They are innumerable about the beds of hogs and dogs. In our houses, soap suds and the broom are effectual remedies, but require frequent application.

Chigoe.—Jigger .A species of flea, confined to a few places in the Territory. It enters the skin of the feet, forms a little bag, in which it deposites numbers of eggs ; as they increase in size, the bag extends to the size of a pea. They inflame the flesh and produce excruciating itching. To cure the part, the bag must be carefully extracted. If broken, each egg, too small to be seen, produces a new ulcer.

Scorpion.—scorpio. Found in various parts. The large brown kind are sometimes three inches long. The smaller kind are lighter colored, and usually live in the ground, or under boards, on old wood. Their bite inflames the part affected, but has never proved dangerous.

Barnacle.—L. antifera and L. narialis. These are most destructive insects to all water craft. They often, in a few months time, reduce the bottom of a vessel to a honey-comb. Vessels are preserved for a short time, by paying them over with tar and brimstone. But coppering is the only effectual remedy. The mangrove and the cabbage-palm resist their attack.

BIRDS.

There are many birds in Florida, distinguished for the brilliancy of their plumage ; and some that are excellent food. But there are fine songsters besides the Mocking Bird.

The Wild Turkey, meleagris Americana, stands at the head of the festive board, and is abundant in most of the new settlements.

The Water Turkey, ichthyophagus, is less than the wild turkey, and usually of a darker color. It is supposed to be the Ibis of the Egyptians. It haunts the streams and lakes of the interior. These birds usually sit over the water on some pendant limb, from which they suddenly drop, when disturbed, and sink to the bottom, where they may be seen walking, if the water be clear. Their flesh is very good eating.

Bald Eagle.	Falco leucephelus.
Fishing Eagle.	F. piscatoreus.
Hen Hawk.	F. gallinareus.
Chicken Hawk.	F pullenareus.
Pigeon Hawk.	F. columbarea.
Marsh Hawk.	F. raniverius.
Horned Owl.	Strix arcticus.
Whooping Owl.	S. acclamator.
Screech Owl.	S. assio.

[The owl is more numerous in the northern, than in the southern parts of Florida.]

Turkey Buzzard.	Vultur. aurea.
Carion Crow.	V. atratus.
Raven.	Cerrus carniverous.
Rook.	C. martimus.
Small Crow.	C. ferugireous.
Florida Jay.	C. floridamus.
Jackdaw.	Granda quiscula.
Crow Blackbird.	G. purpurea.
Bob of Lincoln.	oriole.
Paroquet.	Psitticus carolinaensis.
Whiteback Woodpecker.	Picus principalis.
Red Crested.	P. pillatus.
Red bellied.	P. carolinus.
Speckled.	P. pubescens.
Yellow bellied.	P. varius.

10

Nuthatch.   P. varia ventre.
Brown Creeper.   Centhia rufa.
Pine Creeper.   C. pinus.
King Fisher.   Aludo alion.

Humming Bird, trochilus calubris. We have two other kinds of the humming bird, very small, but very beautiful.

Butcher Bird.—lanius garrullus.

Wren.—muscitapa cantatrix. We have three other kinds of flycatchers.

Pigeon.—columbo migratore. This kind are not so numerous in general, as the turtle dove, and ground dove.

Meadow Lark.—alauda.

Robin.—turdus migratoreus. Seen here only in winter.

Mocking Bird.—T. pollyglottis. These incomparable singers, are numerous in every part of Florida.

Cedar Bird.—amphillis garrullus.

Quail.—tetrao minor.

Grossbeak.—loxia rastro.

Sparrow.—passen palustris. There are two other kinds. The house sparrows are numerous.

Red Bird.—merula merilandica. The loxia cardinalis is also found here, but is less in size, and by no means so fine a singer as the merula.

Tewe.—fringilla. There are four kinds of fringilla.

Cowpen bird.—S. stercatoreus

Blue Bird.—motacilla sialis. There are four kinds of motacilla.

Yellow Bird.—parreus luteus. A species of Rice Bird.

Swallow.—hirundo. There are four or five kinds, of which the Martin is most admired.

Night Hawk.—caprimulgus Americanus.

Nocturnal Goatsucker.—C. Europeus.

Muckawis.—C. rufus. This bird resembles the Whippoorwill in every thing but his note.

Sandhill Crane.—Grus pratensis. This bird inhabits the pine barrens, and feeds on grass seeds and insects. They are usually found in small flocks, or in pairs. Vast flocks of them collect on the coast, or the gravelly bank of some river, to spend the night. They usually stand close together near the water. Each small party as they arrive, in the dusk of the evening, give a cry, which is answered by those at the place of rendezvous. They are three feet high; of a cinerous grey color. They are generally very fat, and are superior eating to a turkey. They are noisy birds, and apparently very intelligent.

Heron.—Andrea herodias. There are several kinds; the grey, white, large and small crab-catcher, frog catcher, grey bittern, blue bittern and poke.

Spoonbill.—Platalea ajaja. This bird is of a peachblow color ; a little smaller than the sea curlew, with which it often associates. They are excellent eating. They rarely appear north of Musquito Lagoon on the east, or the Fresh Water Keys on the west side of the Peninsula.

Black Winged Pellican.—Tantalus loquator.

White Curliew.—T. alba.

Screamer.—T. Pictus.

Godwit.—Numerous. White and red breasted. There is besides six or seven kinds, some of them peculiar to this coast.

Tring.—Tringa rufa. Of this species there are seven kinds, perhaps more.

Dotterel.—Morinella.

Goose.—Anser. There are four species of geese found here during winter. They are usually fat and well flavored.

Duck.—Anas. There is a great variety of ducks. In some of the inland lakes acres of water are covered with them. Their flavor is as various as their plumage.

Cormorant.—Calymbus floridanus. These birds are extremely numerous in the Gulf of Mexico.

Loon.—C. murienus. Is not so common as the pied diver. Both are found in salt and fresh water.

Tropic Bird.—Phaeton Athenius.

Gull.—Laurus. Very numerous. Three or four species.

Sea Pellican.—Onoratus Americanus.

Petrel.—Petrilla pintada.

Sheerwater.—Rynchops niger.

Man of War Bird.—Aquilus. Always soars high in the air during a gale.

Plover.—Atraradnus. Of these there is the kildear, spotted plover and ring-neck.

Oyster Bird.—Ostrealegus.

Coot.—Fulia floridana.

Widgeon.—Bullus Virginianus.

Water Rail.—R. aquateous. and Brown Rail.

Flamingo.—Phoeniropterus ruber. This elegant bird is seen in large flocks, south of the 28th degree of north latitude, particularly on the Gulf side of the peninsula. They are more rare on the eastern coast. They stand from 4 to 5 feet high ; this height being equally divided between the neck, the body, and the legs. Their color is a beautiful crimson when full grown. The young ones are paler; the under side of their wings are black. They have a large, crooked, and clumsy bill; the rest of their proportions are slender and graceful. In flying, their legs form a right line with their necks. While ranged on the shore, they resemble files of soldiers in uniform. They are excellent food.

PRODUCTIONS OF THE SOIL.

These vary with the soils that produce them. They may be comprehended under five heads;—pine-barrens, uplands, hammocks, swamps, and marshes. If we estimate the quantity of land at 10,560,000 acres, and deduct one-fourth part for bays, lakes, rivers, &c., there will remain 7,920,000. Of this quantity, two-thirds, or 5,280,000 acres may be covered with pine barrens; 800,000 with tillable upland; 600,000 with hammocks; 500,000 with swamp; and 400,000 with marsh.

PINE BARRENS.

The pine barrens are composed, principally, of silicious sand, more or less mixed with calcareous and vegetable matter, and often divested of every fertilizing principle, by the frequent fires which run over them. Barrens are found on the sea coast, and on the ridges, between the large water courses. All the lands covered with pine timber, are by no means barren; on the contrary, some of the best uplands are wholly, or nearly all, covered with yellow pines. And some of the burnt barrens will not produce even pine or scrub oaks, but are usually partially covered with clumps of savin. West of Cape St. Blas, the sands are usually of a pure white; east of that point, they become more colored, and of course, more fertile. Very few trees grow on this soil; those most frequent, are,

Pine, pitch. Pinus rigida—a low, poor timbered tree, but produces turpentine and tar.

Pine, many cored. Pinus seratina—a useless tree, found on the banks of lakes and lagoons.

Pine, loblolly. Pinus tæda—a large tree, in valleys, has much sap.

Pine, yellow. Pinus palustris—this is a large and most useful tree; it is the principal timber used for plank and scantling in the southern states; and also produces turpentine and tar.

Oak, high willow. Quercus cinera—on barren hills.

Black Jack. Quercus nigra—on the poorest sand ridges—excellent firewood.

Andromeda. A. rigida—on the edges of savannas and streams.

Shrubs.

Shallow Cup.   Quercus pumilla—round the borders of hammocks.

Live-oak shrub.   Q. maratima—near the sea coast, very fruitful.

Holly-leaved.   Q. ilicifolia,   do.   the branches often bent to the ground with acorns, excellent for swine.

Hickory grubs.   Juglans tormentosa—the better kind of barrens.

Haw, winter.   Cratagus parvaflora—ridges, fruit green or yellow, eatable.

Haw, summer.   C. flava—sea islands and dry plains.

C. apafolia—edges of savannas and streams.

Azalea.   A. Bicolor and nudiflora,   do.   do

Chinquapin.   Castanea nana—dry ridges, edge of hammocks ; nuts fine.

Andromeda.   A. feruginea—dry ridges, edge of hammocks.

Huckleberry.   Vaccineum myrsinites—dry ridges, berry small, black.

Whortleberry.   V. staminium—dry ridges, berry larger.

V. dumosum—plains, dark purple. With several other varieties.

Blueberry.   V. frondosum—damp flat plains, berry blue.

V. glaucum,   do.   larger fruit, on a smaller shrub.

Herbs are abundant, to wit :—

Wild Sunflower.   Helianthes atranubus—pine woods.

H. pubescens—banks of streams.

H. mollis—ridges.

H. hispidulus—ridges and sandy plains.

H. tormentosus—do.

H. decapitatus—do.

Goldenrod.   Salidago reflecta—ridges.

S. laterifolia—pine woods.

S. pyrimidata,   do.

S. bicolor,   plains.

S. pulverulenta,   do.

S. elata,   do.

Aster.   A. ericoides—dry ridges.

A. squarosus—pine woods.

A. concolor,   do.

A. surculasus,   do.

A. undulatus,   do.

A. cenearefoleus,   do.   There are numerous other species.

Dittany.   Cunila mariana,   do.

Wild Pennyroyal.   A. pugloides, do.

Woundwort.   Stachys sylvatica—barren fields.

S. hysopafolia—barren fields.

S. aspera, do.

Wild Mallows.　Hybiscus scaber,　　do.　with five other species.

Origanum.　Monarde punctata,　　do.

Spiderwort.　Tradescanthia virginica,　　do.

T. tripetalous, do.

Wild Indigo.　Baptista perfoliata,　　do.

B. lanceolata—pine woods.

B. tinctorea,　　do.　this is a most valuable plant ; it produces the best indigo, with less trouble than any other of the species, and grows on the poorest soil.—much used in family dying.

Agrimony.　Eupatoreum alleum—barren plains.

E. rotundifolium, do.

E. linearifolium, do.

E. fœniculasceum. do.

Penstemon.　P. pubescens—pine woods.

P. lævagatum,　　do.

Chrysopsis.　C. argentea—dry ridges.

C. graminifolia,　do.

C. pinifolia,　　do.

C. trychophylia,　do.

Ophrys.　Neottia tortillis—sandy plains.

Balsam Cuphilla.　C. viscossima, do.

Gerardia.　G. linifolia—sandy plains, flower blossoms four months.

G. purpurea.

Scull cap.　Scutelaria villosa—pine woods.

S. pilosa,　　do.

Silkweed.　Asclepias phytolachoides—sandy plains, and sea islands. This beautiful plant has already, by the French nation, been cultivated to advantage. The pappus is spun with raw silk for gloves, the juice collected for opium, and the leaf used in dying.

Asclepias connivens—sandy plains and sea islands.

A. obtusifolia,　　do.　　do.

A. amplexicoides,　do.　　do.

A. lanifolia,　　do.　　do.

A. tuberosa,　　do.　　do.

Violet.　Viola villosa.

Button Root.　Eryngia.

Lupin.　Lupinus perennis—pine woods.

L. villosus,　　do.　with three other species.

Glycine.　G. argentosa—dry plains.

G. peduncularis,　　do.

Sensitive plant. Mimosa sensitiva—dry plains.
White Lilly. Crinum—pine woods.
Nightbelle. Ipomea bona nox, do.
Sand Lilly. Convolvulus spithamacus—dry plains.
                C. obtusilobus,   do.   and sea islands.
Granadilla. Passiflora incarnata,   do.
           P. lutea,   do.
Phlox.   P. parviculatus   do.
           P. pyramidalis,   do.
           P. glaberima—damp plains.
Verbena. V. corymbosa.
         V. urticiflora.
Graphalum. G. purpureum.
Annona. A grandiflora.
Ruellia. R. strepens.
        R. oblongafolia.
Salvia. S. graviolens.
      S. lyrata.
Prenanthus. P. virgata.
        P. alba.
Chrysomachia. C. acaulis.
Galega: G. chrysophylla.
Hypoxis. H. folafilia.
Comelina. C. erecta.
Black root. Pychnastaticum.
Blackberry. Rubus villosus.
Dewberry. R. cunefolius.
        R. trivialis.
Strawberry. Fragaria virginiana.
White do. F. canadensis.
Tormentilla. T. officinalis.
Wood-anemony. A. nemorosa.

Vines.

Muscadine grape. Vitis rotundefolia—heads of small streams, thick skin.
Briar, China. Smilax China—grows every where, but best in damp soils, near streams. It often extends one hundred feet; the root is similar to a cluster of potatoes. The Indians grate them, or bruize them in a large wooden mortar, then throw on water, strain the starch through baskets, dry and pulverize it; the color is a reddish brown. They mix it with fine homony, and make cakes; with honey and warm water, it becomes a fine jelly; toasted and mixed with sweet milk, it is a delicious food.

S. Ovata.

S. Caduca.

Morning-glory.　Convolvulus purpureus :—variegated with purple and blue.

C. dracrorhizus—with twenty other species.

Cypress vine.　Ipomea coccinea—a beautiful scarlet flower.

I. nil—a rich coclico flower.

I. dissecta—all found in middle Florida.

Traveller's Joy.　Clematis holoserica.

C. walteri.

C. reticulata.

Crimson woodbine.　Lonicera sempervirens.

Yellow　do.　　L. flavium.

L. parvaflora.

Climbing Ivy.　Cissus hederocea.

Yellow Jessamine.　Gelseminum sempervirens—dry plains.

The grasses are also numerous ; there are very few spots, indeed, of pine barren, that are not covered with grass : in many dry ridges, the heat of the summer kills the stem, while the roots remain entire ; and fire is thought to improve its growth ; the herdsmen, accordingly, fire the barrens, at regular seasons. Deer, as well as cattle, may always be found on places recently burnt over.

Twisted Xyris.　X. flexuosa—flat grounds.

X. fimbricata.

X. brevefolia.

Rough-head Fuerina.　F. squarosa—flat grounds.

Rush-like　　　　　F. scirpoida—savanna edges.

Killingia.　K. pumila,　　　　　do

Rhynchospera.　R. plumosa—dry plains.

Schœnus.　S. Sparsus—pine woods.

Nut grass.　Cyperus hydra—on cultivated sandy land, and almost every place ; it is the greatest curse to planters ; the Riband cane is said to keep it down, but nothing has been found to eradicate it. The root is fibrous like horse hairs, strung at a few inches apart with tubers of the size of a rifle ball, which descend into the sand, in every direction, frequently to the depth of five feet.

C. compressus.

C. mariscoides.

C. odoratus.

C. distans—pine woods.

Mariscus.　M. retrofractus—sandy plains.

Scirpus.　S. Capellaceus—dried savannas, forms a close carpet soft as silk.

S. autumnalis—savanna edges.

S. ferugineus—pine woods.

S. exaltatus,   do. grows to a great height—ten feet.

S. lineatus,   do.

S. divaricatus.

White button.   Duchromena leucocephala—wet barrens.

                D. ciliata,   do.

Cockspur.   Cenchrus tribuloides—old sandy uncultivated fields.

Low cane.   Arundinarea tecta—around spring heads.

            Muhlenbergia erecta—pine woods.

Fringed Aulaxanthus.   A. ciliatus—ridges.

                A. rufus.

Fringed Paspalum.   P. ciliatifolium—old fields which have been cultivated.

                P. floridanum.

Smooth Panic grass.   P. lævigatum—ridges.

                P. glaucum.

Cocksfoot.   P. grus-galli—round savannas.

                P. hians.

Broad-leaved Panic grass.   P. latifolium—pine woods.

                P. amarum—sand ridges.

                P. ciliatum—wet barrens, evergreen.

                P. divergens—sand hills.

Crab Grass.   Digitaria sanguinalis.

Bermuda grass.   D. dactylon—these, as well as P. divergens, ought to be cultivated : these in dry, that in wet soils.

Silky Agrostis.   A. senicea—sand hills—may be cultivated wherever there is calcareous matter in the soil.

                A. trichopodes—sand hills.

                A. juncea—sand hills, not fit for hay.

Purple Aristida.   A. spiciformis,   do

Wooly do   A. lanosa,   do   do

Fringed Andropogon.   A. ciliatus, do. if mown early, the hay is tolerable, but coarse.

Nodding Andropogon.   A. nutans—finer.

                A. purpurea—stem coarse, few leaves.

                A. argentus,   do

Broom Grass. Lateralis—tall, coarse, and often used for sweeping.

Purple Aira.   A. purpurea.—sea islands.

Hairy Poa.   P. hirsuta—old fields.

Green do   P. viridis,   do

11

P. nitida,   do
Rough do   P. rigida—pine woods.
Purple do   quinquefida—makes excellent hay.
Oat grass.   Uniola paniculata—sea islands.
              U. gracillis—pine woods.
Slender Fescue.   Festuca tenella—barren plains.
              F. parvaflora—pine woods.
Hairy   do   F. mycinus—ridges.
              F. nutans—most common in the barrens.
Crows Foot.   Eleusine indica—old fields, an exotic probably.
Tooth-ache Grass.   Monocera aromatica.—This is a singular grass; it
has a naked stalk four feet high, spikelets in two close rows, on one side
of the stem, at top; straight when young, but bends with age, and finally curling in a spiry coil.   It affects the breath and milk of cows, who
eat it when young and tender.   The root is bitter, and affects the salivary
glands.

UPLANDS.

Uplands are formations of clay, which arise gradually on the subtending
limestone; they usually commence about twenty miles from the coast.
The first stratum of clay is usually white; red clay succeeds; while the
surface is covered with a mulatto or chocolate colored loam.   The trees, on
this soil, are abundant, and form the pleasantest groves imaginable.   The
following are most common.
Oaks, Hemispherical.   Quercus laurefolia.
              Q. imbricaria.
Black.   Q. tinctoria.
Red.   Q. coccinea.
Yellow.   Q. rubra.
Spanish.   Q. falcata; triloba.
Post.   Q. obtusiloba
White.   Q. alba—the most useful tree in America.
Yellow Pine.   Pinus palustris.
Black Hickory.   Juglans nigra.
Thick shelled do.   J. sulcata.
              J. tormentoso—the common Hickory of Florida.
Magnolia.   M. grandiflora.
Umbrella Tree.   M. tripetala.
Yellow Poplar.   Liriodendron tulipifera.
Dogwood.   Cornus Florida.
Wild Cherry.   Cerassus virginiana.
Persimmon.   Diospyros virginiana.

Holly. Ilex opaca.
Sassafras. Laurus sassafras.
Mulberry. Morus rubra.
White do. M. alba, or pubescens.
Black Gum. Nyssa sylvatica.
Sorrel tree. Andromeda arborea.
Catalpa. C. bignonia.
Scarlet maple. Acer rubrum.
Plumb, red and yellow. Prunus chicasa.
Annona. Asimina triloba, or Pawpaw.
Gordonia. G. lacianthus.
Hopea. H. tinctoria.
White Locust. Robinia pseud acacia.
R. viscosa.
Beach. Fagus sylvatica.
Chestnut. Castenea vesca.
Birch, white. Betula alba.
Iron wood. Carpinus ostrya.
Sycamore. Platanus occidentalis.
White Ash. Fraxinus epiptora.
F. triptera.
Honey Locust. Gleditschia triacanthos.

The uplands produce few shrubs ; the following are found about spring heads, banks of rivers, lakes, and savannas :
Annana. A. grandiflora.
A pygmea.
Lantana. L. camara.
Stratia. S. virginica.
Hopea. H. pumila.
Shrub Locust. Robinea hispida.
Baccharis. B. Halimifolia.
Carylus. C. americana.
Chinquapin. Castanea pumila.
Myrtle. Myrica cerifera—rare.
Prickley Ash. Zanthoxilon tricarpium.
Service Berry. Prinos verticilatus.
White Fringe tree. Chionanthus virginica.
Azalea. A visciosa—rare.
Hydrangea. H. Nivea—on limestone rocks.

The herbs, vines, and grasses, on the hammocks, are many of them similar, but of more numerous species than those on the uplands ; the same
classes of trees and shrubs also grow on the hammocks, but there is also a
greater variety of species; those which are common to both, will therefore not be again enumerated ; but such as are peculiar to the hammocks
will be noted.

Sweet Bay. Laurus borbonia. This tree produces timber inferior only to
  mahogany, which it closely resembles. The young leaves are often
  used for tea, which is a most pleasant and healthful beverage. Cattle
  eat the herbage with avidity.

Pond Spicewood. L. geniculata.

American Olive. Olea americana.

Spotted Haw. Fothergillia punctata.
                F. coccinea.

Cabbage Palm. Chæmarops palmetto.—The greatest ornament of our
  sea coast; they sometimes rise on a straight column eighty feet. The
  foot stalks of the old branches enclose the trunk like a coarse net work.
  The timber resists the Gulf worm, so destructive to vessels. Hats, baskets, mats, &c. are manufactured from the leaves. The embryo head is
  excellent food.* Bears and other animals feed on the berries. Confined
  to the coast and islands ; not seen farther west than St. Andrew's Bay.

Cotton Tree. Populus grandidentata.
                P. angulata.

Juniper. Juniperus alba.

Red Cedar. J. virginiana.

Sweet Gum. Liriodendron styraciflua—rivers, hammocks.

Live Oak. Quercus virens.

Cettis. C. occidentalis.

Mulberry. Morus rubra.
                M. alba.

Saponaria. Sapindus saponaria.

Sidiroxelon. Bumelia lycoydes.
                B. languinosa.

Halesia. H. tetraptera.

SHRUBS.

Azalea. A. calendulacia—the most beautiful native shrub of Florida.
  Flame colored, pink, yellow, streaked and mottled, with every intermediate shade.

*On removing the large branches the cabbage is discovered lying in many thin, white,
brittle flakes, which taste like unripe chestnuts. It should be boiled in two waters ; the first
thrown away.

Haw. Cratægus grus galli.

C. lucida.

C. flava.

Salicifolia. Spinæa salicifolia.

S. tomentosa.

Andromeda. A. axillaris.

A. acuminata,

A. mariana.

Hammock Berries. Vaccinium myrtilloides—about the size of a cherry, usually grows near streams; ten feet high.

Clethera. C. tomentosa.

Styrax. S. grandifolium.

S. læve.

S. glabrum.

Hydrangia. H. quercifolia.

Annana. A. incarnata—five feet high, flowers large, white, many on a large panicle ; fruit size of a small cucumber ; pulp yellow, and tastes like custard.

Sumach. Rhus vernix.

Sensitive Shrub. Mimosa eburnea—the first plant which grows on the sea sand ; excellent for hedges and ornament.

Herbs.

Scull Cap. Scutilaria hysopifolia.

Blue do. S. laterifolia.

Coral Tree. Erythrina herbacea.

E. coralodendron.

Cassia. Sesbania macrocarpa.

Senna. C. marylandica.

C. tora.

C. occidentalis.

C. ligustrina.

C. aspera.

Lindernia. L. dilatata.

Bellwort. Uvularia sessilafolia.

U. perfoliata.

Fairy Flax. Houstonia cœrulea.

Star of Bethlehem. Hypoxis erecta.

Slender Lobelia. L. kalmia.

Indian Tobacco. L. inflata.

Ladies traces. Neottia tortillis.
Domestic Ipecacuanha. Gillenia trifoliata.
Scabious. Erigeron philadelphicum.
        E. hederophyllum.
Asclepias. A. tuberosa.
Pentstemon. P. pubescens.
Starwort. Aster lineafolium.
        A. solidaginoides.
        A. flexuosus.
        A. sparsiflorus.
        A. reticulatus.
        A. virgatus.
Bird Pepper. Capsicum minium.
Turnera cistoides.
Wild Sunflower. Helianthus truncatus.
        H. longifolius.
        H. multiflorus.
Annemona. A. thalictroides.
Milkwort. Polygala purpurea.
Pogonia. P. verticillata.
Smilacina. S. canadensis.
Cancer Root. Orobanche virginica.
        O. unifolia.
Wormseed. Chenopodium anthelminticum.
Lamb's Quarter. C. alleum.
        C. botrys.
        C. ambrossoides.
Poke. Phytolacca decandria.
Sheep Sorrel. Oxalis acetosilla.
Spanish Moss. Tilandsia usneoides.
Indian Agave. A. virginiana.
Ground Sorrel. Rumex acetosa.
Jimpson. Stramoneum datura.
Phlox. P. carolina.
        P. uniflora.
Broad Thistle. Sonchus macrophyllus.
Cotton do. S. oleraceous.
Narrow leaf. S. floridanus.
Small yellow. S. carolinianus.
Milk Thistle. S. accuminatus.

Wild Baum.   Melissa.
Golden Rod.   Solidago reflexa.
     S. laterifolia.
     S. rugosa.
     S. villosa.
     S. ulmifolia.
Tarragon.   Artemissia caudata.
Wild Parsnip.   Sison trifoliatum.
Ranunculus.   R. recurvatus.
     R. muricatus.
Wild Fennel.   Antherim finiculeum.
Poppy.   Papaver—white and yellow, petals four, stamens many, pistil one, leaves jagged and thorny, sap a yellow juice somewhat corrosive ; these plants are new to me, and although very common on the shores and old fields, it is doubtful whether they are not exotics naturalized.
Mallows.   Malvus virginicus.
    M. militaris.
    M. speciosus.
Water Cress.   Sisymbrium nasturtium.
     S. amphibium.—This plant is found on sea islands in other respects barren, and on the shore ; the sands often drift over it, but it shoots through again ; it is a delicious and most healthy herb, especially in scrobutic affections.
White nettle.   Urtica alba.
    U. pumila.
Domestic Euphorbium.   E. cordifolia.
    E, polygonifolia.
    E. gracilis.
    E. helioscapia.
    E. paniculata.
Aurantium.   A. coccinia.
Veronica.   V. angustifolia.
    V. praealta
Eupatoreum.   E. fœniculaceum.
    E. coronopifolium.
    E. hysopifolium.
    E. aromaticum.
    E. cœlestinum.
Graphalium.   G. polycephalum.
    G. purpureum.
    G. plantaginum.

Senecio. S. hieracifolium.
          S. suaviolens.
Chrysopsis. C. pinafolia.
Verbesina. V. sinuata.
Cancer Weed. Salvia lyrata.
                    S. coccinia.
                    S. azurea.
                    S. aborata.
Madwort Alyssum. halifalius—common.
Jacobean Lilly. Amaranthus formassissima—wet pine lands.

Vines.

Fox grape. Vitis vulpina.
            V. cordifolia.
            V. riparia.
            V. æstivalis—usually cultivated for arbors, it is also a good
wine grape.
Bignonia. B. radicans.
           B. crucigera.
Rhus. R. radicans.
Poison Vine. R. toxicodendron.
Crimson Woodbine. Caprifolium sempervirens.
Yellow   do.   C. flavum.
Supple Jack. Rhamnus volubilis—Twisted walking canes of this vine
are much admired.
                    R. carolinianus.
Yellow Bell Flower. Convolvulus obtusilobus
                    C. panduratus.
Ipomea. I. coccinea.
         I. tricocarpa.
Ivy Vine. Cessus hederacea.
Yellow Jessamine. Gelsemum sempervirens.
Yellow Echites. E. diformis.
Aristolachea. A. tomentosa.
Purple Thyrsa. Thyrsanthus frutescens.

SWAMPS.

These may be divided into three kinds. First, those formed on the borders of rivers, by inundation ; these are the richest swamps, and most extensive. They are usually separated from the stream by a ridge of dry
land, formed by the heaviest parts of the alluvial matter, which is deposited
immediately after leaving the current ; this ridge, or natural embankment,

prevents the waters from draining off, as the surface of the rivers subside. They are, usually, densely covered with heavy timber, and this tangled with innumerable vines, which renders them almost impenetrable. Secondly, pine barren swamps, which are natural basins, containing the waters of the surrounding country. These swamps, when covered with small coast cypress trees and knees, are usually, but improperly, termed cypress galls. Cypress knees are hollow cones, which rise from roots of the cypress tree, from one to six feet high, and terminate in a blunt point. These never shoot up into trees, as has been imagined, from the circumstance of large cypresses being supported on hollow cones, similar in appearance ; in the latter case, the tree first grows up straight, and the cone gradually swells out underneath it, as high as the highest stage of the water. Savannas are no more than natural reservoirs of water like the swamps ; except that they are covered with grass and herbs instead of trees and vines ; they are usually founded on clay or marle, but sometimes only on a hard sand. They are frequently extensive, and form excellent grazing lands. The third kind of swamps are those spongy tracts, where the waters continually ooze through the soil, and finally collect in streams and pass off. These are properly termed galls, sometimes sour, sometimes bitter lands. They are the coldest soils we have, and the waters arising through them are frequently impregnated with sulphur, vitriol, and iron. When their foundation is alluvial matter, it is usually very thin, like quagmire : the land may be shaken for acres in extent. When the base is sand, it is always a lively quicksand, very dangerous for cattle. These galls are usually covered with titi and other andromedas, loblolly and other laurels, vacciniums and vines.

The trees most peculiar to swamps, are,

Cypress. Cupressus disticha.—A large and beautiful tree, often rising one hundred feet, makes excellent boards, scantling, palings, and shingles.

Pine barren do.   C. imbricarea.

Swamp Ash.   Fraxinus epiptera.

White do.   F. acuminata.

Oval-leaved.   F. platycarpa.

Black.   F. pubescens.—Red ash in ponds.

Willow Oak.   Quercus phellos.

Water do.   Q. aquatica.

Lyre-leaved.   Q. lyrata.

Chestnut do.   Q. prinos.

Velutinian.   Q. michauxii.

Pignut.   Juglans porcena.

Tupelo.   Nyssa unifolia.

12.

Ogechee Lime.   N. capitata.

                N. aquatica.

Loblolly.   Laurus carolinaensis—grows in every kind of swamp, from ten to seventy feet high; the beauty and aroma of its flower is well known.

Swamp Magnolia.   M. glauca.

Swamp Poplar.   Populus angulata—river swamp.

Whohao.   Ulmus alata—high pine barren,

Bumelia.   B. lycoides—galls.

Plane Tree.   Planera gmelini—grows in river swamps, and resembles elm.

Soap Tree.   Sapindus saponaria,   do.   near the sea coast.

Winter Plumb.   Prunus hiemalis,   do.   back from the coast

Gordonia.   G. lasianthus,   do.

Shrubs.

Buttonwood.   Cephalanthus occidentalis—near the Atlantic coast.

Swamp Dogwood,   Cornus canadensis.

Amorpha.   A frutescens—river swamps.

Strawberry Tree.   Euonimus americanus,   do.   borders of streams

Viburnus.   Viburnum dentatum,   do.   swamps

Swamp Haw.   V. nudum,   do.   do.

Sambucus.   S. canadensis—deep inland swamps.

Laurel.   Laurus millisafolium,   do.   and in bay galls.

Andromeda.   A. axillaris.

               A. acuminata.

               A. ligustrina.

               A. racemosa.

               A. speciosa.

Sorrel Tree.   A. arborea.

Titi.   A. angustifolia.—this class furnishes most of the shrubs found in our swamps; the titi, in particular, occupies the same situation south of Georgia that the alder does in the northern states. It grows from six to twelve feet high; the stoles are slender and set so thickly together that their shade keeps the small streams cool for a great distance from their fountains. In March, their racemes of white flowers are abundant and very ornamental, and their singular strings of three cornered seeds often hang on the bushes till winter.

Billberry.   Vaccinium corymbosum.

               V. virgatum.

Spice wood.   Laurus benzoin.

Herbs.

Bird Shot. Canna indica—river swamps.

Herbaceous Canna. C. salicornia—savannas.

Spring Callitriche. C. callitriche—bay galls.

Virginian Gratiola. G. virginica—ditches.

Yellow   do.   G. aurea—pine barren swamps.

Hairy   do.   G. pilosa—near swamps.

Round Fruit.   G. sphærocarpa—lake shores, and savannas.

         G. quadridentala,   do.

Square-stemmed.   G. tetragona,   do.

Lindernia. L. dilatata,   do.

         L. attenuata,   do.

Round Micranthemum. M. orbiculatum, do.

Big-leaved do.   M. emarginatum, do.

Floating Utriculare. U. inflata,   do. in still water, fresh.

Purple   do.   U. saccata,   do.

Yellow   do.   U. longirostris,   do.

Small   do.   U. biflora,   do.

Bristle-stalked.   U. setacca—pine barren swamps and savannas.

Narrow-leaved Lycopus. L. europius,   do.

Sallop-leaved   do.   L. sinuatus,   do.

Blue Tripterella. T. cœrulea,   do.

Variegated Iris. I. versicolor,   do. the root is a remedy for
     dropsy. White Iris. I. alba.

Three-petaled. I. tripetala,   do. rare.

Blue.   I. hexagona—rich river swamps.

Yellow Tricoma. Lachranthes tinctoria—pine barren swamps and ponds.

Creeping Comelina. C. communis,   do.

Blue do   C. longifolia,   do.

Moss-leaved Syena. S. fluviatilis—bay galls.

Proserpina. Proserpinaca palustris,   do.

         P. pectinata   do. and savannas.

Coonta. Zamia integrafolia—south of 29° 30′ in rich pine lands, all the
     way to the Capes.

Tetragon. Diorea tetragona—galls.

Three-leaved Galium. G. trifidum,   do.

Centaurella. C. verna,   do.

         C. paniculata,   do. and swamps.

Sanguisorba. S. canadensis,   do.

         S. media.

Potamogiton. P. pinnatum—stagnant fresh water.

P. verticillatum,   do.

Villarsia.   V. trachysperma,   do.

Lysimachia.   L. ciliata—savannas.

Phlox.   P. divaricata—low river swamps.

Cardinal flower.   Lobelia cardinalis, do. beautiful scarlet.

L. amæna,   do. blue.

Pinckneya.   P. pubens—galls and savannas.

Solanum.   S. nigrum—savannas.

S. mamosum—low swamps.

Swamp Milkweed.   Asclepias parviflora, do.   scarlet flower

Hydrolea.   H. quadravalvis—galls.

H. corymbosa,   do.

Erynguim.   E. fœtidum,   do.

E. gracile,   do.

Hydrocotyle.   H. interrupta—stagnant water.

H. umbellata—swamps.

Wild Annise.   Ammi copillaceum—galls.

A. costatum—swamps.

Cicuta.   C. maculata,   do.

Sundew Drasera.   D. rotundifolia—galls.

D. longifolia,   do.

Spanish Moss.   Tilandsia usneoides—swamps.

T. recurvata,   do.

Wampee.   Pontederia cordata—galls and savannas.

Pancratium.   P. mexicanum—savannas and swamps.

Smooth Palmetto.   Yucca gloriosa—galls near the sea shore.

Calamus.   Acorus calamus—muddy galls.

Cats Tail.   Typha latifolia,   do.

Soft Rush.   Juncus effusus—galls and savannas.

J. setaceus,   do.

J. triflorus—river swamp edges.

J. polyuphalos—savannas.

Rumex.   N. britannicus.—shady swamps.

Nectris.   N. aquatica,   do.

Swamp Lilly.   Saururus cernuus—galls.

Rhexea.   R. virginica,   do

R. lutea

Blue Scull-cap.   Scutelaria laterifolia—swamps and galls.

Poylgonum.   P. hirsutum,   do.

P. persecaria,   do. and ponds.

P. mite.

P. incarnatum.

Penthorum.   P. seoides—swamps and ponds.

White Pond Lilly.   Nymphæa odorata—in swamps, ponds, and ditches. The root used by the natives to cure felons.

Sarracena.   S. purpuria—swamps, galls, and savannas.

           S. rubra,   do.

           S. flava.

           S. variolis.—The leaf of this singular plant is a tube which widens towards the top in the two latter species ; in the two former, they are contracted near the top.   The inside of the tube is covered with viscid hairs, which prevent insects from retreating, when once they have entered for shelter or food.   They are always partly filled with insects. The leaf is beautiful, both as to shape and color, and the flower is of a deep gaudy redish brown, and remarkable for having two calyces.

Hypericum.   H. parvaflorum.

           H. amærum.

           H. nudiflorum.

           H. glaucum.

Elodea.   E. virginica.

Ranunculus.   R. hederaceus.

           R. oblongafolius.

           R. nitidus.

Caltha.   C. ficoloides—swamps.

           C. brassera—ponds.

Cyamus.   C. luteus, or Yellow water Chestnut—ponds.   The capsule contains from four to ten edible chestnuts—Hogs will swim in the water to obtain the fruit.

Polygala.   P. lutea—ponds and galls.

           P. corymbosa,   do.

Winged Dolichos.   D. luteolus, do.

Aromatic Liatris.   L. odoratus—galls and savannas.

Purple Veronica.   V. oligophylla—edge of swamps.

Eupatorium.   E. perfoliatum,   do.   A decoction of this plant operates as a gentle emetic.   Indians use it as a sudorific in fevers.

Conyza.   C. marylandica.

Black Root.   Pterocaulon pychnastachum.—The famous Indian remedy for pulmonary disorders.

Butter Weed.   Senecio lobatus—swamps.

Slender Aster.   A. carolinianus,   do.

           A. dracunculoides, do.

Solidago.   S. virgata,   do.

S. pulverulenta—swamps.

Baltonia.   B. asteroides,   do.
Heleneum.   H. autumnale,   do.
            H. quadridentatum,   do.
Yellow Bidens.   B. coreopsis—ditches and galls.
Chana.   C. capitata,   do.
Duck-meat.   Lemma minor—stagnant waters.   Often covers the surface
of the water in form of a green scum.
Bristly Typha.   T. latafolia,   do.
Sparganium.   S. americanum,   do.
Carex.   C. stipata—swamps.
         C. scirpoides, do.
         C. scoparia,   do.
         C. crineta,   do.
         C. trichocarpa, do.
         C. furcata,   do:
Orchis.   O. ciliaris,   do. and galls.
          O. cristata,   do.
Calopogon.   C. pulchellus, do.
Sagittaria.   S. sagittifolia, do.
              S. graminea—swamps and galls.
Arum.   A. dracontium,   do.
        A. triphyllum,   do.
        A. alba,   do.

Vines.

Cissus.   C. ampelopsis—swamps.
Echites.   E. diformis,   do.
Dolychos.   D. luteolus,   do. near salt water. On sand hills.
Apios.   A. tuberosa,   do.   This vine has numerous tubers of the
size of hickory nuts.   The Seminoles raised great quantities for food.
Glycine.   G. reflexa,   do.
Grape.   Vitis labrusca—in all swamps.
Muscadine.   V. rotundifolia—edges of swamps.
Smilax.   S. pastata,   do. very common
Smooth Briar.   S. bona nox.
                S. quadrangularis.
                S. walteri.
                S. sarsaparilla.
                S. pseudo china.
                S. caduca.—These briars cover wet lands of every descrip-
tion.

Pistache. Amphicarpe monoica.—This is a singular plant, stem decumbent, climbing angular, red at the base, light green above, branching, twenty inches to two feet long. They were greatly cultivated by the Seminoles, and are now much used by the Americans of West Florida. This vine produces a large crop on sandy land. They are baked or roasted in the shell, and are much used by the confectioners. The pistache is a native of Spain, from which it was, but a few years since, transferred to the gardens of France and Italy. With us it is perfectly naturalized.

GRASSES.

Rhynchospora.	R. cymosa—galls and savannas.	
	R. distans,	do.
	R. sparsa,	do.
Cyperus.	C. articulatus,	do.
	C. vegetus,	do.
Spanish Grass.	C. virens,	do.
Yellow Cyperus.	C. flavescens,	do.
	C. tenuiflorus,	do.
	C. odoratus—edge of rivers.	
	C. strigosus—galls and savannas.	
	C. speciosus,	do.
	C. enslenii,	do.
Scirpus.	S. filiformis,	do.
	S. validus—in lakes and ponds.	
	S. minimus—galls and savannas.	
Fringe leaved.	S. ciliatifolius—savannas.	
Dichromena.	D. ciliata—margin of ponds and swamps.	
	D. latifolia.	
Trichophorum.	T. cyperinum—savannas.	
Cane.	Arundenaria macrosperma.	
	A. tecta—edge of swamps and marshes.	
Spring Trichodeum	T. laxiflorum—swamps.	
Leersia.	L. oryzoides,	do. inland.
Phalaris.	P. americana,	do. fresh and brackish.
Early Paspalpum.	P. precox, swamps.	
Joint Grass.	P. distichum,	do.
Large Spiked Panicum.	P. italicum,	do.
Cockfoot.	P. grus-galli,	do·

Water Panicum.   P. geniculatum—swamps.
Compressed.   P. anceps,   do
Sword-leaved.   P. ensifolium—galls.
Aira. A. palustris—swamps and savannas.
Proserpinaca. P. palustris,   do.
                P. pectinata,   do.
Arenarea. A. glabra,   do.
Liatris. L. tormentosa. do.
Veronica. V. oligophyla, do.
Awlwort. Sibularia aquatica—river swamps, and wet sea beach.

MARSHES,

Are of two kinds, fresh and salt. The former are usually situate on the borders of some large body of water, in the interior of the country. The latter on the sea coast, or near the estuaries of rivers. There is a great diversity of marshes; much depends on the substratum on which they are based. For instance, the most extensive marshes of West Florida are based on limestone, which renders them extremely fertile in aquatic vegetables; some of the fresh marshes, on the contrary, are merely quicksands, covered with a very thin soil, and are of course quite barren. Others have a clay foundation, and may be cultivated to advantage. Marshes produce no trees; a few shrubs sometimes skirt the edges of them. The salt marsh has been found to be an invaluable manure for our sandy soils. The herbs most common, are,

Micranthemum. M. Orbiculatum—fresh marsh.
Triptaleria. T. cærulea,   do.
Creeping Comelina. C. communis,   do.
Convolvulus. C. sagittifolius—salt.
                C. repens,   do. near the mouth of rivers.
Marsh Rosemary. Statice limonium—salt marsh near the the shores.
Pancratium. P. mexicanum—fresh.
Dracocephalum. D. variegatum, do.
Cardamine. C. pennsylvanica—salt—near the sandy shore.
Pistia. P. spathulata—rivers and lakes in Florida. It floats on the surface, the roots hanging like threads in the water, and often forming floating islands.
Sagittaria. S. lancifolia, do.
Arum. A. virginicum, do. and fresh.
Iresine. I. celosioides—salt and fresh.
Acnida. A. rusocarpa—fresh.

Water Plantain. Alisma plantago—brackish.
Marsh Reed. Phragmites.
Great Reed. Debox.

Grasses.

Schœnus. S. effusus—fresh marsh.
Rhynchospora. R. longirostris, do.
Scirpus. S. simplex, do.
S. palustris, do.
Round-head. S. capitatus—salt marsh.
S. mucronatus, do.
Large Marsh. S. lacustris, do.
Salt Rush. S. spadiceus, do.
Downy Flower. S. ferrugineus, do.
S. maratimus, do.
Eriophorum. E. virginicum—fresh do.—in boggy clumps.
White Rush. Spartina juncea—salt do.—forming also tufts.
S. polystachya—brackish do.
Salt Marsh Grass. S. glabra—salt marsh.
Ceresia. C. fluitans—fresh do.
Smooth Panicum. P. lævigatum—fresh do.
Soft do. P. molle, do.
Sea-shore do. P. virgatum, do.
Johnny Bartram. Lycium carolinianum—salt do.
Black Rush. Juncus acutus—brackish do.
Arenaria. A. canadensis, do.
Aster. A. flexuosus, do.
A. subulatus, do.
Zizanea. Z. aquatica. This is the most common grass at the mouths of
rivers where the marsh is often overflowed ; grows six to ten feet high ;
is eaten freely by cattle and horses. Miliacea is not eaten by either.
Z. fluitans.
Z. miliacea.
Sea Wrack.
Sea Ware.
Indian Grass.
Dulce.
Tangle.
On approaching the 27th degree of N. latitude, the whole vegetation be-
gins rapidly to change. Oaks and yellow pines become rare, and at length
13

disappear. The Hawey, Caccaloba and Gum Elemi, take their place on
the sea-coast, and pitch pine takes the place of the yellow pine in the interior. Among other timbers the following are found about the capes and
keys.

The White Mangrove grows to the size of a forest tree, one and a half
feet in diameter, and often rises to the height of sixty feet, without a limb.
It grows in profound swamps, unmixed with any other timber. Trees are
connected together by large hooplike roots, that rise high above the ground,
that is covered by every tide. Nothing will grow beneath them except a
sickly harsh-looking glasswort. This wood being impervious to the worms,
s useful for boat timbers and for wharves, &c.

The Black Mangrove covers most of the low islands and shores of the
keys, as well as the southern shores of the peninsula. The seeds, which
are abundant, shoot up through the saltmarsh in every direction. A .por-
tion of the limbs hang down in a straight perpendicular line, to the water.
The end is directly covered with young oysters, which grow rapidly as the
limb swings about ; at length they anchor it to the mud. It then throws
out branches and becomes the body of the tree. Thus all the trees of an
island appear to grow together. Sometimes the large body of a tree is
mounted on a few slender roots, ten feet from the ground.

Lignumvitæ—guacum officinalis. This useful wood covers the higher
points, of the interior keys.

It grows to the size of a small apple tree, which it resembles in shape.

Mahogany—Swetonia. This tree grows to a large size, straight and
free from knots. The best are cut off from the keys.

Maderia—S. Niger. This is a tree of the same species, but of a darker and closer grain.

Logwood.—Hæmatoxilon. The four last mentioned trees, are natives of
the keys, but the best part of the timber has been cut off by the Bahama
wreckers.

Sea Grape. (Ovino.) Cacaalobe vivifera.—This beautiful tree resembles
the Fig, in shape and size, its leaf is equally large, but oval; the clusters of fruit are numerous, generally a foot long, and of the size of a
musket ball. They taste much like a clingstone Peach.

Wild Cinnamon.—Called by the inhabitants, Naked Wood. The bark is
strongly aromatic, and flavored much like the Laurus cinnamon, but
is more pungent.

Gum Elemi.—Called by the inhabitants Gumbo-limbo, is a large spreading tree, with a smooth brown bark, which has the appearance of having been varnished. The juice, which is a white milk, is converted into
bird-lime by boiling it to the consistence of a soft gum. This is the
grandest tree of our southern latitudes.

Sattin Wool.—It does not grow large, but makes beautiful furniture.

Mastic.—This is very common. It bears a plum which is much esteemed when boiled. The timber is excellent for small vessels.

White Mastic.—Is a softer wood.

Black Wood.—White Wood.—Dog Wood.—Iron Wood.—These four kinds of wood are all exceedingly hard and heavy, and are altogether different from those trees, which bear the same names in our northern states.

Water Willow.

Sapadillo.

Button Wood, or Bastard Lignumvitæ.—The timber of this tree resembles the real lignumvitæ, but is not as heavy.

Howey.—This tree bears a multitude of little figs, not bigger than a grain of corn. They are of a dark brown colour when ripe. In formation and taste, they are perfect figs.

Papayer.—This tree bears large lobed leaves, like the Palma Christi; which rise directly from the trunk, on long foot-stalks. The fruit is of various shapes, like the long or round garden squashes. These also spring directly from the stalk from under the head of leaves.

Hickok, or Coco Plum.—The fruit of this tree, is of the size of a pullets egg. They are black, yellow and pale red. They are very abundant about the capes ; and extend as high as 27°.

Pigeon Plum.

Dowland Plum.

Corker Plum.

Huesco Plum.

Horse Flesh.

Custard Apple.

Seven-years Apple.

Manchineal, Hipomone.—Extremely poisonous.

Hackberry.

Red Bay. Laurus borbonia.—Much used for cabinet work.

Nopal. Caetus Casti.—This is a tree whose body and limbs are articulated without leaves. Numerous small red flowers spring from the limbs, they nourish the cochineal insect.

Bay Cedar.

Prickly Ash. Different from the northern.

White Stopper.

Red Stopper.

Cocoanut.—This is probably not a native, but is perfectly naturalized.

Palm.

The herbs and plants are not so numerous on the keys, as the trees are.

the Magui or mexican alloe is abundant.   It is a splendid flowering plant ;
its fruit stalk rises to twenty feet high, and is surmounted with a multitude
of splendid white flowers, on long pendulous foot-stalks.   The fruit stalk
when dry, is lighter than cork, and about as soft.   The fibres of the leaves
are worked into white cordage.

There are two kinds of Yucca, and three kinds of Cactus, the palmated,
the triangular, and the round or Napal.   The cotton shrub is common, and
usually grows about six feet high.   The wild Thyme is one of the most
conspicuous plants in the southern region.   Of this is made the Tea Bin-
cum, which immediately cures the Dangue.   The bird pepper is the most
common weed, about the keys ; wherever the woods are cleared from the
land this capsicum immediately covers the ground.

Sesbanea Coccina.—A beautiful scarlet bell shaped flower, very common
on the keys.   It has a strong woody stalk, ten feet high, the leaves
laurel shaped, large and rough.

Guilandina Dioica.   Nicker-nut.—This is a thorny vine, has pods from
four to five inches long which contains hard blue seeds, of the size and
hardness of musket balls ; they resemble marbles.   There are two other
species of Guilandina, one is a beautiful tree with hirsute leaves ; they
grow as high as the 27° of latitude.

FISH.

On this department of the natural history of Florida, we are very imperfect.   The subjects are numerous, but so many of them bear Spanish or
Indian names, and vary, so materially from those found in the Northern
States, that without authorities, which we connot here command, it is impossible to class them.

The Gulph Whale.   This fish, very common on the western coast, is
probably the Grampus orca.   It is usually from twenty to twenty-five feet
long and very broad and thick.   There are many other fish of the Dolphin
tribe, as the—

Porpoise.   Phocenae.   These are very abundant on the coast and very
large, often eight feet long.   They sport in shoals and delight to play
around a vessel sailing near the shore.   In our bays and rivers they pass up
the channels at day break, fishing for the sea bass, when their exertions are
perfectly astonishing.   They usually go in pairs and assist each other in
detecting their flying prey.   There is no doubt, that fisheries might be
profitably established on the coast for them, as their oil is very valuable.

Manatee.   Beluga.   This is a shy fish and is mostly confined to the
grassy bays and particularly to the deep springs on the coast.   They feed
on grass and are considered excellent food.   Their ribs are used for ivory.
They are usually shot while feeding near the shore.

Of the Cartilagenous tribe. The Shark. squalus—stands foremost. Of these there are several kinds. The white carepalus, is the largest and most formidable. They are sometines twenty-five feet long, and delight to sport in the surfs. They are often very dangerous, and have, in the Gulf of Mexico often been known to destroy persons ; yet at other times are perfectly inoffensive. I have seen a boat sunk, at the Pass L' Este, on the western coast, among numbers of the white sharks, as well as other kinds, and not the least attempt was made, by these sea monsters, to seize the men who were for a long time plunged in the breakers, before they could secure any thing to float on.

Dogfish. Caracida. This is a large black fish extremely ferocious.

The small Dogfish. Calutus—is from three to four feet long. Perfectly black, with a broad flat nose, perhaps the most voracious fish that swims.

The Blue Shark. Glaucus—is common in the bay, as well as along the shores of the Gulf. He is from five to seven feet long. He sometimes ascends the rivers for mullet.

The Sawfish. Priscae—is from five to fifteen feet long, and their saw is usually one third the length of their bodies.

Angelfish. Squintina—is broad, with extensive fins and a brilliant silver colored skin.

Catfish. Stettarus—is small in the sea, but in some of our deep rivers, grows to a great size.

Eel, swordfish, conger eel, flounder, perch mackerel, lasher, minna, mullet, flying-fish, herring, cod, mud-fish, black-fish, white-fish, (trout silver, yellow and blue bream, in lakes and springs. Gar, gorupers, porgys, sheep-head, bass, grunts, yellow-tail, barracooter, permits, king-fish, jew-fish, stingray, whipray, moray, hog-fish, ponk-fish, hound-fish, pompano, mutton-fish, snapper, margate-fish, amber-fish, bill-fish, sturgeon, whiting, drum, skate and whip-jack.

SHELL FISH.

Of Multivalves, we have here two species of the chiton ; the C. spinosus and C. larvæformis. The finest I found near Palm Sound, on the Gulf shore, and the latter on St. Rosa Island.

Of the Acorn Shell, or Lepas, there are several kinds ; some of them extremely mischievous, destroying in a short time, not only the bottoms of vessels, but wharves, piles, and every kind of wood that is exposed to the sea. Tar, sulphur, and paint, give way to them in a few days, and nothing but copper can check their devastations. It is said that they will not meddle with the timber of the mangrove ; it is held in high estimation on that account. The tough fibres of the cabbage palm also resist these insects, and for piles it answers a good purpose. The tintinabula and the antifera are the worst of these insects.

Of Bivalves, the mya or gaper holds a conspicuous station. The fresh water pearl muscle is said to abound in our great inland lakes. When Ferdinand De Soto invaded Florida, the natives possessed great numbers of pearls ; and the Spanish writers state that they were found in Lake Myaco, as well as in the Appalache Bay. The latter must have been the mya margaratiferæ, which shell is still found there. The trincata, or thick shelled clam, is found in the sand of all the bays and lagoons.

Razor Shell. Saler.

The Scimetar. S. ensis. Is common.

Violet Radiated is found about Cape Sable, and is much used in ornamental shell work.

Of Telinas there are several species.

Cockles. Cardium: An abundance of different species on every part of the coast. The Common. E. edule. Grow very large on the grassy shores of the Gulf of Mexico. During storms they are often driven on shore.

The Fluted Heart. C. castatum.

Venus Heart. C. cardissa.

Yellow Ribbed. C. magnum. Are very common.

The Bear's Paw. C. Rusticum. Only about the Camachee Fields on the S. W. coast.

Mactra. M. stuttonim. I have in several places on the Gulf discovered these among old heaps of shells, but have not discovered them on the shore.

The Wedge Shells. Dorax. Are very common on the Atlantic coast. They are small white shells, with purple rays. Some are white, with the inner side purple.

The Venus abounds on every part of our coast. The ridges go round the shell, instead of across, as in most shells. The V. edentula is, perhaps, as beautiful as any of the species. It is diaphanous, tinged with red, the inside of a gold color.

The Spandylous I found most numerous about the Hillsborough Inlet. It is eared and spiny.

Arca. Of this class, the tortuosa is the finest species that inhabits our coast. They are thin, but peculiarly delicate. The mouth of Appalachicola Bay affords the finest specimens. The noae is common.

No part of America can boast finer oysters than St. Andrews Bay. I have seen them 12 inches long, and very fat.

Besides the edules, or common oyster, there are the marima, or scallop, the radula, varia and fasicula, besides one or two kinds of sole. The leaf, folium, is rare. A long kind, called racoon, are extremely abundant about the Florida Keys. It is this kind that grow so abundantly on the mangrove bushes.

Anomias. Of these there are green, black, and yellow, on every part of our coast. The white and yellow are translucent.

Mytillus. Sea Muscle. There are several beautiful species on various parts of our coast. Groups of the edulis are found in the bays of the Gulf, attached to the ostrea and especially to the old shells ; they also adhere to various other substances. Some beautiful species are attached to the coralines. The shells of these are variegated with very beautiful colors. I have seen the shell of the margaratiferous both in the Appalache Bay and at Hillsborough Inlet, on the Atlantic coast; and there can be no doubt that the pearls might be found there, if we had persons that understood fishing for them.

Pinna. We have but the pictinata, at least, I have observed no other. They are small and rare on the Atlantic side of Florida. The sea is there too rough ; the pinna delights in calm bays, where it can wave about in security. In the Bay of St. Joseph's they grow to the size of twelve or thirteen inches in length, and have been known to weigh five pounds. Their bysus, or silky cordage, is of a reddish cast.

Argonauta. Paper Sailor. This beautiful little adventurer is frequently driven on shore, about the Inlet of St. Augustine. The coast below Indian River is often covered with them in the winter season.

Nautilus. The spinula is found in various parts, but I have not discovered the pompilius.

Conus. The cone shells are scarce on our coast. The virgo is occasionally found ; and a larger species, crowned with a black epidermis, with a beautiful pearly substratum, is sometimes found near the capes of Florida.

Cypræ. The finest specimens of these shells are found on the Bahama Islands. The finest species of C. arabica, called mikrimak, is found about the roots of the mangroves, on the Florida keys. The limax crawls out of his shell and basks in the sun ; as he covers the shell with his body, no person unacquainted with it, would suspect the shell to exist. On being disturbed he slowly withdraws himself again into his fortress. The shells are usually boiled to extricate the animal. Fine mikrimaks, at Key West, sell from three to six dollars per dozen. The lurida and some other kinds, are rarely found about the keys.

Bulla, or Bubble. Of these, the ficus or fig are abundant, on the St. George Island. The ampulla or pewit's eggs are found about the north entrance of the Caximba. The terebellum or augur are seen occasionally in various places, and the unseemly slug, B. aparta is often seen along the shores of the Gulf.

Voluta. The Olivia, usually called Paramars, are found on every part of our coast, but the finest are about the islands in front of St. Andrew's Sound. The peninsula mistica and glans, are occasionally seen on both coasts.

Buccinium. The Ariola, or dice shell, is found on St. Rose Island, some of a pure white, andoth ers finely checqued. The dalium strigilatum palulum and reticulatum are rare.

Strombus. The Fucus and palustris are common.

The Pes Pelicani are found abundantly in old heaps about the sea, but recent shells of this species are rare. The urcius and geblerulus are found about the capes.

Murex. Several of the kinds are scattered over our coasts. The tribulus, ramosus rana and moncinella are rare. The celebrated Tyrian dye, was contained in one of these species.

Trochus. The dolibratus is the most common of the species; the perspectivus and zyziphorus and several others are occasionally seen.

Turbo. mericatus anguis and tenebra, are common. The chrysostomus rare. The mericatus and littoris, perewinkle, of every color, and variety, are found on the mangroves, about the keys, in great numbers.

Helix. This class is extremely diffuse, inhabiting the ocean, the rivers, and the land. We find on the Atlantic, a large snail, of light brown color. and a small one, of a rich purple. The columna is found in our hammocks, three inches long, of a rich brown color. The nemoralis is common. Our savannas afford a great variety of beautiful small correas. Every different quality of land affords a different kind of Helix.

Nerita. Common in many parts of the coast. The litoralis live upon the bullrush.

Haliatis. This class is rare on our coast. The impertura is most frequent, and is a beautiful little shell.

Patella, Dishes. Called in England, Limpet. This is a very numerous class of shells. The animal is fixed to the rocks, at the bottom of the sea, and the shell covers him like a dish. The granatira would scarcely be supposed to contain any living creature; it is a mere mass of shell. The gracea and sanguinelenta, are very common on the southern coast.

The serpulae lumbrecalis, is common on the western coast, from Sarrazota Bay to Cape Sable. And there are also many other species of serpula wholly new to me.

The Teredro navalis, the destroyer of our vessels, are infinitely numerous, as they are in most tropical regions.

CRUSTACÆ.

The large Cray-fish of the Florida keys have been seen only one or two hundred miles north of the capes. The coral reefs are their appropriate region. Their flavor is equal to that of the lobster, and they are equally large.

The Rock Crab is common on the Atlantic coast. The meat is stronger and less delicate than the Black Crab.

The Black Crabs are abundant in our salt lagoons. Their flesh is very white, and delicate eating.

The white Sand Crab is confined to the sandy shores of the Gulf of Mexico. They are good for nothing but to bait the red bass. They burrow in the dry sandy shore.

The Shrimps are numerous in autumn, and are finely flavored.

Fiddlers and black Water Spiders are infinitely numerous. They afford excellent food for hogs.

The Moluscas on our coast are extremely numerous, comprehending nearly all the known varieties.

AGRICULTURE.

The course commenced in Florida is the same that has generally been pursued, in all the slave holding states, north of us. A course which has destroyed the native fertility of the soil, from the Chesapeake Bay to the St. Mary's River, with few exceptions. The object has been to cultivate as much land and with as few hands as possible. To exhaust the soil and turn it common, and then to remove and pursue the same course again, upon new land. It is greatly to be hoped, that in future, some system may be adopted, which may tend not only to preserve, but to improve the soil we cultivate. Near the sea coast we have boundless means in the sea weed and marsh mud, to improve our lands; and facts abundantly demonstrate, that it is much less expensive to preserve the fertility of a good soil, by manuring it, than to clear up new and heavy timbered lands. Besides, it is something, to preserve the fruits that we have planted, and the improvements we have made in early life, or those which we have received from our ancestors. Besides, we are approaching the limits of our peregrinations, unless we fly off in a western tangent ; and it will be a long journey, in that direction, which will bring us to good uncultivated lands.

The Sea-Island Cotton has hitherto been our principal crop, near the sea coast, and the Green Seed Cotton in the country. But at present the sugar cultivation is taking the lead in the Middle and Eastern Districts. This ought to be the staple of the country. Experiments in every part of the

14

Territory prove, that all our good lands will produce sugar cane as well as any other crop, and that it is more certain and more valuable, in most places. Besides, there can be no danger of glutting the market with sugar. Three kinds of cane are planted in the Territory, the creole, otaheita, and ribon. The creole cane is said to produce the most sugar, when perfectly ripened, but it requires a longer season than either of the other kinds. The ribon cane comes to maturity quicker than either of the other kinds, and of course may be cultivated farther north, but the albumen of the stalk is much harder and requires a stronger power to grind it. When cut, it does not ferment so soon as the creole cane. South of 30 degrees of latitude the yellow kinds are preferred. At the time the cane is fully ripe, it is the best time to plant it, for a future crop. One of our principal planters has raised cane six years from the same roots, without replanting, and there are yet, no signs of depreciation : how long they will continue to yield good crops is unknown. It is a very great saving of labor. But this rattoning cannot be practised in climates where the frost is sufficiently severe to kill the roots. The top of the stalk makes excellent fodder, for cattle and horses. In spring the cane should be headed two or three times. It then covers the ground sufficiently to smother and kill out the weeds. A general opinion has prevailed that sugar could not be made to advantage, unless a great capital is invested; but experience abundantly proves, that a small capital may be as profitably employed in the culture of cane, as any other product. The cane produced on less than ten acres of ground is usually ground in a wooden mill, which does not cost one hundred dollars, the work of the farmer himself, while the juice is boiled in the common utensils of his kitchen, and the produce is usually greater in proportion to the stock worked, than where the machinery has cost ten thousand dollars.

Cane is cultivated with more ease than corn, because it does not require so much hoeing. From midsummer to the time of harvesting, the hands may be employed in other business, but at the time of manufacturing, a greater number of hands will be required.

One hand may tend five acres of cane, with the hoe, or eight acres, with the assistance of a horse and plough. At the same time he may raise his provisions ; 1200 pounds to the acre, is about a common yield. This at 7 dollars per hundred, amounts to 420 dollars for five acres. The molasses is always expected to pay the expense of manufacturing. Fifty acres of cane well managed will produce 4200 dollars ; certainly the most profitable crop, that can be raised in any part of the United States.

The Cuba Tobacco stands next to sugar, in the estimation of our small farmers. It is not a crop fit for a large plantation. It has the finest flavor when grown on old lands that are well manured. Our sandy soil near the

sea coast, is well adapted for this production ; and a usual season will produce three good cuttings from the same stalks. The seed should be sown
in December, on rich beds finely pulverized, and kept constantly damp.
When the plant first springs from the ground, it is very fine and should be
watered by a pot, pierced with very small holes. From February to March,
the plants will be fit to transplant into the field, which ought to be well
ploughed and manured. The plants may be set five feet apart, or six if the
soil be not strong. From this period they must be tended with the hoe, carefully observed from day to day. The grub will cut down some every night,
which must be replaced. If watered with strong soap suds, the grub will
leave them. The ants will then pierce the hill so full of holes that the rays of
the sun will kill the stalk, or they will cover it up with sand. The hoe alone
can cure this evil. A large green catterpillar, next attacks the leaf ; these
must be daily picked off and destroyed, or they will leave the stalk bare.
A small striped catterpillar next attacks the buds and the flower, and lastly
the large striped tobacco worm, feeds on the large leaves, and cuts them
full of holes. There is no crop that requires such constant attention as
tobacco. And it is remarkable that so noisome a plant, should harbor such
a variety of insects. When it is properly cultivated, suckered and topped,
and the leaves carefully gathered and cured, 700 lbs. is an average crop, to
the acre, which will make 100 boxes of cigars, worth from 10 to 14 dollars per box. Deduct for rent three dollars, one hand six months, 60 dollars,
and making the Cigars 250=313, and 687 dollars will remain for the nett
proceeds of one acre of ground. The objections to this crop, are, the constant attention required, not only in the cultivation, but also in curing the
tobacco ; the risk of damage by storms, which in some seasons, blow
the leaves in pieces, and third that the market is easily glutted with cigars.

Sea Island Cotton is peculiarly adapted to our sea coast and islands,
and although good crops may sometimes be made at some distance in the
country, yet they are uncertain, and always degenerate in proportion to
their distance from the sea. Our islands and coast are made up of the debris of sea shells, a small portion of clay, and vegetable matter, with a
large portion of silicious sand. The larger the proportion of vegetable matter and clay, the larger is usually the crop of cotton, but the less of these
matters contained in the soil, the finer and more glossy will be the staple of
the cotton, and no kind of manure has been found that will increase the
quantity, without at the same time injuring the quality of the cotton, except
it be sea-weeds, or marsh mud. These do increase the quantity, without
materially injuring the staple. By means of these exhaustless manures,
our poorest pine barrens may be rendered fertile, and thus all our lands
near to navigable waters may be improved to advantage. In order to cul-

tivate a good crop of cotton, the land should be well ploughed; the seed should be chosen with great care; that which contains a small bunch of hairs on the end is said to be the best. The distance of the drills should be determined by the quality of the soil, say six or seven feet. The plough may be used to great advantage in clearing out the weeds. After the first hoeing, the soil ought not to be drawn up to the stalks. The pods sometimes begin to open in August, but generally in September. The cotton ought to be picked soon after the capsules open, as the fine gloss of the herl is injured by exposure to the weather, and particularly by rains; the wind also dislodges it from the pod. It is usually exposed to the sun on scaffolds a short time before ginning. The smooth roller gin is the only machine that has been discovered to extricate the seed without injuring the herl. In ginning, the cotton should be equally distributed upon the rollers, for a hard pressure destroys the elasticity of the cotton. The best planters do not average more than three acres of cotton to the hand. The best land will produce in good seasons one bale to the hand, but in general half that quantity can be depended on. The value of this crop depends, more than any other, on the manner in which it is handled and put up for market. Some of the crops raised on the islands of South Carolina bring 1 dollar per lb., but here it usually sells from 20 to 50 cents. The crop is liable to many accidents. The caterpillar sometimes destroys whole fields in one night. The red bug pierces the pod and discolors the cotton, and heavy winds destroy the pods; besides, it is a tedious crop to clear and prepare for market. It ought never to be cultivated on lands that will produce either sugar or tobacco, but to be confined to light hammock lands, within the range of the sea-breezes.

The Mexican and Green Seed Cotton is still cultivated in the country. High oak land is the only kind which produces this crop to advantage, and at the price now given, it does not, in Florida, pay the expense of cultivation.

Rice is a valuable crop, where fresh water can be had to flow the ground during the dry season. The borders of St. Mary's River afford the finest lands for this crop of any in the Territory. There are some excellent lands for this culture on the Appalachicola River. There is not tide enough in the St. John's, above the salt water line, to render rice planting profitable. The upland rice however, may be cultivated without water. Our pine lands, when trod by cattle, has often produced sixty bushels of rough rice to an acre. This is a profitable crop. With one months' labor, one hand with a horse and plough, can raise ten acres of rice, which is worth $450. The rice sells at seventy-five cents per bushel, besides, the straw makes excellent fodder for cattle. Deducting ten dollars for the hand, the same for the

horse and plough, and three dollars for the rent of the land, and we have
$400 left, beside the straw. On marsh land where water may be comman-
ded, three barrels of six hundred pounds each, are raised on the acre ; and
one hand will cultivate three acres with the hoe. The value of each
hand at this culture, is estimated at one hundred and fifty dollars per annum. Nett profit, one hundred and twenty dollars.

Indigo was the principal staple of the Florida planters, while the British
possessed the country. It brought the highest price of any brought into
the London market, with the exception of that from Caraccas, which was
said to have been manufactured in a better manner. Except cane, this is
the most certain crop raised in Florida. It is a native of the country, our
pine barrens are covered with it. The old fields cultivated by the English,
sixty years ago, are still covered with it, in spite of time and cultivation. It
is subject to no risk, the only objection to its culture arises from the un-
healthiness of its manufacture. This may now be avoided by curing
the leaves and sending them in bales to market. The highest price is offered in New-York, for the article prepared in this way. While it was raised
and manufactured on the same plantation, the usual product to each hand
was one hundred and seventy-five pounds, and it sold at one dollar per
pound.

Silk. As our climate is the best in the world for the production of this
article, and as we have considerable districts of country, that will produce no
crop, so well as the mulberry tree, the culture of silk ought certainly to be
encouraged. Every species of mulberry will grow as far south as the 27th
degree of latitude. South of that they are smaller till you reach the
capes, where the tree is rarely seen. Cocoons of the silk worm are often
found on these, as well as on other trees in a wild state. Our native red
and black mulberry are said to produce silk equally as good as the white.
The rough pubescent leaved mulberry, is said to produce a larger quantity,
but of a coarser staple than either. The best way to obtain a grove of
mulberry trees, is to take cuttings from old trees, just as the bud begins to
push out. These should be planted in beds made rich and mellow. The
butt of the stalk should be inclined say twenty degrees, with a bud just
at the surface of the ground. Twenty feet is a proper distance apart. In
four or five years you may begin to feed from them.* But the leaves

*Since writing the above, the Multicaulis has been introduced into the United States,
and bids fair to supercede all other kinds of mulberry. They are more easily raised, their
foliage is more abundant, and it is much easier to gather the leaves from this shrub, than
from trees ; we are also assured that the silk is at least equal to that made from any other
species of plants. After having planted at Bayard, twenty-five cuttings of the Multicaulis,
at the expense of half as many dollars, they were all eat down by the mules of a company

ought never wholly to be stripped off.   It would be better to leave one-half at least, for several years.

The worms should be kept in a light, airy room, on shelves of thin boards, planed, and bored full of holes; while another should be placed underneath, to catch the dirt that falls through.   It is very important that their dwelling should be kept sweet and clean.   They eat sparingly in the first stages of their existence, but grow extremely voracious as they increase in size, and they must then be well supplied with fresh leaves, as often as they are required.   The under shelves ought to be frequently washed in lime water, and particular care should be taken that the ants do not approach them ; they are so numerous in this climate, that they would very soon destroy all the worms.   From the time that the mulberry puts forth its leaves, until the insect accomplishes its whole work is about forty days.   At this period the cocoons should be laid up in a cool place until the next season, unless a second crop should be required.   For this, there is plenty of time in this climate, nor do I know any good reason why it should not be improved.   The manner of reeling the cocoons is a matter to be learned by experience, and a detail here would be useless.   We have not had in Florida, a sufficient number of experiments to ascertain the expense, or the value of this pursuit, in comparison with other crops.   We can only say that the culture is appropriate, and easily carried into effect.

The Cochineal insect is a native of Florida, and as the male nopal is also a native plant, found about the Florida Keys, it is confidently believed that it might be cultivated to a certain extent.   The insect is seen hovering about the leaf of the prickly pear, quite in the northern parts of the Territory.   The female nopal is cultivated in Guatimala to support the insect. It is planted in rows on rich land well prepared, and must be kept perfectly loose and clear of weeds.   When twenty months old they are fit to inoculate, which is the placing of the insect on the plant.   The seed insect is very minute ; it is preserved in boxes and sold by the pound.   Twenty-five pounds will inoculate one thousand plants.   About a tea spoonful is put in a small piece of gauze, and attached to the plant with a thorn, from this they crawl over the plant, and in about two months come to maturity.   It

of volunteers, in the winter of 1836.   Three sprouts only were found rising from roots left in the ground.   These were taken up, and planted at Picolata in December.   Much care was taken to lay down the stoles, when about three feet high, and in May, 1837, we successfully transplanted from these three stocks, four hundred and twelve plants.

During the last year, a gentleman from the city of New-York, planted four hundred stalks of the Multicaulis, on a poor lot of ground in St. Augustine, that cost him, with the buildings, about eight hundred dollars.   His crop of Multicaulis was carefully cultivated, and in one year he sold the lot for sixteen hundred dollars, besides having sold enough of the plants to pay the original cost of the lot.

is then scraped off the nopal with a feather, and exposed to a hot sun for twenty successive days, on a piece of polished tin or other metal. It then assumes a silvery grey color, and is called grana. The granilla and cascarilla are inferior qualities procured by scalding. Great care is taken to pack it in several mats to preserve it from the least moisture, which would spoil it.

Corn is the most important article of food in a southern climate ; to the negro it is indispensable, and many of the white inhabitants prefer corn bread to wheat. Although Florida is south of the best corn climate, still very good crops are raised in many parts of the Territory, and every planter ought to raise enough for the consumption of his family. This crop is cultivated most successfully in the Middle District, and on the Chattahooche River. Forty bushels are often produced to the acre on the best land, while in the Eastern District from twelve to fifteen bushels to the acre, is an average crop on good land. In the Middle District it is usually worth more than thirty-seven and a half cents per bushel, while at St. Augustine and Pensacola, it is more frequently worth one dollar per bushel. It is therefore worth cultivating for use, but not as an article of commerce. The weavil destroys corn very soon after it is harvested. When stored away in the husk, it resists these insects for a longer period. Our seasons are long enough to produce two crops, but the late crop is usually much injured by the corn worm, which is the same that preys on the cabbage.—Phalæna oleracea.

The Guinea corn, Otaheite corn, and Millet, succeed very well. The latter in particular, is a useful and safe crop.

The Sweet Potato is next to corn, in the estimation of the Florida planter. The pine land furnishes its natural soil. This root is agreeable to almost every taste, is very healthy, contains much nutriment, and will often produce 400 bushels to the acre. The potato is planted in seed beds, and when the vines have grown three or four feet long, they are cut and transplanted into ridges, thrown up lightly for that purpose. The top of the ridge is opened with the hoe, and from four to six vines laid side by side, in a row extending the length of the ridge ; the earth is then hauled over them in spots one foot apart, the intermediate space left uncovered ; from thence the vegetation spreads above ground, while the covered spaces throw off roots, to furnish the tubers. This is altogether a laborious cultivation. One hand can scarcely attend more than five acres, for weeds must not be suffered to grow among the vines. But supposing them to produce only one thousand bushels of potatoes, it is a valuable crop. At Pensacola, and St. Augustine, 75 cents per bushel is a common price, and they are worth fifty cents, for the purpose of feeding to cattle and hogs.

The Irish Potato produces a good crop, if planted in the winter. They ought always to be covered with seaweed, or coarse compost, to shield the roots from the heat of the sun, which is powerful in the spring. The clayey soil of the middle district suits this crop, better than the sandy soil of the sea-coast. The potato raised here will not keep, as well as those brought from the north, nor will they answer to plant again, as they run to vines, without producing any tubers.

Pumpkins, squashes, water mellons, and musk mellons are produced with great ease, and are equal in flavor to any in the world. Cucumbers, gherkins, &c., succeed well in wet seasons. Turnips are a valuable winter crop; beets, carrots, onions and radishes, as well as most other garden roots, succeed well in quantity and quality.

The English pea succeeds only in the winter. The cow pea, lady pea, and chickasaw pea, produce excellent crops during the heat of summer. They also ameliorate the soil and prevent extreme evaporation. Cabbages succeed best in winter, but Tomatoes and Egg plants as well as acras require a warm sun. The pea nut produces a large crop, with little care, and is a useful article in the desert.

Of fruits the orange stands preeminent in the eastern section of the Territory. Groves have, for many years, been increasing in the neighborhood of St. Augustine, and St. John's River. They are now extending to every part of the eastern coast, 2,000,000 are annually shipped from St. Augustine, and forms the staple commodity of the country. The western and middle parts of the Territory are too cold for the successful production of this fruit. The china orange tree requires a rich sandy soil. It produces fruit in about seven years from the seed. By engrafting, this period may be shortened two or three years. The tree grows larger here, than in the West Indies. One hundred is as many as can grow profitably, on an acre. When full grown they will usually average 500 to the tree, each year, and they are worth 7,50 per thousand, which would amount to 375 dollars per acre. Some groves produce much more than that. One tree in Mr. Alvarez' grove has produced more than 6000 in one year. A grove is, on the whole, a valuable property. The care and attention necessary in pruning and manuring, bears a small proportion, to the labor necessary in raising other crops. It is necessary to keep the head of the tree pruned often, so as to throw the weight of vegetation to the extremity of the limbs. No moss ought to be suffered to grow on the bark. The ground about them should be kept clear of weeds and grass, and the roots ought to be annually manured. The frosts of the winter 1835, destroyed all the china orange trees, and most other fruit trees in Florida, as far south as the 28th degree of latitude. South of that, the wild orange and lime groves were injured, but not destroyed. See page 20.

The Seville, or Bitter Sweets, are common forest trees, indiginous to the eastern and southern districts. The pulp of the fruit is equally pleasant as that of the China orange ; but the pellicle, which separates the pulp into lobes, is bitter. To a stranger, this is usually very unpleasant, but custom soon reconciles the taste to it. It is thought to be very healthy. The sour orange is also abundant in the hammock lands, but is used only for its acid juice, which is often converted into shrub.

Very few of the shaddocks are cultivated in Florida. Forbidden fruit, citrons, lemons and limes are rapidly increasing.

The Pomegranate is a useful as well as an ornamental shrub. The fruit is used as a healthy and cooling desert. The blossom is among the most beautiful of our native flowers. It arrives to perfection in almost every part of our territory. Most of our gardens are enriched with its blossoms and fruit. Mr. Darby recommends it for hedges. If intermixed with our poppinac, (mimosa eburnum,) it would doubtless form a hedge equally splendid and formidable.

The Apple and Quince both succeed very well in the north and western parts of Florida, but neither of them will bear fruit near the sea coast.

Figs are abundant and richly flavored. They are raised with great ease. A limb cut from a bearing tree will produce figs the second year after planting. No attempts have been made to preserve them, but there is little doubt that it may be done successfully.

Peaches and nectarines succeed perfectly. Large orchards of them are cultivated in the middle and western districts. They do not succeed so well near the sea coast.

The Persimmon of Florida exceeds that of the Middle States. The fruit is larger and more soft and juicy. It is ripe about August. It is sold in our markets as a delicate article of the desert. The former natives pressed the pulp into cakes, which were dried and eaten as bread during the year.

The Hawey is a fig in miniature ; it grows upon a large and beautiful spreading tree, in the southern district. The fruit is the size of a hazlenut and springs from the limb of the tree, without any apparent flower. It is of a dark brown color, is soft and in taste resembles the black fig.

The Cocoanut is a native tree, or at least naturalized, south of the 27th degree of latitude. It rises above all the trees of the forest. This fruit ought to be extensively cultivated. It is about fifteen years coming to perfection, but then it bears abundant crops, without any farther attention, for a long period of years. Many of these trees planted in 1824, are now in full bearing at Key West.

The sugar apple and custard apple grows perfectly well, about the capes,

15

and keys of the southern district. The few planted at St. Augustine flourish and bear fruit.

The Caccalobe or sea grape ornaments all our southern coast with its abundant clusters. The tree is about the size of our fig tree, its leaves large and woolley and the clusters usually a foot long. The grape tastes much like a cling-stone peach.

Of Plumbs, we have the chickasaw, the hickok, corker, dowland, huesco, mastic and pigeon ; all these are natives. The plumbs of the northern states succeed better in the middle and western districts, than at the east and south.

Of Cherries we have only the black wild cherry. The fruit of this is indifferent, but the timber is far superior, to that of the Northern States.

The plantain and bananna succeed to perfection in the southern district. At St. Augustine and Tallahasse, the bananna has been cultivated with success. The Papayer is a native on the waters of Musquito and thence south. The Guava usually produces abundantly, but it is occasionally cut down by the frost. The Tamarind and the Olive are growing in many places and will doubtless become productive.

We have native blackberries, dewberries, billberries, whortleberries and strawberries, in abundance.

MANUFACTURES.

Except domestic clothing made in the families of the planters, for their own use, little can be expected for many years. The staple articles of commerce, sugar, cotton and rice, will for many seasons, employ the inhabitants of the Territory, more profitably than manufactures. Some of the most important productions of the country indeed, require to be manufactured on the spot ; such are, sugar, indigo, myrtle wax, quercitron, sumach, sessamy and palmachrystie. Bricks are sent in considerable large quantities, from Pensacola to New Orleans. Fire bricks, in particular, are in high demand. Some lime, has also been made, for exportation. Rum and peach brandy will presently make considerable items in our list of manufactures. Cigars have already been made for exportation in considerable quantities. They are considered, in no respect, inferior to those made in Cuba. The cultivation of this article ought to be extended.

Our shores are peculiarly well calculated to produce salt in large quantities. Many of the southern keys are covered with salt ponds, which with little preparation would produce sufficient for the consumption of the southern States. At Key West several hundred bushels are annually collected from the natural salt ponds. Extensive works have been for some time preparing at Duck Key for evaporating the sea water, as well as at Key West.

COMMERCE.

Our commerce, like our manufactures, is in its infancy. A moderate coasting trade is all that Florida yet can boast. Dry goods are brought from New York, and provisions from New Orleans and Charleston. Our exports consist of live oak and cedar timber, cotton, bricks, pine lumber, staves, hides, horns, tallow, bees-wax, peltries and oranges. At St. Joseph's a line of packets has lately been established to run to Liverpool.

MANNERS AND CUSTOMS.

These are various, as the different originals which make up the population of the country. This having, at different periods, been conquered by the French, Spaniards and English, the inhabitants of these various countries were much intermixed when Turnbull introduced into East Florida a colony composed of Minorcans, Greeks and Italians. The Greeks for the most part perished, but the Minorcans, even now, form one of the strongest portions of the eastern population. The creoles had, before the transfer of Florida to the United States, assumed something of a national character. But between Pensacola and St. Augustine there was very little communication, and considerable difference of habits and manners existed between them. They were both military posts. The inhabitants were almost entirely confined to these fortifications. A few cow-pens in the country formed the only exceptions. Most of the respectable inhabitants held commissions in the army, or in some of the departments of the government; they lived on their salaries, paid no taxes, and were rarely called to a strict account for their actions. The balance of the people, the military excepted, kept little shops, cultivated small groves or gardens, and followed fishing and hunting. They were a temperate, quiet, and rather an indolent people; affectionate and friendly to each other, and kind to the few slaves they held. The even tenor of their way was not often interrupted. Dances, card parties and patgoes were the diversions of the west, and posey balls and masquerades of the eastern portions of Florida. Sherivarees were common to both.

The exertion and bustle, of a mixed American population, for a time threw the old inhabitants into the back ground; but the new comers met with little success, in the first attempts at speculation, and at present they seem disposed, rather to settle down to the easy habits of their neighbors, than to pursue a course of active industry themselves. To this, however, there is some honorable exceptions. It was a misfortune, that most of the American emigrants to Florida brought with them the expectations of accumulating rapid fortunes ; being disappointed in their hopes, many left the country in disgust, and most relaxed in their exertions. The few who settled down to a course of patient industry, are realizing a decent independence. Nothing is now wanting, but for the old and new inhabitants of the Territory, to unite in establishing a common system of education. That once performed, all distinctions will soon be lost, and Florida will enjoy a most happy population.

Balls are the most common amusements of the Floridians. The Patgoe of West Florida is rather the introduction to a dance. A wooden bird is fixed on a pole and carried through the city, by some slave ; on presenting it to the ladies, they make an offering of a piece of ribon, of any length or color that happens to suit their fancy or convenience. This is fixed to the bird, which soon becomes decked in a gaudy and abundant plumage. A time and place is then set apart for the fair patrons of the Patgo to assemble, who are usually gallantly attended by their beaux, with rifles or fowling pieces. The Patgo is set up at a proper distance, and shot at, the fortunate marksman who first succeeds in striking it, is proclaimed king of the entertainment. The Patgo becomes his property, by right of conquest, and is, by him, presented to the fair lady of his choice, who by accepting the present, becomes queen of the festivities ; his majesty then becomes entitled to the enviable privilege of paying the expense of the entertainment, over which he with his royal consort presides.

The Posey Dance, of St. Augustine is introduced in a different manner, but results in the same amusement. The females of a family, no matter what their rank or station in life may be, erect in a room of their house, a neat little altar, lit up with candles, and dressed with pots and festoons of flowers. This is understood by the gentlemen as a polite invitation to call and admire the taste of the fair architects. It is continued for several successive evenings ; in the mean time the lady selects from her visitors, some happy beau, whom she delights to honor, and presents him with a boquet of choice flowers. His gallantry is then put to the test : should he choose to decline the proffered honor, he has only to pay the expense of lighting up the altar. But if he accepts the full dignity offered him, he is king of the ball, which shortly after succeeds, and the posey lass becomes queen, as a matter of course. The posey ball is a mixed assembly. People of all ranks meet here on a level, yet so far as we have been acquainted with them, they have been conducted with the nicest decorum, and even with politeness and grace.

Sherivarees are parties of idle people, who dress themselves in grotesque masquerade, whenever a widow or widower are married. They often parade about the streets, and play buffoon tricks for two or three days ; haunting the residence of the new married pair, and disturbing the whole city with noise and riot, until they can be bought off with money or whiskey. This foolish custom is common to West Florida. It has become a disgusting bore to the inhabitants, and will soon be forgotten.

The Carnival is a scene of masquerading, which should commence three days before Lent. It was formerly celebrated by the Spanish and Minorcan population, with much taste and gaiety; but since the introduction of American population, it has, during the whole winter season been prostituted, to cover drunken revels; and to pass the basest objects of society, into the abodes of respectable people, to the great annoyance of the civil part of the community. It is not one of those pastimes that ought to be upheld, by the fostering hand of a moral society.

Dancing is the favorite amusement of all our southern inhabitants. The Spanish dances are still preferred, by the natives, while the Americans consider cotillions as more genteel, and object to the waltzing that is practised, and indeed mingled in all the Spanish parties of pleasure. They are easy and graceful, and will probably preserve their present standing in Florida.

Private entertainments are frequent in our old towns; perhaps more frequent than prudence might dictate. We are a social and friendly people, but few of us have fortunes, to justify excess of fashionable amusements. Simple habits are commendable in a republican government, and all attempts at useless splendor ought to be discouraged.

With our country people, hunting is a favorite amusement, and the abundance of wild game, that stocks our woodlands, renders the amusement useful and interesting. The training of our frontier inhabitants to the use of the rifle, is not the least of its benefits.

TOWNS.

St. Augustine is the oldest city in the United States. It was first settled by the Spaniards under Pedro Mendez, in 1564. It is situate two miles back from the Atlantic shore, near the southern point of a peninsula, nearly surrounded by water; defended from the surf by Anastasia Island, which is not high enough to obstruct the sea breezes, or a view of the ocean. The situation is peculiarly serene, healthy and pleasant. The site was originally a shell hammock, scarcely twelve feet higher than the surface of the sea. The soil, although sandy, is rich in calcareous and vegetable deposites, finely calculated for horticultural pursuits. The town is, in fact, embosomed in a grove of orange trees.* Abundance of fresh water is found near the surface of the ground, which, although it is not so pure as that of the country, is used without any inconvenience for all the purposes of drinking, cooking and washing. The climate of St. Augustine is probably equal to any on earth. Snow is almost unknown, and frosts are felt in one or two months only of the year, and many winters pass without

*1834, before the great frost.

discovering a mark of frost. In the summer season the air is tempered daily by the sea breezes, while the land breezes render the evenings cool and pleasant. Heavy rains are frequent during the summer months, but from October to May the air is usually temperate, and the sky serene.

In form, the town is a parallellogram, fronting to the east, on the Matanzas Sound, which spreads a half mile in width between the town and Anastasia Island, forming a harbor sufficiently capacious to contain a large fleet in perfect safety. From the old magazine on the south to the gateway on the north side of the city, the distance is about one mile, and from the Matanzas to the St. Sebastian's on the west, is about three fourths of a mile. Not more than one half of this extent is compactly built. It contains upwards of three hundred houses, more than half of which are built of shell stone, called by the Spaniards coquina. Most of the old houses are two stories high, the lower floor of which is of tabby* ; in some instances the upper floor and roof are of the same material. These are now generally removed, on account of their great weight, from the upper parts of the buildings. The principal streets cross each other at right angles, but they are narrow, and many of them very crooked. A fine large square opens from the Matanzas into the eastern part of the town, in the centre of which stands a monument, dedicated to the constitution of the Spanish Cortez. On the west side of the public square, where the old government house formerly stood, in the centre of the botanic garden, enclosed by high walls, a neat court house has been erected. It is two stories high ; in form of an L. It is built of coquina stone, and contains, besides the hall of justice, and jury rooms, apartments for all the public offices of the district. On the north stands a splendid catholic church, and the ruins of the old custom house, which was burnt down in January, 1825. On the south side are several elegant dwelling houses, and the new trinity church, a very neat edifice of the gothic order. In front of the harbor stands a neat market place ; dwelling houses and orange groves fill up the intervening spaces round the square, which give it rather a rural than commercial appearance.

Fort Marion stands at the north end of the town, directly opposite to the entrance of the harbor, which it perfectly commands. It is built after the system of Vauban, and is said to be a very good specimen of military architecture. It is a trapizum with bastions at each corner, the walls are 21

---

*Tabby is formed by mixing a quantity of lime with the fine coquina shell cast on shore by the tide. These materials are with fresh water mixed into a stiff mortar, and then spread from four to six inches thick, either on the ground, or on a flooring of boards. It is then beat with a heavy stamper, similar to that used by pavers to smooth their work. When beat till no more water appears on the surface, it is left to dry. It is then in substance very similar to the coquina rock, except that the surface, by beating, becomes very smooth.

feet high. The whole work is casemated, and bomb proof. The ditch is forty feet wide. The covered way, glacis raveline and place of arms are entire, but the water batteries are giving away to the tides, which are rapidly undermining its base, and require immediate repairs. The fort is calculated to contain one thousand fighting men, and formerly mounted seventy pieces of heavy ordinance. They are at present dismounted. A small part of the fort is still occupied as an arsenal ; the balance is used as a jail for criminals. The following inscription is sculptured in stone, under the Spanish arms, which are placed over the principal gate.

Reynando en Espana el son Don Fernando sexto, y sierdo Governador y Coptan General di esta Plaza de san Augustin, de Florida, y su Provincia el Mariscal de campo Dⁿ Alonzo Fernandez de Heredia se conduyo este castillo el ano de 1756, dirigiendo las abras el capitan ynginero Don Pedro de Brazas y Garay.

Don Ferdinand the sixth being King of Spain, and the Field Marshal Don Alonzo Fernandoz de Hereda being Governor and Captain General of this place, St Augustine of Florida, and its province. This fort was finished in the year 1756. The works were directed by the captain engineer Don Pedro de Brazas y Garay.

From the fort, a sea wall seven feet high, and five feet thick, was extended from the fort to the public square. This wall is now rebuilding at the expense of $50 000, under the superintendence of Mr Daney, late of the army, and will be extended in front of the whole city, to check the inroads daily made by the tides. Great injury has already been sustained, by one or two eastern gales, for want of this barrier.

In the south part of the town, fronting the Matanzas, the barracks occupy an important situation. It is erected on the ruins of an old pile of buildings, formerly constructed by the Franciscan order of Friers, as the head quarters of their fraternity. The vessel which brought their General and principal men from Cuba, was wrecked on the coast, in sight of their dwelling, and the passengers and crew all perished. Since that time it has been occupied as a barracks, successively by the Spaniards and British, until it was destroyed by fire. Since the change of governments, it has been rebuilt at an expense of twenty-five thousand dollars. An extensive garden is attached to the building, which affords at times, abundant vegetables for the troops stationed there.

The city contains 1739 inhabitants, of which 498 are males, 519 females, 151 colored persons free, and 571 slaves. Of this population, nearly one-half are natives of the United States, the balance are descendants of the Minrocan families introduced by Doct. Turnbull ; Spaniards, French, English, Greeks, and Italians, who are all rapidly amalgamating into one people, and will, ere long, assume a general national character. They are social and friendly in their manners, kind and hospitable to strangers, industrious and frugal in their habits, fond of amusement, void of intemperance and public spirit, but 'content with their situation. The religion of at least one half of the inhabitants, is the Roman Catholic, the balance who profess any religion, are Presbyterians, Episcopalians, and Methodists.

The market is rather scantily supplied with meat and vegetables. Fish are abundant, of various kinds and finely flavored. Fowls are rather dear and scarce.

Of schools there are few, and in the whole department of education, there is great room for improvement. We need schools to be established on a liberal foundation, such as would enable the poor as well as the rich to receive instruction, and above all, the children of the old inhabitants should be encouraged to attend the same schools as the Americans, that their habits and manners may the sooner become united.

Directly behind the town, an inlet of salt water enters from the southern marshes, and extends nearly to the north ditch. It is called Mary Sanches Creek. The space between this and the Matanzas River, is divided into squares of irregular dimensions. The western division between the creek and St. Sebastian's River, is laid off into lots of different size, from two to twenty acres. Most of these are covered with fruit trees, such as mulberry, plumb, peach, fig, pomegranate, and oranges. Across the creek, an excellent stone causeway is erected The St. Sebastian's is crossed by a bridge 500 feet long, and a causeway is extended over the marshes, about seven hundred yards. The soil of the city and neighborhood is excellent for horticultural improvements, and much of it is cultivated in gardens, as well as groves. The timber which was originally abundant around the city, has in a long course of years been cut off to a considerable distance. Wood and fencing materials are consequently scarce and dear. Most of the lumber used here, is brought from northern parts. This renders building rather expensive. Notwithstanding this circumstance, the inhabitants are beginning to repair most of the old dwellings, and to erect some new and elegant buildings. The Presbyterian church in the south part of the town, has lately been enclosed, and finished in a plain but neat style. A small Methodist church was built in 1833, on Charlotte-street.

The old Government House has, heretofore, been occupied by all classes of Protestants as a meeting-house, and also as a hall for the courts of justice. This was once a large and splendid building. The extensive garden, enclosed by a formidable stone wall, and still containing a few ancient fruit trees, the remnants of Governor White's old and valuable botanic garden, now serves for the pen of a herd of swine, who appear the only tenants of a spot lately devoted to the choicest gifts of Flora.

The powder magazine, situated at the extreme south part of the town, is a large, plain, well-built house, constructed of stone and covered with tile. It is going rapidly to decay.

At the opposite part of the town stands the gate-way. Its two bold pilasters remind us of years long past and gone. The old moat, also, and ditch, extends from the fort to the St. Sebastian's River. The public road crosses it over a decent stone bridge, under which the tide regularly ebbs and flows.

The city contains ten lawyers, three doctors, one printer, seven dry goods stores, six boarding houses, thirteen groceries, one painter, seven carpenters, four masons, two blacksmiths, one gunsmith, two shoemakers, one baker, two tailors, one tanner, five segar makers, one regular packet which runs to Charleston.

The city is governed by a mayor and four aldermen ; they are chosen from any part of the city. The revenue amounts to about fifteen hundred dollars. It is raised by licences on stores, taverns, groceries, carts, and slaves. The languages usually spoken are English, Spanish, French, and Lingua França.

St. Augustine has become a place of great resort for invalids, affected by pulmonary and bronchial complaints. To this circumstance and the sale of oranges, the place owes her prosperity. The accommodations for strangers are rapidly improving, and it is believed, that in a short time, persons of the first rank, will be under no necessity for visiting Italy or the south of France, for the improvement of their health, as our climate is equally salubrious and the conveniences and luxuries of life may easily be obtained, when it is known that they will be required.

Tallahasse, the seat of government for the Territory, is situated in Leon County, about twenty-two miles north of St. Marks, and about midway between the eastern and western extremities of the Territory, on a high and commanding eminence, in the bosom of a fertile and picturesque country. A pleasant mill-stream, the collected waters of several fine springs, winds along the eastern border of the city, until it falls fifteen or sixteen feet, into a gulf scooped out by its own current, and finally sinks into a cleft of limestone rock, at the base of an opposite hill. Numerous springs flow from the southern border of the town. In every part of the place good water may be obtained by sinking wells, from six to thirty feet, through a clay formation. In the spring of 1824 the first house was erected in Tallahassee. The first legislative council sat there, in the winter of the same year. In the winter of 1825 it was incorporated, and the government of the city was vested in an intendant and five aldermen. It now contains little short of fifteen hundred inhabitants, and three hundred houses. The corner-stone of the state house was laid in January, 1826, and one wing of the building was erected during the same season. Several religious societies have since been established there. An academy, masonic lodge and chapter, an agricultural society, and many others; —two printing presses, and several public offices. The market is well supplied with meats of various kinds; vegetables, fresh butter, cheese, fowls, eggs, &c., are abundant, and excellent of their kind. The situation is healthy and pleasant, and few places in the southern part of America are more rapidly improving. Within four years past, the limits of the town have been greatly extended, by grants of land from the United States, which have been laid off into lots, and many of them improved. It must, in a few years, become a charming place of residence; it never was expected to become a place of extensive commerce. A railroad, however, has been constructed to St. Marks, and much of the commercial business of the country will now be transacted here.

Pensacola is situate on the north side of the bay of the same name about ten miles from the sea, in latitude 30° 23′ 43″ and in 10° 5′ longitude west from Washington City. An establishment was made at the entrance of the bay by Ariola, in 1696, as a check on the French at Baloxi Bay. In 1719 this post was broken up by Bienville. The Spaniards then removed to the west end of St. Rosa, across the channel, and two wooden forts were erected to protect their village. But as the land was poor and water scarce, they obtained permission of the Pensacola Indians to plant on the north side of the bay an extensive field. Here, in time, a village was built round their corn field, now the public square. At length, the natives vanished by degrees, and the whole Spanish population concentrated here. In 1763, when the English took possession of Florida, this was laid out in form of a city on an excellent plan. The streets were wide and crossed at right angles, making squares of four hundred by two hundred and fifty feet, with the large common fronting on the bay, one thousand six hundred feet long, by nine hundred wide. This square is now sold out in lots, except two small squares of 500 feet, at each end of the original common, and will soon form the most important part of the city. Most of the principal buildings were erected during this period. The two barracks, and Cassa Blanca, the residence of the governors, were superb buildings; they have since been burned down at different periods. Agriculture was greatly encouraged, and commerce in lumber, naval stores, indigo, skins, peltries, &c., was greatly extended. The gardens of Pensacola were the pride of Florida. Every city lot had appended to it a garden lot in the suburbs; their ruins are still apparent, though overrun with weeds and bushes. In 1781 the Spaniards, under Count Galvez, again attacked and conquered West Florida. Pensacola was defended by General Campbell, but the magazine at Fort St. Michael being blown up, the place surrendered. From this period the city declined. In 1814 the plan of the city suffered a reformation, like many that occur in our times. The gardens in the suburbs were sold at auction, in arpent lots, after which, none of them were ever improved. A slice was cut off the public square and built up. The body of the square was sliced into irregular lots, some of which were sold by the Intendant, and some by the Ayuntamento, to suit their private purposes. Streets were laid off to meet the general confusion, of various lengths and widths. Two small squares of five hundred by three hundred feet were saved from the confusion. The western, called the square of Ferdinand, and the eastern, the square of Seville.

The public buildings in Pensacola are a court house, church, market house, custom house, and public store. An episcopal church has lately been erected.

There is a wooden building two stories high, formerly the government house of the Spaniards. It stands near the bay, on the old common. It has lately been fitted up and painted by order of the government, and the yard has been enclosed with a handsome paling. But the orangery and out houses have been suffered to go to ruin.*

The catholic church stands on the beach. It was formerly a warehouse, and is large enough for present use, but very inconvenient and illy calculated for the purpose to which it is appropriated.

The market house is a very neat building, situate at the foot of the square of Ferdinand, near the beach. The productions of the market are yet small, but improving. The beef is plenty and good. Pork, mutton, veal and venison rather dear. Fish are plenty and cheap; oysters and crabs are also plenty. Vegetables have, within two years, increased in quantity and quality. The government of the city is vested in a mayor and nine aldermen, to whom is committed the police and fiscal concerns of the place. The health and quarantine regulations are referred to a board of health, appointed by the city council. The revenue amounts to about two thousand dollars per annum, drawn from a tax on real estate, slaves, pleasure carriages, saddle horses, and licenses on shops, stores, taverns, billard tables and carts. A large and extensive wharf is among the most useful of the late improvements. The number of inhabitants is less than two thousand.

Magnolia was established in 1827, by some enterprising individuals, under the expectation that from its position on the river St. Marks, it would command the trade of the adjacent country. In this however, they have

* The building since torn away.

16*

not been successful, as the trade has found its way to St. Marks and Tallahasse.

Quincey, the seat of Justice for Gadsden County, was laid out in 1825
in a rich tract of country, on the waters of Atta'pulgas Creek. It has improved into a pleasant village.

Monticello was surveyed for the country seat of Jefferson County, at the
beginning of 1828. It has improved very considerably. A court-house
and several respectable dwelling houses have been erected, and several
stores established. The situation is high, and surrounded with springs of
fine water. The site was formerly an old Indian town. It is twenty-five
miles N. E. from Tallahasse, and two from the Micakasookey Lake.

Marianna is situate on the Chipola River; it was incorporated in 1829,
and is a thriving country village.

Webville had grown into a considerable village, before it was laid off
into lots. It was incorporated in 1829, when one half of the lots sold for
8000 dollars, at public auction. It is situate on the high grounds, about
six miles west of the Chipola River, in a country of very rich land.

Fernandina is a small village, established about the year 1808, on the
north end of Amelia Island, and is the seat of justice for Nassau County. It became a considerable sea port, during the embargo times of Jefferson's administration; but it has since that period, diminished to an inconsiderable village. Its fine harbor, that used to contain at one time, 300
sail of square-rigged vessels, is now scarcely visited by one ship in a year.
It may still, at some future day, become a place of consequence.

Jacksonville is the seat of Justice, for Duval County. It is situate on the
north side of St. Johns River, at the Cowford, thirty miles from the bar.
Here the Kings road crosses the river. It contains a large courthouse, a
jail, and several private dwellings.

Appalachicola is a sea port town situated on a bluff, at the mouth of the
River Appalachicola; west side. It was incorporated in 1830. The
plan of this town was re-modelled and improved in 1836, since which 42
brick stores and ware-houses, besides many wooden dwellings and stores,
have been already added to the improvements of this thriving place.

This town has one large hotel, three taverns and private boarding
houses. It has two banks; is a seat of admiralty jurisdiction, and issues
one newspaper, the Appalachicola Gazette.

The exports of Appalachicola were last year, 58,500 bales of cotton,—
and including its foreign as well at domestic trade, there were 300 entries,
and the same number of clearances at the customhouse, from the 1st September, 1836, to 1st July, 1837, a large proportion of them ships and square
rigged vessels. There are twenty steam-boats besides barges and small
crafts employed in the navigation of the river Appalachicola.

Shell Point, a few miles west of the Appalache, is a pleasant and healthy situation, which the proprietors are laying off into lots, for the accommodation of those who wish to avail themselves of a pleasant summer retreat, on the sea shore.

St. Josephs, a new town commenced in 1836, on the east shore of St. Josephs Bay, from which a rail road is constructed to lake Wimeco, is a thriving town where considerable capital is embarked. It has already a Printing Office, a Hotel, &c.

Mico is the seat of justice for Hamilton County. Ochesee is a town laid out at the Ochesee bluffs, on the Appalachicola River. Vernon is another laid off eight miles below the junction of Chattahooche and Flint Rivers. Aspalaga is situate between the two last mentioned towns.

Key West is a town on the north end of the Island, of the same name. It is finely situated for commerce, admitting into the harbor, vessels drawing 27 feet water ; and capable of being well fortified. It may yet become the key of the Gulf of Mexico. It was incorporated in 1829, and laid off into lots the same year. It contains a court house and jail, two extensive ware houses, 14 stores, 8 groceries, and about 60 dwelling houses, 10 Lawyers, 2 Physicians, and about 600 inhabitants. The wages of mechanics are high, and there is good encouragement for every species of industry. There is a channel passing by the west side of Key West, into the Gulf of Mexico in a N. W. direction, through which vessels may pass, drawing 9 feet water. This is not only safer than the circuit round the Tortugus's, but it shortens the distance 90 miles.

COUNTIES.

The Territory is divided into twenty counties, Escambia, Walton, Washington, Jackson, Gadsden, Leon, Jefferson, Madison, Hamilton, Allachua, Nassau, Duval, St. Johns, Musquito, Monroe, Fayette, Columbia, Franklin, Dade and Hillsborough.

Escambia county is bounded west by the Perdido Bay, north by the 31st degree of north latitude, which divides it from Alabama, east by Walton, south by the Gulf of Mexico. It is about fifty-four miles long, from east to west, and fifty miles wide, from north to south. A large portion of the land in this county, is poor pine barren. The Bay of Pensacola enters the heart of it, and the lagoons and rivers connected with it, spread through every part, and bring a good navigation, to the very doors of the inhabitants. Small hammocks skirt these navigable waters, presenting eligible situations for country seats.

The pine lands, on the waters of the Perdido, afford excellent grazing and much good pine timber. The bottom lands on the Escambia River are very rich, but are subject to be overflown. A kind of second bottom, or hammock rises between the interval and the pine lands : these are generally cultivated and produce very good crops. Excellent springs of pure water burst out from the foot of the pine ridges. The peninsula between the Pensacola and Yellow Water Bays, is covered with pine and black jack timber, some savannas of good moist grazing land and a few hammocks.

The pine level is an extensive tract of land, spreading from the Escambia to the Black Water River. It is watered by numerous springs that unite in the Cold Water Creek, a branch of Black Water. The best farms in this country are situated here. The soil is a sandy clay, which yields good crops of corn, potatoes, peas, upland rice and green seed cotton, peaches, grapes and vines. Apples and figs do well, and will in future, be greatly increased. The peninsula between Pensacola Bay and St. Rosa Sound, is a mixture of pine and black jack ridges, bordered with hammocks of live oak, black oak, red bay, magnolia, &c. with strips of wet savanna, giving rise to abundance of fine streams that fall into the bay and sound at short intervals. The land on this peninsula, from Town Point, to Williams Creek, was purchased and appropriated by the former administration, for a live oak plantation, as an appendage to the Naval Depôt, at Tartar Point. Notwithstanding the favorable reports of the commissioners of the Naval Deparment, appointed to examine and report on this location, it has furnished to the ignorant and the designing a fruitful source of complaint, against the Delegate in Congress. Much of the land had been formerly cultivated, and the large timber cut off. A new growth of young trees, of various descriptions, had succeeded. The course of improvement has been to cut away all other timber, except the young live oaks, to prune them and keep out the pines. In this way, thirty thousand trees are preserved in a rapid state of growth, which will be ready to supply the navy, when the old trees are all cut from the public lands. This live oak plantation is about twenty-five miles long and from one to three miles wide. From the live oak plantation to the Chactawhatche Bay, the sound presents many picturesque scenes, and several tracts of excellent land, especially at the west end of the lake; and the main land, on the east side of Pensacola Bay, affords excellent grazing land and fine timber; it is traversed by many streams of good water which rise on the high lands, north of the Chactawhatche Bay. Between the Black Water and Yellow Water Rivers, the pine ridges are usually poor land.

In all the waters that traverse this county, fish and oysters are abundant, and excellent of their kinds. It is generally speaking, a healthy country; the see breezes cool the air during summer, and generally prevent the effects of frost during the winter season. The establishment of a Naval Depôt, and the erection of a large fort on the west end of St. Rose Island, have, and will for a long time to come, give employment to every species of industry, and afford great facilities to commercial speculation. A great

COUNTIES. **127**

quantity of good land remains uncultivated. Exhaustless banks of clay render brick making a lucrative employment, and the grazing of cattle is still pursued with great success.

Walton County is fifty-four miles long, from east to west, and thirty-six miles wide, from north to south. It is bounded north by the thirty-first degree of north latitude, east by Washington County, south by the Chactawhatche Bay, and west by Escambia County. This county is diversified with knolls and ridges of very poor land, and hammocks of great extent, of a very excellent quality. The most extensive tracts are the Uche and Aliqua vallies, the Yellow Water Settlement, the hammocks of McDavids pond and those on the north side of Chactawhatche Bay. A high ridge divides the waters that descend easterly into the Uche Creek, and Aliqua River, south into the Chactawhatche Bay, west into Pensacola Bay, and north into Shoal River. The north and south sides are steep and cut up with deep ravines, the east end terminates in sharp peaks, the west end slopes gradually into the low pine lands. This ridge is more than thirty miles long, generally sandy, but, in some parts covered with iron sand stone, which does not appear to enter deeply into the earth : the noblest springs issue from its sides, descending with rapid currents to the Bay on the south, and to Shoal River on the north side. At a distance of three or four miles from their sources, they become deep enough to navigate with large boats. These waters are very pure and cold. Five considerable streams are thus formed and pass into the Bay. Twin Creek is the first that enters Lafayette Bay, a western arm of the Chactawhatche. This Bay extends 7 miles into the country. There are three principal branches that unite and form Boggy Creek, which is navigable four miles from the Bay. Rock Creek is also navigable seven miles from the bay. Aliqua is the largest of the streams, that rise in this county. It is navigable, fifteen miles from the Bay. It then divides into three principal streams, that head in the knolls, which terminate the great ridge ; they interlock with the heads of Shoal Creek. The two eastern branches undulate through extensive cane brakes, and water a large extent of good land, supported by a substratum of soapstone. The Aliqua enters the bay, over a bar of five feet water.

The Yellow Water Settlement is in the north part of the county, on both sides of the river of that name. Here is a tract of excellent land, very well improved for a new country. The droughts of summer, affect this tract of country less than any other part of Florida. Cotton, corn, potatoes, rice, peas and vines make up the principal sum of the crops. Fruits, especially peaches, succeed perfectly well. Mills were early established, and since the river below has been opened, this settlement enjoys a convenient market for their produce.

The Uche Creek rises north of the Aliqua, and after running a course of thirty miles S. E. it falls into the Chactawhatche River, twenty miles from the bay. The valley watered by this creek is among the best land in the county. It is founded on limestone. Here is a large settlement of industrious Scotch farmers, who till their lands with their own hands, assisted with very few slaves, and are rapidly increasing in wealth and respectability.

On the north line of the county there is a thriving settlement of farms around McDavid's pond, a very handsome sheet of pure water, of an oval form, about three miles long and two broad. The land on its borders is formed of a rich clay and sand, which produces excellent crops of corn, cotton, etc. From this pond a large creek issues and unites with Shoal Creek. The farmers of Walton County are generally a stout, industrious, hardy and healthy class of people, very attentive to their own business, and are calculated to support a very fair standing in the mixed population of Florida. About one-third of this county is good, tillable land. On the east side of the Aliqua river the streams head in gentle vales, like grass savannas, from which they pass into brakes of reed cane, and then titi thickets succeed, and ultimately the banks become covered with forests of oak, hickory, magnolia, gum, and poplars. It is, on the whole, a beautiful country.

Washington County is about fifty-four miles long, from Hickory Hill to St. Joseph's Bay on the south, and ninety from the Pass L' Este on the west, to St. Joseph's Bay on the east. It is an irregular triangle in shape. This county boasts of one of the finest bays in Florida. The St. Andrews occupies the heart of the county. The hammocks on its banks contain live oak sufficient to build a navy, and although there is much poor land contained in its limits, especially along the sea-shore, yet there is already two very good settlements. Holmes Valley on the east side of the Chactawhatche River, extends eastward ten or twelve miles, parallel with Holmes Creek, from which it is separated by a sand ridge from one to two miles wide. It contains from eight to ten sections of good land, sunk nearly one hundred feet below the level of the surrounding pine country. The soil is a dark sandy loam, covered with white, black, red and water oak,— white ash, black gum, wild cherry, red bay, and magnolia, with witch hazel, pawpaw, sassafras, and haw shrubs, the whole mixed with wild cane of an extraordinary large growth. A good mill stream runs through it, collected from springs which issue abundantly from the sides of the valley. Near these springs, in the pine woods, the inhabitants usually fix their residences, while they cultivate their fields in the valley below. The lands in this valley are well cultivated by a hardy, industrious people.

Holmes Creek rises in Richmond County, Alabama, passes through the north-west corner of Jackson County, and falls into the east side of the Chactawhatchee River, about seven miles above the Cow Ford. This creek has a channel deeper than the river, and the enterprise of Messrs. Shackleford and Merlet has rendered it navigable, as far as Hard Labor Creek, by clearing out the timber, which had before that time obstructed the channel. They have erected warehouses about forty miles from its mouth, to receive the produce of the Chipola planters. The Big Spring of Chactawhatche rises near the mouth of this creek, with which it unites its waters. Six feet of water can be carried from the bay into this spring, which will be hereafter more particularly described. Groves of fine cypress clothe the margins of this creek, and a few good hammocks skirt its banks.

There is another very good settlement on the Econfina River, which is navigable fifteen miles from the Bay of St. Andrews. The limestone lands on this stream are very fertile, producing in a natural state, the finest groves of white oak in Florida : there is also a large quantity of wild cherry and red cedar of superior quality. All the productions of this country are raised in abundance here. Numerous springs of fine water are found convenient to every farm, and the county is healthy as it is fertile.

The hammocks on the north side of the main body of the bay and of the eastern arm are extensive and rich, and will afford excellent farms, for ten or twelve miles, with good grazing lands in the rear. They will also enjoy every facility of commerce, with the finest fish and oysters at their doors. The lands north of this arm of the bay are clayey, and although covered with pine timber, are, for the most part, capable of successful cultivation. The banks of the Chipola are in many places very fertile. The western arm between the sea and Chactawhatche Bay is covered with sand hills, scrub, and miserable swamps. The borders of the bay are an exception, having some very good hammock lands. From the east end of the bay to the Econfina River, there are extensive ranges of ponds, with poor pine ridges between. In progress of time its commercial advantages may render this county one of the most important in the Territory.

Jackson County is bounded north by the Alabama line ; east, by the Chattahooche and Appalachicola Rivers ; south, by Washington County ; and west, by Walton County. It is forty-eight miles in length, from east to west, and thirty-two from north to south. It is one of the most populous counties in the Territory. Near the centre of the north line arises Spring Creek, from several very large springs which rise on both sides of the line ; this is the largest tributary stream of the Chipola River, which rises in Richmond and Columbia Counties, Alabama. It meanders through the heart of Jackson County, more distinguished for the good lands on its borders, than for its size or beauty.

From thè natural bridge, to the head of Spring Creek, a distance of nearly twenty miles, the rich land extends three or four miles west of the river, but narrow on the east side. The soil is a soft chocolate colored loam, on red clay, and amorphous limestone. The timber in a state of nature, large white oaks, gum, hickory, and dogwood, thickly filled up with cane. The lands also, on the borders of the Chattahooche and Appalachicola, are very fine. There is also a considerable extent of good land about the Big Spring of Chipola, near the south line. Here also are some excellent farms under cultivation. In the western part of the county, oak and hickory hills, almost the only eminences in the country, stand insulated in the pine barren, which extends a great distance around them; above this plain they are elevated some hundreds of feet, covered with a rich soil and forests of oak and hickory timber, of a very large size; the finest wild cherry in the Territory, white ash, chesnut, black gum, sorrel and red bay, with an under-growth of cane. Oak hill is nearly round and may contain one and a half sections of good land. Hickory hill stands about two miles distant, in a western direction ; it throws off a spur or ridge, which extends about six miles to the S. W. Both these hills derive their names from the timber that predominates on them. Hickory hill contains four or five sections of good land, some of it excellent. Abundant springs gush from the sides of these hills, many of which are absorbed by the sands of the plains below. Dry Creek, and Hard Labor, are the only two streams that convey currents through the pine barren. The balance of this county consists of pine barrens, intersected with ponds and sink holes. The caves, natural bridges, and noble springs of this country, are noted under the head of natural curiosities. The limestone that subtends the whole region, varies considerably in quality in different parts, which has an evident effect on the natural productions of the soil.

Gadsden county extends from the Georgia line, to the Gulf of Mexico, a distance of sixty-six miles, and from the Appalachicola to the Oclockony River, from thirty to thirty-six miles. Dog Island, on the coast, is attached to it. The lands on the Appalachicola are very rich, covered with very large timber, interspersed with luxuriant cane brakes. Musquito Creek and Sweet Water, small b anches of the Appalachicola, water considerable tracts of good land on the west, while Little River and its branches, spread over the N. E. quarter of the county, and irrigate some of the finest land in the Territory. The Oclockony is navigable for large boats. Vessels drawing six feet water, can enter the bay, and ascend as far as the crooked stream will render it profitable. The principal settlements are on the Attapulgas, Rocky Comfort, and Robinson's Creek, branches of Little River, which enters the

Oclockony, about five miles below the Tallahasse road. The high grounds between the Appalachicola and the waters of the Oclockony, are usually pine barren. The south part of the county is covered with palmettoes, ponds and swamps. Low marsh lands border the Oclockony bay. Alligator Harbor lies south of this bay, in front of James Island, which is formed between the two arms of the Oclockony River. This county already embraces a valuable population, which is daily increasing. Quincy, the seat of justice, is situate on the west side of the Attapulgus Creek.

Leon County is bounded west by the Oclockony River, north by Decatur County, Georgia, east by Jefferson County, and south by Appalache Bay. It is forty-eight miles long, from north to south, and thirty-eight, from east to west. The sea coast is generally marshy. Four miles east of the Oclockony Bay, there is a little archipelago of islands, some of them covered with live oak and cedar, but many others only with grass and reeds. The Appalache Bay makes a sweep, of something like one hundred miles ; the circle is very gradual. The water is shoal, for many miles into the sea. The bottom, an amorphous limestone, with nodules of flint or hornstone. Oysters grow to the rock, in large masses, and grass is so abundant, even to the depth of several feet, that the coast at low tide, has the appearance of a green meadow. The forests rarely approach within three or four miles of the tide. On these marshes however, there are frequent keys, which rise like small islands, covered with live oak, cedar and cabbage palms. These are most frequent, where streams of water enter the bay. The high grounds, bordering the marshes, are usually rocky, but covered with a great variety of heavy timber. A ridge of rocks, runs parallel with the coast, at about six to nine miles distance ; it does not rise high, above the surface of the earth, but causes ripples and falls, in all the streams that pass into the bay, east of the Wakully. There are many rich hammocks, on the borders of the Appalache Bay, and the streams, that fall into it. There are also detached hammocks that are surrounded by fine lands. The latter kinds are most frequent, between the Oclockony and Wakully. Much of the pine land near the bay, has a rich soil and is very productive. The streams are usually so full of grass, as to impede the navigation.

The whole county abounds in lakes, ponds, subterranean rivers, sink holes and large springs. To the distance of about twenty miles, from the coast, on the rocky pine lands, the waters are strongly tinctured with lime, but upon the uplands, the springs and streams are very pure. The flat country abounds in fine yellow pine timber, under which the wild grass grows luxuriantly. It is a good grazing county, and much of it might be profitably cultivated, especially with sea island cotton, where the quality of the cotton is far superior to that produced on the uplands. From this level tract of pine land, the county rises in gentle swells, of red and white clay, covered with an excellent brown soil, and crowned with wide spreading oaks, tall hickories, liriodendrons, magnolia and gum trees. Between the swells, every valley is enlivened with streams of pure water. They however generally sink into the earth, before they leave the upland country. This kind of land, in many places, extends into Georgia. In other parts, the low pine country makes deep indentations among the hills. The argilaceous re-region extends through this county, from east to west; in width, it is from ten to twenty miles. The traces of subterranean rivers, which sometimes burst from the earth, only to sink again; the very great diversity of soil, scenery and timber, renders the county of Leon, a situation of much interest to the curious. One half of the lands in this county is considered to be very good and the greater part of the other moiety, tolerable. This part of Florida is rapidly settling by men of wealth and enterprize. The face of it is covered with extensive fields of cane, cotton, and corn. Ease and opulence are the certain results of a moderate industry.

Tallahasse, the capital of the Territory, is rapidly increasing in wealth and population. Magnolia has already become a place of considerable commerce, and St. Mark's, since the completion of the rail road to Tallahasse, has become a place of active business, and, if not retarded by fevers, may become a port of great commercial consequence.

Jefferson county is bounded west by the county of Leon, north by the Georgia line, east by the Ocilla and its eastern branch, and south by the Gulf of Mexico. It is about 39 miles long and 18 miles wide. The north end of it is very good land. The best is, perhaps, in the neighborhood of Monticello, the county seat. It was formerly an old Indian town. The principal Mickasooky towns were situate on the eastern borders of the lake, which bounds this county on the west. There is also considerable first rate land in the forks of the Ocilla river. These lands were occupied and cultivated by the Seminole Indians after the Mickasooky towns were broken up by General Jackson. The Massasaugea Sinks are situated about two miles S. E. from the lake, on the line between Leon and Jefferson counties. Here the waters of the lake, with several other streams unite, and together plunge into the earth. On one of these streams Col. Baily has erected extensive mills, &c. Colonels White, Gadsden, Murat and Gamble, and many other gentlemen of distinction, have extensive plantations in this county.

Madison county is bounded by Jefferson county on the west, the Georgia line on the north, the Withlacooche and Suwanne rivers on the east, and the Gulf of Mexico on the south. It is about 96 miles long and 48 wide. It is diversified with very good and very poor land. The north and west have excellent tracts of considerable extent. The centre is generally poor.

The S. E. has many sections of very superior sugar land. The principal settlements are north of the road leading from Tallahasse to St. Augustine. This part of the country is rolling oak land, interspersed with fine springs and streams of water. Old Hick's Town was formerly a favorite settlement of the Seminoles. The borders of San Pedro Lake were early occupied by the Spaniards as a missionary establishment. Much of the pine land on the great road, east of the Ocilla, is rich and productive. The Histahatchee, Chattahatchee, and Achenahatchee, and Fœnahalloway, a large branch of the Ocilla, water the southern part of the county. A great number of small lakes are scattered over it; of these, the largest is San Pedro, which is the source of the Chattahatchee. The south-east corner, near the Suwanne, contains some excellent cane lands; some valuable settlers are opening plantations here.

Hamilton county is bounded west by the Withlacooche River, north by the Georgia line, east and south by the Little Suwanne River. It is about 36 miles long and 20 in the widest part. This county has acquired a considerable population in a short time. It is said to contain much good land, and is finely watered. The Little Suwanne skirts it for 40 miles. The Allappahaw passes through the centre, and the Withlacooche washes the western side. The line which separates it from Georgia, runs on a ridge that divides the waters which fall into the Suwanne on the south, and the Oquefanoke Swamp on the north. Mico, situate in the forks of Allappahaw, is the seat of justice.

Columbia County is bounded west by the Suwanne River; north, by the Georgia line; east, by the St. Mary's River and Duval County; and south by Allachua County. It is about seventy-two miles long and sixty wide. It contains much poor pine barren land. In the northern part there are detached spots of good farming land. In the southern part, about the Santaffe and its tributary streams and lakes, there is considerable good land. The settlements are much scattered over the county. It is almost surrounded by the Suwanne, the St. Marys, and the Santaffe Rivers.

Ocean, or Randolph Lake is situated about twelve miles from the St. Marys, on the north side of the road leading to St. Augustine; it is about seven miles long and five wide; it discharges its waters into the St. Marys. Alligator Lake is, in a wet season, three miles long and two wide; but in a dry season, the waters of six considerable streams sink into the earth :— the surface of the land is soon covered with grass, and herds of cattle are seen during summer, where shoals of fishes and alligators swim during the winter season. When a sudden drought has withdrawn the waters, millions of fish have been left to perish on the muddy bottom. The alligators are more provident,—they withdraw with the water to the great

sink hole. Whether the waters of the lake arise again at New River, a
branch of the Santaffe, or at Echatucne, a great spring south of the
natural bridge, is uncertain ; both are large creeks that arise at once from
the earth, not many miles distant.   There are several other large lakes
in this county, but little known.   Gadsdens' Spring is celebrated for its
medical qualities ; it is situated in the seventeenth section of the first township in range fourteen, on the south bank of the Little Suwanne.   It is
situated on the bank of the river, is about sixty feet across, and thirty to
forty deep.   A small village is here incorporated.   This county is a fine
grazing tract both for cattle and hogs.

Duval County is bounded north and north-west by Nassau ; east, by the
Atlantic and St. Johns River ; south, by Allachua ; and west, by Columbia
Counties.   It is about eighty-four miles long and thirty wide.   The seat of
justice is at Jacksonville, on the north side of the St. Johns River, about
thirty miles from the sea.   The eastern part of this county is low and
marshy.   The Nassau River separates it from the county of that name
on the north.   On the bar of that river there is eight feet water, but the
country affords but few objects for commercial enterprise.   Some live oak
has been cut.   In some future time, rice plantations will be cultivated.
Considerable business is done on the St. Johns.   Live oak to a considerable
amount is annually exported—cotton, oranges, lemons, moss, jerked beef,
and lumber.   Both sides of the St. Johns is cultivated by industrious farmers.   There is a safe inland passage from the St. Johns to Savanna.
Steam Boats have already passed back and forth from that place, and it is
confidently expected that much business will hereafter be done in that line.
Groves of fruit trees are rapidly extending, cotton farms, and sugar plantations are increasing in number and extent.   Black Creek, a tributary of
St. Johns, is a fine navigable stream for fifteen miles.   Should the canal
ever be carried into effect across the peninsula, the forks of Black Creek
will become a valuable situation for business.   The islands of Fort George
and Talbot are well cultivated, and produce abundance of provisions and
fruit.   The first is wholly owned by Mr. Kingsley, the second by Messrs.
Houston and Christopher.

Nassau County is bounded west and north by St. Marys River ; east by
the Atlantic ; and south, by Duval County.   The lands of Nassau are
generally low and level, but it is well settled by an industrious and thriving
population.   Amelia Island extends the whole length of its eastern line,
and is divided from the main land by a navigable sound, which has lately
been improved by a canal about half a mile in length.   The Harbor of
Fernandina is the best south of Chesapeake Bay.   Some of the plantations on the St. Marys are very productive in rice and sugar.   The plan-

tation called White Oak while it belonged to Z. Kingsley, Esq., is said to have produced crops of the value of ten thousand dollars in one year. In 1829 he made five thousand bushels of rough rice, fifty hogsheads of sugar, besides a large quantity of cotton, corn, peas, potatoes, &c. The seat of justice for Nassau County has lately been removed from Fernandina to a settlement north of Nassau River.

Allachua County extends from the south line of Columbia, south to the Talassee pond, and Paines Landing, a distance of sixty-six miles. And from Orange Lake, on the east to the Wakasasse Bay, and Suwańne River on the west, forty-eight miles. It embraces one of the largest tracts of good land in the Territory. It was from the time of its first discovery, by de Soto to the present day, covered by a dense population. In 1812, the seat of the Seminole nation, governed by Paine, and Bowlegs was in this county, and so continued till their power was broken by Col. Newnan. The site of their principal towns, is comprehended in the grant of land made to Arredondo. This county embraces the great Lakes of Orange, Pithlachucco, and Hogmasters, and the Prairies of Allachua, Kanappaha, Wakahoota, and many others. The great plantation of Lang Syne, Oakland and Tarvers, and many others, produced great quantities of sugar and provisions. The herds of cattle, and droves of horses that ranged over these prairies, were almost innumerable ; good judges have estimated that the Seminoles have, since this war commenced, driven off more than thirty thousand head. The Allachua savanna, is during the winter season, usually covered with water if the season be very wet ; a stream flows from it into Orange Lake. But, as the dry season approaches, the water withdraws into a sink hole, near the north shore, and leaves a green meadow fifteen miles from east to west, and six from north to south. It is probably one of the best spots for grazing in the world. The grass is often so tall as to hide the droves of cattle, and deer from sight. The sink hole that receives these waters is a deep rocky dell in the north bank of the prairie, shaded with lofty oaks, and here in the dry season may be seen innumerable fishes and alligators. A large stream runs from the Pithlachucco Lake, through part of the savanna into this Sink Hole. Almost any quantity of fine trout may be caught in this stream. The hammock lands, on the borders of this great prairie, are very rich and afforded many delightful prospects, and many rich farms, before the Seminole war.

From the Allachua uplands the country descends westward, about twenty miles, to the Wakasasse River, is covered with pine timber, and is diversified by a variety of grass ponds and swamps. The Wakasasse is formed by the collection of many springs and drains, from the wet savannas. The whole country is excellent for grazing.

From the Wakasasse to the Suwanne, the country is rolling pine land until you approach the coast, when it becomes flat and wet, in many places very swampy.

Dade County, erected expressly in memory of the lamented officer, who was massacred by the Seminoles, is bounded by Allachua County on the north, the Seminole reserve on the east, Tampa Bay on the south, and the Gulf of Mexico on the west. Ouithlacooche River gives a leading feature to this county. At some future period, this river will be the great thoroughfare across the peninsula. There is no other place where the Atlantic and the Gulf can be connected at so small an expense, nor where the fertile lands of the east, can be so generally benefitted by such a communication. From the Ouithlacooche to Chicuchatte Settlements, there is a great quantity of excellent land, but it is interspersed with very poor lands in a singular manner. The Big Hammock, is the largest tract unbroken by waste lands in this part of Florida. The Olocklikane, or Spotted Lake, is a tract of grass meadow, covered from one to six feet deep with water, sprinkled all over with islets of rich land and cypress swamps. Many of these spots were, before the war, and perhaps are at this time, thickly settled with Seminoles. Col. Lane explored two of them, on which he found 150 cabins, cultivated fields, and 700 head of cattle. One of the old Indian negroes, long ago, informed us that on one of these islands the Seminole chiefs kept their magazine of ammunition concealed from the great body of their own people. West of the Olocklikany, the country falls westward over rather barren pine lands to the Gulf. The country around Chicuchatty, is high table land formed of the rich red clay, so predominant in Middle Florida. In this part of the country there are many delightful situations for planters, with pleasant and extensive prospects, fine air, abundant springs of good water, and excellent grazing land.

Hillsborough County, is bounded north by Dade, east by the Indian Reserve, south by Charlotte Harbor, and west by the Gulf of Mexico. This County embraces Tampa Bay.

On the east side of Hillsborough Bay the pine lands have a good sub-soil of rich clay. Southwest of Manatee River, on the borders of Tampa, and progressing towards the Sarrazota Bay, there is considerable live oak hammock, interspersed with cane and tall palmettoes. The soil appears to be rich. The best part of these hammocks are about Oyster Creek. On the east side of the Sarrazota there has been a considerable tract improved, and would now afford a fine settlement. From this to Charlotte Bay, the lands, so far as they have been explored, are poor. Some beautiful situations are found on the coast, especially about Palm Sound ; below which, the pine lands extend to the Gulf for a distance of 12 or 15 miles, to Cleni Sound, an arm of Charlotte Bay. In addition to Arridendo's Allachua grant, there is another of eight leagues square, 308,640 acres, claimed by the heirs of Miranda, situate on the heads of Hillsborough and Tampa Bays. This grant contains a fine commercial situation and considerable good land. The title is now before the Superior Court of this District, and will probably be soon decided. The tract of country embraced within the boundaries of this county, would probably have been well settled by this period, had the titles been decided.

The seat of justice is established at Newnansville, now in Columbia, until another be selected, south of the Santaffe, and a little village is rising around it.

St. John's County is bounded north by Duval, east by the Atlantic, south by Musquito, and west by Allachua and Duval. It is about 72 miles long, and from thirty to forty-eight miles wide. This county contains much valuable land, and most of it is situate on navigable waters. The St. John's river passes through the western part, while the eastern side is abundantly watered by the North River and Matanzas Sound, branches that disembogue at the St. Augustine Inlet. The north part of the county embraces the Cabbage Swamp and Diego Plains, both containing superior land. They are separated from Durbin and Twelve Mile Swamps by a ridge of pine land, three or four miles wide, which extends from the north line to St. Augustine. There is a considerable settlement around Julington Creek. Although the hammocks are not extensive, yet the pine land five or six miles from the river, has a rich clay foundation, and produces excellent crops. The shores of St. John's river are generally clothed with forests of live oak and orange trees. In many places the soil has been exhausted by long cultivation; but there are still more than have ever been improved. It is generally believed that the eastern side of the St. John's produce better lemons, citrons and oranges than the west; that fruit is larger, and the trees less liable to receive injury from storms; we think these opinions incorrect. Cotton and corn grow equally well on the west side, and the few experiments made, in cane, have been perfectly successful. While the English occupied Florida, this fine river was skirted with rich plantations, nearly to Lake George. Some of their distinguished nobility and statesmen had seats on its waters. The ruins of their mansions are now mouldering in dust.

At this time there is but one considerable establishment above Palatka, which is a little south of St. Augustine, except the hammocks, which border the small streams running into the St. John's and the Atlantic. There are in this county several swamps of very rich land. Cabbage, Durbin and Twelve Mile have already been noticed. There is, besides,

18

Turnbull, which extends from Six Mile Creek to the south end of Twelve Mile Swamp. Pivit lies two and a half miles west of St. Augustine ; in which Mr. Hanson has now in successful operation a large sugar plantation. Cowan Swamp lies two miles west of it, at the head of a western branch of Moultrie Creek. The last mentioned swamps contain several sections of good farming land within 4 miles of St. Augustine. All the lands on the North River, which extends 25 miles north of St. Augustine, are good. Many of them have been exhausted by long cultivation, but the means of renovating them are at hand, in the salt marshes that skirt the river. The tract situate between the river and Guanna Creek, has all been cultivated time out of mind, and was nearly abandoned, when Mr. Jenckes, a gentleman from Rhode Island, purchased New Waterford, near the head of the river, and has already rendered it a delightful spot. Mr. Perpall is now cultivating a plantation lower down the river. These lands afford excellent orange groves. South of St. Augustine, the lands are not so good as they are in the northern part. Near the Matanzas bar, however, there is considerable excellent land. Dunn's Lake and Lake George, both furnish some good hammocks and much excellent grazing land.

Kingsley's Island contains two or three thousand acres of superior land. It is situate near the outlet of Lake George. The plantation of Esperanzee, on Dunns Lake, is a beautiful situation. Considerable improvements had been made on it by the proprietor, Mr. Joseph M. Sanches, before his death. It is at present purchased by a gentleman who will cultivate it. A superior sugar plantation might be made here. Schooners enter the lake in front of this plantation. On Pallaciers Creek, there is a large extent of good hammock land, some of which has been long under cultivation. Mala Compra the seat of General Hernandez, is situate at the head of the Matanzas Lagoon. It is an extensive cotton plantation. The large sugar plantations of Major Samuel Williams, and that of Col. Williams of Maryland, are situate on the north end of Graham's Swamp. Live oak, oranges, and cotton, have hitherto been the principal articles exported from this county, but sugar will probably hereafter, supercede the cotton crop. The culture of oranges is rapidly increasing. Lemons, limes, guavas, and figs, are increasing, and some successful attempts at the cultivation of the vine, has lately been made. Within two years, this county has made much improvement in agriculture, in population, and in the value of property. Since the Seminole war commenced, all these plantations have been laid waste.

Musquito County is one hundred and ninety miles long, and sixty broad. It is bounded on the north by St. John's and Allachua counties, west by Allachua and the Seminole reserve, south by Monroe county, and east by the Atlantic Ocean. There is a considerable settlement on Tomoko and Smith's Creeks, on the Halifax River, and at New Smyrna ; the balance of this county is unsettled.

In so great an extent of country, as Musquito, there must necessarily be a great diversity of soil and climate. The north line, which cuts Graham's Swamp in the centre, passes over some excellent land. The savanna that extends from Mala Compra, to Smith's Creek, a distance of thirteen miles, has a superior soil of rich clay and marl, covered with vegetable mould. But it is too wet to cultivate without draining. A company is formed to cut a canal through this savanna, from Mala Compra, at the head of Matanzas Lagoon, to Mr Bulow's plantation, on Smith's Creek, a water of Halifax River. From this savanna, to Graham Swamp, the pine land is of a good quality, and there is some hammock intermixed. Graham's Swamp is a narrow strip of land, that runs parallel with the coast, commencing at the head of the Matanzas Lagoon, and extending to the Tomoko River. It is scarcely over two miles in width, but the lands are of a superior quality.

The plantation of the late Mr. Bulow, is one of the finest in Florida. About eight hundred acres were under cultivation before the war. Messrs Lawton, Mr. Dummet, Mr. Andrews, and Mrs. Anderson, have all extensive and valuable plantations. All these were in full operation before the Seminole war. The land cultivated by Col. Dummet, is salt marsh drained. His fields have produced excellent crops, six years in succession from rattones. He made about fifty hogsheads of sugar a year, with a very small force. On all the water courses in this quarter of the country, there are extensive marshes, equally valuble, as the expense of draining is less, than that of clearing the heavy timber from our swamp lands.

On the west side of Halifax River, Messrs Armstrong and Simmons, Harriet and Williams, had opened extensive sugar plantations ; and at New Smyrna Messrs Crugher and Depuyster and Mr. Hunter were also commencing very extensive sugar establishments. The former had their manufactory erected and had commenced making up their last years crop, when the war broke out. This part of the county affords extensive tracts of swamp and hammock lands, of the first quality. Turnbulls swamp, which extends from Spruce Creek, to about five miles south of New Smyrna, was drained by Doct. Turnbull, in 1768. Two large canals were cut from the Hillsborough River, three miles back into the swamp, and one cut nearly the same distance, into Spruce Creek. These are connected, by ditches, that drain the swamp in every direction. It is thought that one hundred thousand dollars would scarcely procure the labor, that has been expended here. It has fully prepared the lands for cultivation, except taking off a second growth of timber, which has sprung up, since these improvements were made. What

is of still more consequence, it has rendered the country healthy.   McDou
gals swamp commences, where Turnbulls ends, there is only a narrow
grass savanna, that separates them.   This swamp embraces the heads of
Indian river ; and extends in length, on the west side, at least thirty miles ;
on the east side, it terminates in a hammock, west of Ross place, about 14
miles from its commencement.   It is, in many places, more than two miles
wide.   Some places, in the centre of the swamp, are overflowed in wet
weather, but the borders are, at all seasons, fit for cultivation.   The country
west of Graham, Turnbull and McDougal swamps, is, for about twenty
miles, a piny glade, diversified with cypress swamps, grass savannas and
ponds.   There is no line marked, between this county and the Indian reser-
ervation.   The St. Johns River runs through the heart of this county, until
it terminates in broad grass savannas, deeply covered with water.   The
lands on this river, towards its head, are usually low, rich hammocks.   In
the forks between this river and the Ocklawaha, the sand hills and ridges
rise to a consideradle height, often chequered with ponds and bay galls.

From the head of Indian River to Jupiter Inlet, a distance of more than
a hundred miles, the country is greatly diversified.   The sea shore below
Cape Canaverel is cut up into islands which are not usually more than a mile
in width, the eastern slope being washed by the sea; the sand hills are
raised very high, in the centre ; behind them range the shrub oaks and palmettoes, while the eastern shores of Indian River are usually covered with
a rich forest of hammock trees and vines.   In several deep bends of this
coast, very good plantations might be cultivated.   These islands are covered by a grant of the Spanish Government to Eusebio Gomez of twelve
thousand acres.   Merritts Island claimed by Gen. Clinch, lies within Indian
River.   The western shore of Indian River, is skirted with cabbage hammocks on a rich but rocky surface, which usually extends some distance
up the tributary streams.   One of these is the N. W. Branch, which rises
in the vicinity of the St. Johns River, between which and this stream there
exists a very narrow pine ridge.   On both sides of this stream there is excellent land for some distance into the country.   Delespines large grant of
forty-three thousand acres is situated on the west side of Indian River, and
nearly west of Cape Canaverel.   Between Hillsborough Lagoon and Indian River, there is a narrow portage of nineteen hundred and eighty feet.
The land which it crosses, is dry savanna or prairie, quite rocky, but has a
tolerable soil.   Boats appear to have been hauled across this portage time
out of mind.   The land cannot be more than four feet above the water.
Very little tide is perceivable on either side.

Elbow Creek enters Indian River opposite the south end of Merritts Island.   It opens into a fine large cove with hammocks on each side, upon a

low rocky shore. This is however a short stream, rising in a swamp five or six miles back. The pine lands soon succeed the hammocks, and cypress covers the swamp.

Crane Creek enters two miles below Elbow. It has a very narrow entrance, but widens for half a mile, into a broad lagoon ; a marsh succeeds in which the creek again becomes narrow. Above this, pine lands succeed, with high banks and a clay soil, and appears to be good land. This is a beautiful stream and abundantly stocked with fresh water trout.

Turkey Creek enters two miles farther south. It is a short stream and the land on its banks appears to be light and sandy. South of this creek the bluffs of yellow sand rise very high, on the west bank of Indian River, and here the coquina rocks cease to appear, on this shore of the river. The bluffs are marked on the old charts, Les Tortolas. Shells succeed the rocks on this shore of the river, and the quality of the land is not so good.

St. Sebastians Creek is a considerable river ; it enters eighteen miles south of Merritts Island. A high bluff of very yellow sand, rises on the south point of the entrance. The banks of this creek are generally high, and usually covered with pine timber. This river appears to rise about thirty miles south west, nearly opposite to the narrows, in ponds and extensive savannas. For several miles, from its mouth, it traverses a high and rolling country, of pine lands of a tolerable quality. On both sides of this creek, is located Flemmings Grant, of twenty thousand acres.

St. Lucia River enters twenty-six miles south of St. Sebastians. From the western shore, in this space, the land rises into sand hills and again recedes into low pine lands, which extend back, a few miles ; the savannas then become very frequent. A fine cabbage hammock rises about two miles north of the St. Lucia and extends up that river, about eight miles ; it then terminates in good pine land. On the north shore, the coquina formation again appears, in high rocky bluffs. The south shore near the mouth, has a deep hammock of hard timber, but it does not extend so far up, as on the north shore. The pine lands that succeed, are mixed with oak and hickory shrubs. The river divides into three large branches, about nine miles from its mouth. In these forks the country is covered with pine, but the soil is good ; near the south branch, there are large islets of hammock land, surrounded by pine. South of St. Lucia, an extensive tract of mangroves extend from the coast, three or four miles back, and seven or eight miles south, to Hobe Sound. This tract is cut up by numerous deep, but narrow channels, which traverse it in every direction. On the west, a rich low pine country succeeds, covered with high grass, forming an excellent grazing country, for several miles ; when wet savannas succeed, which terminate in cedar swamps.

On the west of Hobe Sound, the land rises into hills and ridges of light sand, scattered over with shrub pines and vacciniums. This tract is marked on the old charts, the Bleach Yard. On Gomez Island, north of Jupiter Inlet, is the old plantation of Padre Torry, now grown up with bushes, but embracing several fruit trees, that contend with the cabbage-palms for possession.

No person has penetrated the country, many miles west of Indian River. West of Delespines tract, an extensive grass savanna, is bounded by a large water course, which by the surveyor was supposed to be the St. John's. But it is more likely to be one of those lakes, that in many places intersect the interior of the country, to a great extent. Occasionally cabbage hammocks of considerable extent, rise in the midst of these glades. Near the heads of St. Lucia, a broad savanna was coasted many miles north, and at length was crossed, where it was from four to five miles wide, and the water was from three to four feet deep, but wholly covered with grass. Still farther west, numerous branches traversed the pine lands, and run in the direction of the St. John's.

Greenville Creek, Middle Creek, Jupiter Creek, and Fresh Water Creek, all enter the south end of Hobe Sound, near Jupiter Inlet. The country through which these streams pass, is unexplored. Jupiter Creek is said to head in a large lake, about four miles west of the Rio Seco, forty-five miles south of Jupiter inlet. Between this creek and the coast, is Fresh Water Lake, which extends near forty miles, parallel with the coast, and only two or three miles distant. Some very rich marsh lands separate Fresh Water Lake from the Lagoon of Rattones and Hillsborough Inlet. The northern branch of this inlet, which receives the waters of the Rattones Lagoon, is named Potomac, and this stream is the southern boundary of Musquito County.

Monroe County is bounded on the north by Allachua and Musquito Counties, east by the Atlantic, south by the Florida Channel, and west by the Gulf of Mexico. It embraces all the south end of the Peninsula, from Charlotte Bay to Hillsborough Inlet, a distance of one hundred and fifty miles ; together with the Florida Keys. These have been described under the head of islands. The coast has also been generally described, and the interior is very little known. A very few additional facts we shall here state.

The Sandwich Gulf, or Bay Biscayne, extends from Key Biscayne, in a N. E. direction, about eighteen miles, and receives the Miami and Rattones Rivers from the glades. New River, that enters the Atlantic, nine miles south of Hillsborough Inlet, also communicates with the glades, and boats can ascend any one of these rivers into the glades, and from thence descend the others into the Sandwich Gulf, and from thence into the Atlantic. On the south side of Hillsborough, there is a large prairie, which may contain one thousand acres. It appears like an old Indian field, but the land is rather poor. It is surrounded with pine lands, broken by lagoons, which extend with some interruptions, to New River.

On the west side of New River, there is a considerable tract of rich hammock land, part of which is cultivated by a few families that reside on the coast. At the east side of the river, a sand beach extends nearly six miles S. W. from this settlement, passing the mouth of the river over a sand bar of six feet water.

On the west side of Sandwich Gulf, there is for two or three miles, above and below the Miami River, a tract of rocky land, but which has a rich soil. The shore is high and precipitous, with cocoanut trees jutting from the fissures of the rocks. A considerable settlement has been established here for 22 years past, but they have made very little improvement. On the north side of the Miami, is located the large grant of Aronbede, of ninety thousand acres of land. It has not been surveyed, but embraces the head of the Gulf, and the River Rattones, with the inclined plane that descends from the glades to the sea.

Below Cape Florida, the coast declines again into sandy pine lands, for several miles, until Fresh Water Creek enters the Gulf. Here again is a small quantity of good hammock land, called Cocoanut Point. From this to Cape Sable, the prairie approaches near the coast, extending into the country, usually about fifteen miles. It is interspersed with pleasant hammocks of good land. This prairie usually terminates in cypress swamps, and those in the interminable glades.

Fayette County was organized in February, 1832. It is bounded north by the Alabama line, west by Jackson County, south by Washington County, and east by the Chattahooche, and Appalachicola Rivers. It is about 36 miles long, and 24 miles wide. The lands on the rivers are generally very fertile. The centre of the county is generally pine barren, and water is scarce. The Big Spring of Chipola, rises in the S. W. part of the county. It is particularly described, under the head of curiosities. The greatest population is on the borders of the Chattahooche, but the lands on Spring Creek and Chipola, are rapidly selling.

Franklin County was established at the same time as Fayette. It is in shape, nearly a triangle, each of whose sides are about 48 miles. It was cut out of Washington and Gadsden Counties, embracing the Appalachicola River, below the Chipola inundation, and embracing also the Islands of St. George and St. Vincent. The lands of this county are very low and wet. Ponds, swamps, and marshes are liberally distributed over the face of it. The lands bordering the river, are very rich, but have not been considered healthy. Collinton, laid out on the site of Fort Gadsden, 25 miles above the bay, is not increasing. But the Appalachicola Town, at the mouth of the river, is rising to a place of commerce. Few places in Florida, export more produce.

ROADS.

When Florida was ceded to the United States, there was but one road of any consequence in the Territory. That called the King's Road extended from St. Augustine to the River St. Marys. It had been well constructed by the English, and at first extended to New Smyrna, but the lower part was wholly grown up, and the balance much out of repair. Trails leading from Pensacola to Mobile, and up the Escambia, were scarcely passable for carts. In 1824, twenty-five thousand dollars were appropriated for a public road, to be opened from Pensacola to St. Augustine. Unfortunately for the Territory, it was located through a wilderness part of the country, a great proportion of which has never been inhabited, and the road, in those parts, has never been used. Another appropriation was made, for a road from Jacksonville to Tampa Bay ; this was well constructed, and has proved a useful route. In 1828 the King's Road was reopened as far as Tomoko, forty miles south of St. Augustine, and to about ten miles north of Jacksonville. It has lately been opened to New Smyrna.

Attempts were made to open roads as far as Charlotte Harbor, on the west, and Cape Florida on the east side of the Peninsula ; but the face of the country was found to be covered with extensive swamps, and it was thought that the expense of constructing the roads could not be justified by any advantages likely to accrue.

A great variety of public roads have within the last three years, been constructed by the several counties of the Territory ; so that in general, communications from one part to another are much more convenient than formerly. Much, however, still remains to be done, to facilitate travelling, through the Territory. In 1830 congress granted an appropriation of two thousand dollars, for repairing the road between St. Augustine and Talahasse : also, two thousand for opening a road between Marianna and the mouth of the Appalachicola River : also, a large sum for constructing a road between Pensacola and Blakely. In 1835, seven thousand dollars were appropriated further to repair the road from St. Augustine to Pensacola. Part of this sum was expended in repairing the road from Bayard, on the St. Johns, to Newnansville, when the Indian hostilities put a stop to the work.

CANALS.

A Canal across the Peninsula of Florida has been located, by the Engineers of the United States, under an Act of Congress ;—a report of which was made in the spring of 1829. The first project of this canal submitted to Congress, proposed a ship canal, but on examination, the table land of the Peninsula was found to be much higher than was anticipated, in consequence of which, a steamboat canal was recommended by the Engineers. A speedy execution of the work has been strongly recommended to Congress, as highly important to the commercial interests of the eastern and western parts of the Union. The location commences at the south branch of Black Creek, twelve miles westward of St. Johns River, in Duval County, and proceeds by Kingsley's Pond, down Alligator Creek to Sampson's Ponds; thence to the Santaffe River and along its channel to the natural bridge, thence westward to the Suwanne River, and from this river ultimately across the country to St. Marks, and the ce to the Gulf of Mexico. When completed, much of the produce of the western country is expected to be conveyed across the Peninsula to the port of Fernandina, at the mouth of St. Marys River. To facilitate which, the inland communication between the Rivers St. Johns and St. Marys is to be considerably improved by deepening and straightening the channel,—an appropriation of fifteen thousand dollars having been made and expended on this route to very little purpose. A dredging machine is still slowly at work at the Sisters, a little north of the St. Johns.

A company has been incorporated to connect the waters of Oclockony River with Lake Jackson ; should this be accomplished, it will greatly add to the commercial importance of Tallahasse.

Another company has been incorporated to connect the eastern arm of St. Andrews Bay with the Chipola, and thence, with the Appalachicola River. When the titles to the country about St. Andrews are set at rest, this project will afford one of the most promising speculations in the Territory. The countries watered by the Chattahooche are extensive, and rich in commercial products. The Bay of St. Andrews is one of the pleasantest, as well as the healthiest situations in Florida. It affords an entrance and safe anchorage for any number of vessels drawing eighteen feet water. These water-courses are separated by a level tract of land only eight miles wide.

The Legislative Council of the Territory in 1832 incorporated a company to open a canal from the head of Matanzas Lagoon, to Smith's Creek, a tributary of Halifax River. With this act, a memorial from the company was presented to Congress, asking for a grant of land for the location, and

19

to assist in carrying into effect the purpose of the company; five sections were appropriated for that purpose. The company propose to commence this canal at the plantation of Mala Compra, the seat of General Hernandez, and carry it through a rich wet savanna, parallel with the coast, to Smith's Creek, about 4 miles above Mr. Bulow's plantation. The distance may be 11 or 12 miles at most.

A similar act was passed, incorporating a company to construct a canal from Six Mile Creek, below Picolata, on the St. John's River, to St. Augustine. The distance from the navigable waters of Six Mile to the St. Sebastian's, will not exceed twelve miles. An excellent steamboat now plies between Savannah in Georgia, and Six Mile Creek, through the inland passages, touching at Darien and St. Mary's, in Georgia, and at Jacksonville, on the St. John's.

A survey has lately been completed between Mobile Bay and Pensacola, and a canal to connect those waters is located and levelled.

Indeed, the whole of our extensive sea coast is lined by inland water courses, that might, at the expense of a few miles cutting, be rendered navigable for steamboats, and the whole danger from our southern reefs, keys and currents, be obviated.

RAIL ROADS.

A company has been incorporated for the purpose of constructing a rail road from Tallahasse to St. Mark's; a distance of about 20 miles; which has been completed.

Many of our projected canals will probably be superseded by rail roads. Where the elevation requires much lockage, rail roads will be far preferable, and less expensive. Stone for locks is scarce, the soil is light, and scarcely solid enough to support heavy dams, and they are very easily undermined by the water. Near the coast, where thorough cuts can be made, canals may answer, but in the rolling country, rail roads are both cheaper and more expeditious, besides, they are far more permanent.

CURIOSITIES.

Florida is, itself, a natural curiosity. It is a curiously shaped and curiously formed terminal appendage to the great United States. Not absolutely a sand bank, as alledged by Mr. Seagrove, but a calcareous fragment of the Appalachian mountain, clothed with some sterile sand banks, some rich variegated clay banks, and some beautiful coralines. It is traversed, also, by many beautiful streams and lakes, but some of them have a curious fancy for traversing a considerable part of their course under ground. It is common to observe pleasant streams of sweet limpid water plunge headlong into some wild cavern and disappear altogether. It is equally common to see navigable streams jet forth from the earth with all their inhabitants of fish, turtles, and alligators. Most of our readers, it is presumed, have observed Bartram's description of the springs near Lake George, the Allachua, and Suwanne; as well as the article of Mr. Shepherd on the same subject, in the Journal of Science, for October, 1823, which it is not my intention to repeat, but will add a few other specimens not less extraordinary, merely remarking *en passant*, that Mr. Shepherd has mistaken Tallahassache, an old Indian town on the Little Suwanne, for Tallahasse, the seat of government of this Territory, one hundred miles south west from the Alligator Hole.

The Wakully River rises about ten miles N. W. of St. Mark's, from one of the finest springs in Florida, or perhaps in the world. It is of an oval form, the largest diameter of which, is about six rods. It is of an unknown depth and perfectly transparent. In looking into it, the color resembles a clear blue sky, except near the border, where it has a slight tinge of green from the reflection of the surrounding verdure, which hangs over it in drooping branches and waving festoons. The eastern side presents a rugged rocky precipice, all else is an abyss of boundless depth. Squadrons of fishes are seen careering round "their own world" in perfect security. The water is moderately cold, and highly impregnated with lime. The beauty of the fountain, the luxuriance of the foliage around it, and the calm retirement of the whole scene, renders this one of the most charming spots that West Florida affords.

The Big Spring of Chipola, offers a very different scene. Here also, a river bursts from the earth, with giant force, from huge masses of rugged rocks, with furious rapidity, as though impatient of restraint. The orifice opens to the south west, from a high swelling bank, scattered over with large oak trees. East and west, the orifice may be thirty feet by eight feet wide. A large rock divides the mouth almost into two parts, at a considerable depth below the surface. The water acts as a prism : all objects seen through it on a sun-shiny day, reflect all the colors of the rainbow. This spring at once forms a river, six rods wide, and eight feet deep, which joins the Chipola River, at about ten miles distance.

The Wakully rises gently from a retired dell, in a low flat country, surrounded by deep embowering groves, from which hang numerous vines, in rich festoons, waving gracefully in every breeze. The Chipola bursts from the side of a hill, in a rolling country sparsely covered with oaks. There, all is calm unrufled quiet ; here, all is life, activity, animation.

The St. Mark's River rises in a small pond at Rockhaven, about fourteen miles from St. Mark's, where it forms a junction with the Wakully, and from thence, both rivers lose their name in that of Appalache.

Besides these, the springs already described, there is one on the Chactawhatchee, another on the west side of the Chipola, five or six on the Su-wanne, and five times as many on the St. John's River, some of them lar-ger and very beautiful. Some of these are highly medicinal, containing iron, sulphur, vitriol, and lime. One of these fine springs, quite warm, and highly impregnated with sulphur, iron, and other minerals, is situate six miles belowBayard, and on the west side of the St. John's.

LIME SINKS.

Nearly allied to these springs, are the sink holes, or lime sinks that are scat-tered all over the Territory, and mark the course of the subterranean rivers. They are formed by holes in the earth, above these subter-rene reservoirs, like the sand in an hour glass, the earth caves in and the hole is filled with water. They are often very deep, and from them I have often taken fine strings of trout. Many large ponds are formed on the same principle. Two instances have occurred within our own knowledge, where persons have camped under the pines one night, and the next, earth, trees, and all have disappeared, and an unfathomable sink has supplied the place. The water in the sinks as well as in the large springs, are all strongly impregnated with lime, and many of the springs deposite a bluish white coagulum on the bottom and sides.

Several considerable rivers sink under ground and rise again. The San-tafee sinks about a mile above the Tallahasse road, in Allachua County, and it rises again about two miles below. During the rainy season, the orifice is not able to receive all the river, and then a broad torrent passes across the road, often so deep, as to swim a horse. Such also, are the Ocilla, the Chipola, Econfina, and others

Several considerable lakes also, sink through the summer season in dry weather, the bottoms become rich meadows of grass, and feed vast herds of cattle, but during the heavy rains of winter, the sinks cannot receive the water, which soon fills the vallies and swarms with myriads of fish. The river Styx drains the waters from Pithlachucco Lake, into the Allachua savanna, where it is joined by several other streams, which all fall into a sink of a semicircular form, about one hundred and twenty yards across, which is almost surrounded by high rocky banks, from which the orifice may be discovered. It is a vast abyss, situate on the north side of the sav-anna. At the begining of summer, when the waters are withdrawing, it is crowded with alligators and fish. The grass quickly sprouts up from the savanna to such a height, as almost to conceal the heads of cattle that graze over its surface. During the winter the same valley presents a lake fifteen miles long, and six wide. The Alligator Lake in Columbia County, presents the same phenomena ; it is about three miles long, by two wide.

This last lake is probably the alligator hole, spoken of by Bartram and Shepherd, as the place where the great river bursts from the earth.

An account of an extraordinary fountain, bursting from the Atlantic coast, about nine miles south of St. Augustine, and from one to two miles from the east shore of Anastasia Island, has been published on the authority of Captain Sisson. The subject had been mentioned to me several times by persons who alledged that they had not only sailed across it, but had drawn from the fountain buckets of tolerable drinking water. Fearing that there might have been some mistake in the matter, I have heretofore hesitated to introduce it. As the subject has now been published from an authentic source, I think myself justified in stating the matter as it has been represented to me. On approaching the place, says my informant, the sea appeared to be ruffled with short waves, as though rocks lay beneath the surface, and the color assumed a yellowish cast, which led him to fear that they were approaching a shoal : as the wind was light, he ordered the lead to be cast, and found from seven to eight fathoms quite across the rippling space, that in some places boiled and whirled, at intervals, in a very singular manner. The whole space agitated was, perhaps, six rods across, and the water was considerably deeper here than on the adjacent coast. The captain, who left the above account, is now dead.

CAVES.

Nearly allied to the sinks, are the subterranean Caves.

The Arch Cave is situate in Jackson County, about three miles west of the Chipola River. An aperture opens to the east, beneath a vast limestone rock, about five feet high, and thirty feet wide. The passage descends gradually for about four rods ; the cavern then opens to the extent of a hundred feet wide, and fifty feet high. A deep channel of cold transparent water skirts the south side for some rods, it then breaks off into wells and finally disappears altogether. The course of the cave now bends to the north-west, grows narrow, and resembles an arch of the gothic order. After proceeding about sixty yards, the cave is crossed by another stream, twenty feet wide, and five feet deep, in which are seen a great number of white cray-fish. The passage now turns north east, and opens into a hole one hundred feet in length, with a very uneven floor of red clay, in which are piles of debris from the decomposed rock above. A cluster of stalectite columns support the centre of this room, while thousands of stalectites of various lengths and sizes, hang from the roof dripping upon the white bases below, to assist them in their growth, that they may be joined in solid columns. Many large holes in the rock above, are filled with myriads of bats. These on the approach of lights, flit off to other dark recesses with a roaring sound like a heavy wind or a torrent of water. The passage now becomes crooked and intricate for a few rods, it then leads into another lofty apartment, from which there are many avenues, but these were bounded by water courses at the time we visited the cave in 1825. Since that time, we are informed that it has been examined to a much greater distance. It is evident that the debris of the rock, is in rainy seasons carried off by the currents of water that pass through these caves, and thus they become more and more enlarged, and when the rock is fritted quite through, the earth losing its support, falls into the cave, and forms a sink hole.

This cavern has been penetrated near six hundred yards. The chrystalizations on the sides, as well as on the stalectites, present the appearance of a brilliant gray ice ; they often project in curling and folding masses, representing draperies, mouldings and bas reliefs of singular appearance ; the projections are nearly white, but they present the same sparkling chrystaline appearance. The regular stalectites are hollow, the outsides are soft and chalky from recent deposite, the inside almost as hard as flint, and often enclose irregular chrystals of spar.

In the neighborhood of this cave, Col. Stone attempted in three several places to dig wells, but in every instance the workmen came to hollow spaces in the earth, and at length became frightened at the danger of falling into some fathomless abyss, and the project was abandoned.

The Ladies Cave is about one mile south east from the arch cave ; it opens to the north west ; the entrance is wide and easier of access, than the former; it is also more spacious within. About fifty paces from the entrance it is divided into two passages, the left, about fifteen yards in extent, terminates in a deep stream, which passes to the north, under a bold arch of sparry congelations, which has not, and cannot, without a boat be explored ; the banks are bold, rocky and difficult of access. The right hand passage is also pushed forward among rugged masses of rock, bold projecting columns, curious excavations, and fanciful galleries, which it would be difficult to describe. The congelations are fine and infinitely various. The passage terminates in a narrow chasm, which appears to have been a water course ; through which, at about three rods distance, another room appears, which however has been but imperfectly explored. To the right of this last branch of the cave, the clefts have been traced about one hundred feet ; many small passages lead off in different directions and may terminate in other rooms.

EVERGLADES.

That part of the peninsula of Florida that lies south of the 28th degree of north latitude, declines towards the centre in form of a dish, the border of which is raised towards the coast. Near Cape Florida, this border is from twelve to twenty miles from the sea beach. It is formed of the same calcareous rock which skirts the Gulf of Mexico as far west as the Appalache River. This vast basin is filled with marshes, wet savannas, intersected by extensive lakes and lagoons, forming a labyrinth which taken together, is called the Everglades. It is very little known. It is drained on every side by rivers of different dimensions. The St. Johns drains it on the north, The St. Lucia, Greenville, Jupiter, New River, Rattones and Miami on the east, and Snake, Swallow, Delaware, Caloosahatche, and Macaco on the west. Behind Cape Florida, the glades approach within twelve miles of the coast. The inlets may here be ascended in one day, notwithstanding the swiftness of their currents.

On reaching the level of the glades, a vast grass meadow is expanded, apparently as boundless as the ocean ; you then pass on the winding lagoons from six to twelve miles westwardly and the grass, by degrees, disappears and you are left in an unexplored grassy lake to which you can discover no bounds. It probably extends near to the eastern shore of the Gulf. The grassy borders of this lake is usually covered with water during the winter season, not so deep however, as to hide the grass which is very thick and tall. During the summer, the ground is often dry and hard for ten miles from the timbered land. This tract is at all times stocked with wild game, and would afford a superior range for cattle. On viewing for the first time, this singular region, I was led into many reflections on its origin, capabilities and future destination. Has it recently risen from the ocean ? Is the land still rising on the border and encroaching on the lake, from the masses of grass and other plants so abundantly produced from this very productive limestone rock ?

Could it be drained by deepening the natural outlets ? Would it not open to cultivation immense tracts of rich vegetable soil ? Could the water power, obtained by draining, be improved to any useful purposes ? Would such draining render the country unhealthy? Can the Spanish tradition be true, that pearl fisheries were formerly established in these lakes ?

Many queries like these passed through our minds. They can only be solved by a thorough examination of the whole country. Could the waters be lowered ten feet, it would probably drain six hundred thousand acres ; should this prove to be a rich soil, as would seem probable, what a field would it open for tropical productions ! What facilities for commerce ! La Vego relates that pearls were abundant among the natives of Florida at the time of the invasion of De Soto. An old manuscript in my possession, asserts that a governor of Florida appointed a commission, for the purpose of seeking pearls in these lakes, and that they were successful.

HISTORY.

1497.   Sebastian Cabot, sailing under the flag of England, first discovered the coast of Florida and sailed along its easternshore, but did
not land to examine the interior of the country.

1512.   Twenty-two years afterwards, Ponce de Leon, a Spanish adventurer of Hispaniola, was led, by the fictions of a Carib girl, to explore the country in search of a fountain, which she stated would renovate
old age and restore departed youth.   But old age and infirmities grew upon
him during his search, for which he was never so fortunate as to discover
a remedy.   He landed at a place called Punta Tanchi, now Cape Sable.
It is the southernmost point of Florida.   It was on Easter Day, and the
country being covered with a verdant foliage, induced him to bestow upon
it the name of Florida.   In attempting to penetrate the interior of the
country, which is low and marshy, he lost many of his people, and the rest
re-embarked, greatly distressed for want of food, which they could not
obtain till they arrived at the islands.

1516.   A second voyage made by de Leon, to search for gold, was not
more successful, for being attacked by the natives in their swamps,
they lost several brave men, and the remainder were obliged to retreat on
board of their vessels.

1518.   Two years after, Luke Valasquez sailed from Cuba and landed
at St. Helena, S. C.   The natives received him in a friendly manner, and supplied his crew with provisions.   He returned their kindness
with apparent civility, and invited a great number to go on board his vessel,
which they had no sooner done, than they were seized and bound in chains.
Some few jumped overboard and swam to the shore, where immense
numbers being gathered, they were fired on by Velasquez, and many of the
astonished natives were wantonly killed and wounded.   Velasquez having
arrived at Cuba, disposed of his cargo for the purpose of working the
Mexican mines.   Numbers of them had starved themselves to death ;
others died of grief.   The white monster was so well satisfied with
1520. his success, that he tried the event of another voyage, and it were
greatly to be wished that all kidnappers might meet the same
punishment.   The natives were not a second time deceived, but fell upon
them as soon as they had decoyed them from the coast, and killed two
hundred.   The rest fled to their vessels and immediately set sail, but
encountering a terrible storm they were shipwrecked and all perished
except Velasquez himself; he was picked up, and returned to pass the
remainder of his life in misery and remorse.   Spanish historians assert that
he incurred the King's displeasure, and was recalled.

1524.   Florida had by this time acquired considerable importance in the
eyes of the Spaniards.   They could not conceive that any people

fight with so much determination, unless they had mines of gold to ...end. Francis de Guerray obtained a grant of the country from the King of Spain, but dying soon after, he was succeeded by de Allyon, who raised forces and invaded the country. Instead of gold mines, he found only swamps filled with armed savages ready to attack them at every natural defile. He soon fled from the coast with the loss of half his men.

1528. Four years after Pamphillo de Narvaes, succeeded to the honor of sacrificing himself, and a small army of adventurers to the prevailing thirst for gold. He set sail with 400 foot, and forty horse, from St. Jago de Cuba, and arrived on the coast of Florida on the 12th day of April, and took formal possession of the country, for the King of Spain. It is uncertain at this period, at what place Narvaes disembarked his troops, but from the length of time he spent in traversing the country to Appalache, he must have landed as far south as Charlotte Bay. He landed in a deep bay, in sight of Indian wigwams, but the natives had deserted them. He proceeded inland with his forces, and struck another still larger bay, and soon discovered savages, who offered him corn. Among them he discovered some wooden cases containing dead Indians, covered with skins, ornamented with paintings, together with pieces of cloth, and sprigs of gold. On being informed that the gold was brought from Appalache, Narvaes immediately ordered his troops to march thither by land. His treasurer, Cobeca de Vaca, endeavored in vain to dissuade him. He commenced his march on the first of May, with 300 foot and his 40 horses, having distributed to each, two pounds of biscuit, and half a pound of pork. Fifteen days they traversed a desolate country, void of inhabitants and food. They at length reached a large river, which they crossed, partly by swimming, and partly on rafts ; the opposite shore was inhabited by Indians, who furnished them with corn. Having rested and explored the coast, they found it shoal and without ports. They then proceeded 15 days without any signs of an inhabitant, till the 17th June, when they fell in with a tribe of savages, whose sachem was clothed in a deer's hide, elegantly painted. The Indians took them to their town, and supplied them with corn and venison ; informed them that they were enemies of the Appalacheans, and pointed out to them the course to pursue. After exchanging presents, the Spaniards departed, and travelled six days through swamps and marshes, almost impassable. On the 25th they reached Appalache, an inland town, and at once fell upon the natives, without warning or parley, and slaughtered them without mercy. The town consisted of forty comfortable wigwams, well stocked with corn, skins and garments made of bark cloth.

20

But they found no gold. They continued 25 days at this village, during which time, they were twice assaulted by the natives.

Narvaez divided his troops into three companies and directed them to scour the country, but their labor was vain ; they discovered neither gold nor food. They kept the Indian Chief in chains, and travelled south for nine days, when they reached another savage town. During this route they were constantly harrassed by the savages, who continually lurked about their camp, and killed many of their horses during the night. On approaching the town of Auta they were attacked by the natives, and a bloody battle ensued, in which many Spaniards, but more Indians, were slain. The wild troops at length were broken and the town sacked and plundered. A great quantity of corn, peas, gourds and fruits were found which furnished a seasonable supply to the starving Spaniards.

De Vaca was then despatched with an exploring party to examine the coast. In three days he returned with information that the sea was distant, and that the deep bays were lined with dismal swamps and marshes. Their horses were nearly all destroyed, they could proceed no further by land, and they had no boats to convey them to sea.

In this distressed situation they moved slowly down the river, and at its mouth killed the few remaining horses, made boats of their hides, and twisted ropes from the hair of the manes and tails, cut up their shirts for sails, and by the 20th of September they set sail in five boats, directing their course towards Mexico. During this extreme exertion, the natives retaliated upon them the cruelties they had before inflicted at Appalache. Ten of the Spaniards were picked off while they laid at Auta.

They set sail on the 22d of September, but made little progress. They wandered seven days in unknown bays. At length they found their way into the open sea, and stretched northward along the shore, but they suffered excessively for want of water. Fish they caught in considerable quantities, but no fresh water could be found near the beach, and they hesitated to penetrate into the country, from fear of the savages. At length, with great difficulty and danger they weathered the southern point of a long cape, (South Cape,) and again approached the continent. Here the natives appearing friendly, they ventured on shore, and were supplied with fresh water and fish. This treatment lulled them into security, and they went to rest after so many sufferings : but in the dead of night the Indians made a sudden and fierce attack upon them, and rescued the imprisoned chief. The Spaniards broke in confusion and fled to their boats, which they were happy to regain, short as they were of provisions and water. Narvaez here received a severe wound.

They sailed three days, and then were again obliged to put in shore for water. Here they took the precaution to exchange hostages with the natives, before they proceeded to the watering place; but the savages soon retook their hostages, and kept the Spanish hostages prisoners.

Narvaez was obliged to run out to sea and leave these men to the mercy of the enraged savages. The surf beat so violently on the coast that they were obliged to keep far from the shore, where they were soon separated by stress of weather, and but one of them was ever heard of afterwards. That commanded by Cabecca De Vaca was driven upon an island, where they found about one hundred Indians, who at first attacked the Spaniards, but being allured by some gaudy presents they became friendly, and supplied them with water and provisions. These, however, were soon exhausted and the Spaniards were again obliged to proceed on their voyage. Their sufferings were extreme, for a great length of time, on a barren coast, lined with savages, and fifteen, only, of the eighty soldiers that embarked at Auta, under De Vaca, reached the province of Mexico.

It was customary at this period for the Indians on the coast of Florida, to destroy all their prisoners. A singluar exception to this practice, soon after occurred. Among the few of Narvaez soldiers, who were so fortunate as to escape, there was a man named Ortez, active and enterprizing, who among others, got back to Cuba in a small boat. In detailing the events of their defeat to the wife of Narvaez, she was led to suspect that her husband might have been abandoned by his troops, and might still be living on the Florida Coast. She prevailed upon Ortez, by a great reward, to return and search for him, and fitted out a small pinnace to convey him back to the hostile coast. Ortez returned, but being watched by the natives, he was taken prisoner.

While on the point of being sacrificed, the daughter of the Indian Chief interceded in his favor, and obtained him from her father, and he lived several years with her. But being honored with the defence of a burying ground, where some chief was lately deposited, he suffered a wolf to disinter and drag out the body, and although he pursued and killed the wolf, yet he was a second time sentenced to death, when his wife again privately released him, and directed him to flee southward until he should reach the confines of the Tampa Bay; where he should find Macaco, a powerful chief, a friend of hers, who would protect him. He fled accordingly, and found an asylum from his enemies until the conquest of De Soto.

1539.   It was eleven years, before a leader could be found to reassert the Spanish claim to Florida. Ferdinand De Soto, a brave Spanish cavalier who had greatly distinguished himself in the conquest of Peru, and thus rendered himself an object of suspicion to the ambitious conquerors of that important kingdom, was induced to relinquish the path of glory, at the price of a million and a half of dollars.

Hearing the country of Florida described, and the destruction of his countrymen lamented, he seemed disposed to make an essay, to redeem the national honor. He therefore applied to the King for permission to fit out an expedition for that purpose. His petition was readily granted. He proceeded to purchase seven ships, and three cutters, which he armed and equiped for the expedition. He enlisted one thousand men, three hundred of whom were cavaliers, well mounted on excellent horses; he sailed in the spring of the year, as far as Cuba, where he made some stay, and here he married the sister of the famous Bovadilla. He at length proceeded to Florida, and landed at Tampa Bay. The country bordering this bay was governed by an Indian chief, named Hiriga, who also gave the same name to the province, as was the custom among these people.

De Soto forbid his followers to molest the natives, as they had shown no hostile disposition towards the Spaniards, and he was desirous of cultivating their friendship. But Porcello, one of his captains of horse, had observed the old chief Hiriga, to enter a deep swamp, very frequently, and he thought that he might distinguish himself, by seizing the old man and conveying him to his general. He therefore watched an opportunity to surround the swamp, with his squadron, and beat up the old man's quarters. Hiriga was not to be surprised, he poured a shower of arrows on the Spaniards, accompanied with hideous yells. The horses were frightened, and fell into confusion, and Porcello was obliged to retreat. He became a subject of sport to his companions, which mortified him to such a degree, that he begged a cutter of the General, to convey him out of the camp; this was granted to him, and he returned to Cuba.

Soon after this event, a reconnoitering party was sent under Col. Mucaco, to explore the interior of the country. They were one day suddenly surprised by a small party of men rushing upon them. Taking them for enemies, Mucaco ordered a charge, when one of the assailants cried out, in the Spanish language, begged them not to kill their countryman. Mucaco was astonished, and witheld his men from the assault. An explanation ensued, and Ortez, of whom we have before spoken, made himself known to his countrymen. He had remained a prisoner twelve years, had acquired the language of the country, and was from this period, of infinite service to de Soto, in his intercourse with the natives.

Mucaco, the chief who had protected Ortez, governed a Province which was situate fifty-one miles east of Hiriga, and was near the present Indian town of Hichapucksassy. Through the mediation of Ortez, this chief became the friend and ally of the Spaniards. He also induced his kinsman, Uribarricuxi, who governed the next district, to become also an ally.

Acuera, was the next province, it was divided from Uribarricuxi, by a deep swamp, beyond which it extended northwardly sixty miles. De Soto also acquired the friendship of Acuera, and during twenty days that the Spanish troops traversed his dominions, he supplied them with abundance of food. The province of Acuera, probably embraced the Indian towns of Oakahumky, or Piclaklakaha.

The next province entered by the Spaniards was called Ocala; it must have been the neighborhood of Fort King. For thirty miles they marched through a country of tall pines, more fertile than the lands near the sea. The population was more dense, and the lands were well cultivated. For some leagues, the houses were thickly scattered along the road, before they reached the town. Ocala contained six hundred houses. The chief was friendly, and supplied the Spaniards abundantly with walnuts, sun-raisins, beans, millet, and other provisions. For eighteen miles beyond Ocala, the lands continued fertile, with pleasant rustic dwellings, the country spotted with ponds and small streams.

The Spaniards left Ocala, and marched twenty-four miles in two days. On the evening of the third, the weather being fine, they marched all night, and early in the morning they reached the town of Ochili, perhaps Chichile. This was a large town in the province of Vitachucco, and must have been south of the Allachua prairie. It was fortified with pallisadoes, it contained near five hundred houses; that of the chief, was one hundred and twenty feet long, contained a great many rooms, and was placed on an artificial hill.

De Soto here departed from the pacific course which he had hitherto pursued towards the natives. His army dashed suddenly into the town, the astonished inhabitants flew to arms, and made a short resistance; it was wholly useless against the arms and discipline of their invaders, they submitted wondering what kind of enemies had assailed them. De Soto then endeavored to conciliate them with kind treatment, and believed that he had secured their friendship.

Vitachucco was governed by three brothers, who alternately assumed the reins of Government, during which time they resided at the Capital, while the other two retired to the country. At this time the last mentioned brothers came into the city, appeared friendly, and presented vegetables (legumes) to the troops, who with great pleasure returned their good will. Two days march brought the Spaniards to Vitachucco, the Capital. Here the chief received them in a very friendly and hospitable manner, and lodged De Soto in his palace.

This town contained about twenty houses, for the chiefs, that were very large, and a great number of smaller ones. Here the Spaniards continued four days, during which time, some of them discovered that great quantities of arms were brought into the city, and that large bodies of men were concealed at a short distance, behind a copse of woods. De Soto was immediately notified of these facts; he concealed the information from Vitachucco, who continued to treat his enemies with great hospitality.

On the morning of the fourth day, De Soto led forth his troops in order of battle, attended by Vitachucco and a large guard of Indians. Just as they were emerging from the wood into a large prairie, Vitachucco snatched De Soto's sword and made a violent pass to stab him. De Soto parried the stroke, and beat the savage to the ground; he was saved by his guards, and a fierce battle succeeded. Six thousand Indians occupied the wood and the prairie, they fell upon the Spaniards with hideous yells, and the battle raged most of the day. The Spaniards were faithfully supported by their Indian allies, especially by the Uribarricuxians, who fought most bravely. The Vitachuccans were at length driven into an extensive grassy lake filled with water, where the Spaniards could not follow them. De Soto placed sentinels around the borders of the marsh, and rested on the field of battle. During the night the Vitachuccans rallied in the marsh, and broke into the prairie, but great numbers of them being killed, the rest retired.

In the morning De Soto proceeded on his march towards Osachili, the Tallahasoche of the Seminoles, near Mico, in Hamilton County, twelve miles. At evening they encamped on the banks of a large river. This river (probably the Suwanne) separated the provinces of Vitachucco and Osachili. On the western side the natives had assembled in great numbers, to oppose the passage of the Spaniards. Early on the next morning the troops were in motion; several large rafts were constructed, on which were pushed over one hundred fusiliers, and sixty cavaliers with their horses. Their landing was sharply disputed, but the natives at length gave way before the fire-arms and discipline of their invaders, and the whole army followed in quick succession. A beautiful country opened here to the Spaniards; the earth was covered with corn, vegetables, grapes, and nuts. The capital of the province was at no great distance. It contained about two hundred houses; the possession of it was sharply and resolutely contested by the inhabitants, but the Spaniards at last forced a passage and entered in triumph. De Soto, by great kindness, soon quieted the fierce savages, and when he learned that the Appalacheans were making war on Osachili, he volunteered his services to assist in conquering that rich and powerful province, where, he took it for granted, that he could spend the winter in peace and plenty. He spent but three days at Osachili to recruit his troops, and to collect a stock of provisions for the journey. On the morning of the fourth day they commenced their march for Appalache, and in three days they had progressed thirty-six miles, through a barren country of pine trees, destitute of inhabitants. On the fourth day they arrived at an immense swamp (Oscilla,) covered with weeds and vines, with water from two to six feet deep. It was more than two miles across; the devious path which led through it had been fortified by the Indians in the best manner their ingenuity could suggest, by floating logs, trees and brush across it, and fastening them with vines and wythes. They also dug many holes under the water and stuck down sharp stakes to maim the horses. De Soto was anxious to avoid this place and to find another crossing. He therefore encamped his army, and sent an exploring party of two hundred infantry and thirty horsemen to examine the country, but the swamp continued in front of them, with no other pass across it. On their return, De Soto drew up his army and made a desperate attack with his whole force, but was beaten back and obliged to retreat to his camp.

The battle was renewed the next day, with no better success. The pass swarmed with Indians, who closed in with the Spaniards, hand to hand and fought with desperation, and being perfectly acquainted with the ground, had many advantages over their invaders. Besides, they had twelve years before successfully attacked Narvaez in this very place, and felt certain of defending the pass.

On the third day, De Soto placed himself at the head of his troops and led them to the charge, and was bravely supported by Col. Mucoco, at the head of his guards; they bore down all opposition and after six hours desperate fighting, they forced a passage through the swamp and encamped on the western side, upon a low savanna. Here they rested the next day and sent out reconnoitering parties, to examine the country. These parties were constantly waylaid, and many of the soilders were severely wounded by arrows. They discovered that another swamp (Mickasukee) lay before them, at a few miles distance. During the night, the savages hovered about them, howling like wolves, but made no attack. At an early hour in the morning the army took up the line of march, and having reached the other swamp they made no stop, but plunged in amid the howling savages, who received them with a perfect shower of arrows.

Every obstruction, that savages could invent, was here opposed to the Spaniards, and they fought for their last stake, like brave men. The fire-locks and horses of the Spaniards confounded them. Inch by inch, the passage was contested, until every obstacle was demolished, and the Spaniards at length found themselves again on solid ground. At two o'clock in the afternoon a small village was gained, on the west side of the swamp, where the army encamped for the night. The Indians gave them no rest, but attacked the sentinels in every direction. At day light, they proceeded towards the capital, through rich and highly cultivated lands. Fields of millet and other vegetables covered the ground. Scattering houses formed an irregular village the whole way.

Towards evening they arrived at a deep brook, with tall trees of hard wood on its banks; here the Indians kept them at bay another night. The Spaniards made several unsuccessful attempts to carry a palisade, but at each attempt they were beaten off by the Indians, who fought with desperation. Early in the morning, De Soto made a final assault and forced a passage.

From this place they marched without farther opposition, over highly cultivated fields to Appalache, the capital of the province. It was situated sixteen miles from the first swamp, (probably on the western side of Mickasookee Lake.) It contained two hundred and fifty large houses, handsomely built, and the adjacent country was thickly sprinkled over with buildings.

Small villages of 60 to 70 houses lay in different directions, to the distance of six or eight miles. Provisions were abundant for men and horses. Fish in particular were caught in great quantities in lakes and streams, both here and at Ochili. Reconnoitering parties were sent out to examine the country in various directions. They found the country fertile for 20 miles generally. Towards the sea it became cold and and wet, and northward and westward piney and thin land. One party, under Mucoco, discovered the bones of Narvaez' horses at Auta Bay, thirty miles distant.

When De Soto had become quietly settled in these quarters for the winter, he despatched a party of twenty cavaliers under the command of Dalhusco, to Hiriga, ordering the vessels to be brought round into the mouth of the Appalache River. This service was performed at great risk. The party escaped pretty well, by the rapidity of their movements, until they reached the Big Swamp, here they could not evade an attack; it was a pass always guarded by the natives, but the intrepidity of the Spaniards beat down all opposition, and the swiftness of their horses soon bore them out of danger. At Osachili they were obliged to construct a raft to bear them across the current; here the Indians collected again and showered arrows upon them, but they landed without any loss, and arrived in safety at Tampa. The vessels soon after set sail and arrived in safety at Appalache River, at a place called Auta.

About Christmas De Soto despatched Maldonado with a small body of infantry, to explore the coast to the westward of Auta. He returned in January and informed De Soto that he had discovered a good harbor, of excellent depth, 180 miles to the west, which the natives called Ochuse, and that there were considerable signs of gold in the neighborhood. De Soto was much pleased, and despatched Maldonado to Havana for warlike implements, as well as for tools to work the mines. The Indians, in the meantime, often attacked the Spaniards, and beat up their quarters in the adjoining villages, but they were usually repelled. About this time a young Indian was brought before the governor, who had been taken prisoner at Napetaka. He stated that he was a native of the eastern coast, at a country called Yupaha. That it abounded in gold, and he went on to describe the process of extracting it from the ore so minutely, that he imposed on those who were best acquainted with the subject. They stated to De Soto that it was impossible for the Indian to describe the matter so correctly, unless he had seen the process of smelting, refining, &c. This raised the spirits of the whole army, and De Soto determined to march for Yupaha in three days. Every man was ordered to prepare for himself provisions for a journey of 60 leagues. These consisted of corn, dried grapes and dried persimmons, with a little dried fish. They marched four days over a barren country, when they arrived at a large river, rapid and deep, (the Flint, in Early county, Ga.) They obtained a large canoe, and with the help of a long rope crossed the army over in a day and a half. On the 11th of March they arrived at an Indian town, called Copochique. Here the Indians became very hostile, often attacking the foraging parties, and were sure to cut off all stragglers. When pursued they threw themselves into marshes, where it was in vain to follow them. De Soto left this place as soon as provisions were renewed, and marched to Toalli, which he reached on the 21st of March. At this place the houses were covered with reeds ranged like tiles, the walls built of pales, and so plastered as to appear like stone. In these houses they built large fires, because the winter was rather cold. Their granaries were raised on four posts, with floors made of canes. Both in their dress and buildings, these people were more civilized than the Indians near the coast. Their deer skins were dyed of beautiful colors, and from the inside bark of a tree they made quite a handsome kind of linen cloth.

They staid but two days at Toalli; on the 23d, they approached Achesi; the inhabitants retired, but the Chief being sent for, he appeared before de Soto, and made a handsome speech, desiring to know what the Spaniards sought in his country, and whether he could serve them. De Soto told him he was the son of the sun; that he had left his abode, to seek the greatest land, and the richest province in the country. The chief said, that Acuta was the richest country, he knew, and that he would send guides, and an interpreter to assist him. Soto was much pleased, and directly set at liberty, all the prisoners he had taken at Achesi. At the same

21

time he set up a wooden cross, and explained it to the Indian, who promised to treat it with great respect. The next day they marched to Allaraca ; and on the tenth of May, they reached Acuta. The cassique of this place, sent 2000 Indians to Soto, with provisions, consisting of paniers, loaded with cakes of dried persimmons, and a great quantity of dogs, which were killed and eat instead of mutton. The natives supplied themselves with abundance of wild game; but the Spaniards had not time to search for it. Soto staid but two days here ; the Chief gave him 400 Indians, to carry his baggage, and he proceeded to an Indian village, called Cofaque, and thence to a larger one called Potofa. The country as far as Acuta, was found by the Spaniards, to be flat and wet, covered with pine trees, and rough bushes. But from Acuta to Patofa, it was a delightful country, of hard timber, with cultivated fields, and fine streams of sweet water. The natives were friendly, and cheerful. They told Soto, that there was no rich country, to the eastward of them, to their knowledge. To the north west, they said that the province of Coca, was fertile and populous. But the chief said, he would supply guides, to go with the Spaniards in any direction they should choose. It is not stated what course was chosen, but it is pro- bable N. W. La Vega states, that the young Yupaha Indian led them into a wild barren country, where there were no roads, and finally told them he did not know where he was. Soto was enraged, and determined to kill the guide, and give him to the dogs ; but Ortez representing that he was the only Indian that could understand the native language, Soto smothered his rage from necessity. For nine days, the army continued in this wilderness ; at length, their provisions failed altogether, and the soldiers, and horses became weak from fatigue and hunger. They had crossed se- veral large rivers, which were rapid and deep, and they at length, came to one, which ran to the S. W. (the Chatahooche,) and which in their feeble state, they could not cross.

While the troops rested, the General himself mounted a horse, and with a few soldiers, rode the whole day in search of a road, but returned in the night quite disheartened, not having discovered the least trace of a human residence, or trail. The next morning, he called a council of war, to consider whether they should proceed, or retreat. The latter was op- posed, because the country was exhausted, and the Indians ready to fall upon them. It was concluded to reconnoitre the country more extensively, and a party was sent out for that purpose, but they returned in the evening without success. The next day, Macoco, Danhusco, Romo, and Labhillo, each at the head of a party of cavaliers, were directed to take different routes, and explore the whole country. Several hogs had been brought over by the army, and had multipled very fast ; they had attended the camp during all the marches, they were now put in requisition, and afforded about half a pound of flesh to each man, for a short period. The Patofa Indians were dismissed; they departed with much regret, at leaving the Spaniards in so much distress.

On the fourth day Danhusco returned, with the pleasing intelligence, that he had discovered an Indian town, thirty-six miles down the river.

This intelligence revived the spirits of the whole army; they immediately formed the line of march, and in three days arrived at Aymay, where they found extensive granaries filled with corn. The inhabitants fled, but Soto took four prisoners, who informed him that another town, called Catifachique, lay near that place. The General proceeded in advance of the army, and on the way took three prisoners, who informed him that a great lady governed the country. The General sent a messenger to present his compliments, and offer her his friendship. She in return sent her sister, to bid him welcome. Her majesty soon after appeared, in a large canoe, full of Indians, and an awning supported by a lance, shaded the poop. Her seat was formed of two cushions, where she reclined, surrounded by her women; many other canoes accompanied her. Soto stood on the bank to receive her; she landed and made a very handsome speech to the General, and then presented him with many presents, especially a necklace formed of very large pearls. Here the army rested several days, and were supplied with fowls, and other provisions in abundance, and here the army wished to make a final settlement. The country was rich in nuts, mulberries, and persimmons. The natives were a tawney, plump, well made people, well clothed in their style of dress. They were much more polished in their manners, than the coast Indians. The river was navigable, and they were not more than two or three days journey from the sea.

It is difficult to trace the course of the Spaniards from Apralache to Catafachique. It is pretty certain that the latter situation was upon the Chattahooche River, about two hundred and fifty miles above Appalache·

They appear to have marched northeastwardly at first, and it is difficult to determine when they should have changed their course, unless it was at the time they lost the road. It appears that the Chiaha, in Chicasa country, was at this time twelve days journey to the north, and the sea three days journey to the south; these data with the description of the place of their stay, must designate the place to be on the waters of the Chattahooche. But Soto could not be detained here, the riches of Peru swam in his imagination, and he prepared for new toils, conciliating his troops, by stating that the provisions of the whole country here would not supply them for one month; that he must at all events, meet Maldonado at Ochuse. That in case of any misfortune, they could return here, when the Indians would have their fields replanted.

On the third of June, they left Catafachique, taking the queen along; she had been greatly dissatisfied with the conduct of the Spaniards towards her people. Soto's conduct towards her was very inhuman ; he ordered that she should walk on foot, with her attendants, alleging, that she wished to escape, and with her people to leave him without guides or laborers. She endeavored to sooth him, by ordering the Indians to carry his baggage; they obeyed her orders with great alacrity. The country was wretched. They passed a village called Chatague, whose chief presented Soto with two deer skins ; they were all he could give. They had come from Ocala, one hundred and thirty miles, eighty of which were a perfect desert. They now had to pass a mountainous country, two hundred and fifty miles to Hualla. During the march, the queen gave them the slip, and carried off with her, a casket of reeds, containing pearls of great value. Parties were sent in pursuit of her, in every direction, but in vain.

In five days after the army arrived at Quaxulla, but found so little provision, that Soto sent an Indian to the chief of Chiapa, requesting him to send provisions to refresh his troops. This request was granted, and twenty men were sent, loaded with mulberries and other provisions, which were presented to him. The country from Catafachique to this place abounds in fruits. For five days they marched through a desert; they were then met by fifteen more Indians loaded with corn from Chiapa, who informed Soto that much more was at his service, as well as himself, his people, and his country. Soto sent a messenger to return his grateful thanks.

The town of Chiapa was situate on the banks of a large river ; (the Mobile) opposite was an island, one mile long and two bow-shots across. The lands on the river borders were sown with rice. Such was the friendly deportment of the Indians, that the horses were turned loose to graze, and the Spaniards encamped in groupes among the trees, without order. This relaxation was a great relief to both troops and horses : the latter became fat in a short time. For thirty days the army enjoyed this necessary repose, and the hospitality of the Indians remained unchanged, until Soto was prevailed on to request the chief to send some of his men to carry the baggage of the Spaniards, on their march. The chief drily replied, that he would propose the matter to his subjects. But the inhabitants all left the town and fled to the island, fearing the Spanish horse. Soto was about to pursue them, but the chief came to excuse them, and offered himself as a guide. The General took sixty men and the chief, over to the island, and explained the matter to the natives, who agreed to return.

While these matters were transacting, the chief of Acoste came to offer Soto his services. The General, as usual, inquired for gold. Acoste told him that farther north, in the province of Chisca, copper was found, and another metal, purer and more lively; but though more beautiful, was little valued, on account of its softness. Soto was charmed, and ordered the troops to be ready to march for Chisca. In the mean time he sent forward an express, to learn whether the mountainous country could not be avoided, by taking a circuit through the low country.

Soto now took leave of Chiapa, making him some valuable presents, and proceeded to Acosta, where he arrived on the 12th of June; and having pitched his camp at a small distance, he entered the town with eight men only. He was respectfully received by the chief; but while they were in conversation, some Spaniards entered the town to look for corn, and not finding any to please them, they began ransacking the houses. This conduct was so highly resented by the natives, that they gave them a good drubing with their clubs. Soto saw his danger, and being in their hands, made a merit of necessity, and snatching up a stick, joined the Indians in beating his men; despatching, at the same time, a man to the camp, to bring up the horse, without delay, to his assistance. He then took the hand of the chief, and insensibly led him, in conversation, towards the camp, until the horse rode up and surrounded them both, and took them into the camp. The chief and several of his principal men were confined until he agreed to furnish guides for the army, and also until his express returned from Chisca.

Three days after, the express returned and stated, that the country was utterly impassable; that the road shown them, by the guide was mountainous, rocky and barren. On receving this information, Soto directed his march to Tali, and the chief having furnished guides was set at liberty. They arrived at Tali on the ninth of July, and were kindly received, the chief giving them provisons, and sending some of his subjects to carry the baggage. For six days they marched in the province of Cosa and reached the chief town, on the 16th. The chief of Cosa came out to meet the Spaniards, in great style. He was seated on a kind of palanquin, carried on the shoulders of his subjects; surrounded by his troops, attended by musicians, singing and playing on some singular instruments. The chief was dressed in a robe of martin skins, with a diadem of feathers on his head. He received Soto with much civility and they entered the town together, well pleased with each other. The Spaniards were made welcome to the houses and granaries, which were well filled with corn, beans, gourds &c., and the trees were loaded with two sorts of plumbs, and persimmons. The houses of the town were placed in the midst of cultivated fields. Rivulets of charming water meandered through the fields; their banks were clothed with grass and flowers, and luxuriant vines hung in festoons from the tops of the trees. Soto had been acustomed to carry a chief along with him, until he entered the territories of another; making use of such of the natives as chose to follow him, for the service of the army, dismissing them when he arrived at another province. But the Indians of course were indignant when they beheld their chief kept in confinement, by strangers, who had been treated so liberally, and they fled to the woods for shelter, against such oppression. Soto sent armed troops to intercept their flight, and several severe conflicts were had, before they could be humbled, to perform the drudgery of the Spaniards. Their chief finally persuaded them to submit. Cosa was abandoned on the 20th of August; Soto marched first to Tallimuchasse and thence to Itava, where he was obliged to wait for the waters to decrease, in a river whose banks were overflown. When the waters had sufficiently fallen, he marched to Ulliballi. This town was fortified with pallisadoes; a beautiful stream skirted its borders. On the other side of this stream, dwelt the chief, who was surrounded with so many Indians, in warlike attiude, that the Spaniards were induced to guard against surprise. Soto sent messengers to the chief, requiring his attendance, and he came without delay ; bringing with him several male and female Indians, for the service of the general. The Spaniards marched next to Toasi. In a cultivated country, the army usually progressed about eighteen miles a day, but, when in a barren country, they increased their speed as much as possible. From Toasi they arrived in five days at Tallisse. It was a large town, surrounded with a well cultivated country. Here the chief of Cosa was dismissed with presents. Soto permitted the army to repose here for twenty days. He then marched for Tascaluça and encamped in a wood, near the town. The next morning, he sent Lewis De Moscoso to wait on the chief. Moscoso found him seated on cushions which were raised on a fine carpet. He was surrounded by Indians; the most considerable of which, were allowed to approach pretty near him ; the rest were kept at a respectable distance. A servant held an umbrella over his head ; it was made of deer skin, so beautifully colored, that it looked like taffety ; it was about the size of a target. He was a great warrior and had rendered himself terrible to all his neighbors, and his dominions spread over wide extended and populous countries. He was large and well proportioned.

As soon as Moscoso had made his obeisance, the squadron of horse, which attended him, performed many evolutions : riding at full speed, close up to the chief, making passadoes to and fro. The old man observed them with fixed gravity, but without any surprise. In the mean time, Soto arrived. The chief making no motion to meet him, he went up and took him by the hand and set down by him. The chief then rose and made an eloquent speech, offering his services to the Spaniards. Soto thanked him and told him he should be under the necessity, of taking him along with the army, to the next province, to which he submitted, and the army marched the next morning. In two days, the army reached Piache ; it was situated on a large river, over which, they passed on rafts, made of cane reeds. Soon after a Spaniard pursued an Indian woman who attempted to flee into the woods, the Indians killed the Spaniard and relieved the woman. Soto declared to the chief, that he should be kept prisoner, until the man was found and restored. The chief submitted and requested Soto to permit one of his Indians, to go forward to Manilla, one of his towns, which lay upon the road, to order provisions to be got ready for the army. Soto readily consented, but suspecting treachery, he sent a Spaniard to watch the motions of the Indian. This Spaniard met them, before they reached the place and informed the general, that the Indians were collecting in great numbers and with very hostile appearances, at Manilla. The army reached that place, on the eighteenth of October. The Indians had erected pallisades around the town; no resistance however was made, to his enterance. He kept eight of his foot soldiers and a few horsemen about him, as a guard. He entered a house, with the chief; when they were seated, Tascaluca used his endeavor, to persuade Soto to proceed no farther into the country : Soto refused. The old chief withdrew into another house and refused to return. Soto sent for him, but he fiercely answered that he would not return, and advised Soto to retreat out of his dominions, without molesting him any more. Soto was aware of the danger of his situation, he therefore waited on the chief and tried to sooth him, but Tascaluca turned from him, with disdain, and refused to answer him ; nor would he see Soto any more.

The Spanish officers were consulted ; they advised to offer the chief his liberty, if he would furnish guides and baggage carriers, to the next province, and a chief was requested by Soto, to convey the message to Tascaluca. The Indian peremptorily refused ; a Spanish officer resented the insult ; a scuffle ensued, in which the Indian was killed. This was the signal for a general attack. The Indians showered arrows from all quarters on the Spaniards, who charged them in turn, but in vain, they were too numerous and too well sheltered, by the houses. Soto was obliged to retreat. The Indians pursued, with true savage fury, wounding Soto and all of his guard, killing five Spaniards outright. They then attacked the Spanish baggage, which they took and carried into the town, releasing and arming the Indian carriers. The Spaniards here lost all the riches they had collected among the Floridians, consisting of rich pearls, robes of fur, arms &c.

The moment Soto reached the plain, and obtained a reinforcement of ca-

valry, he made a charge on the Indians, with such fury that he slew three
with his own spear, and pursued them to the palisades.

A monk, a secular, and a servant, were left in the town ; seeing the tumult,
they barricaded the doors of the house, which they occupied. The Indians
mounted the roof in order to uncover it, and play their arrows on the Spaniards. The army was brought up by Mascoso, to the pallisades. A halt
became necessary, and a consultation of the officers, whether to storm, or
besiege the town ; the former, although more dangerous, was resolved on.
The best men were dismounted, the army was formed into four battallions,
and each was led to attack one of the gates. The Indians, resolved to die
rather than to submit, urged their old Chief to take the baggage, and retire to the woods ; he complied, though very reluctantly. Soto was soon
apprized of the retreat, he ordered the battalions to extend their lines so as to
surround the place, and to set it every where on fire. The signal was then
given to engage, and a horrid carnage ensued. The Indians fought most
bravely, and repulsed the Spaniards, several times. In the midst of the
fight, the monk and his companions found means to escape, but two brave
Spaniards, who protected them, were cut in pieces by the savages. The
fight lasted several hours, the sun was hot, and the thirsty Spaniards drew
off to drink at a pool, near the palisades. It was nearly half blood, but they
were forced to drink it. They then returned to the charge with renewed
vigor. The Indians were driven from their pallisades, Soto entered at the
head of the horse, and scoured the streets, while the soldiers set fire to the
houses. The miserable inhabitants, attacked at all points with unusual
weapons, were no match for the Spaniards, who, with their sabres, swept
them away in files ; but they fought hand to hand, until they were nearly
exterminated, and the few that remained, cast themselves into the flames
and perished. Two thousand five hundred Indians were killed, and many
wounded, but all the clothes, arms, and baggage, except what they had on
their backs, and in their hands, was lost.

This was the first severe loss that the Spaniards had sustained, since
they landed in Florida, and it was a severe mortification to Soto, who had
just received intelligence of Maldonado's arrival at Ochuse, now Pensacola,
with the tools for mining. His present situation was seven days journey
from Ochuse. He had marched his army in a circuit quite round the
northern parts of Florida, in the space of one year ; he had discovered no
mines, and the pearls he had obtained, were all lost. He came to a conclusion, to repair his loss, before he let it be known to his countrymen ; he
therefore forbid Ortez to mention the arrival of Maldonado, to the troops.

After recruiting his men and horses one month in this fertile country, he
collected his troops, and on the eighteenth of November, he marched north,

still in search of gold. We shall not follow his perigrinations
1553. out of our own region, except to mention that he proceeded as
May 1st. high as the Cumberland River, then turned west, crossed the
Mississppi, and reached Red River ; in the course of two years,
from this period. Here Soto died from fatigue and disappointment.

After the death of De Soto, the Spaniards elected Col. Moscoco, their
General. He immediately proceeded to build boats, and collect provisions
to enable him to evacuate a country, where, instead of finding gold, they
had found diseases, hostile enemies, and total ruin. As soon as the annual
floods had rendered the river navigable, they descended it, entered the Mississippi, and thence proceeded to the Gulf of Mexico. They were pursued
down the river by the natives, and attacked at every opportunity, but without
any material loss. After entering the Gulf they proceeded westward to the
river Panuco, in Mexico, where they joined their countrymen, with three
hundred and eleven souls, the sole survivors of the gallant army that
1553 invaded Florida. Maldonado having waited a long time at Ochuse,
Sept. and learning nothing from De Soto, he returned to Cuba with the
10. fleet.

The Spaniards, at length became discouraged, at so many fruitless
attempts to settle a country that yielded only misfortunes, and the natives
remained undisturbed for twenty years.

1562. At this period, religious persecution raged in France. The Hu-
gunots under the protection of Admiral Coligny, conceived the project of withdrawing from their native country, and of seeking an asylum in
the wilds of America. To effect this purpose, application was made to
Charles IX, who readily granted them two ships, which were manned with
zealous Calvinists, commanded by John Ribault, an experienced navigator.
They set sail on the 18th February, 1562, intending to enter the River
Santee, but they made land about the lat. of St. Augustine. They proceeded north, and entered a large river on the first day of May, and therefore
named it May River. They left this river and proceeded north, and finally
disembarked at a place near where Beaufort now stands, and erected a fort
which they named Fort Carolin. They found the country pleasant, abounding in mulberry and persimmon trees, and inhabited by a race of hospitable
Indians, who supplied them with food for the merest trifles.

Ribault being desirous to establish a colony there, while he returned to
France to report his success, twenty-six of his crew volunteered to stay
and keep possession of the fort, and Albert, his Lieutenant, was left to command them. A little field sixteen rods long, and thirteen wide, was stockaded in around the fort. It was near the middle of July, when Ribault set
sail for France ; on his arrival he found the country so involved in broils

and confusion, that he could draw no attention to his colony, which was neglected for two years. In the meantime, Albert visited the Indian Princes in his neighborhood, cultivating their friendship and paying every attention to their wants, and such was his success, that they readily supplied his people with provisions, and made them many presents of pearls, chrystals, silver, &c. The Colonists, however, were licentious, lazy and quarrelsome, and to preserve peace between them and the natives, he was obliged to exercise a very strict discipline; this they would not endure. Among the Colonists, was one Lachan, who was a popular demagogue; he endeavored to reduce some of the Indians to slavery, which Albert would not permit, and compelled him to do justice to the natives. A mutiny was the consequence, in which Albert lost his life. The Indians then refused to supply them with provisions, and none being likely to arrive from France, the Colonists resolved to leave the fort, and return to their country. They chose Nicholas Bornu for their Captain, and having constructed a small vessel, and collected a very small quantity of provisions, they set sail for France. They had not been long at sea, before they were becalmed, and remained in that situation for twenty days; this reduced them to a state of starvation. They cast lots to select one who should be butchered to sustain his companions, when Lachan the mutineer offered his throat to the knife, which was accepted. Soon after this, they were discovered, and picked up by an English ship, which landed them on the coast of England. They were conducted to Queen Elizabeth, and their account of Florida, first turned her attention to this country.

1564   Early this year, Coligny obtained permission to send three ships to Florida, under the command of Rene Lardoniere, who had before accompanied Ribault in the first expedition. A great many volunteers of respectable connections flocked on board this expedition, which was well supplied with arms, provisions, and tools for agriculture. They arrived at Fort Carolin in the month of June, but found it abandoned. Lardoniere distrusting the natives, left the place and sailed south to May River;* here he built a small town, fortified it with palisadoes and a rampart of earth, and named it also Carolin. It was about six leagues above the mouth of the river, on the south side. The friendship of the natives was assiduously cultivated, and they supplied the colony with provisions and afforded them every facility for exploring the country. Lardoniere improved this peaceable disposition by settling the petty disputes of the natives,—soothing their rough passions, and in preparing their minds for exploring the interior of the country, where he designed to search for gold, which was, at that time, the universal passion. Small quantities of the precious metals and some pearls had been discovered, and the natives pointed to the

* Probably the St. Johns.

S. W. as the direction from which they were procured. Two of his best officers, with a strong escort, were despatched on this service, who penetrated to the Mississippi River, but they found no gold. In this expedition, however, the French exhausted all their trinkets and goods, so that they had nothing to offer to their neighbors for provisions ;—a famine was the consequence. Lardoniere had sent a vessel to France for provisions, but it never returned. He fitted out two more ; the crews mutinied, turned pirates, and cruised against the Spaniards.

Had the governor on his first arrival employed his men in the cultivation of the soil, all the necessaries of life might have been procured independent of the natives, and all these evils would have been avoided. A council was now called, and they resolved to build a brigantine, sail for France, and abandon Florida. At this time an English vessel, commanded by a Capt. Hawkins, sailed up the coast. This vessel Lardoniere purchased at a reasonable price, and after dismantling the fort, prepared to sail for his native country. This was prevented by the appearance of Ribault with nine vesssels equipped with all the supplies necessary for the 1565. colony. Ribault now assumed the command, re-established the fort, renewed a friendly intercourse with the Indians, and was about to get up another gold seeking expedition, when a Spanish fleet appeared on the coast, and furnished the Frenchmen with other employment.

At this time France and Spain were at peace. Philip the Second had leisure to reflect on the importance of propagating the gospel among the heathen of Florida, a patrimony granted to him by the Pope on that condition. Don Pedro Menendez de Avilla was appointed Adelantado, who is said to have equipped at his own expense twenty sail of vessels for the expedition. It was at this time that Charles the Ninth gave notice of Ribault's establishment on the east coast of Florida ; this information at once fixed the course of the Spaniards. Volunteers flocked on board the fleet, zealous to destroy the heretics, so that in a short time Menendez found himself at the head of three thousand men. The fleet had scarcely sailed when they were overtaken by a storm, which sunk and destroyed two thirds of them ; the balance were collected at Porto Rico in so shattered a condition, that a general despair pervaded the troops. But Menendez revived them by assuring them that the Almighty had reduced their numbers that his own arm might achieve the victory without any human aid. Ribault had arrived on the Florida coast but a few days before Menendez. Four of his ships were too large to enter May River, and lay at anchor off the bar. Menendez hoped to have taken them with the six ships still left him, but Ribault slipped his cables and ran to sea, where he was closely pursued by Menendez for a short time, when he returned to the coast; fearing to enter the river with his small force, he retired down the coast and entered the Inlet at St. Augustine, where he disembarked, and laid the foundation of the first permanent town in North America. Expecting an attack from Ribault, he fortified the post in all haste, determining to defend himself until reinforcements could be obtained from Cuba.

Ribault was not behind him in exertion; he returned to May River, collected his whole force, withdrew from the fort all the artillery, arms and men, except eighty, who were mostly invalids. These, with the women and children, he committed to the care of Lardoniere, and sailed in pursuit of Menendez. He found the Spanish vessels anchored off the bar of St. Augustine, and bore down for them, expecting to make them an easy prey, when he was struck by a sudden tempest, which forced his fleet down the coast, and finally wrecked the whole near Cape Canaverel.

Menendez saw the tempest continue and was satisfied that his enemy could not collect his vessels on the station short of several days. He therefore selected his best men with eight days provision, and marched across the country to attack fort Carolin, which he knew must be undefended. The fatigue of traversing these forests and wet swamps was extreme, but he arrived in the forest, in the rear of the fort, without alarming Lardoniere. Here the Spanish historian states, that Menendez prepared his men for the attack, by kneeling and praying for success. From prayers they rushed to slaughter, and very few escaped the onset; seventy women and children are said to have escaped death and submitted to slavery. Lardoniere with about twenty men leaped from the parapet of the fort and made for some small vessels which had been left in charge of young Ribault, which having reached, they dropped down the river out of the reach of the enemy. Those who escaped instant death were hung to the limbs of a tree and left for the buzzards and crows to feed upon. Menendez had a stone monument affixed near the spot on which was written "Not as Frenchmen, but as Heretics." This scene of horror was left immediately, lest Ribault should return and attack the post at St. Augustine. On his return he was hailed as a conqueror. Te Deum was solemnly chanted. He soon learned that the Frenchmen were on the coast below the Matanzas bar.

Ribault had collected about six hundred men from the wreck of his fleet; a considerable quantity of small arms had also been saved. With this force he might either have reached his fort, or have attacked Menendez in his, with a fair prospect of sucess. But the extraordinary reverse of fortune, had broken down their spirits and distracted their councils. They finally concluded to surrender themselves prisoners at discretion. They formed into two companies; the first consisting of two hundred men, proceeded up the coast as far as Matanzas Inlet. Here they were met by Menendez who had, with forty soldiers sailed up the sound to reconnoitre. A French soldier was sent across the inlet to learn what terms could be obtained ; the messenger was detained. The boat was then sent across for ten Frenchmen, who were taken behind a sand hill and murdered. And in this manner were the two hundred men decoyed across the stream, by tens, and all massacred and left on the sand, to be devoured by the birds and beasts of prey.

In two or three days Menendez again repaired to the scene of butchery with his main force, where he was soon met by Ribault with the balance of his wrecked companions. Here Ribault endeavored to enter into negociations to ransom himself and his men. Menendez treated him civilly and offered him food, but demanded unconditional submission. Although Ribault was shewn the carcasses of his murdered men, still he had the madness to submit, and induced one hundred and fifty more to follow his example. They were murdered to a man. The rest of the French retreated back to the wrecked vessels, built a small fort and began to construct a small vessel to bear them from the coast. The natives informed Menendez of their situation, who fitted out a fleet of small craft and attacked the fugitives, who were obliged to abandon their fort. They however rallied on a sand hill out of the reach of the large guns. To these Menendez offered terms of peace and safety. Their leader would not listen to any terms, but finding a majority disposed to surrender, he with about twenty of his followers fled to the woods and they were never heard of more. The rest being too insignificant to injure the Spaniards, had their lives spared.

Thus the whole colony was destroyed. All France was indignant when informed of this infamous transaction. But the king seemed satisfied, and no public notice was taken of the matter till 1569, when the chevalier Dominique de Gourgas, revenged the insult offered to his nation, at the same time that he gratified his private revenge.

1569

De Gourgas was a Catholic, born of a respectable family in Comminges, at Mount Marsan. His youth had been spent in arms, and his reputation was of the first order. In Italy he served against the Spaniards, by whom he was taken prisoner, and consigned to the gallies. From this situation he was released by the capture of the galley by an Algerine pirate. The prize was soon after retaken by a vessel of Malta, and De Gourgas restored to liberty. He then betook himself to the seas, and in several cruizes against the Spaniards he acquired considerable wealth. He had just retired to private life when the news of the Florida massacres reached France. He immediately sold his property, purchased two gallies and a tender, under pretence of trading to Africa. His first care was to procure one of Lardoniere's men who knew the coast, and had acquired the

Indian language. One hundred and fifty picked men, many of them gentlemen adventurers, were enlisted for a cruize of twelve months. His purpose he kept a profound secret, until he reached the coast of Florida. In a masterly speech he then informed his crews of the object of his voyage, pointed out to them the cowardly atrocities of the Spaniards, and the disgraces that their nation had sustained from suffering the murderers to go unpunished. His fellows showed their readiness to revenge the wrongs of their countrymen.

The fleet soon entered the river and passed the forts without suspicion; salutes being interchanged as though they were Spaniards. De Gourgas not thinking himself safe to attack his enemies until he could collect reinforcements. The Indians were numerous on the coast, and as they knew Lardoniere, they were greatly rejoiced at meeting their old friends, the French, and readily combined their warriors with them, for the purpose of revenging the injuries done to both parties by the Spaniards. Besides Carolin, the Spaniards had built two other forts, nearer to the mouth of the river, and had mounted on the redoubts the cannon taken from the French; the whole were garrisoned with four hundred men. Gourgas left his vessels and marched his combined forces down the north bank of the river to attack the forts in the rear. He calculated to have reached them before day light, but the paths being intricate, the sun had risen just as they came in sight of the lowest fortification; they turned again into the woods and led the troops in a circuit across a small river, and were close upon the fort before the Spaniards discovered them. A few cannon were fired from the ramparts, when the Indians rushing forward, scaled the palisades, and being closely followed by the French, the place was soon taken. Gourgas made no delay here, but jumped into a boat, crossed the river, followed by the Indians swimming, and in a few minutes another fort was taken by storm. Fort Carolin still remained; there the Spanish governor resided, with a garrison of three hundred men. Gourgas learned from a prisoner that his forces were estimated much higher than they really were, thought it good policy to attack the fort before the terror of his arms should be dissipated by a knowledge of his weakness; he therefore collected eight skiffs, and compelling a Spanish prisoner to act as guide, he came early on the next morning in sight of the fort; after planting groups of Indians around the place, in every copse of wood, to cut off the retreat of the Spaniards, Gourgas led the French to attack a low situation which he had discovered in the fortifications. This was immediately carried. The governor sent sixty men to guard the spot, but they were all cut in pieces by the assailants. This event frightened the governor so much, that he attempted to fly to the woods with his garrison; there they were intercepted by the Indians, and scarcely a man escaped death.

On entering the fort, they found some of the skeletons of the former colonists hanging to the limbs of the trees, and the stone engraved, " *Not as Frenchmen, but as hereticks*." Gourgas ordered the bones to be buried, and the Spaniards to be hung in their places, and affixed this label, " *Not as Spaniards, but as murderers*." Gourgas being aware that his force was too small to hold possession of the country, joined the Indians in demolishing all the forts, and then embarked his troops for France.

1574. When the Adelantado Pedro Menendez, heard of the destruction of his garrisons at Carolin, his indignation was great, but his enemy had escaped him. He thought it better to preserve his force entire at St. Augustine, than to weaken it by rebuilding those places that he had held at so uncertain a tenure. He continued to govern that post for twelve years, during which period he was indefatigable in reducing the natives of Florida, to the catholic faith. • At his request, the King of Spain, sent out missionaries from most of the religious orders; but the greatest number, and the most enterprising, were franciscans. These men were sent among the Indians, in every part of the country, and by the mildness of their manners, and by teaching the arts of civilized life, they acquired a complete ascendency over them ; so that at the time the Adelantado left Florida, the King of Spain was acknowledged ; and the catholic religion was professed by all the tribes, from St. Helena on the north, to Bocca Rattones on the south, and from the Atlantic, to the Gulf of Mexico.

1578. On returning to Spain, Menendez invested De las Alas with the authority, and title of Governor of Florida. He assembled a council of the province, and imparted to them his instructions, which had been left by the Adelantado. In pursuance of the advice of this council, he despatched embassies to all the tribes of Indians, for several hundred miles to the west, and north of St. Augustine. In this he was so successful, that all the tribes east of the Appalachicola River, received into their towns

1581. Spanish garrisons, and many Spanish families to instruct the Indians.

1583. This year the Chickasaws, Taçoposcas, Apacas, Tamaicas, Apiscas, and Alabamas, joined in allegiance with the Spaniards,

1584. and during the next year, the Chischemacas came into the same terms, so that the Spanish authorities were acknowledged as far west, as the river Missisippi, (Empalaçada) and north one hundred and forty leagues to the mountains of Georgia. It was at this period that the Missionary establishments, and convents were founded, whose ruins are at this time a subject of curious investigation, in the middle district of Florida. It was here that the see of Rome chartered a great religious province, under the order of the Francisçans, it was called St. Helena, and all the minor

establishments throughout the province, were represented at the great
Francisçan house, at St. Augustine.

1585.   Some private adventurers, about this time, fitted out a fleet of
twenty-six vessels, in England, to cruize against the Spanish commerce. Sir Francis Drake, was appointed Admiral, Forbisher Vice, and
Knolles Rear Admiral. This fleet sailed in September. They sacked St.
Jago ; raised a contribution of twenty-five thousand ducats on St. Domingo, and took Carthagena, after a hard fought battle. From thence they
steered for Florida, doubled the cape and sailed up the coast. On
1586. the eighth of May, they espied on the shore a tower, which appeared to be a look out station. The Admiral suspected it to be some
Spanish establishment, ordered the pinnaces to be manned and landed the
troops on an island. On marching up the shore, he discovered across the
sound, a fort, and farther up a town, built with wood.

General Carlisle, of the land forces, took a skiff and crossed the sound to
reconnoitre. Although very cautious he was discovered by the Spaniards,
who took the alarm, and after discharging a few cannon, fled, believing the
English were at their heels. The General, however, returned without discovering their retreat. At length they observed a French fifer, crossing
the sound in a little boat, playing the Prince of Örange's march ; he informed the guard, that he had been taken prisoner by the Spaniards, and that in
the recent panic he had recovered his liberty, and offered to conduct the
English to the fort. Drake then crossed the sound, and took the fort,
which was deserted. It was a wooden entrenchment, enlarged by palisades
of cabbage trees. The platforms were made, by placing large pine trees
horizontally across each other, and earth rammed in to fill the space. This
fort was called St. John, and fourteen pieces of brass cannon, were found on
the platforms ; a chest of silver was also found, containing two thousand
pounds sterling, intended for the payment of the garrison, which consisted
of one hundred and fifty men.

The next day he marched towards the town, but some unfavorable rains
intervened, so that they were obliged to return, and embark in the pinnaces,
and so proceed up the sound. On approaching the town, the Spaniards
made a show of resistance, but on receiving a volley from the fire arms,
they fled into the country, leaving the town defenceless. The Admiral had
intended to attack St. Helena, but the surfs on this shore are dangerous,
and he had no pilot on whom he could depend ; he therefore sailed for
England.

1665.   Captain Davis, an English Buccanier, sailed from the West
Indies to attack St. Augustine, and meeting with no opposition, he
plundered the town, although it was fortified by an octagon fort, and two

round towers, garrisoned with regular troops. It was about this period that the English made a permanent settlement at St. Helena, on the banks of what was at that time called May River. The Captain General of Cuba, was by the court of Spain, ordered to dislodge them, but it was never done.

1680. This year, the Spanish Governor of Florida, Don John Menyers de Cabrana, become jealous of the Yamasee chief, Nichosatly, whose tribe was, at that time, very powerful in numbers and in bravery, possessng many flourishing towns in various parts of Florida. This chief resided near the new settlements of the English at St Helena. He denied that he had afforded any assistance to these new settlers, and professed much loyalty to the King of Spain, and allegiance to the catholic church. Yet he was condemned as a traitor. He exhibited a very christian temper, forgiving his enemies, and exorting his friends not to revenge his death. Nothing could appease Cabrana, and Nichosatty was publicly executed. The English took advantage of this event, to excite the Yamasees to a fierce war

1686 against the Spaniards, who were shortly driven from all the islands north of St John's River. Cabrena was soon after recalled and punished by the King of Spain, but from this period the Spanish influence declined among the natives of Florida.

1689. During this year an English colony was settled on Ashley River, where Charleston now stands. This settlement was patronized by Governor Sayle. It was also during this year that Monsieur Bienville planted a French colony on the Bay of Baloxi, opposite Ship Island on the Gulf of Mexico, and the Spanish court despatched Count Ariola to establish a fortified post at the entrance of Pensacola Bay to check the progress of the French. The post was named Anchusa, from an ancient Indian name of the bay. Ariola built a square fort with bastions, a church, and a few dwelling houses, near the site of the present fort of Barrancas.

1693. The Count de Galvez, Viceroy of New Spain, being informed that the affairs of Florida were in a bad situation, he despatched Don Andrea de la Paez with an armament to Pensacola Bay ; he landed at Point Sequenza, on the west end of S. Rosa Island, where he planted a small village. He then made another establishment across the bay on the site of Pensacola. To this bay Don Tristan de Luna had given the name of St. Maria, and De Paez added the name of the Viceroy de Galvez. Before De Paez left Pensacola he erected a castle for its defence.

1702. By this time, the English settlements in North and South Carolina had become strong and wealthy. Governor Moore, of South Carolina, projected an invasion of Florida. To promote it, the Legislature voted two thousand pounds sterling. Six hundred volunteers were raised, and six hundred Creek Indians engaged and armed to accompany them. Several schooners and other merchant vessels were impressed as transports to convey the troops to Port Royal, the place of rendezvous, where the governor in person joined the expedition in the month of September. Col. Daniel was appointed second in command, and was ordered to take with him one division of the army and to proceed through the inland passages to the St. John's River, and from thence to scour the country to St. Augustine, and to attack that city in the rear, while the governor should enter the harbor and assault it in front. Col. Daniel was an officer of spirit, he pushed forward, entered and plundered the town before Governor Moore arrived. But the Spaniards had collected provisions and withdrew into the fort of St. Mark's with their most valuable effects, and prepared for any emergency. On the arrival of Moore, the fort was regularly besieged with a force against which the Spaniards could make little resistance, and they lay quietly within their walls. Moore directly found that his artillery was altogether too light to injure the place. He therefore despatched Col. Daniel in a sloop to Jamaica for cannon and mortars. During his absence two Spanish vessels hove in sight. One of them carried twenty-two and the other sixteen guns. Moore was struck with such a panic, that he fled through the country by land, and abandoned his whole armament, ships, stores and all, to the Spaniards.

Col. Daniel soon after returned, and was entering the harbor when he discovered that Moore had raised the seige. He narrowly escaped capture. The Creeks were indignant at the conduct of their ally and abandoned the English with disgust. When the Governor returned to Carolina, very severe reflections were cast upon him. The expedition had cost the colony six thousand pounds sterling, which they were not then in a condition to pay ; and this great sum had purchased nothing but disgrace. In order to defend himself, Moore was obliged to keep himself surrounded by armed troops, and with these he put down all opposition.

1704   Two years afterwards, Moore wishing to retrieve his character with his countrymen, applied to the Legislature to furnish him with troops to attack the Appalache and Yamasee towns in the western part of Florida, but they refused. They told him that he might raise volunteers and make war on the Indians if he chose, but declared their inability to supply him with funds. He therefore collected about twenty-five resolute Carolineans and proceed to the Creek nation, whose various tribes had long been at war with the Appalache, Yamasee and Attamasco Indians. He soon engaged one thousand warriors to march under him. With this army, he proceeded down the Flint River and entering Florida, made his first attack on Lewis' fort, situate about twenty miles from the sea and east of the Oclockony River. The Governor of Appalache, was Don Juan Mexia. The fort was garrisoned by four hundred men, a number amply sufficient to have defended the place against any number of men who were destitute of artillery, but led by a foolish spirit of chivalry, he marched out to meet the Creeks on their own ground. A terrible battle ensued, which terminated in the death of Mexia and nearly all the Spaniards under his command. The fort was taken and burned. A scene of general devastation succeeded, monasteries, convents and missionary establishments, sunk in succession beneath the flames, and such of the inhabitants as escaped the tommahawk and scalping knife were driven into captivity. Fourteen hundred Yamasees were driven into Georgia, some of them were made slaves and the balance were settled on the north side of the Savanna River. From this time the Spaniards abandoned middle Florida except the fort on the Appalachicola River, below the junction of the Flint and Chattahooche, which was presently abandoned and the armament and stores removed to St. Marks, a new fort which was begun at the forks of the Appalache at the request of the Uche tribe of Indians. This was never finished, but a garrison was kept there until Florida was given up to the United States.

1706.   This year the French and Spaniards under Mons. La Febour, entered the port of St. Augustine on their way to attack Charleston. After taking a part of the garrison from the fort they sailed for Carolina, but on their arrival they found the country so perfectly defended by Gov. Johnston, that they found it necessary to retreat, after loosing three hundred of their best men. The combined fleet retired to Havanna.

1715.   On the 31st of June of this year, a Spanish fleet of fourteen sail of galleons on their return from Mexico through the Gulf of Florida, ran foul of the reef near Carysford, through the ignorance of the Admiral Don Rodrigues de Torres. Every ship but one was destroyed. The Captain of the ship that was saved disobeyed the signal of the Admiral and bore away. An immense treasure was lost. The Spaniards, some time afterwards, fitted out a company of wreckers and divers, and sent them to attempt a recovery of the specie and bullion that was on board the galleons, were very successful, and raised a large quantity of the treasure.

1716.   The English in Jamaica, learning how the Spaniards were employed, fitted out two ships and four sloops, under the command of Captain Henry Jennings, who immediately sailed to the Florida Keys, anchored his fleet, and sent three hundred men on shore to attack the Spanish guard, which consisted of sixty men, who fled into the woods and abandoned to the English three hundred and fifty thousand pieces of eight, which was carried in triumph to Jamaica.

1717.   This year, the Spanish authorities in St. Augustine procured a general combination of the western Indians against the English settlements of the Carolinas. The Yamasees, Creeks and Appalaches, attacked the southern frontier; while the Congarees, Catanbas and Cherokees, killed, burnt and destroyed the western settlements. Governor Craven, however, fortunately brought their united forces to a general battle, near a place called Saltcatchers, and totally defeated them, and pursuing his success, he drove them all across the Savanna River and ended the war.   The Yamasees, thus humbled, retired into East Florida.   For a long time they cherished the most deadly hatred against the Carolineans, and for many years they occasionally sent out scalping parties, who cut off the frontier families, and usually inflicted on them the most cruel tortures.

1718.   This year Governor Ayola was succeeded by Don Antonio de Benavuedi Barini y Malini, who put a stop to the hostilities against the English, and it was thought that he treated his Yamasee allies with much ingratitude.   He published an ordinance exiling them to the distance of 6 leagues south of the city of St. Augustine and also to the same distance from the Fort of St. Marks in West Florida.   This fort had been erected by Governor Ayola at the special request of the Uche and Yamasee Indians, that resided near Coweta.   At the beginning of this year the first garrison of Spanish troops took possession of it, and fortified it with cannon, in order to protect the natives from the frequent incursions of the northern Indians.

The Yamasees remonstrated with the new Governor against his order; stating to him, that, although they had at one time joined the English, to wit, after the execution of their chief Nichosatly, yet they had since repented of that fault, and fought against them in behalf of the Spaniards. They said it would be a grievous act to drive them from their fields of corn, and their houses, while the English were their enemies.   That they revered the catholic King, and the holy church, and desired to have its rites administered to them, that they were content to live in peace with all nations. Malina was immoveable, and instead of granting any favor to their reasonable requests, he sent Captain Lewis Ortagas, with an armed troop to quicken their obedience.

The Yamasees complied without further reply, abandoning their fields almost ripe for the harvest, their cattle, horses, hogs, furniture &c.   Many of these poor wretches died of hunger, fatigue, and broken hearts.   Great numbers of women, children, and infirm persons, were left on the island of St. Mary's,* being unable to travel.   These were presently discovered by the English, who pursued the fugitives in their launches, on which they had mounted swivels; these they brought to bear on the miserable starving

* Amelia.

rabble, who had not a tree or bush to protect them, but were murdered in cold blood. Four hundred were thus slaughtered ; and of three thousand that now survived, more than two-thirds died in less than a year, by hunger and diseases.

Thus was this once powerful and warlike nation, almost annihilated by those friends, for whom they had fought and bled in vain. The English soon occupied the fields thus abandoned. They planted a town on the river Jordan, which they called Savanna, and the surrounding country, they called new Georgia.

1718.　　During this year also, the French established a fort on the north shore of St. Joseph's Bay, and planted about it a small settlement. The fort was named Crevecoeur ; but the Spaniards protested against this settlement, as an invasion of their rights, and the next year it was abandoned. The same spot was afterwards occupied by a garrison, sent there by the Marquis Salino Vive, under the command of Don Gregorio Salinas Barrera, but it was soon afterwards also abandoned by them, and the fort destroyed.

1819.　　About the latter end of May, Mons. de Serigny, Governor of Louisiana, sent Mons. Chateaugue, with eight hundred Indians, to invest the fort at Pensacola. It was built about twenty-two years before by de Pez ; but little progress had been made in settling the country. Mons. de Serigny proceeded himself, by water, with three ships. The Philip, and Thoulouse, carried each twenty-four guns, and the Hercules fifty six, and bore the Admirals broad penant ; they also carried out four hundred men. The Spaniards made a show of resistance, but fired only two or three shots, before they beat the chamade, and had the privilege of marching out, with their arms and baggage ; their arms were, however, to be delivered up on the esplanade. It was also agreed that they should be sent to Havanna, in French vessels. Accordingly the Thoulouse, and Marischal de Villier, which were about to sail for France, were ordered to land the Spanish garrison at the Havanna. They sailed on the beginning of June, but when off the Havanna, they were captured by a Spanish fleet, that were destined to break up the settlements of New Georgia. The ships were taken into the Havanna, and fitted up to return with a new force to Pensacola, to which place the whole fleet was now ordered. They arrived in August, with eighteen hundred troops, six hundred of whom were regular forces. The French withdrew the companies of two ships into the fort. They were summoned to surrender, but refused. However, a mutiny was soon after raised, which resulted in a capitulation, without a gun being fired. The garrison consisted of two hundred and eighty men.

About the month of September Mons. Champslen appeared off the bar, with six ships ;—the Hercules, of fifty-six guns ; the Mars, of sixty ; the Triton, of fifty-four , the Philip, of twenty-four ; and the Union, of thirty-six ; with a brigantine. The Spaniards having heard of their arrival at Dauphin Island, were prepared to receive them. They constructed on the western point of St. Rosa Island a stockaded fort, with ordnance and men to defend it. But it was found too weak to withstand the heavy artillery of the French ships It was soon battered in pieces, and most of the garrison killed. The Spaniards then drew up their fleet, consisting of eleven small vessels, and fought gallantly until all their ammunition was expended : then they were obliged to strike their colors. The fort continued the action warmly for two hours longer, but finally sent out a flag and offered to capitulate, as they greatly dreaded the Indians who had invested the fort by land, under Mons. Bienville. The French refused any other terms than a surrender as prisoners of war. These terms being accepted, the fort was given up on the 17th of September; six hundred men laid down their arms. The French immediately demolished the fortifications, burnt up the houses, and left the place a scene of perfect desolation.

This year a dispute arose between the governors of St. Augustine 1725 and South Carolina. The Spaniards charged the English with intruding on their lands, and the Englishmen charged the Spaniards with enticing away their negroes, and in urging the Yamasees to murder the frontier inhabitants. Gov. Malina recalled Antonio Macono, with those Yamasees that had survived their banishment, and having armed and equipped them, despatched them across the country into Georgia, where they ravaged the frontier settlements with horrible carnage, sparing neither age nor sex. Col. Palmer raised about three hundred militia and Indians, and entered Florida with a resolution to retaliate these injuries. He burned and destroyed nearly every settlement in the colony, to the very gates of St. Augustine. The inhabitants flew to the fort for refuge, but the poor Yamasees were most of them killed or made prisoners. The Spaniards saved nothing except what was protected by the guns of the fortress. Among other devastations, the Georgians plundered the chapel of Nostra Seniora de la Lache, which stood without the walls of the city, stripped it of the gold and silver ornaments, and took the infant image from the Virgin Mary and carried it as a prize to Col. Palmer, who lay at Fort Mosa, two miles north of the city. He cast the image into the field, and angrily told the soldiers that the Spaniards would one day punish them for their sacrilege. Palmer well knew that without cannon he could make no impression on the fort, he therefore retired with an immense booty, in cattle, horses, and other plunder.

1740. Fifteen years elapsed before any event of importance occurred in Florida. The spirit of enmity was kept up between the Spanish and English settlements, by the Spaniards sheltering and protecting the negroes who ran away from the English colonies. This, they said they were bound in conscience to do, in order to convert them to the catholic religion and save their souls. General Oglethorpe, Governor of Georgia, projected an invasion of Florida, and wrote to the other colonies for assistance. They raised four hundred men and sent them to him, under the command of Col. Vanderdussen. He also engaged a large body of Creek Indians, so that in May he rendezvoused at the mouth of St. John's River, with more than two thousand men of all kinds. Commodore Price, commander of the English ships of war on that station, acted in concert, but neglected to blockade the harbor of St. Augustine in season.

Oglethorpe selected four hundred men and a party of Indians, with which he invested Fort Diego, situate on the Plains of that name, twenty-five miles from St. Augustine. This fort, after a short resistance, capitulated. In this fort he placed a garrison of sixty men under the command of Lieut. Dunbar, and here the General committed an error, which in the end rendered the whole campaign abortive. Instead of pushing directly to St. Augustine, and taking the Spaniards by surprise, he returned to St. John's, where he was joined by more troops. While there, the Spaniards received into the harbor six half gallies, with a number of long brass nine pound cannon, and two sloops loaded with provisions, and all the cattle in the country were driven into the town. Thus provided, the Spaniards bid defiance to their invaders.

Oglethorpe marched his army in a few days to the Fort Mosa, two miles north of St. Augustine; this being destroyed, he proceeded to reconnoitre the town. The observations he made, and the report of prisoners tended much to discourage him. The fort, that had been a long time building, was now in a fine state of defence, from the cannon lately received; besides, the town was entrenched with ten salient angles, on each of which, more or less cannon were mounted. The garrison consisted of seven hundred regulars, two troops of horse, and four companies of armed negroes, besides militia and Indians. It was utterly in vain to think of carrying the place with his means; he therefore changed the siege into a blockade. The ships were moored across the harbor, and lines were established around the town by land; Colonel Palmer with a company of Highlanders and forty-two Indians, stationed at Fort Mosa; with orders to scour the woods and intercept all supplies of cattle, &c; and for greater safety, they were directed not to come to action, but to keep strict watch, and encamp every night at a different place. He sent Col. Vanderdussen to erect a small battery on Point Quartell, and he, with his regiment of Georgians and the main body of Indians, passed over to Anastasia Island. From a battery erected at the north end he intended to bombard the place. Capt. Price stationed one of his ships off the mouth of the Matanzas River, to prevent supplies from that quarter. With the assistance of the sailors, cannon were soon mounted on the batteries. The Spanish garrison was then summoned to surrender. But the Governor answered that he should be happy to shake hands with the General in the fort.

Oglethorp was indignant, and renewed his exertions to reduce the place ; his batteries opened a hot fire, and a great number of shells were thrown into the town. The Spaniards returned the fire, with equal spirit, both from the fort, and from the half gallies. But the combatants were too far distant from each other, to do much execution. Capt. Warren, a brave naval officer, offered to attack, and carry the gallies in the night : a council of war was called, to consider on the subject, but the plan was relinquish- ed, because the water was too shoal, to bring up any heavy vessel, to cover the attack, and the galleys laying under cover of the guns of the fort, it was thought, that the risk was too great. The Spanish Governor observing that some embarrassment had relaxed the fire of the besiegers, he sent out a detachment of three hundred men, with some Yamasees, against Col. Palmer. They surprised him at fort Mosa, while asleep and unguarded. The Highlanders, with their Colonel, were cut in pieces ; a few only escaped, who obtained a small boat, and joined the Carolina regiment, at point Quartell. The Spanish historians, assert that Col. Palmer was killed by Wakona the Yamasee Chief, on the spot where he had cast the infant image into the field.

Another misfortune soon followed : a Cherokee encountering a Spaniard, cut off his head, and brought it to Oglethorp, but he spurned the savage, with abhorrence, and calling him a barbarous dog, bid him begone. The Cherokees said, that the French would have treated them very differently. They soon after drew off, and left the place.

Soon after this, the ship placed off the Matanzas sound, was removed. Immediately several small boats entered, and brought several hundred men to reinforce the garrison ; with an abundant supply of provisions. The troops of Oglethorpe now lost all hope. They were enfeebled by the heat of the cli- mate ; dispirited by sickness, and fatigued by fruitless exertions, in a despe- rate cause. They deserted in large bodies. The fleet being short of provi- sions, and the stormy season approaching, the Commodore judged it impru- dent to risk the ships any longer on the station. General Oglethorpe him- self, fell sick of a fever, and the flux raged in his own regiment. The siege was raised, and the troops retired to Georgia.

* This is denied by the Spanish historians.

The General was blamed for his delay at Diego, for want of energy, in not attempting to carry the place ; for placing so small a party at Fort Mosa, exposed to the sallies of the enemy. The General alleged, that he was not supported by the troops, that he could place no confidence in them, that Palmer was lost on account of disobedience of orders and negligence. It is not probable that he could have taken the place, with double the force he possessed, unless by surprize.

1742.   Two years had scarcely elapsed, when the English colonies were, in their turn, made to feel the terrors of invasion. An army of two thousand men was raised in the Havanna, and Antonio de Rodondo appointed Adjutant General, and Don Manuel Montiano General of the army. They were embarked in a number of vessels, which put into St. Augustine, about the middle of May. It was however, discovered, by Captain Haymer, who was cruizing on the coast. He immediately gave advice to General Oglethorpe, who sent to Glen, Governor of Carolina, requesting assistance. He at the same time, despatched advice to Admiral Vernon, in the West Indies.

The people of Carolina, had lost all confidence in Oglethorpe and refused to send troops to his assistance, but, in as much, as Georgia had proved a great barrier against the Indians, it was thought necessary to fit out some vessels, to cruise down the coast and see what could be done, for their re-relief. Oglethorpe made every possible exertion, to prepare for the event. He procured great numbers of Indians, from the Creek nation, with whom he was very popular. A company of Highlanders joined him, anxious to find an opportunity of revenging their companions, who were massacred at Fort Mosa. A company of Rangers also joined him at Frederica, where he fixed his head quarters. The Spanish fleet hove in sight on the last of June. It was under the command of Don Manuel de Monteano, governor of East Florida. It consisted of thirty-two sail of vessels, bearing more than three thousand men. The fleet came to an anchor, outside of St. Simons' bar, and boats were sent to sound out the channel. After which they entered, with the tide, and stood in for Jekyl, (called Oboloquina sound.) The batteries on St. Simons were opened upon them as they passed, and the fire was returned, by the fleet, until they were out of reach. They passed up the river Altamaha. There the enemy hoisted a red flag, at the mast head of the largest ship ; landed their forces upon the Island and erected a battery, mounted with twenty, eighteen pounders.

The Spaniards had a fine company of artillery, commanded by Rodondo, and a well disciplined regiment of negroes, whose officers dressed, ranked and associated with the Spanish officers, without reserve.

Oglethorpe found that his situation on the island of St. Simons was too

24

dangerous, he therefore spiked his cannon, burst the bombs and cohorns, destroyed such stores as could not be carried away, and retreated to Frederica; determined to act on the defensive and with the greatest caution. He kept one part of his troops busily employed on the fortifications, while the balance scoured the woods, in every direction, to avoid surprise and to check any incursions. His Indians often fell upon the outposts of the enemy, and at length they brought in five prisoners, who informed him of the enemies force. His provisions were bad and scarce, but this he was obliged to keep secret, from his own troops. He still expected assistance from Carolina. And while the enemy commanded the river and harbor, no supplies could be expected. His whole force, Indians, militia and regulars amounted only to seven hundred men. He exposed himself to the same fare and the same fatigues as the meanest soldier.

Several attempts were made to force a passage through the woods, in order to attack the fort of the Georgians ; but the deep morasses and thickets were so lined with wild Indians and fierce Highlanders, that the Spaniards said, that the Devil could not get to Frederica. In two skirmishes with the exploring parties of the Spaniards, the latter lost one captain, two lieutenants and one hundred men, taken prisoners. Monteano then sent some gallies up the river, with the flood tide, to reconnoitre the fort, and to attract the attention of Oglethorpe to another quarter. A party of Indians were placed in ambush to prevent their landing.

About this time an English prisoner escaped from the Spanish camp, and informed the General that the Cuba troops and the Florida troops had quarrelled, so that each had formed a separate encampment. He immediately determined to surprise one of them. Being well acquainted with the woods, he marched out in the night with the Highlanders and rangers, in all, three hundred men. He approached within two miles and halted the troops, going himself forward with a small party to examine the situation of the enemy, but he was betrayed by a French deserter, who fired his musket and gave the alarm. Being thus discovered, he retreated back to Frederica, perfectly aware that the deserter would discover his weakness to the enemy. Oglethorpe was greatly troubled ; but on reflection he determined on a plan to avert the consequences. For this purpose he wrote a letter to the Frenchman, directing him to use every art to induce the Spaniards to make an attack on Frederica, by stating its weakness and defenceless situation. But if he could not succeed in that, by all means to prevent them from retreating, if it was only for three days, until the arrival of six British ships, when he expected to give a good account of the Spaniards. This letter was confided to one of the Spanish prisoners, who was bribed to deliver it to the Frenchman. The Spaniard, as was expected, gave the letter to Monteano. Various were the speculations and conjectures that this letter created; some of the officers believed it to be true, and that the Frenchman was a spy, others gave no credit to the matter, believing it all a hoax. The Frenchman, however, was put in irons, and a council of war was called. While the Spanish officers were in conclave, consulting about the letter, three ships sent from Charleston appeared off the coast. This corresponded so well with the letter, that every man was convinced; a general panic ran through the camp, the Spaniards set fire to the fort and embarked in perfect confusion, leaving behind them several cannon, and a large quantity of provisions and military stores. The wind opposed the entrance of the Carolina ships all that day; before the next morning the Spanish fleet had slipped out, and were under way for St. Augustine. In this affair Oglethorpe retrieved his character with the colonies, both for personal courage and military skill.

Monteano was fifteen days on a small island, with three thousand men and a powerful fleet, opposed to seven hundred troops of all kinds; lost several of his bravest men, with several cannon and many stores, and gained nothing. On his return to Cuba he was imprisoned and tried for misconduct. General Oglethorpe was also recalled and tried on nineteen charges, brought against him by Lieut. Col. Wm. Cook, who owed his preferment to the friendship of the General. He was honorably acquitted.

1743. The next year Governor Oglethorpe retaliated upon the Province of Florida another secret expedition. He proceeded by land from St. John's River, attended by a numerous collection of Creek Indians. He proceeded with great caution to the neighborhood of the city of St. Augustine, where he planted an ambuscade, and then took possession of a small fort that had been erected to protect the King's workmen. A troop of cavalry was sent out to succor the workmen, and by accident the ambuscade was discovered. Had this not been done, the cavalry would probably have been intercepted, and the gates would have been entered by the enemy. This stratagem having been frustrated, Oglethorpe perceived that an assault would be useless, he retreated back to Georgia after spending in the Province seventy-five days.

A Yamassee chief, Pedro Christano, applied to Governor Monteana for permission to attack the Georgians on their retreat through the narrows of Fort George and Talbot Islands. But the governor thought it not prudent to make the attack until the enemy should be dispersed over the frontier settlements. He then furnished Christano with arms and ammunition, and supported him in several bloody incursions, until all the settlements of the English were broken up, as far as St. Simond's Island.

1748. A treaty being concluded between Spain and England, the war ceased. But the English immediately pushed their settlements south as far as the mouth of the Santilla River. Notice was immediately sent to Governor Monteano, but he paid no attention to the subject.

1755. This year Don Alonzo Fernandez de Herreda was appointed commandant of the Fort at St. Augustine. He ordered Captain Don Leo Joseph de Leon, with a company of mounted dragoons to go and recover the invaded territory. On the first summons, the English agreed to retire immediately, and being satisfied with their apparent willingness, De Leon returned. But the English kept their ground. The ambassador of Spain soon after obtained an order from the Court of London commanding these intruders to withdraw, but the order was never enforced.

1763. This year the King of Spain ceded Florida to Great Britain. There was but six hundred inhabitants in the Province, besides the regular troops, and they were very poor. Nearly all of them removed to Cuba, and left the country to be parcelled out among the half pay officers and disbanded soldiers, who had served in the American campaigns. Emigrants also arrived from Great Britain and from many other parts of Europe. Several of the English nobility settled plantations at Hillsborough River, on the St. John's River, and on Amelia Island. A few also settled at Pensacola.

Lord Rolle obtained a grant of land on the St. John's, which he named Charlotia. To this place he transported nearly three hundred miserable females, who were picked up about the purlieus of London. His object was to reform them, and make of them good members of society. They all died in a few years.

1767. Doct. Turnbull tried a different speculation. He sailed to the Peloponesus, and for the sum of four hundred pounds sterling, obtained permission from the Governor of Modon, to convey to Florida, a large number of Greek families. In 1767, he arrived with one small vessel, and took as many Greeks as he could obtain. On his way back from Modon, he put in at the islands of Corsica, and Minorca, and recruited his number of settlers to fifteen hundred. He agreed to carry them free of expense, to find them in good provisions and clothing, and at the end of three years, to give fifty acres of land to each head of families, and twenty-five acres to each child. If they were dissatisfied, in six months, he agreed to send them back. They had a long voyage, of four months ; many of the old people died. Twenty-nine died in one vessel. They arrived in the fall season. Sixty thousand acres of land, were granted them by the Governor of Florida. They built huts of palmetto, to shelter them through the winter, and in the spring they planted provisions. Their settlement was named

New Smyrna. It was about four miles west of Musquito Inlet, and seventy-four miles south of St. Augustine. After a sufficient quantity of provisions were raised, Turnbull, turned his attention to indigo. In five years, they had nearly three thousand acres of good land, highly improved, and in one year, the nett value of the indigo crop, amounted to three thousand one hundred and seventy-four dollars. Turnbull, however, did not fulfill his agreements, with these people, his avarice seemed to increase with his prosperity. He selected a few Italians, and made them overseers and drivers. The rest, men, women, and children, were reduced to the most abject slavery. Tasks were assigned them, as large as they could possibly perform during the week. The food of the laborers, was seven quarts of corn per week, for the whites, and ten quarts a week, for the negroes, a number of which had been placed on the settlement ; to the sick, three and a half quarts were allowed.

Most of the Minorcans, and Corsicans, had brought a good stock of clothing with them; when that was worn out, they were furnished with a suit of osnaburgs, each year. One blanket, and one pair of shoes, for the whole term of service were given to the men, but the women had no shoes, although many of them had been accustomed to live in affluence, in their own country. In this state of slavery, was this people kept for nine years. The tyranny exercised over them, was not exceeded, by the savage Spaniards of St. Domingo. The three last years, no clothing was given them at all, but they were permitted to buy it at a public store, and the debt thus incurred, was assigned as a reason for their confinement. On the most trifling occasions, they were beaten excessively, and the negroes were usually chosen as the instruments of diabolical cruelty. They were often compelled to beat and lacerate those who had not performed their tasks, till they died. After scourging the skin from their backs, they were sometimes left naked, tied to a tree all night, for the musquitoes to suck their blood. These usually swelled up ready to burst, with their tortures. If induced by despair to run away, they were stopped, and taken up by the negroes on the neighboring plantations, who were paid for returning them. Some wandered off, and died in the forests. At the end of nine years, six hundred only were left, of fifteen hundred and their natural increase.

1776. Some time in the summer of 1776, several English gentlemen from St. Augustine, on an excursion down the coast, called at New Smyrna, to see the improvements, especially a very large stone building, that was commenced for a mansion house. In the course of conversation, some of them made the remark, that if the people knew their rights, they would not suffer under such slavery. This was remarked by an intelligent boy, who told it to his mother. The old lady summoned a counsel of her friends in the night, and they devised a plan to gain more intelligence.

Three of them were to ask for a long task, in order to gain time to go down the coast, to catch turtle. This was granted them, as a special favor. They were assisted in finishing their task, by their fellow slaves. They then set off for St. Augustine, by the coast, and had to swim the Matanzas. They arrived safely, and the first man they met, was Mr. Younge, the Attorney general of the province. They made known to him their business, and he promised to protect them. A change of Governors had lately taken place ; Governor Grant, had been superceded by Governor Tonyn, Grant was supposed to have been connected with Turnbull, in the slavery of the Minorcans, Greeks, &c. Tonyn, on the contrary, had it in his power, to render himself popular, by doing an act of justice, to these long injured people.

The envoys returned, with the glad tidings that their chains where broken, and that protection awaited them. Turnbull was absent, but they feared the overseers, whose cruelty, they dreaded. They met in secret, and chose for their leader, a Mr. Pallicier, who was head carpenter of the Mansion House. The women and children, with the old men, were placed in the centre, and the stoutest men armed with wooden spears, were placed in front, and rear. In this order, they set off like the children of Israel, from a place that had proved an Egypt to them. So secretly had they conducted the transaction, that they had proceeded some miles, before the overseers discovered that the place was deserted. Some of them were well pleased, and joined them. Others informed the tyrant, who was at some distance from the place. He rode after the fugitives, and overtook them, before they reached St. Augustine, and used every exertion to persuade them to return, but in vain.

On the third day, they reached St. Augustine, where provisions were served out to them, by order of the Governor. Their case was tried before the Judges, where they were honestly defended by their friend, the Attorney General. Turnbull could show no cause for detaining them, and their freedom was fully established. Lands were offered to them, at New Smyrna, but they suspected some trick was on foot, to get them into Turnbull's hands, and besides, they detested the place, where they had suffered so much. Lands were therefore assigned them, in the north part of the city, where they have built houses, and cultivated their gardens to this day. Some by industry, have acquired large estates ; they at this time, form a respectable part of the population of the city.

1781.   This year Don Galvez, Governor of Louisiana, and Admiral Salano entered west Florida, and laid siege to Pensacola. The place was strongly fortified, and General Campbell, at the head of a thousand regular troops, defended the place, for a long time, with great bravery. Fort St. Michael commands the town, and harbor: The officer of the day observing that the gate of the principal Magazine was often opened, opposite the Spanish camp; ordered it to be closed, and another opened on the opposite side. While some fixed ammunition was taking out, to serve the ordnance, a bomb struck the eastern glacis, and rebounding back, it entered this back gate, exploded, and blew up the magazine. The principal redoubt was carried away, and several lives were lost. Count Galvez availed himself of this misfortune, and immediately occupied the place. Dispositions were now made, to take fort St. Bernard, by assault. General Campbell, aware that the place could not be defended, entered into a capitulation. He obtained the most honorable conditions, and surrendered the city.

The Floridas had been the most important acquisition which the English had obtained by the French war. These provinces rounded off their empire in America. But an attempt to oppress their colonies, was punished by the loss of those colonies and the Floridas besides.

1763. Very great improvements were made by the English, during the twenty years they held possession of the country. They encouraged agriculture, in the east and west, by offering bounties on Indigo. Similar bounties were shortly after, given for the increase of naval stores. The country became cultivated to a great extent. They had commenced the culture of the sugar cane, and the manufacture of sugar and rum in East Florida, was nearly as far advanced as it is at present. Some of the iron machinery, of their sugar works, have been dug out of the ground, below Tomoko, and again appropriated to the purpose, for which it was originally intended. Some of the old boilers had wild orange trees of considerable size growing in them.

The re-cession of the country to Spain operated as a blight over the whole land. The English population removed, as the Spaniards had done before *enmasse;* abandoning their gardens, fields, villages and towns. They sought shelter among the islands of the West Indies, and many from competency and ease were reduced to penury and want. A military government succeeded. A sparse population who barely existed on their pay, wholly inattentive to improvements of any kind. Their gardens, fences, fields and houses were suffered to grow up, with briars, or rot down, with time, or were burned up for fuel. In the space of forty years, the once flourishing settlements of Florida, dwindled down to two dirty towns, which, with all their dependencies, could not muster six thousand inhabitants.

The persevering Minorcans and Greeks were an exception; they continued to fish, make canoes and cultivate their gardens, and still do the same, without any perceptible change.

1792. Considerable disturbance was this year occasioned by an Englishman named Bowles. He sailed from New Providence in a schoon-

er with about sixty adherents. They landed on the Musquito coast, and proceeded to attack a large Indian store, situate on the west bank of the river St.
Johns, called Hamblys store. In order to facilitate the expedition, Bowles
took with him from the vessel several iron swivels, but his progress had
been observed, by the retainers of the house of Penton and Lesley, proprietors of the trading house, and they anticipated the attack of the marauders,
by garrisoning the store with fifty Spanish troops and a large number of their
own negroes.

Finding the place too strong, Bowles sought for subsistence at Cuscowil-
la, a Seminole town commanded by Payne, a very intelligent Indian. His
men being broken down by fatigue and hunger, deserted him. Finding that
Payne would not protect him, he fled to the Creek nation. There he married the daughter of Perryman, an intelligent Indian, and there he was joined by Daniel M'Girty, a white subject of East Florida. They made the
Creeks believe, that the stores establised by Panton Lesley and co., had
been sent by the English, as gifts to the Indians, and that they had a good
right to take and make use of them. Kenhutry, Little Prince and several
other chiefs were induced to join him. They established their head quarters
at Mickasookie old town. While here, a small vessel arrived at Appalache,
with goods for Bowles ; with these he made liberal presents to the Indians ;
whom he told, that they were part of the same goods, that the English
had sent to Panton for their use. The house of John Forbes and co. had
much influence with the Seminoles, they sent a Mr. Forest, to collect a
body of Indians, to take Bowles prisoner. Kennard, Payne, Bowlegs and
White King, with seven hundred Seminoles joined him, and they proceeded
with the expedition, to Mickasookie. But M'Girty was on the scout, and
gave notice to Bowles, who escaped to Oclockony River and hid himself.

When the Seminoles arrived, the Creeks professed to give up all hostile
views, and offered to go to St. Marks and make a treaty. The proposal
was acceded to; they went to St. Marks, and under the direction of the
commandant, they entered into a treaty to retire home in a peaceable manner. The Seminoles dispersed. Perryman and Kenhutry returned to
Mickasookie, where they were met by Bowles. He immediately led them
to the great store on Wakully which they took, carried off the goods, and
destroyed the store. A scene of drunkenness and confusion succeeded for
several days. At length an armed schooner called the Sheerwater, arrived
at the fort ; she was deeply laden with dry goods for the store. Bowles
had immediate notice of it. He placed a large number of Creeks in ambush, where the river was very narrow, and when the schooner entered
the river, the Indians rose and took the vessel by surprise. During all
these proceedings Bowles professed great friendship for the Spaniards.

But when he found that the garrison at the fort of St. Marks were off their guard, he made a sudden assault and took the place. Here he rioted for several weeks with his Indians, until Gov. O'Neil arrived from Pensacola, with a detachment of Spanish soldiers and retook the fort. He found Bowles and all his Indians drunk and happy. He drove them off, but punished none of them. Orders were, however, sent to take Bowles ; he fled to the hickory ground in the Creek nation, where a reward being offered, the Indians gave him up. He was conveyed in chains to Cuba, and confined in the Moro Castle, where he is said to have died.

1811.   In January, Mr. Monroe, Secretary of State of the United States, wrote to Gen. George Matthews and Col. John McKee, informing them that he had appointed them Commissioners to carry into effect certain provisions of a late act of Congress, relating to the provinces of Florida. By this commission they were instructed to repair as privately as possible, to Folch, Governor of Pensacola, in the first place, and to accept from him a voluntary cession of the province, if he should deliver it up. If he would not, " should there be room to entertain a suspicion, that a design existed in any other power, to occupy the provinces," the Commissioners were then directed to occupy them by force, if necessary. They were also invested with discretionary powers to arrange the subjects of debts, land titles, offices, and laws :—to remove the Spanish troops, to pay money, etc. The conduct they were to pursue in regard to East Florida, " was to be regulated by the dictates of their own judgment," always recurring to the above instructions as the paramount rule of their conduct. All ordnance and military stores were to be held as Spanish property, to be accounted for by the United States. If the governors should insist on a re-delivery of the provinces at a future day, the Commissioners were directed to stipulate accordingly.

In pursuance of these instructions, the Commissioners proceeded to Pensacola and St. Augustine, and made these propositions to the Spanish governors, but they refused to surrender the provinces. By this time, however, an idea had been generally circulated through Georgia and Florida, that the United States intended to occupy the provinces at any rate. It is said that Gen. Matthews and Mr. McIntosh gave currency to the idea.

1812.   In the month of March, a large collection of Georgians and Floridians, with all the wood-choppers and boatmen in the neighborhood of St. Marys, met at the dwelling-house of Col. Ashley and organised a provisional government, and chose John Houston McIntosh, Esq., Director. He appointed Col. Ashley commandant of the troops. Boats were then collected to convey them to Fernandina, a town on the Spanish shore. Here nine American gun-boats, under the command of

25

Commodore Campbell, formed a line in the harbor and brought their guns
to bear on the fort. A flag was then sent to Don Jose Lopez, who commanded the fort and the Island of Amelia, demanding of him the surrender of the place. He entered into a capitulation, a copy of which here
follows :—

"ARTICLES OF CAPITULATION, made and entered into between Don Justo
Lopez, Commandant of Amelia Island, in the Province of East Florida,
part of the dominions of his C. M. Ferdinand VII, on the one part; and
John H. McIntosh, Esq. commissioner, named, and duly authorised by
the Patriots of the district, of the Province, lying between the Rivers St.
John's, and St. Mary's, including the islands of the same, on the other
part, viz :

1. In consequence of superior forces, all communications and other re-
scources cut off from St. Augustine, being impossible to defend the port and
town of Fernandina ; Don Justo Lopez, agrees to surrender the said port,
and town, to the forces of the Patriots, with all the arms, public provisions,
money, &c., that are in his possession, and all the duties owing to Government.

"2. The Commandant and troops, shall march out with the honors of
war, and after laying down their arms, shall receive their parole not to take
up arms against the Patriots, during the present contest.

"3. Individuals who are considered bona fide residents, who have grants,
or just claims to obtain lands, or lumber by memorial, or evidence, or purchase, shall have them fully guaranteed, and in case of memorial, having
complied, or not, with the conditions specified.

"4. The property of persons, of every description, shall be considered
sacred, and neither examined, or touched, but remain, and be used in the
same manner, as before the capitulation.

"5. The island, twenty-four hours after the capitulation, shall be ceded
to the United States of America, under the express condition, that the port
of Fernandina, shall not be subject to any of the restrictions in commerce,
which at present exists in the United States ; but shall be open as heretofore, to British, and other vessels, and produce, on paying the lawful ton-
nage, and import duties ; and in case of actual war between the United
States and Great Britain, the port of Fernandina, shall be open to British
merchant vessels, and produce, and considered a free port, until the first of
May, 1813.

"6 The inhabitants, who have been bona fide residents of the district,
and have had permission to cut lumber, shall have the same continued until
the first of May, 1813, to the exclusion of others, and exactly as heretofore.

" 7. All vessels of every description shall be protected, and clearances given to any port, as before, (excepting to the coast of Africa,) as well as all vessels of every description, arriving before the first of May, 1813, which have cleared from a Spanish port, three months before the capitulation, and being the property of Spanish subjects of this Island.

" 8. All British, and other merchandise, which has been regularly entered, according to the laws and regulations of the Spanish Government, shall be exported from here, and admitted in the ports of the United States free of duties, until the first of May, 1813 ; and all vessels now owned by Spanish subjects, of this island, shall have the right, and receive registers in the same manner as American vessels.

" 9. The inhabitants of this island who wish to remove shall have twelve months time to sell their property, or remove it, as may be most agreeable, without molestation, and in case of war between the United States and Spain, in said time, said inhabitants shall be allowed to appoint agents to sell their property.

Fernandina, at 4 o'clock P. M. 17th March, 1812.

Signed,

George Atkinson,	Justo Lopez,
George I. F. Clarke,	John H. McIntosh.
Charles W. Clarke,	
Archibald Clarke.	

Fernandina is, at this time, an inconsiderable village, on the North West point of Amelia Island. During the memorable embargo, this place was a resort, for vessels of all nations, wishing to procure American productions, provisions, and lumber, in particular. At the time of this revolution, the town contained about six hundred inhabitants, and was rapidly increasing. Smuggling was carried on to a great extent, and the slave trade was fostered, by speculators in human flesh, from all quarters. There being five fathoms on the bar of St. Mary's, at high water, it affords greater facilities for entrance, than any inlet on the coast ; and the harbor before the town, is capacious and safe.

The day after the capitulation, Lieut. Ridgely was appointed by the director, to take command of the place, and Col. Ashley, with three hundred men, were marched towards St. Augustine, by the Cowford, now Jacksonville. From this place, a detachment was sent to the Laurel Grove, to seize Zephaniah Kingsley, Esq. one of the most able planters in Florida. When brought to head quarters, he was offered his liberty and protection, on condition of joining the Patriots, and was threatened in case of noncompliance, with imprisonment, and confiscation of his goods. He joined them, and was a distinguished partizan, until the whole revolution was checked by the government of the United States. Ashley then proceeded to Fort Mosa, within two miles of St. Augustine; where he was reinforced by Col. Smith, with one hundred American regular troops. Here the Patriots became dissatisfied with Col. Ashley, and deposed him, and elected William Craig, Esq. a planter, and one of the Spanish judges, as commander. Ashley retired with his staff, carrying with him, a large number of horses, that had been collected from the plantations in Florida.

About the middle of June, Estrada, Governor of East Florida, *pr. interim.* fitted up a schooner, with one twenty-four pound, and two twelve pound cannon, and two gun boats, to attack Fort Mosa. The schooner came to anchor before the fort, and began firing, before the gun boats could arrive, little execution was done for some time; at length, a ball passed through the old fort. The Patriots having no cannon, were unable to defend themselves, and retreated to Four Mile Creek, where they encamped. In a short time, Craig removed to the St. John's River, and established a camp, called New Hope.

Here a deputation of the Seminole Indians arrived, and offered their services to the director. They were met in council, by General Mathews, McIntosh, and Kingsley, who advised them to remain peaceably in their towns, and not to interfere with the quarrels of white men. The young warriors, headed by Bowlegs, took this as an insult, and presented themselves before the Governor of Florida, who received them with open arms, and supplied them with arms and ammunition. They immediately planned an attack, to sweep the settlements on St. John's River, and then to cross the St. Marys, and carry fire and sword into the heart of Georgia.

The invasion of Florida, under the direction of General Mathews, an accredited Agent of the American Government, excited the attention of the Spanish and British Ministers, and strong remonstrances were made to our Government, by Don Onis, and Mr. Foster. In consequence of which, General Mathews received from Mr. Monroe, a letter, stating that the President disapproved of the invasion of Florida; inasmuch as neither of the contingencies had occurred, which were to precede all offensive measures. His conduct was attributed to a laudable, but mistaken zeal, for the public welfare. His commission was superseded by the appointment of Mr. Mitchel, Governor of Georgia. Who was instructed " to direct his efforts, in the first instance, to the restoration of that state of things in the province, which existed before the late transactions." To communicate with the Governor of East Florida, and to act in harmony with him, in the attainment of it. But inasmuch as the people, who acted under General Mathews, relied on the countenance and support, of the United States, Governor Mitchel was directed not to expose them, to the resentment of the Spanish authorities, but to require full assurance and satisfaction of their safety : and to apprize all the parties concerned, of his full reliance on it. Governor Mitchel was also requested to use the greatest delicacy towards General Mathews, who, the Secretary observes, " is held in high estimation by the'Government, for his gallant, and meritorious services, during the American revolution, and for his patriotic services since that time." General Mathews withdrew from Florida, and Governor Mitchel, on the 9th of May, wrote to Governor Estrada, in conformity with his instructions. While these commmunications were passing, Captain Williams of the Marines, kept open a communication between Col. Smith, at Four Mile Creek, and Colonel Craig, at Camp Hope,

In the meantime, a company of negroes was collected in St. Augustine, headed by a free black, called Prince. They were sent to form an ambuscade in an impervious thicket, called Twelve Mile Swamp, through which the convoy under the command of Captain Williams had to pass. It was on the 12th of May, about 8 o'clock in the evening, that the wagons entered the swamp. They were escorted by Captain Williams, attended by Captain Fort, of the Milledgeville volunteers, a non-commissioned officer and nineteen privates, besides the drivers. They had but just entered the swamp, when a deadly fire was poured in upon the escort, some of the horses being killed, the wagons blocked up the passage. The non-commissioned officer was killed, both Captains were wounded, Williams mortally, he was shot in eight places ; six privates were wounded. On the second discharge of the regulars, a charge was ordered, but the negroes fled into the woods. After this affair, Governor Mitchell ceased to communicate with Estrada. He wrote to the Secretary of State requesting that a reinforcement might be sent, that St. Augustine might be attacked, and shewed no disposition to withdraw the troops from Florida.

On the 11th of June, Governor Kintelan wrote to Governor Mitchell, stating that if Colonel Smith did not remove from Four Mile Creek within eleven days, he should be obliged to resort to disagreeable measures to compel him. Mitchel answered that the arrangements for the withdrawing the troops were making, but were stopped by the wanton attack on Williams ; that now he should await further orders from the government. The President finding that Congress would not support him in the occupation of Florida, determined to abandon it. Gov. Mitchell was, therefore, very politely superseded by General Pinckney about the middle of October.

About the 20th of September Col. Smith removed his camp to Davis' Creek, twenty miles north of St. Augustine ; the troops had dwindled to two hundred and seventy, and many were sick, all of them nearly naked. The Seminoles, under Bowlegs, were ravaging the country, burning houses and orange groves, and driving off slaves and cattle from every quarter. Certain information was received that Payne, the civil chief, finding it impossible to check the young warriors, who called him an old woman, for withholding them so long at bay, had finally taken command of one party, which was destined to sweep the St. John's settlements and meet Bowlegs at the head of another party in Georgia. Col. Nunen, Inspector General of Georgia, was a volunteer among the Georgia troops in Florida. He solicited permission to march at the head of a party of volunteers and attack the Seminoles in their towns. Permission was granted him, though with considerable hesitation, as it weakened the posts at Davis' Creek and New Hope. One hundred and ten men, many of whom had been discharged, volunteered their services in this expedition. About twenty of them were marines from Captain Williams' company, the balance were from Humphrey's riflemen and Fort's infantry. They rendezvoused at Laurel Grove, the seat of Mr. Kingsley, who sent them in his boats to Judge Facio. Here they received an order to join Col. Smith at Four Mile Creek, from thence they accompanied the party to Davis' Creek, and were then again sent to New Switzerland, the seat of Judge Facio. They were marched the next day to Picolata, and crossed the river. In three days they arrived within seven miles of Payne's Town, situate near the great Allachua Savanna; here they were met by a party of Seminoles, consisting of one hundred and fifty, headed by Payne and Bowlegs, who had just set out on their intended war expedition. It was about twelve o'clock. Col. Nunen immediately formed his little army to receive the Indians. Capt. Humphreys, with the marines, was placed on the right. Captain Fort, of the infantry, on the left, and Lieutenants Reed and Broadnax formed the centre with twenty-five choice men. Two fallen pines shielded the centre in a partial manner against the enemies' fire. The right was defended by a pond, and the left by the head of a swamp.

Payne and Bowlegs led the principal part of their Indians from a swamp, and very gallantly formed them in two columns, in full view of the Americans, and each took the command of a column. Payne was conspicuously mounted, on a white horse, and displayed much judgment during the action. The Indians commenced firing from the swamp, in rear of their main body. A smart firing continued about two hours, to very little effect. Nunen finding that the Indians kept close to their swamp, ordered a hasty retreat. The Indians pursued them with great joy and some confusion, when Nunen charged suddenly upon them; killed a great number and Payne was himself mortally wounded. In a few minutes there was not an Indian to be seen. The Americans then began cutting pine trees, for the purpose of a fort; but half an hour before sunset, the Indians under Bowlegs, returned with a large reinforcement. They rushed from the swamp and charged within one hundred yards of the American line. They were received with a cool and incessant fire, which continued with little intermission, till about nine o'clock at night. It was very dark, each party fired at the flashes of their opponents' guns. Five times, the Indians attempted to force the centre, approaching within twenty paces yelling like devils, but Reed and Broadnax kept their men behind the breast work, and poured in such deadly discharges of buck shot, that the Indians finally retired, carrying off all their dead and wounded, except six, which they probably could not find. Nunen had but one man killed, he received a ball in his forehead, while peeping over the log. The men although extremely fatigued, fixed up their logs in form of a pen, and encamped in it. The Indians besieged them on all sides, and kept them eight days in that situation, killing all the horses except one; that the Georgians killed themselves and eat him, having destroyed all their provisions.

A straggling fire was occasionally heard, and some ineffectual attempts were made, by the Indians, to cut off small foraging parties. On the third evening after the battle, eight men under the command of Lieut. Reed, were detailed to scour the woods, for provisions. They fortunately killed a large bull, about twelve miles north of the fort, and conveyed it in, without molestation. In the night of the eighth day of the seige, Nunen ordered a retreat, despairing of receiving relief. Eight wounded men were placed on litters, and the fort was silently evacuated, while the tents were left standing. At day light, they had proceeded about six miles. The Col. being sick, they halted till afternoon. Here Captain Humphreys made an exertion, to draw off the troops and leave the Col. and the wounded men behind, but the troops would not consent. About three o'clock, they again proceeded towards Picolata. The Indians had discovered them, and fifty of the best warriors, under the young Governor, were placed in ambush in a hammock, beside the trail, where the troops had to pass. They had proceeded about three miles, when the Indians rose upon them. At the first fire, three men fell, two were killed outright, and the other mortally wounded. Nunen ordered a sudden charge, which effectually dispersed the Indians. They were seen no more. The young Governor was killed. The retreat was continued eight miles farther, although the troops were almost famished. They encamped on a ridge of ground between two ponds, where a breastwork was hastily thrown up. An express was sent forward to procure provisions, and foraging parties sent to a short distance to hunt. Two alligators were killed and eaten. On the fourth day, it was determined to conceal the wounded men in a hammock, for the troops had not strength to carry them, while they should attempt to reach the settlement. This step was rendered unnecessary by the arrival of sixteen horsemen with provisions. The wounded men were mounted, and the detachment arrived in two days at Picolata with seventy-five men.

During the first battle, seven men, including the quarter master, surgeon and rear sentinel, deserted, and took away with them the best horses. They reported that the whole detachment was cut off. Mr. Kingsley raised twenty-seven men and sent them to pick up any stragglers they might find, and to collect intelligence. This party reached the battle ground the night of the retreat. Seeing the tents unmolested, they entered the fort, but were surprised to find no occupants ; they concluded that the garrison was killed, and therefore retreated, as fast as possible, the same path they came.

Nunen's expedition deranged the plans of the Seminoles, altogether. The loss of Payne was a serious misfortune to them. They were never successful afterwards. They kept small parties constantly abroad, taking cattle and horses, as well as negroes, from the patriots. Mr. Kingsley's plantation was besieged for nine months ; about forty negroes and all his cattle were stolen. These injuries were again retaliated on the loyalists ; they, also, took every species of property they could carry off, and burnt and destroyed houses, fruit trees, and crops of every description. East Florida became a scene of universal desolation, from which she has never yet recovered.

1813.   In the month of May, the American troops were withdrawn from Florida, and Fernandina was delivered to the Spanish authorities. At the same time a general pardon was proclaimed to all persons concerned in the insurrection.

1814.   In the month of August, Col. Nichols brought into the bay of Pensacola, a British fleet, from which he manned the forts of Barrancas and St. Michael with troops, and hoisted the British flag. On the 31st, he published a proclamation, dated at "Head Quarters, Pensacola," in which he called the people of Louisiana and Kentucky to join his standard, and release themselves from the slavish yoke of the United States. The Indians were abundantly furnished with arms and ammunition, and commissioned to butcher the defenceless inhabitants of the frontier states ; ten dollars a-piece were offered for the scalps of men, women, or children.

On the 6th of November, General Jackson, with five thousand Tennessee militia, and a considerable Indian force, arrived in the neighborhood of Pensacola, and sent Major Pierre with a flag, to inform governor Manrequez of the object of his visit. On approaching one of the fortifications, the flag was fired on by the cannon of the fort, on which the major returned. General Jackson, with the adjutant-general and a small escort, immediately reconnoitered the fort, and found it manned with British and Spanish soldiers. He returned, encamped for the night, and prepared to carry the town by storm in the morning. On the morning of the 7th, he marched with the regulars of the third, thirty-ninth, and forty-fourth infantry, part of General Coffee's brigade, the Mississippi dragoons, part of the West Tennessee regiment, commanded by lieutenant-colonel Hammond, and part of the Chactaws, commanded by Major Blue of the thirty-ninth, and Major Kennedy of the Mississippi troops. Jackson had encpamed on the north side of the town, on the Blakely road, which passed by the forts St. Bernard and St. Michael.

The British naturally supposed that the attack would be made 1814. from that quarter, and were prepared to rake the road with their Nov. 14. batteries; to improve this idea, a part of the mounted men were ordered to show themselves in that direction, while the army was marched past the rear of the forts, to the east of the town, undiscovered, till within a mile of the streets. They were now fully exposed to Fort St. Michael on the right, and seven armed vessels on the left: several block-houses and batteries of cannon defended the streets. They however marched into the town with perfect firmness, and with trifling loss. As the centre column, composed of the regulars, entered, a battery of two cannon was opened upon it, with ball and grape, and a shower of musketry from the houses and fences. They had made but three fires, when the battery was stormed by captain Laval, who was severely wounded, but afterwards recovered. The fire of the regulars soon silenced the musketry of the English. Governor Manriquez met the troops in the streets, and begged Colonels Williamson and Smith, the first officers he met, to show mercy to the town; which request, by orders of the general, was granted, on an unconditional surrender of the town and forts. This was agreed to; and the citizens, with their property, were protected: the fort St. Michael was withheld till twelve o'clock at night. On the morning of the 8th, the fort of Barrancas was blown up with a tremendous explosion, all the cannon spiked except two, and every combustible matter burnt to ashes. This act enabled Nichols to escape from the harbor with his fleet. Captain Woodbine and the Red Sticks were conveyed by Nichols to the Appalachicola River, where a strong fort was built, about twenty-five miles above the mouth, and manned with three hundred troops, to which there was an immediate resort of Indians and runaway negroes. A small fort was also built, about two miles below the junction of the Chattahoochee and Flint Rivers, and one mile south of the old Appalachicola fort.

The principal fortifications of the harbor being destroyed at Pensacola, General Jackson evacuated the town, after holding possession only two days. Major Blue was despatched, with a thousand mounted men, against the forts on the Appalachicola, while the General proceeded to the defence of New-Orleans.

The Spaniards immediately commenced rebuilding the fortifications at Barrancas, in which Nichols proffered his assistance, but the governor answered him, that when he needed any assistance, he would call on his friend General Jackson. The conduct of the General appears to have been satisfactory to the Spaniards. At parting, he notified them, if any injuries had been done to private property, to draw on him for payment : no demands were made ; and although many thousand dollars damages were in 1825 proven to have been suffered, yet General Jackson always insisted, that five hundred dollars of damage had not been sustained.

About the first of August, 1816, Colonel Clinch received advice from General Gaines, that he had ordered a supply of provisions, two eighteen pounders, a five-inch howitzer, and a quantity of ordnance stores, to ascend the Appalachicola River to Camp Crawford ; and in case any opposition should be made by the negro fort, he was instructed to reduce it. He immediately despatched Laforka, an Indian chief, to the bay, for intelligence. He returned on the 15th, with news of the arrival of Lieutenant Loomis in the bay, with two gun vessels, and two transports, laden with provisions, ordnance, stores, &c. On the 17th the Colonel descended the river with one hundred and sixteen chosen men, in two companies, the one commanded by Major Muhlenberg, and the other by Captain Taylor. On the same evening, he was joined by Maj. M'Intosh, with one hundred and fifty Indians ; and the next day, by Captain Isaacs and Mad Tyger, with a large body of Indians, badly armed. The meeting was accidental : the Indians were on a long projected expedition against the negroes, with an intention of restoring them to their owners. A council was held, and an agreement entered into, respecting the campaign. The Indians were ordered to keep parties in advance, and secure every negro that could be found. On the 19th, they brought in a prisoner taken with a scalp, who said that the black commandant of the fort, and a Chactaw chief, with a party of men, had returned the day before to the fort from the bay, where they had taken a boat and killed several Americans. On the 20th, at two o'clock in the morning, Colonel Clinch arrived within cannon-shot of the fort, and landed behind a skirt of woods. Major M'Intosh was ordered to surround the fort with one-third of his men, and to keep up an irregular fire, while Laforka was sent to notify Lieutenant Loomis of the arrival of the troops. The enemy retired within the fort, and kept up a constant roar of artillery, which did no execution, except to frighten the Indians.

On the 23d, Lieutenant Loomis sent intelligence that he had ordered out a watering party, who were attacked by the negroes and Indians ; that a midshipman and two sailors were killed, one sailor taken, and one made his escape : he asked assistance to convoy up the boats. In the evening, the Indians demanded a surrender of the forts, but were treated with great contempt by Garçon, the commandant, and the negroes, who hoisted a red flag with the English jack over it.

On the 24th, Lieutenant Wilson was ordered to descend the river with a party, to assist in bringing up the boats. On the 26th, they arrived within four miles of the fort; and the Colonel went on board the gun-boat 149. After reconnoitering the river in company with the commander of the boat, he ordered Maj. Muhlenberg, and Captain Taylor to cross over to the west side of the river, with their companies, to erect a battery; while Lieutenant M. Garrick, with a party of men and the main body of Indians, were left to secure the rear.

The battery was immediately commenced ; the vessels were ordered up, and the transport Similante was directed to be in readiness to land the artillery under cover of the night. At six in the morning, the two gun-boats sailed up in handsome style, and made fast near the battery. In a few minutes after, they received a shot from a thirty-two pounder : it was immediately returned in a gallant manner. On the fifth discharge, a hot shot from gun-boat No. 154 entered the magazine, and blew up the fort—the explosion was awful, and the scene horrible beyond description. The fort contained about one hundred men, and two hundred women and children : not more than one sixth part were saved. The cries of the wounded, and the yells of the Indians, rendered the confusion most dreadful. The fort was situated on a beautiful high bluff, with a large creek below, and a swamp above, which rendered an approach with artillery extremely difficult. The parapet was fifteen feet high, and eighteen thick, and was defended by one thirty-two, three twenty-four's, two nine, and two six pounders, with an elegant 5½ inch howitzer.

The property taken and destroyed, amounted to two hundred thousand dollars ; three thousand stands of arms, and six hundred barrels of powder were destroyed ; one magazine, containing one hundred and sixty-three barrels of powder, was saved by the victors.

The negro force had been rapidly increasing for one or two years, from runaways : their fields extended fifty miles up the river. The Chactaw chief, and the negro commandant, named Garçon, were put to death by the Indians.

On the 30th, the ordnance and stores, were sent to Camp Crawford, in small boats.

On the 1st of September, Colonel Clinch received notice that a large Seminole force was descending the river to attack him. He immediately placed himself in a position to receive them ; but they dispersed without making an attack, or even showing themselves to the American troops.

The Seminole Indians, together with many vagabond Creeks, excited by Nichols and Woodbine, began, soon after the establishment at Appalachicola, to commit depredations on the frontiers of Georgia. General Gaines, stationed at fort Scott, demanded the murderers ; the Seminoles refused to give them up.

A requisition was made on Georgia for five hundred more troops. The Seminole force was estimated at two thousand five hundred troops. The whole force under General Gaines, when joined by General Glasscock from Georgia, and six hundred Cherokees, amounted to two thousand five hundred. But the Georgia militia were raised for a term of two months only ; they were scarcely collected before they were dismissed, without having effected any essential service.

In December, General Gaines despatched Major Twigs with two hundred and fifty men, to an Indian town, near Flint River, with orders to bring the chiefs to the fort. He arrived early in the morning, and was fired upon by the Indians ; he then returned their fire, and killed four warriors, and wounded many more. In the cabin of Neamathla, the chief, was found a British uniform, of scarlet cloth, with gold epauletts, and a certificate, signed by the secretary of Nichols, stating that Neamathla was a faithful British subject, &c. In a few days after, Colonel Arbukle, with three hundred men, was attacked about twelve miles from Fort Scott ; one of his men was killed, and three wounded. The Indians were defeated with a loss of ten killed. General Gaines despatched Lieutenant Scott, with fifty men, down the river, to meet and support Major Muhlenberg, who was ascending with two boats loaded with provisions. The Seminoles formed an ambuscade on the bank of the Appalachicola, about a mile below the junction of the Flint and Chattahoochee Rivers, at a place where the boats had to pass near the shore. On the first discharge, Lieutenant Scott and the best of his men fell : only six men escaped ; four of these were badly wounded : there were seven women on board, who shared the common fate of the soldiers. Lieutenant Scott had met Major Muhlenberg ; and had left twenty of his men, receiving as many sick, and the women, with some regimental clothing, and was returning to the fort. Two covered boats were sent down the river, under the command of Captain Clinch, to support Scott ; he passed the scene of action on the night after the engagement. On the 15th, the transports, under Major Muhlenberg, were attacked by an Indian force, amounting to twelve hundred, placed on both sides of the river.

The attack was continued, with little intermission, to the 19th; but no impression was made, as the boats were fortified with bulwarks, to secure the men from the enemy's shot. During the four days of the attack, two men were killed, and thirteen wounded. The boats finally arrived safely at Fort Scott. About this time, Captain M'Intosh was attacked in a small house, twelve miles from Fort Scott; although surrounded several days, he defended himself without loss. The Indians at length retired with considerable loss, and the party was called into the fort.

On the 22d of January, 1818, General Jackson concluded a treaty with the Creek Indians; and in February, the Creek warriors agreed to march, under their chief M'Intosh, to fight the Seminoles in Florida.

About the 1st of March, General Jackson arrived at Fort Scott, and took command of the southern army. M'Intosh, with his Creeks, marched down the west bank of the Chattahoochee, with provisions for six days only. On the 12th of March, they arrived at Chaubulle Creek; the waters being high, the Indians were obliged to leave their baggage and provisions, and swim a considerable distance, as the swamp was six miles wide. Hitche-taw town, commanded by the Red-ground King, Econchatti Micco, was surrounded; but he escaped. The Indians were starving; but here they obtained food, and then pursued the fugitives; came up with them, and took fifty-six men, and one hundred and eighty women and children: the rest escaped. A quantity of cattle were taken.

On the 26th, General Jackson left Fort Gadsden, and marched towards the Mickasookie towns, in East Florida. On the 14th, he met an abundant supply of provisions. His force consisted of five hundred regulars, one thousand militia, and eighteen hundred Indians. M'Intosh had not joined him with his seven hundred Creeks. On the 1st of April, the Mickasookie towns were destroyed, and the Fowl towns directly after. The Indians made little resistance. One thousand head of fine cattle, and many thousand bushels of corn, were taken. Jackson then proceeded to St. Mark's: the fort surrendered. Arbuthnot, the prophet Francis, and another Indian chief, were taken here. The two latter were immediately hanged. The fort was strongly fortified, and mounted twenty pieces of heavy ordnance. The garrison were sent to Pensacola. M'Intosh here took about one hundred Indian prisoners.

At Mickasookie, three hundred scalps were found; fifty of them were suspended over the square, on a painted war-pole. They were of every description; men's, women's, and infants': and most of them fresh.

Early in April, General Jackson marched for Suwanne, where about two thousand Indians and negroes were collected, acting under the orders of Arbuthnot, who had a schooner, loaded with arms, ammunition, and military stores, lying opposite the mouth of the Suwanne River, in Wakasasse Bay. On the approach of our troops a show of resistance was made; but the main body of the Indians fled to St. Augustine. They were pursued some distance, when a camp of negroes was discovered in the night; they fought desperately, and did not give way until eighty out of three hundred and forty, were killed. Three hundred Indian women and children, and a great many cattle, were taken prisoners; and the Indians killed many more, to prevent their falling into our hands.

Arbuthnot, ignorant of the proximity of Jackson, approached the camp in a canoe, with two negroes and an Indian, in the evening, and was taken; some boats were then sent down the river, or a raft, and the schooner seized. On the 1st of May a court martial was held on Arbuthnot and Ambrister, of which General Gaines was president. The charges were, exciting the Indians and negroes to commit murders, and supplying them with arms and ammunition; and, secondly, acting as spies. They were both found guilty; Arbuthnot was sentenced to be hung, and Ambrister to be shot. The sentence was immediately executed. Arbuthnot was the bosom friend of Woodbine;* had been in every part of Florida, exciting the Indians and negroes; and was the author of this war. Ambrister was, in appearance, a fine young man, about twenty-five years old, and was a lieutenant of engineers. He was sometimes called Warburton. He died like a weak woman.

The Indian war being thus despatched, the General discharged the Tennessee volunteers; and, with the regulars and friendly Indians, marched for Pensacola.

On the 13th of April, M'Intosh met M'Queen, with a party of Seminoles and fugitive Red Sticks, thirty miles east of Mickasookie; a running fight took place; M'Queen retreated, and M'Intosh pursued, about three hours; killed thirty-seven, took one hundred women and children and six men prisoners, and seven hundred head of cattle. M'Intosh then joined General Jackson at Suwanne.

About the last of this month, Lieutenant Eddy was attacked by a party of Indians, while ascending the Escambia River with a boat loaded with provisions: he had one man killed, and two wounded. Major Young, at Fort Montgmery, put himself at the head of seventy-five mounted men, and pursued the murderers within one mile of Pensacola, were he encountered them at the bayou Texar, killed thirty, and took seventy-four prisoners.

When Jackson had arrived in the neigborhood of Pensacola, and learned that the governor had refused permission for boats loaded with provisions,

---

* Woodbine was lately murdered with his family, at Campeachy, by negroes.—(1837.)

bearing the American flag, to ascend the Escambia, to furnish his troops—while they had issued provisions, arms and ammunition to the savages—he determined to enter the town again, and expel the treacherous Spaniards. The governor was apprised of his approach, and sent to warn him that he would be opposed by the whole Spanish force. The General said he would answer him the next morning, and continued his march. At nine o'clock the next morning he took possession without opposition. The governor had abandoned it, and taken shelter in the fort of Barrancas.

1818. Three days after, (May 28) the army was marched to the Barrancas, and a situation taken about four hundred yards west of the fort, where the men were set to work during the night, to erect a breastwork. In the morning it was discovered by the Spaniards, who commenced firing on it with two twenty-four pounders; the firing was returned with a howitzer. At three o'clock a flag was sent by the fort, and a capitulation followed. The governor and garrison were sent to Havana.

Captain Girt was sent with a company to scour the country between the Pensacola and Perdido Bays; and Captain Bowles to perform a similar service about the Uche and Holmes' old fields, on the Chactawatchee.

Colonel King was left in the command of Pensacola, while Gen. Jackson marched with the volunteers to Tennessee.

A treaty of amity, settlement, and limits, was at length concluded 1819. between His Catholic Majesty and the United States, by which the two Floridas and the adjacent islands were ceded to the latter. West Florida then extended westwardly to the Appalachicola River. The exchange of flags under this treaty took place on the 17th of June 1821, when General Jackson was appointed Governor of the Floridas, with very ample legislative, judicial and executive powers.

Soon after the arrival of Governor Jackson at Pensacola, he received information that the Spanish ex-governor, Calleava, was about to send to Cuba certain papers and documents relating to the titles of lands, in violation of the second article of the treaty of cession : he proceeded to make a demand of them. The ex-governor not complying in the manner and form that was thought proper, an order was issued for his imprisonment, and he was committed to the calabosa, some boxes of papers were seized, and Calleava was soon after released. Several Spanish officers feeling themselves insulted by this degradation of their late Governor, sent to Governor Jackson a spirited remonstrance. This was so highly resented by Jackson, that he issued an order of banishment against twelve of them, and they were hurried from the Territory with the loss of nearly all their property.

It having since been suggested to our general government that many important papers relating to land claims were still detained at the Havana, they sent an agent to examine the archives, and to collect other evidences on that subject. This agency was continued some years at a very great expense, but probably to little advantage.

Governor Jackson removed the dividing line between East and West Florida, from the Appalachicola to the Suwanne River, thus rendering them more equal in size; and established in each, courts with civil and criminal jurisdiction. At the same time he published several ordinances for their direction in the distribution of public justice.

1822.   On the 30th of March, 1822, Congress passed an act, erecting into a territory the two Floridas ; and his excellency, William P. Duval, was appointed governor for three years. A legislative council was formed, which held its first session in June. At this council, West Florida was divided into two counties, Escambia and Jackson. East Florida was also divided into Duval and St. Johns Counties. Congress had, at their last session, established a Superior Court, to be held in each district of the Territory, corresponding to Jackson's division.

The Legislative Council, in June, 1823, passed an act, appointing Dr. William H. Simmons, of St. Augustine, and J. Lee Williams, of Pensacola, Commissioners to locate a common seat of government. In October of the same year, they fixed the site, near the old fields of Tallahasse, the centre of the Fowl towns. In 1824, the town was surveyed, and the public offices were soon after removed to that place ; where the seat of territorial government has since been established.

Two more counties were this year established. Gadsden in West, and Monroe in East Florida. The first embraced the country between Appalachicola and Suwanne Rivers, and the other all the tract of country below Charlotte Bay and the Gulf south, together with the Florida Keys. This year Congress extended the term of the governor to four years.

1824.   The Legislative Council this year established the counties of Walton, Leon, Allachua, and Nassau. Congress established also a Court of Appeals, to be held by the several judges of the Superior Court, each year, in January, at the seat of government : and the Territory was divided into three Judicial Districts. The Eastern, to extend to the Suwanne River ; the Middle to the Appalachicola ; and the Western comprising all the country west of that river.

The Court of Appeals has been found of very little use. The judges having once decided the causes in the Superior Courts of each district, usually confirm their own judgments.

1825.   The counties of Washington and Musquito were this year laid off.

The privilege of electing members of the Legislative Council, was, this year, extended to the citizens of the Territory, by Congress, and the governor was empowered to divide the Territory into thirteen election districts.

1827.   Jefferson County was, this year, set off from Leon.

The Southern Judicial District, was this year established, to em-
1828.   brace the Florida Keys, and the south end of the Peninsula, as far as Indian River and Charlotte Bay.   Hamilton and Madison Counties were set off from Jefferson.

The privilege of electing all officers of the Territory, civil and military, except such as are by law appointed by the President, was
1829.   this year conferred on the citizens of the Territory.

INDIANS.

When Ponce De Leon visited Florida in 1512, the natives were represented to have been a brave and warlike people, who wanted neither courage nor ability to defend themselves.

In the succeeding invasions of Velasquez, in 1518, and of Pamphillo de Narvaez, in 1528, their bravery is equally well supported, but little more of their character is developed.   The Spanish historians of that period were so engrossed in detailing the disasters of their own countrymen, that they did not trouble themselves to examine the character, policy or resources of their enemy.

In 1539, Ferdinand de Soto invaded Florida with an army that bore down all opposition, and for four years swept the face of the country like a desolating tempest.   During this invasion the Indians did not exhibit less bravery than heretofore, but they had to contend with a distinguished chief, and men accustomed to overcome all opposition ; besides, De Soto carried with him a train of artillery and four hundred horses, neither of which had before been seen by the Floridians, and they were utterly astonished by their power and effects.   Notwithstanding these disadvantages they fought many battles with desperation, hand to hand with their invaders, and in some instances, were killed to a man rather than retreat.

In this campaign De Soto was accompanied by men who were capable of making correct observations as to the character, manners, policy, and resources of the natives.   One of these, a Portuguese gentleman, has written a history of the invasion, which is now extant ; the others were carefully examined by Garcilasso de la Vega, the historian of the New World, and by him their narratives were committed to writing.   Both of these writers have painted the natives minutely, and apparently with faithful colors.

27

It is not easy to determine, from what quarter the Florida tribes derived their origin ; or whether they were all connected with the Natchez. At the time the French settled in Louisiana, this nation extended up the eastern bank of the Mississippi, from near its mouth, to the Ohio River. Their traditions bore marks of probability, which have been confirmed, by the discoveries lately made, near the Gulf of Californa and on the Rivers Gila and Yaquisila. These traditions state, that the Natchez came from the South West, from a pleasant country and a mild climate, where they spread over an extensive territory of hills and plains, on the latter of which, their cities were built of stone, the houses several stories in height. Some of these people having been conquered by their enemies, their Sun, or Cacique, sent some of his subjects to discover a place of retreat ; on their return, they reported so favorably of the Mississippi country, that a large colony was sent to take possession of it, where they resided in peace for many years. In process of time, the chief, Sun, came with the balance of the nation, stating that warriors of fire, who made the earth tremble, had visited their country, that the Natchez had assisted them to conquer their enemies, but the strangers then endeavored to enslave their allies; but rather than submit, they had abandoned their country, and joined their friends on the Mississippi.

Whether these people extended over Florida at the time of De Soto's invasion, or whether their example had tended to civilize the neighboring tribes, it is not easy to determine, but they were certainly far ahead of the other American savages, in civilization and all the arts of life. Those in the interior of the country, were also more civilized than those of the sea coast and islands.

At the time of De Sotos' invasion, the country must have contained, according to La Vega, five times the number of inhabitants, that it does at this time ; this would have rendered wild game scarce, and would have necessarily induced the natives to adopt habits of industry and improvement. At the same time, the abundance of fish and turtle on the sea coast, would lead to an erratic and idle life. The lands on the sea coast are also much poorer than those near the heads and sources of the rivers. There is no doubt that the mildness of the climate and the facility of procuring vegetable food, both tended to improve the social habits of the people. Accordingly, at Ocala, perhaps near Fort King, La Vega describes a town of six hundred houses, and a few miles farther, another at Ochile (Chichila) of five hundred houses, enclosed with a regular palisado, and containing some buildings one hundred and twenty feet long. At the capital of Vitachucco, the cacique raised an army of six thousand men in four days. for the purpose of repelling their invaders. These people subsisted on fruits and grains, the produce of their industry, and they had abundance to spare to the Spanish army of twelve hundred men and four hundred horses.

After the evacuation of the country by the Spaniards, the inhabitants were greatly diminished; during the invasion vast numbers had perished, both by the sword and by their extreme fatigues, in consequence of their being obliged to convey the Spanish baggage from one province to another. Indeed, they were so much weakened, that their enemies gained advantages over them, which they never could have done, but for these disasters.

In 1564, Philip the II of Spain, conceived the project of converting the Indians of Florida, to the Catholic faith. For this service, he selected several missionaries, from the several orders of Spanish Friars, the most numerous as well as the most intelligent, of which, were Franciscans. These he sent under the protection of three thousand men, commanded by Don Pedro Menendez De Avilla, who was appointed Adelantado. The fleet anchored in the sound west of Anastatia Island, about the middle of September and a village was immediately commenced, on the western bank of the sound, and called St. Augustine. A convent was also established for the missionaries and called St. Helena. From this place, they extended their labors over the whole country, as far west as the Mississippi and north to the Appalachean mountains. Few men have been more zealous or more successful than Menendez and his successor Alas, in the propagation of the Catholic faith. During the twenty-five years which they resided in Florida, they established several hundred societies of Indians, who sent regular deputies to the great convent of St. Helena. The missionary posts were establishments of much importance; they were permanent stations where some special missionaries were permitted by the Indians to reside, to preach and to instruct the children of the natives, in the Spanish language, religion and the arts of life. In order to assist in these labors, several Spanish families were permitted also to settle at the posts; they often encouraged marriages between the young persons of each nation, until they became like one people; the country was extensively improved, and became very populous and very prosperous.

At this period, Florida was divided between the Appalaches, who dwelt west of the Suwanne, and the Yamasees, who spread over the district between the Suwanne and the Atlantic, extending as far north as South Carolina; these nations had long been at war with each other, but were reconciled by the Spaniards, and lived from that time in friendship and peace.

De las Alas succeeded Menendez, as Adelantado of Florida; the same policy pursued by his predecessors, was improved by him. In 1583, he united under the protection of Spain, the Chickasaws, Tocaposcas, Apacas, Tamaicas, Apiscas, and Alabamas; and during the next year, the Chischemacas joined the confederacy.

In 1680, de las Alas was succeeded by Don John Menyers de Cabrane. He became a bitter enemy to the Yamasees, suspecting them of being too friendly with the English of Carolina ; so far did his resentment extend, that he publicly executed their Cacique, Nichosatly. The English taking advantage of this event, engaged the Yamasees in a furious war with the Spaniards, which continued several years, until Cabrane was recalled to Spain. He was succeeded by Ayola as Governor.

From this time till 1704, a space of fourteen years, the Indians of Florida were alternately courted by the Spanish and French colonies in West Florida, and some of the young warriors were induced to take arms, but the body of the natives, remained peaceably at home, cultivating their lands. From this happy state, they were at length roused by the invasion of the Creeks, under the command of Governor Moore, of South Carolina. Two years before, Moore had attacked and beseiged St. Augustine, but was driven from thence with disgrace. To wipe off this stain, he, with a few more daring Carolinians, put themselves at the head of one thousand Creek warriors, who had ever been the enemies of the Florida tribes, and pro- ceeding down the Flint River, their first attack was made on Lewis's fort, on the east side of the Oclockony River, and about two and a half miles west of our Tallahasse ; this fort being carried, the whole country was swept of inhabitants, to the gates of St. Augustine. Many were destroyed, and the balance carried as slaves to the north side of Savanna River, and made to till the land. Two or three succeeding inroads cleared the islands and coast of the Gulf of the Muspa and Caloosa tribes, as far as Cape Sable, and the Florida keys. The ruins of the Spanish monasteries and other im- provements, are still seen through middle Florida, and have for a long time been subjects of wonder, to inquiring travellers.

In 1717, Governor Ayola succeeded in reconciling the Florida Indians with the Creeks, and planned a general attack upon the English settle- ments, in Carolina. The fragments of the Yamasees, and Appalaches, were united with the Creeks on the southern borders of the English settle- ments ; while the Congarees, Catowbas, and Cherokees, fell upon their western borders. The Indians being totally defeated by Governor Craven, the confederacy was dissolved, and the Florida Indians retired under the walls of St. Augustine.

The next year, 1718, Ayola was succeeded by Malina, who put a stop to the Indian incursions against the English. He even drove them from their homes, near St. Augustine and St. Marks. This latter fort had been built by order of Governor Ayola, at the particular request of the scattering natives, and the Uchees who had removed from the neighborhood of Coweta, and was intended both to protect a trading house, and guard against the northern Indians. The natives were also ordered to remove from the neighborhood of the English colonies, and were compelled by an armed force to abandon their fields, then nearly ripe, and to encounter starvation in the forests, exposed to those enemies that the Spanish cupidity had created against them. The consequence was, that vast numbers of them, men, women, and children, died of want and disease.

After this, the surviving natives having retired to the southern part of the peninsula, rested from war; but in 1725, Governor Malina, got embroiled with his English neighbors. He then sent to Macono, the Yamasee chief, to assist him, and defend the catholic faith against the heretics. This was ever the prevailing argument with those dupes of the catholic church. They forgot their injuries, and returned to fight the English; and they ravaged the frontier settlements of Georgia, with fire and sword, until Colonel Palmer again drove them for shelter, under the walls of St. Augustine. Trifling incursions were kept up between the Indians and the English, until 1748, when a treaty between Spain and England laid the Savages at rest.

In 1763, when these provinces were ceded to the English, the natives generally, retired from the towns, and commenced raising horses and cattle, in the deep forests. Here they continued to increase both by natural population, and by accessions from other tribes. The country was extensive, and became full of game : the climate was mild and produced many fruits; all these circumstances tended to invite the neighboring Indians to collect and settle, especially around those pleasant prairies and old fields, abounding in peach and persimon orchards, and wild orange groves. By degrees they grew to a small nation, and were called Seminoles, or wanderers.

Except some trifling disturbance made in 1792, by an Englishman named Bowles, who joined the Seminoles, and excited them to some acts of hostility against the Spaniards, Florida remained quiet, until the Americans under Mathews, and McIntosh, invaded East Florida, during the years 1812, 13, and 14. At this time, being excited by the Spaniards in St. Augustine, their young warriors could not be restrained, but contrary to the advice of Payne, their civil chief, they committed many depredations on the American inhabitants. They were at length attacked near their towns, in Allachua, by Colonel Newnan of Georgia, where Payne was killed, and many of his warriors were cut off.

In 1818, the Creek Indians under McIntosh, their chief, attacked, and burned the Fowel towns on the borders of the Mickasookee Lake, and shortly after, General Jackson broke up the main force of the Seminoles, near the Suwanne River, taking most of their women and children. The remaining warriors under Bowlegs, a brother of Payne, being wounded, took refuge under the walls of St. Augustine.

Payne was the civil, and Bowlegs the military chief of the Seminoles; they were the sons of Cowkeeper, a distinguished chief of East Florida. After the death of Payne, the eldest son of Solachoppo, or Long Tom, succeeded him, but dying early of a debauch, his younger brother, Micanopy, became chief of the Seminoles. His father resided at Wealusta, or Black Creek, and owned many cattle, aud some slaves. He is a large fat man, rather obtuse in intellect, but kind to his people and slaves. One of them, Abraham, has long been an interpreter, and as such accompanied his master, and a deputation of Seminoles to Washington City. After his return, Micanopy gave him his freedom; he is a sensible shrewed negro, and has ever been a principal counsellor of his master. Jumper was a Creek, and one of the leaders at the massacre of Fort Mimms, in 1811. He came to Florida after Jackson's campaign, and married a sister of Micanopy; since that time he has continued with the Seminoles.

In 1823, 18th September, a treaty was concluded at Moultrey Creek, in East Florida, between the United States and the Indians of Florida, by which the latter agreed to surrender all their improvements in the Territory, except a part of the eastern peninsula, where they were to reside for twenty years. To this district they were removed during the winter of 1824, except some of their chiefs, who were granted reservations in West Florida. Hicks, one of the chiefs of the Mickasookies, removed with them, and retained the principal control of them till 1825, when he is said to have been shot or poisoned by some of Jumper's partisans. The Mickasooke Indians were principally Creeks, who, at the close of the campaign of 1818 had taken refuge in Florida; they had settled on the borders of the Mickasooke Lake, the Oscilla River and Tallahasse; their settlements were usually termed the Fowel Towns. Neamathla, a fugitive Creek, was their principal chief. Hicks lived near San Pedro Lake. Neamathla was opposed to the treaty of Moultrey Creek, but Hicks was in favor of it. Neamathla was with difficulty induced to sign the treaty. Two miles square of land on Rocky Comfort Creek, embracing the Tuphulga village, were reserved to him. He never resided on it, but returned to the Creek nation. The Mickasookies always expressed great unwillingness to leave the middle district of Florida. After settling on the Peninsula, they petitioned the government, through their agent, Col. Humphreys, to extend their lines farther north, which was finally granted, together with additional issues of provisions; still they continued dissatisfied, and during the years 1835 and 6 many of them were disposed to emigrate, and had their agent then been permitted to accompany them, it is believed that the whole nation would have left the Territory; but he was soon after superseded by Major Phagan, and he was in turn succeeded by General Willey

Thompson. Complaints were often made by the inhabitants of Allachua that the Indians stole their cattle, and one or two acts were passed by the Legislative Council to restrain them within their boundary lines, and to prevent any intercourse or trading between them and the white inhabitants of Florida. In May, 1835, an Indian named Olapotha Hajo, who had a camp at the head of Salt Spring, on the west side of Lake George, came to Switzers, a new plantation at the mouth of Silver Spring, and shot one of the laborers, a Captain Farnham, through the left shoulder. Farnham recovered, but it was evidently the intention of the Indian to kill him, as he took deliberate aim with his rifle. The plantation where this took place belonged to General Clinch; the family of Switzer soon after abandoned the country, and the Indians, about nine in number, presently after came and robbed the house of such articles as they could carry away, and then burned the buildings to the ground, taking away with them a negro boy, who soon after escaped and returned to his master, Mr. Woodruff. About this time, Mr. Kerr, a public surveyor, while running lines west of Lake George, was fired on by the savages and driven off. Near the same period, Captain Willy, of the schooner Jane and Mary, ascended the St. John's as far as the mouth of the Ocklawaha, with a cargo of ammunition and military stores for Fort King; the schooner was visited first by a few Indians, but afterwards by more, until about the third day their numbers amounted to forty or fifty. They grew impudent, and camped nearly around him. The schooner was well armed, but the crew consisted of the Captain and only three men. There can be no doubt of the intention of the savages to take the schooner, but Captain Willy, elevating one of the six pound field pieces over one of the Indian camps, fired it off. It had the desired effect; the Indians soon scattered and left him.

About the month of October, Major Lewellen Williams, and six of his neighbors, discovered a party of Indians near the Kenopaha Pond, butchering one of their beaves. They disarmed five of them, and flogged some of them, but one got away, and two Indian hunters at the same time coming up fired on the whites; a smart skirmish ensued, in which two of the Indians were killed, and three of the whites wounded; one afterwards died of his wounds.

Soon after this affair, the express riding from Tampa Bay, to Fort King, was murdered in a most shocking manner, by these Indians.

Many other indications of the hostile feelings of the Seminoles and Mickasookies were manifested during this summer, but they were but little regarded by the Floridians; they had long been accustomed to hold them in contempt, and treat them with indignity.

General Willey Thompson, the Indian agent at Camp King, however, about the 28th of October, notified the secretary of war, that about two-thirds of the Indians manifested an obstinate determination to disregard the treaty of Payne's Landing, and to resist a removal.

The agent further stated, that immediately after the Indians had received their annuities, they purchased an unusual quantity of powder and lead, which he was informed, they had added to much greater stores, that they had before hoarded up. He advised that a large military force should be immediately placed in the nation, both to overawe the savages, and control designing persons, who he supposed were exciting the Seminoles to war. Those Indians disposed to emigrate, were commanded by the chiefs Holaste, Emathla, Fucaluste, Hajo, and Charley Emathla; their numbers are supposed to amount to four or five hundred, but great exertions were made to prejudice them against the white population, and to make war rather than remove.

In this exertion, none were more zealous than Powel or Oseola, a mixed blooded Creek of the Red Stick tribe, whose mother was a half breed, and his father an Englishman. He was without property or rank, until a daring spirit, about this time, distinguished him, before all his countrymen. It was at a talk held sometime during the summer of 1826, with the Indian agent, that Powel gave him the lie, said the country belonged to the Seminoles, and the whites had better be off; flourishing his knife in defiance. General Thompson reported his conduct to Colonel Fanning, who commanded the post, and Powel was seized by the guard, and put in irons. For some time he manifested great obstinacy and sullenness; finding this a useless course, he assumed a cheerful countenance, and pleasant demeanor, professed a willingness to sign the articles for removing, and many of his friends the Mickasookies, of whom he had about seventy-five attached to him, came and voluntarily signed the treaty with him. He was at length released, and for some time he kept up the mask of friendship, and assisted the agent in restraining the Indians, especially the Mickasookies, from wandering out of their boundaries; in some instances he inflicted severe chastisements on them.

About the first of October, however, he cast off all connection with the agent, and united with Jumper and his adherents, and was the first to dip his tomahawk in blood. Charley Emathla was his first victim. The United States had agreed to purchase the cattle of the emigrating Indians, at a fair valuation: to this end, commissioners were sent to appraise them, on a certain day, which was generally advertised. The hostile chiefs forbid the collecting and penning of the cattle, and threatened death to any that should disobey the order. Charley Emathla, one of the most sensible and prudent chiefs of the Seminoles, disregarding the threats of the hostile chiefs, about the 26th of November, came into Fort King, with his three daughters, and notified Colonel Yancey, one of the commissioners, that his cattle would be duly penned for appraisement; on his return from the fort, he was beset by Powel, and about twenty of his followers, who pierced him with sixteen bullets. This murder struck such a terror through the Seminole tribe, that a stop was put to the further collection of cattle. A great number of people, who had collected from every part of the neighboring country, to purchase cattle and horses, quickly retired to their homes. As no attempt was made by the officer in command at Fort King, to obtain satisfaction for, or to restrain these repeated aggressions of the hostile Mickasookies, the friendly Seminoles became impressed with the idea, that the whites were too weak to defend them, and they reluctantly submitted to the Mickasookies; many of them at length joined in their war parties. From this period, Powel's authority and importance daily increased, which he supported by daring acts of hostility against the Florida troops.

In October, General Clinch advised the Secretary of War, that there was danger to be apprehended from the hostile chiefs, and required an addition to the troops, located in that vicinity. It seems that, in consequence of the representations of the General, and the Indian agent, fourteen companies of regular troops, were ordered to hold themselves in readiness, to march to Florida, from different posts, but such was the distance, and difficulty of transportation, that none of them had reached Fort King on the first of January.

On the 21st December, Major Dade arrived at Tampa Bay, from Key West, with Company A. Infantry, thirty-nine men, and a small supply of cartridges; to this was joined Gardner's Company of 2d Artillery, and Frazier's Company 3d Infantry, fifty men each. This force marched for Fort King on the 24th, attended by a 6 pounder, drawn by oxen, and one light wagon with ten days provision. They proceeded that day to Little Hillsborough River, seven miles from Tampa. The field piece was, however, left four miles from Tampa, the oxen having failed. Major Dade sent back an express, requesting Major Belton to furnish another team, and push forward the field piece; this was done the next day, and the piece reached the camp about nine o'clock in the evening. On reaching the Big Hillsborough, the detachment was delayed some time, on account of the bridge. having been burned by the Indians.

On the 27th they reached the Big Ouithlacoochee. On the 28th, they continued their march about six miles, when they were suddenly attacked in an open pine country, by an unseen enemy. The attack commenced on the advance guard, but immediately extended along the front and left flank; several volleys were fired before an enemy could be seen. The first dis-

28

charge was the most fatal ; Major Dade was killed and nearly half the command disabled. The remaining troops immediately took shelter behind trees, and Lieut. Bassinger poured in five or six rounds of canister upon the Indians, which checked them for some time ; they retreated over a small ridge and disappeared. When the Indians commenced the attack, they were squatting behind trees in the high grass ; after firing several vollies, they rose simultaneously, and yelled horribly. Capt. Frazier fell probably at the first fire, as he rode to the advance guard. Lieut. Mudge was mortally wounded, Lieut. Keys had both arms broken, they were bound up, and he reclined against some logs until he was killed late in the action ; Lieut. Henderson had his left arm broken, but continued to load and fire his piece, until late in the second attack, when he was killed. Capt. Gardener, Lieut. Bassinger and Doct. Gatlin were the only officers who escaped unhurt by the first volley.

On the retreat of the Indians, Capt. Gardener immediately commenced cutting pine trees, and erecting a small triangular breast-work, with the logs. In about three quarters of an hour, their labor was interrupted by a return of the Indians. They came in vast numbers with horrid yells, and commenced a cross fire on the breast-work with deadly execution. Lieut. Bassinger continued to fire the six pounder, until all the artillerists were cut down by the enemy's shot. Capt. Gardener was at length shot down ; Doct. Gatlin with two double barreled guns, continued behind the breast-work firing on the Indians, until late in the action, when he fell and Lieut. Bassenger was severely wounded. About two o'clock the last man fell, and the Indians then rushed into the breast-work, headed by a heavy painted Indian, who believing that all were dead, made a speech to the savages. They then stripped off the accoutrements of the soldiers, and took their arms without offering any indignity ; they retired in a body in the direction from which they came.

Soon after the Indians had retired, about fifty negroes galloped up on horesback ; when they reached the breast-work they alighted, and tied their horses. Then commenced a horrible butchery. If any poor fellow on the ground shewed the least signs of life, the thick lipped savages sank their tomahawks in their brains, and with their knives stabbed and mutilated them amid yells and blasphemies. Lieut. Bassenger being still alive, started up and begged the wretches to spare his life; they mocked at his prayers, while they mangled him with their hatchets till death came to his relief.

After stripping all the dead, the negroes took the field piece and cast it into a pond which was not far distant, shot the oxen, and burnt the wagon and gun carriages. Shortly after the negroes retired, a soldier named Wilson, of Captain Gardener's company, crawled out from among the mangled bodies, and discovering that Rawson Clark was still alive, he asked him to go with him back to Tampa. As he jumped over the breast-work, Clark was about to follow, when an Indian started from behind a tree and shot him dead. Clark again crawled down among the dead bodies, and laid still till nine o'clock in the evening; he then crawled out, and with De Coney, another wounded man, made the best of their way for Tampa. The next day they met an Indian on horseback, with his rifle; they separated, one ran to the right and the other to the left. De Coney was pursued and shot by the savage; Clark, after reaching a scrub, hid himself; the Indian came near him, searching the bushes, but at length rode off. Stiff and cold, Clark camped that night in the woods, surrounded by wolves, who scenting the blood, howled fearfully around him. The next day he reached Tampa and recovered of his wounds. Another soldier, named Thomas, who was partly suffocated beneath the bodies, recovered and found himself in the hands of an Indian that he knew; he gave the Indian six dollars and was permitted to escape. He reached the Fort at Tampa in safety.

Jumper took the command of the Indians in this massacre, although it is stated that Micanopy was compelled to commence the attack by firing the first gun. Lewis was the guide of Major Dade; he was frequently absent from the troops in the march; he fell on hearing the first gun, but directly after joined the enemy, and read to them the despatches and papers found upon the dead. He was a free negro, formerly the property of General Clinch.

The number of Indians engaged in the above horrid affair was very great, and when it is recollected that a large party were at the same time at Wakahoota, and another party at Allachua, under Powell, we shall discover that the numbers of the Indians had been greatly underrated, and that their courage and ability to carry on the war, had been utterly misunderstood by the American government.

The news of Emathla's murder reached General Clinch at St. Augustine, about the 1st of December. He was too well acquainted with the savage character to doubt the object of this daring stroke of Powel. He immediately started for Micanopy by way of Jacksonville. From the latter place he addressed a circular to the inhabitants of Duval and Nassau counties, inviting two hundred volunteers to repair to the frontier posts, to check any attempts of the hostile Indians against the inhabitants. The population of these counties cheerfully responded to the call, and by the 15th, several companies, under the command of Colonels Warren and Mills, were at Newnansville, on their way to Fort Drane, where they were met by Gen. Call, at the head of five hundred men from Middle Florida.

On the 17th they arrived at the Allachua Prairie, where they were met by news that the enemy had appeared in force at Wakahoota, where they had burned and ravaged the plantations of Capt. Priest and others, and had wounded several men, among whom was a son of Capt. Priest. Gen. Call ordered a detachment under the command of Capt. Richards, to escort three wagons and a cart containing the ammunition and stores of Col. Warren's command, to proceed by the Allachua Prairie to Micanope. They proceeded round the west end of the prairie, it being full of water, until they reached Black Point, on the south side. W. Ives was placed one hundred paces in front with five men, and J. Sumeral with the same number in the rear; thirteen continued in the centre with the wagons. The advanced guard had passed the point unmolested, but when the teams came opposite, and about forty yards from the point, a severe fire was opened upon them from the bushes. The front and rear guards were ordered to the centre, but five only obeyed, to wit: Ives, Sumeral, Sparkman, and two teamsters without guns. Tillis fired three times and was then shot through the body. The Captain and all the rest ran off on the first fire. One horse was killed in the harness, and one broke loose. Ives and Sparkman placed Tillis in the cart and were driving it off, when three Indians ran from the brush to stop them ; they were all cut down by the fire of those at the cart, who then retreated back, until they were met by Col. Warren. During their retreat the cart-horse received three balls and on reaching a spot of dry ground he fell dead. The Indians took the ammunition from the wagons and burned one of them. Soon after Capt. M. Lemore arrived and charged up to the hammock with his Orderly Sergeant, Hurst, but was not followed by his company. Hurst was shot through the body and fell. Another attempt was made to charge the hammock, but the troops, with the exception of fifteen, refused, and the whole retreated to Fort Crum. One of the men, named McKee, was shot dead, Weeks and Tillis died of their wounds, Hurst recovered.

On the 20th the troops again marched for Micanope ; the Indians had left Black Point, but on proceeding to Malachi Hagan's, half a mile north of Micanope, they saw his buildings on fire, and Indians running from them into a wet dense hammock. General Call ordered the hammock to be surrounded and scoured. On this service Capt. Lancaster received a dangerous wound from a rifle ; his company soon disposed of five of the savages : no more were found. Capt. Lancaster since recovered.

On the 28th, the same day that Major Dade was cut off, Powel, with twenty of his band, came to the house of Mr. Erastus Rodgers, the suttler at Fort King, situated about two hundred and fifty yards from the pickets. Rodgers was at dinner with a party of friends, when the Indians fired on them through the door, and then burst into the house. Rodgers and his company jumped out of the window and fled, some towards Fort King, and some towards a neighboring hammock ; the former escaped ; the latter, consisting of Rodgers, Siggs, and Hitzler, together with Gen. Wiley Thompson, the Indian Agent, and Lieut. Constantine Smith, who were walking out in that direction, were shot dead. The body of Gen. Thompson was pierced with fifteen balls, and that of Rodgers with sixteen. All of them except Suggs, were scalped and horribly mangled. All this occurred in open day light, in the face of a company of men, who heard the Indian rifles, but suffered the savages to escape unmolested. A negro woman, cook of Rodgers, hid behind a barrel and escaped observation. Powel entered the house, looked around, kicked over the table, and retired.

On the 24th, General Call, with the volunteers from Middle Florida, and Colonel Warren's command of East Floridians, in all, five hundred men, formed a junction with General Clinch, at Fort Drane. These troops had been levied for one month only, and their time was nearly expired. In order to avail himself of their services, General Clinch ordered Colonel Fanning from Fort King, with three companies of artillery ; they arrived on the 27th, still they were detained till the 29th, for two detachments that had been sent out on the 25th, to scour the neighboring country. These having arrived, the little army marched for the Ouithlacooche, in the direction of Powel's town.

On the morning of the 31st, at four o'clock, the baggage was left under the care of Lieutenant Dansy, three miles from the Ouithlacooche. General Clinch pushed forward the troops, in hopes to surprise the Indians on the bank of the river. Several friendly Indians, among whom were Holate Emathla and his son, served as guides, and promised to lead the army to a ford that should be only waist deep. They were mistaken ; when the advanced guard reached the river at early day-light, they found it both deep and rapid. A hammock of thick woods, two hundred yards deep, lined the river's bank. The negro guide stated that the Indians probably occupied this ground. The army was halted, and Adjutant Talcot was ordered forward with a few soldiers to reconnoitre the forest ; he was accompanied by Major Lytle. No Indians were found, but their tracks were numerous ; a pen extended into the water, and showed that cattle had lately been crossed. Opposite the pen, they perceived, on the other side of the river, a small canoe.

These facts being reported, Captain Mellon, and Lieutenant Talcot, offered to swim across the river, and fetch the canoe, but General Clinch forbade them ; he, however, permitted two of Captain Mellon's soldiers to cross, who soon bailed out the water, and brought the fragile bark to the shore ;it could bear only seven or eight men at a time. Captains Mellon and Drane soon had their companies across the stream, and paraded on the other bank. About seventy yards below this crossing, there was a small island, and some of the troops fell to chopping trees on the bank and lodging their tops upon the island, to form a temporary bridge; many of the trees were swept down the current. Impatient of this delay in crossing, Maxey Dill, one of Warren's volunteers dashed his horse into the river, and although two or three times dislodged from his back, he safely reached the other bank. Colonel McIntosh and Major Lytle, aids of General Clinch, then swam their horses across; a few of the men, but none of the officers followed them. Two or three of the friendly Indians swam, and drove across about three hundred of the horses. It was eleven o'clock before General Clinch, Colonels Parkhill, Reed, Warren, Mills, Major Cooper, Captains Scott, Bailey, and some others got over. All the regulars, one hundred and ninety-five, and twenty-seven volunteers under Warren and Mills, were crossed. The south bank was a wet swamp, for two hundred yards; this was succeeded by a thick scrub, beyond this there was a dry plain; the trail led through this plain, and here the regulars were formed by Colonel Fanning, in double files, while Gen. Clinch was superintending the construction of the bridge, in order to facilitate the crossing of Call's volunteers. The regulars were surrounded on the south-west and north by thick scrub; about forty yards on the east there was a dense hammock. The soldiers being weary were permitted to sit at ease, some were lying on the ground, sentinels having been posted, some of them in the hammock. The timber, vines and brush were so thick that the Indians crept up very near to them before they were discovered. The sentinels were compelled to fly, and gave the alarm. The regulars were immediately in line on the plain; an Indian soon discovered himself, when Capt. Mellon immediately fired at him. The savages then raised their yell, and opened a galling fire upon the troops, wholly unsheltered as they were. It was one o'clock.

The moment of alarm brought General Clinch, with his Aid, Major Lytle, to the plain, where he assumed the command of the regulars. To extend the line and reduce the ranks was a matter of some difficulty, and occupied considerable time, under the heavy firing of the enemy. Several charges were made to the edge of the hammock, but it was too thick to enter in any order, and the line was ordered to return. It was believed that some soldier gave this order; who he was, could never be discovered. It passed along the line twice, and was in both instances obeyed.

The Indians made an attempt to turn the right flank, but Captains Gates and Mellon, being ordered to charge them, they fled from the bayonets. The Indians continued their fire on our front, and also upon the left flank beyond the line of regulars, where the twenty-seven East Florida volunteers were stationed ; these men however, being sheltered by the trees, gallantly sustained their post. This however was a critical period, many of the officers were badly wounded and the volunteers, though every moment expected, did not cross the bridge to the support of the regulars. Gen. Clinch's horse had received two wounds, and was staggering under him, Maj. Lytles horse was shot through and ultimately died ; Col. Warren and Major Cooper, Capt. and Lieut. Graham and many of the soldiers were badly wounded. All fought for their lives, but the advantage was in favor of the savages. After the last charge, the line had retired thirty or forty yards. The word halt was given by Gen. Clinch and loudly repeated by all the officers. The line halted, the Gen. dismounted, drawing his sword, approached the line and addressed his men. He spake with much feeling, told them they must defend their post, that he was there ready to die in the discharge of his duty, and there must be no retreat. He remounted, ordered another charge, the enemy fled at every point and the battle ended.

After the last charge was made, Gen. Call rode on to the field, and addressing Gen. Clinch said, sir you must retreat across the river. Gen. Clinch asked him why he must retreat. Call answered that the militia would not support the regulars, and as their time expired the next day, they would return. Under these circumstances Gen. Clinch was compelled to submit, and accordingly gave orders to withdraw the regulars across the river. In this, the enemy, though numerous, did not attempt to molest them.

Col. Parkhill, Ajt. Gen. from the beginning to the close of the battle, distinguished himself by constant active services. Col Reed continued on the field, although he and his horse were both wounded, till he was ordered to the river for the volunteers, who were in vain ordered to the scene of action.

Majors Welford and Gamble, aids of Gen. Call were engaged in most of the action. Col. M'Intosh, who lost his horse, took post with his rifle on the left, with Majors Cooper and Gamble, Captains Scott and Baily with the other twenty-seven volunteers, five of whom were wounded. Gen. Clinch was shot through his cap and coat sleeve. The dead and wounded were removed under the care of Doct. Waightman, who came over to the scene of action to attend them. Four men were killed and fifty-two wounded. After the last charge, many of the Indians were found dead on the field, but their whole loss is unknown.

This battle was fought within three miles of Oseola's town ; the Indians were flushed with their triumph over poor Dade, and fought with desperate firmness ; their line at one time, extended more than half a mile in a circular form and threatened to surround the little band of regulars, until they were broken by the last effective charge.

Could the General have availed himself of even half of the volunteers it is more than probable that he would have ended the Seminole war at once; *but his repeated orders to bring them into the field were disobeyed,* and had the regulars and the 27 veteran militia been cut off, to a man, their five hundred brethren would probably not have been allowed, by their commander to afford them any assistance. For this disobedience of orders, he was afterwards promoted to the command of the army in Florida, and we shall see to what purpose.

Gen. Clinch was now left with one hundred and fifty men, worn down with fatigue, to protect Forts Drane, Micanopy and Oakland, and to guard the trains of wagons necessary to bring from Gareys Ferry, sixty miles distant, the provisions and stores for their support.

On the first of Jan. 1836, Maj. Stephens arrived with twenty volunteers, at Picolata, from Savanna, with two fine brass field pieces. They were followed the next week, by forty more volunteers, and from this time, companies from different parts of Georgia continued to arrive, during the winter. Provisions and military stores also were sent to Picolata, and thence by trains of wagons to Fort King, Fort Drane and Micanopy. The settlements were generally broken up in the centre of the Peninsula, part of the inhabitants left the Territory, and the remainder erected stockades and defended themselves.

Philip, with his gang of murderers, commenced hostilities on the eastern sea coast. The settlements at Musquito were destroyed, and the slaves carried off. Two companies of militia were sent to Tomoko under Maj. Putnam and Capt. Keogh. The settlements on the Halifax River were abandoned.

On the 17th, Major Putnam embarked his company on board three boats, and proceeded down the Halifax River, to Dun Lowton, to bring away the corn, and other stores left there, by the family of Mrs. Anderson; they found the house burning, but encamped near the ruins, for the night. Early in the morning, two Indians were discovered near the encampment; these were fired upon by Mr. Dummet; one of them fell, the other ran off. A brisk engagement ensued. About forty Indians first appeared, in the direction of the Sugar House; they were soon driven back, but other parties of ten and twelve, came in from different points, and in a short time out flanked them, so that the ruins of the building were no longer a shelter. As they were greatly out numbered by the savages, a retreat was ordered to the boats, which were anchored in the stream. In regaining the boats, most of their ammunition was wet, and rendered useless. The savages pursued them to their boats, one of which they took, compelling two young men, Marks and Gould, to swim to Pellican Island. Marks swam the east arm of the river, to Anastatia Island, and escaped, but Gould was overtaken by the savages, and shot. Seventeen were wounded, two mortally, and two more so badly, that they will never entirely recover.

About this time, information was received, that General Scott had been appointed to the command of the troops in Florida, and that General Clinch, was, of course superseded. This act was achieved by the same influence, that has constantly poisoned the ears of the present administration, in most of the appointments made for this devoted Territory, by which her prosperity has been for eight years checked, and the exertions of her best citizens blasted. Our delegate in Congress was not consulted. General Clinch, who conquered the foe on the banks of the Ouithlacooche, without the charge of a fault, without an intimation of dissatisfaction, was placed under the command of an officer, who, although one of the ablest, was utterly ignorant of the country, and equally ignorant of the enemy he was sent to encounter ; what better could have been expected, than that which resulted from his labors.

General Clinch, instead of retiring in disgust, sacrificed his feelings to the duty he owed to his country, and although a cypher in command, was looked up to by the soldiers as a warrior, and by the inhabitants as a patriot, without fear, and without reproach.

About the 15th of January, General Gaines left his head quarters, at Memphis, Tennessee, on a tour of inspection. On his way to Louisiana, he heard of the war in Florida, and of Dade's massacre. He at once wrote to the Governor of Louisiana, for a body of volunteers, and proceeded to Pensacola, to get the assistance of the naval force there. Commodore Dallas, had anticipated his purpose, by sending down the coast, marines and munitions of war.

General Gaines had ordered Colonel Twiggs, to take command of eight companies of volunteers, and all the regulars that could be drawn from the posts in Louisiana, and proceed to Tampa Bay. This force, eleven hundred strong, embarked in three steamboats, on the 4th February, under the command of the General, who had returned from Pensacola. They reached Tampa on the 9th, and marched for the Indian country on the 13th.

He first proceeded eastward, towards the Allafia River, expecting to find a body of the enemy, who had the day before attacked some friendly Indians, that had been scouting from Fort Brook ; after two days search, and finding no signs of an enemy, he changed his course, and marched for Fort King, to obtain provisions, having seen the Quarter Master's order, dated 21st January, directing twenty thousand rations to be sent to that post.

On the 20th they passed Dade's Battle Ground, and interred the bodies of one hundred and six men. After this sad tribute of respect they proceeded, and on the 22d reached Fort King. Here they were able to obtain

29

but two days rations; the horses were therefore sent with an escort to Fort Drane for further supplies; they returned on the 24th with eight day's rations. No more could be obtained in the country. The road from Bayard, opposite to Picolata, had been thrown up late in the autumn, and had not firmly settled. The season was very wet, and the heavy wagons directly cut it up so deeply, that horses could scarcely travel, even without loads. The inland posts were therefore destitute of provisions and forage.

Thus circumstanced, General Gaines determined to return to Tampa by the trail of the Indian towns. He marched on the 26th, and reached the right bank of the Ouithlacooche at Clinch's Battle Ground. The army halted, and several officers rode down to the river to examine and sound the depth of water; it was about 2 o'clock, P. M, when the Indians commenced a spirited fire on the left flank of the army from the southern shore, it was accompanied with the savage yell, and continued about half an hour, during which time eight of the soldiers were wounded, and one killed. The next morning the army moved down the river to a place where the banks were less shaded with woods; here the advanced guard were attacked, and Lieut. Izard mortally wounded. As he fell, he commanded his men to lie close and keep the line. He died on the 5th day, and was buried on the banks of the river. During the whole of this day, except a short interval, the fire and the yells of the enemy were kept up, and one more man was killed. Captain Saunders, who commanded the friendly Indians, and Captain Armstrong, of the schooner Motto, were badly wounded. This evening, an express was sent to General Clinch at Fort Drane, requesting him to co-operate with what force he could spare. But his force was barely sufficient to protect the post and without provisions; besides, he was now under the command of General Scott; of course, he was unable to leave the fort. On the 29th, one-third of the troops were ordered to strengthen the breast-work that had been erected, by piling a few logs upon it, and digging a ditch inside. The remainder of the force was employed in making canoes and rafts for crossing the river. About 9 o'clock, the laborers and the guard were at the same time assaulted by a vigorous fire from every side, except that side next the river, which was continued incessantly for two hours, during which time one man was killed, and three officers, and thirty non-commissioned officers and privates, wounded. General Gaines was among the wounded; a ball passed through his under lip, and broke out three of his teeth. The enemy at length retired, leaving one of their dead; they had dragged him a considerable distance, then took his rifle, and abandoned him with his powder and about sixty bullets. A field piece had been used to some effect, but its ammunition was expended, except six cartridges reserved to meet an assault. On the 30th another express was sent to Fort Drane soliciting provisions and a reinforcement. In the meantime General Clinch had sent an express to Picolata. General Scott on receiving it sent a messenger twenty miles on the road, towards Fort Drane, to stop the march of Major Cooper with his brigade of Georgia volunteers, who returned to the river St. John's, and Major Douglass' battalion was also detained much against its will, at Garey's Ferry, on Black Creek.

On the receipt of the second message, General Clinch put himself at the head of all his disposable force, together with Captain Robertson's Augusta blues, and Captain Bones' company of hussars, and a large company of volunteers from Allachua, who drove about forty beeves collected by Mr. Dill; the General also took a large quantity of corn from his own private stores, and marched to relieve General Gaines.

The provisions of the besieged army were so far exhausted that their remaining corn was issued a pint per day to each man, and this could last but a few days, and had to be parched, or eat raw. They had no covering, the ground was wet, and they were confined to the ditches day and night. Some horses were killed and eaten, and every dog was considered a luxury; one biscuit sold for five dollars; yet there was no murmuring, and no talk of a retreat. They were generally surrounded, and every night rows of fires were made by the Indians a little out of gun shot.

On the five first days of March, the enemy continued both day and night to fire at intervals; and the best marksmen in the camp watched every opportunity to pick off the Indians, whenever they approached sufficiently near, or left their covert of trees.

On the night of the 5th an Indian called from the woods and hailed the camp; he was answered, and asked his wishes; he said the Indians were tired of fighting, and desired to make peace. The General directed an officer to tell him to come in the morning with a white flag, and he should be heard; he answered, very well. Expecting some stratagem, a peculiar caution was kept up all night. This day one man had been killed and two wounded. These were the only casualties that had occurred since the 29th.

On the 6th, about 10, A. M., three hundred Indians filed out from the river, and took a position five hundred yards in rear of the camp; at length a few advanced with great caution near to the camp, and waved the white flag. Captain Hitchcock was ordered to meet them; he went with Capt. Marks, attended also by Major Lear, officer of the day. They all sat down upon a log. Powel, Jumper, and Alligator, on the part of the Indians, stated that they were tired of fighting and wished to remain in peace on the south of the Ouithlacooche, and they would leave the whites unmolested on the other side. Abraham, Micanopy's sense keeper, acted as interpreter.

On reporting this talk to the General, he directed his officer to state to them that he had not power to treat with them, but advised them to leave the country, stating the force that was on their march to overwhelm them, &c. They said they would go and hold a council, and give an answer in the evening. They returned in the afternoon, and said they wished to consult Micanopy, their Governor, and asked a cessation of arms. They were answered, that if they retired south of the river, and abstained from hostilities, and would attend a council when called upon, that their request would be granted ; they promised to do so. At this time the body of the Indians, at a distance, were seen to break, and run for the river, and General Clinch was seen to advance. His advanced guard of mounted men formed a hasty line on the left, and fired briskly on the flying Indians, but they were directly out of the reach of a rifle shot. Powel and his friends were advised to retire also, which they did without delay.

This relief was most grateful to the besieged army, wholly unaccustomed to privations and exposure of that kind. Several beeves were slaughtered, and an abundant meal, soon made them forget their recent hardships. Powel had, at the conference, told Captain Hitchcock, that General Clinch would be there in three hours ; he also told him that he well knew the army was out of provisions, and offered him three cattle, and a bottle of brandy, if he would send over the river for them. He stated the number of his warriors present, at eight hundred, said that many had been killed and wounded, and that the Indians were tired of fighting.

On the 8th, a Negro man, whose wife and family, were in the Indian nation, was sent over the river to learn the situation of the warriors, and ascertain their intentions ; he returned on the evening of the 10th, and stated that they were seriously desirous of peace, and had dispersed two or three miles, in several encampments, said that they had seen our men fishing, but did not wish to molest them ; also that they had lost in the several engagements with this army, thirty warriors killed, and many wounded.

On the 9th, General Gaines delivered up the command of the army, to General Clinch. On the 10th, the whole marched back to Fort Drane, which they reached on the eleventh.

Before proceeding to detail the events of another campaign, it may be well to pause, and for a moment reflect on the present situation of the war. Are the Indians sincerely desirous of peace ? if so, it would be worse than folly, for General Scott to push the war again into their settlements. The evidences of their disposition, are discovered from their overtures, and their future conduct.

Their proposition to General Gaines, was " that they were tired of fighting, and wished to remain in peace, on the south side of the Ouithlacooche, and they would leave the whites unmolested, on the other side." On these terms they undoubtedly desired peace. But having (says our government) agreed to leave the country, war was made to compel them to leave it.

They asked for a cessation of hostilities, it was granted them upon condition of retiring to the south side of the river, and attending a council when called upon. They promised to comply, and retired, but never returned to attend a council. When Primus was sent to invite them, they kept him a prisoner, and sent no answer, except from the bore of their rifles.

That the Hero of Erie, was completely hoaxed by the savages, is the universal belief in Florida. It was perhaps good policy in him, to put a different face on the affair. We give General Gaines credit for the best intentions, in visiting our Territory, and most sincerely regret that he was not more successful.

On the 13th Gen. Scott arrived at Fort Drane, with two companies of regulars. He had left at Tarver's, on the Allachua Prairie, Douglass' Battalion of Georgia volunteers, and Wharton's dragoons. Col. Twigs, Maj. Mumford, Maj. Lear, of the army, and Capt. Marks, of the Louisiana troops, left Fort Drane, and Gen. Gaines started for Tallahasse on the 14th.

The army was ordered to penetrate the hostile country in three columns. The right, commanded by Gen. Clinch, was to march by the Ouithlacooche. The left, commanded by Gen. Eustice, to leave Volusia, above Lake George, to pass by the upper crossing of the Ocklawaha, and thence to Pilacklakaha. While the centre, under Col. Lindsey, should march direct from Tampa to Chicuchatty. Here the three wings were expected to enclose the Indians and dispose of them. Gen. Scott's great fear was that they should slip by him and retreat south to the everglades. Each column as it arrived at the place of destination, was directed to fire signal guns. The distance that each column had to march to reach Chicuchatty, was about sixty miles. The 25th was the day appointed for the columns to meet. Such was the difficulty, however, of collecting the troops and procuring transportation, that neither the right or left wing took up the line of march before the 26th ; the centre marched on the 22nd from Tampa.

The right wing, under Gen. Clinch, attended also by Gen. Scott, took the route by Fort Izard, on the Ouithlacooche, so named by Gen. Gaines. The rains had been incessant for several days, and the pine lands were very soft, so that the wagons moved very slowly ; they reached the river on the morning of the 28th. The savages directly let them know that they were at their old post, by firing a few vollies across the stream into the camp. Col. Gadsden immediately reconnoitered the spot, and selected a place for crossing; the boats which had been brought from Fort Drane were launched, and every thing prepared for crossing the next morning. By four o'clock on the 29th the field pieces were brought up to the bank, and the sharp shooters ranged to cover the crossing column. Foster Blodget, of Robison's Augusta Blues, stripped and swam across the stream with a rope, which he fastened to a tree, and thus greatly accelerated the passage of the boats. Two companies of mounted men crossed the river one and a half miles below this ford; another company swam the river at the ferry. By evening the whole army had crossed. The rear under Col. Bankhead were attacked, but the enemy shortly dispersed. During the night a few shots were fired into the camp.

On the 30th, the wing marched up the river, as General Clinch was satisfied that their enemy were concentrated near that place. About 10 o'clock small numbers of Indians were seen on an island, in a chain of lakes that lay on the right, and ranged along parallel with the river. These Indians were attacked, and pursued about four miles; but they escaped, and the wing encamped for the night. Early the next morning, the enemy were discovered on another island, of Cypress Swamp. This island was attacked by Colonel Smith at one end, and by Colonel Bankhead on the other. The swamp was surrounded by a deep boggy savanna, which prevented the horse from acting. As the columns approached the higher points of the island, they received a sharp fire from the enemy; but a rapid charge drove them from the island three or four miles, and they finally crossed the river, and again escaped. During this pursuit through hammocks, swamps, and savannas, the Indians availed themselvs of their knowledge of the paths and coverts, and never failed to attack our troops at every opportunity, in 'front, flank and rear. The troops encamped on the bank of the river, and the next morning returned to the baggage waggons for provisions, having fasted twenty-four hours.

April 1st, marched along the west side of the Lake Oloklikany, or Spotted Lake, which spread out between the army and the river. On the second, in the morning, reached the south extremity; the pine woods were open, and afforded a good road for the waggons &c. At the S. E. end of the lake a post was established, and garrisoned by Major Cooper with his battalion; here was left seventeen days' provision, and the wing with five days' provision proceeded to Tampa, where they arrived on the 5th. The last twenty miles the country was rough and difficult to travel; the sick had increased to one hundred and fifty. Killed during the march, four, wounded, nine.

About the middle of February, General Eustice despatched Major Kirby with two companies of regulars, and Colonel Brisbane with a battalion of S. C. volunteers, to scour the coast south of St. Augustine, as far as Musquito Inlet. They saw few of the enemy ; three men of Brisbane's were killed and scalped at Tomoko.

On the 9th, Colonel Goodwin's regiment arrived at St. Augustine, and on the 15th, Colonel Butler was ordered to proceed down the coast, and put in motion the several corps for Volusia. The trails were so bad, and the country so wet, that it was the 22d before they generally reached the place of destination ; and Colonel Butler did not arrive until the 24th.

On the 22d, Ashley and Trip's volunteers crossed the St. Johns, and were preparing to encamp, when one of the men in passing over a natural bank close at hand, was shot dead by the Indians, who rose from behind the bank and poured a galling fire on the volunteers ; they were answered with interest. Col. Brisbane, with two more companies, hastened to the scene of action, when a rapid charge dispersed the enemy, who left one of their dead on the ground, four more were by the Indians dragged to the river, and probably thrown in. Three of the volunteers were killed and nine wounded. The number of Indians seen, was about fifty.

On the 24th, twenty-five men under Lieut Arnold, were sent out to scour the woods ; they fell in with fifteen Indians in the open pine woods, two were killed and the rest were permitted to escape. Arnold ordered a retreat, when the savages were in his power ; for this cowardly conduct, he was dismissed.

On the 26th the left wing crossed the river, except two companies of the South Carolina volunteers, under Major Gates, who were left to protect the post. The wing took up the line of march at one o'clock P. M. and proceeded three miles and encamped; 27th marched eight miles. Thus far the roads are flat, wet and bad ; 28th they found the roads better, and marched twelve miles ; 29th marched twelve miles to the upper crossing of the Ocklawaha, and built a pole bridge. The stream deep, about sixty feet wide. Lake Eustice about fifty rods above the crossing.

A fire being discovered on the west side of the stream, a party was sent to reconnoitre ; four Indians were seen with some cattle, one was wounded by General Shelton, a volunteer from Georgia. The Indian fled but was overtaken by Shelton, when the savage raised his rifle and wounded him severely in the hip. He was soon despatched, and proved to be Yaha Hajo, or Crazy Wolf, chief of the Oclawahas. His village stood on the borders of the lake, but it had been for some time abandoned. The other three Indians escaped. The army encamped two miles west of the river.

30th. Proceeded about nine miles, when the advanced guard were attacked by the Indians, concealed in a hammock near Oakhumky; four men were wounded and two horses disabled. Kirby's regulars were brought up, the hammock was charged through by the advanced guard, but no Indians found. After passing a strip of pines, a fire was discovered near another thicket, where about sixty Indians in the edge of the woods, commenced a fire with rifles, which was returned with muskets. The enemy held their ground until the troops were within forty yards, they then retired, firing. A charge was made into the thicket, but it was found too close and too muddy to penetrate ; the battalion then joined in the line of march.

31st. No Indians were seen this day ; one hundred and twenty head of cattle were taken, and the army reached Pilacklakaha near evening. An express was sent to Fort King, who on his return, reported that Gen. Scott had crossed the Ouithlacooche three days before, and that no provisions could be got there. Cattle were plenty about Pilacklakaha, this was Micanopys town, but it had been for some weeks abandoned. It was burned by order of the General. When cattle were first found, the Carolina troops made a free use of beef, but the General afterwards restricted them to regular rations ; in consequence of which, or from some other cause, the cattle were permitted to run away and provisions soon became scarce. On the 2d April, the wing marched for Tampa. On the 4th they encamped fifteen miles from Tampa, where the baggage was left under charge of the foot companies, while the General with the horse proceeded to Fort Brook at Tampa Bay.

Col. Lindsey arrived at Tampa about the 4th of March, with eight companies of Alabama volunteers, under Col. Chrisholm ; where he found Maj. Reed, with a battalion of Florida militia, and on the 10th, Captain Marks arrived with a company of Louisiana volunteers. On the 12th, large fires were seen about the Allafia River ; Major Reed, with his battalion, was directed to scour the woods in that direction, and give an account of the enemy. They executed the duty promptly, by attacking the savages in the night, killing three, capturing six, and driving the main body across the river.

Col. Lindsey then marched to the Hillsborough crossing, on the road to Fort King, and built a stockade, which he named Fort Alabama. Major Reed was left in command, and the main force was marched back to Camp Brook.

On his return, Col. Lindsey found at Fort Brook, Gen. Scott's plan of the campaign, and an order to be at Chicuchatty on the 25th, for the purpose of co-operating with the other wings. The order had been brought by some friendly Indians. In compliance with this order, he left Tampa on the 22nd. At Fort Alabama he was joined by Major Reed, and Capt. Marks, with the Louisiana volunteers, was left in command of the fort. About thirty sick were also left there. The great road was left to the right, and the wing marched over the hilly country to the north-west. After passing Elo Chute Ka, the Indians lay concealed in the numerous hammocks and thickets, and harrassed the flanks and rear of the wing. On the 26th one of the volunteers was killed, and another badly wounded; as the force was passing through a dense hammock, the rear were briskly attacked by the enemy. Captain Benham charged the savages, and was sustained by Major Talliafero, with Blount's company. The savages were soon driven from the hammock, but shewed themselves in a large body, dancing and yelling; they were beyond the reach of our muskets. During the night the wing encamped by a pond; while getting water, the men were constantly fired upon, from a hammock beyond the reach of our muskets; a round of canister silenced them. On the 27th the wing sustained repeated attacks from thickets; they were soon repelled, but one man was killed and two wounded this day. On the 28th the wing encamped near Chicuchatty; the Indians made an attempt to take the horses; they were repulsed and driven off by detachments of the Florida and Alabama troops, under Captains Roulette, and Allison, Blount, and Nott.

On the 30th, provisions becoming scarce, Captains Roulette and Taylor were sent, with two hundred and fifty men under Col. Cross, to forage. They procured beef for four days, but the men had neither bread nor salt. This day, the hostile chief, Charley Fiscico was killed by the friendly Indians. During the night, the sentinels were fired on; the same thing occurred frequently. On the 31st another attempt was made to forage, but without success; the Indians had driven all the cattle from the neighborhood. Colonel Lindsey had now remained at Chicuchatty eight days; his signal guns had not been answered, and he was now destitute of provisions; he was therefore obliged to fall back to Tampa, where he arrived on the 4th of April.

Before the return of Colonel Lindsey, the enemy had collected at Fort Alabama to the number of three or four hundred, and made a violent attack on the post from eight o'clock in the morning till twenty minutes past ten, during which time they lost fifteen men killed and many wounded. Capt. Marks had one man killed and two wounded. They lay around the fort until the return of the main force, and then retreated in a body before them during a whole day.

All the columns of the army rested in the neighborhood of Tampa, until the 12th of April, when the right wing, under General Clinch, was ordered to return to Fort Drane by the cove on Ouithlacooche. Colonel Lindsey, with the centre, to scour the country on the upper part of the river, and penetrate the forks from above. Colonel Smith, with the Louisiana volunteers, to proceed to Charlotte Harbor, and ascend the Macaco, or Charlotte

River.   Colonel Goodwin to march to Peas (Peace) Creek, and break up
any settlements in that quarter.   Major Reed to explore the mouth of the
Ouithlacooche, and General Eustice, accompanied by General Scott, to
return to Volusia.

On the 17th, Generals Scott and Eustice reached Camp Shelton, where
his foot troops had remained eleven days, most of the time on half rations of
pork and flour, which had created great displeasure among the troops.
On the 18th he marched to the Hillsborough, at Fort Alabama ; 19th,
marched 12 miles ; 20th, they passed Colonel Lindsey's column at the
Big Ouithlacooche ; 21st, marched 16 miles ; 22d, 18 miles, and encamped four miles north of Dade's Battle Ground ; 22d, marched 17 miles, and
encamped two miles from the Ocklawaha :—the guard was fired upon this
night without damage :—23d, encamped nine miles east of the river ; 24th,
pass the long scrub eighteen miles.   On the morning of the 24th the
wing reached Volusia.   General Scott here took a steamboat and ran up
the river to Lake Monroe, and returned on the 27th, reaching Picolata on
the 28th.

Colonel Goodwin's command marched about forty miles east of Tampa,
and burned some large Indian villages on Peace Creek, containing three
hundred huts, but they had been abandoned.   He rejoined General Eustice at Fort Alabama.

During the absence of Gen. Eustice, from Volusia, that post had been
attacked by a large Indian force and two men killed.   The discharge of a
howitzer among them, set the Indians scampering and they were heard of
no more.

On the 26th, Gen. Clinch, with the right wing of the army reached Fort
Drane without encountering the enemy.

Col. Lindsey marched round the heads of the Ouithlacooche, while the
Indians remained quietly in the forks ; of course he had no better success
than Clinch, and returned to Tampa, without meeting an enemy.

On the 26th, Col. Chrisholm was sent, with six hundred troops to Fort
Alabama, which it was determined to evacuate.   Eighteen miles from that
place, large Indian trails were discovered, apparently concentrating in a
large hammock near Clonato LassoLake.   Near the same spot, one of Gen.
Eustice's men was found disinterred.   On the 27th, fort Alabama was
stripped and abandoned.   A keg of powder was left, with a musket, whose
spring triger was concealed in the magazine. The troops had proceeded about
a mile, when a tremendous explosion proved that the enemy had entered
the place and proved the fire-works.   On reaching Clonato Lasso Creek, a
regular soldier was found mutilated in a shocking manner, and stretched
naked across the trail ; he had been intoxicated, and straggled from the line

the day before. While a crowd was gazing at this body, a galling fire was opened from the hammock, first on the guard, then on the crowd collected about the dead body ; it directly extended to the artillery, and to the rear guard, near half a mile in extent. The first fire killed some brave men ; caused the team horses to run away with the wagons, and created some confusion. The fire was however returned from every part of the line, and the field piece was run up to the hammock and fired among the enemy with great effect. The hammock was then charged in every direction, and in one hour the enemy were completely driven and silenced. The detachment marched five miles farther and encamped wholly unmolested.

The Alabama troops were soon after embarked for Mobile.

Col. Smith proceeded up the Macaco River instead of the Peace, which enters Charlotte Harbor, near the same place. After ascending the largest branch as far as the boats could go, he then proceeded by land several days, on the south side, through a pine barren country, but discovered no Indians; he therefore returned to the harbor and embarked for New Orleans.

Major Reed made a reconnoisance off the coast, at the mouth of the Ouithlacooche and then returned to St. Marks.

Thus ended the winter campaign of 1836. The regulars were ordered to summer quarters, and the volunteers discharged and sent home.

Shortly after the close of the Campaign, Gen. Clinch resigned his commission and retired to his family, at St. Marys in Georgia.

At this period of our history, our readers may inquire for the causes that gave rise to this Seminole war, and the reasons of the failure of a campaign, commanded by one of the most conspicuous Generals of the United States ; a campaign that cost more than a million of dollars, and many valuable lives—and resulted in the devastation of a valuable and highly improving district of country.

In order to settle these questions, it will be necessary to take a retrospective view of several facts in our civil history, which have heretofore been omitted.

When East and West Florida were purchased from Spain, they contained only two settlements of any consequence, Pensacola, at the western extent of West Florida, and St. Augustine, at the eastern extent of East Florida. Between these two towns, the distance is four hundred miles ; the intermediate space was occupied by the nation of Seminole Indians. There was no means of communication from one to the other, of these towns, except by water, through the Gulf of Mexico, a distance of one thousand miles. These facts suggested the idea of attaching West Florida to the state of Alabama, and East Florida to Georgia ; and much interest was used to accomplish this arrangement. To this division of the new purchase, however, the General Government, as well as a majority of the inhabitants of the country, were opposed. It was therefore proposed to remove the Indians from the middle district of the Territory, to locate therein a common seat of Government, and to cover the country as soon as possible, with an efficient population. To this end commissioners were appointed to hold a treaty with the Seminoles, to induce them to give up their settlements west of the Suwanne River, and to locate themselves on the eastern peninsula. The treaty was held at Camp Moultrie, five miles south of St. Augustine, in 1823.

This treaty bound the Seminoles to remove from the country west of the Suwanne River, and confine themselves to a district of the eastern peninsula, that was afterwards surveyed to them. In consideration of which, the United States agreed to grant them an annuity of five thousand dollars per annum, for twenty years; and tools, subsistence &c. to six thousand men. This arrangement was strongly opposed by Micanopy, the legitimate and hereditary chief of the Seminoles, and by Jumper his brother-in-law. Neamathla, and most of the Mickasookees, were also opposed to leaving the rich fields which they occupied on the borders of the Mickasookee Lake, and Oscilla River. Hicks, however, was disposed to remove, and his influence, together with several reservations, made to Neamathla, Bacca, Pechasse, E. Conchatte, Micco, and Colonel Blunt, procured the signatures of nearly all the chiefs. Micanopy utterly refused, and was by the commissioners treated with that indifference, that rendered him unpopular with his nation; while Hicks was encouraged to assume the chief authority.

Soon after the Indians were condensed within their limits, they experienced a scarcity of food; they were too idle to clear up and cultivate new land; game was scarce, and from moving about, they became indisposed to labor. The Government extended their boundaries, and once or twice, furnished them with provisions; but more than half the donations made to them, stuck in the pockets of the agents.

Difficulties soon arose between them and their white neighbors, about their cattle, ponies, and negroes, and some legislative acts were passed to prevent any intercourse between the white and red men. These acts, tended rather to increase than to allay the prevailing animosities, and the Government came to a determination to remove all the Indians across the Mississippi. For the purpose of disposing of the Seminoles, Colonel Gadsden was commissioned to hold another council with them, and endeavor to remove them altogether. To this end a treaty was obtained at Payne's Landing, on the 9th of May, 1832.

The great objections made to removing, were their ignorance of the country proposed to them, their doubts of security there, and their repugnance to being incorporated among the Creeks, who still held out claims against them, for negroes alleged to have been stolen by the Seminoles; and perhaps a fear of losing the distinction of an independent nation, especially the chiefs, who would necessarily be shorn of power and distinction.

The Commissioner assured them, that the country on the Arkansaw, was a good one; that the title to the soil, should be secured to them, and their descendants forever; that their nation, although it must become a constituent part of the Creeks, yet that their chiefs should be continued as their public officers, and their property should be secured. They finally agreed to send a deputation of their chiefs, to examine the tract of country proposed for their residence, and further, that if on the return of the deputation, they reported favorably, and to their satisfaction, that then, the following articles should be binding on them, viz:

1st. The Seminole Nation relinquish to the United States, the tract of country reserved to them, by the second article of the treaty of Camp Moultrie, and become a constituent part of the Creek nation. One third part of the nation, residing in and about the Big Swamp, to remove as early as practiable in 1833; one third in 1834, and one third in 1835.

2d. The United States to pay to the Seminoles, for the improvements which they abandon, fifteen thousand four hundred dollars, and also to Abraham, the interpreter, and to Cudjoe, both free and influential negroes, two hundred dollars each.

3d. Each Seminole to be supplied with a blanket, a homespun frock, and with corn, meat, and salt, for one year after their arrival at the place assigned them.

4th. To be furnished a blacksmith, at one thousand dollars per annum, and a schoolmaster.

5th. The United States to pay the Seminoles three thousand per annum, for fifteen years, succeeding the treaty, in addition to the annuity of four thousand dollars, agreed on at Camp Moultrie, making in all seven thousand per annum.

6th. The United States agree to investigate, and liquidate all claims on the Seminoles for negroes, to the amount of seven thousand dollars.

This conditional treaty was signed by

HOLATE EMATHLA.—*Leader, or go before.*

JUMPER.—*Hoithle-matte.*

BLACK DIRT.—*Fucta luste Hajo.*

CHARLEY EMATHLA.

ALLIGATOR.—*Coa Hajo.*

SAM JONES.—*Arpiuka.*

MAD WOLF.—*Yaha Hajo.*

MICANOPY.—*Pond Governor, principal chief.*
JOHN HICKS.—*Tokasa Amathle.*
LITTLE CLOUD.—*Catsha Tustenugge.*
BLUE KING.—*Holate Micco.*
BROKEN STICK.—*Hitchitti Micco.*
BUZZARD.—*Enchah.*
WOLF LEADER.—*Yaha Emathla Chopko.*
SLEEPER.—*Moke Is She Larni.*

Holate Emathla, Jumper, Black Dirt, Charley Emathla, Alligator, Sam Jones, and Mad Wolf, were sent under the direction of Major Phagan, the Indian agent, to explore the country; while the United States sent three commissioners* to meet them there, and attend them in the examination of the country. When the Deputation were ready to return, the commissioners induced them to sign, what General Jackson called " an agreement, by which they signified their satisfaction on these subjects, and finally ratified the agreement, made with Colonel Gadsden." Neither the Seminole delegation, nor the nation ever considered it in that light. The chiefs reported to their people on their return, that the land was good, but it was situate near the Pawnees, and other thieving Indians, who robbed them of their horses and packs, and they feared that their situation would be unsafe. That the distance was great, and that removing would be troublesome, and dangerous.

In the course of this examination and the incidents connected with it, the time had elapsed, in which, by the terms of the treaty, one-third of the Indians were to have removed. In 1834, Hicks, the friendly chief, was destroyed by some of his countrymen, that were jealous of, or dissatisfied with him, and it is said, that the agent dictated to the Indians the choice of Tustinuc Hajo, a half-breed, instead of Charley Emathla, who was a man much better in every point of view; in particular, he was friendly to the whites, and a good man. Tustinuc, on the contrary, was sullen, obstinate, and has ever been our enemy. Major Phagan was, in 1834, superseded by General Thompson, as Agent of the Seminoles. In October, 1834, Gen. Thompson called a council of the chiefs to inquire whether they would join with the Creeks at the west;—whether they would be paid for the cattle and poneys which they must leave in Florida, in money, or have them replaced in Arkansas after their removal;—whether they would remove by water or by land;—and whether their next annuity should be paid in money or in goods. With the exception of Holate Emathla, they answered that they were unwilling to go at all. Holate here appeared as

---

* Montford Stokes, H. L. Ellsworth, and J. T. Schermerhorn.

the speaker of the nation. Micanopy appeared to act under the control of Powel and Jumper. Thus the affairs of the Seminoles remained until April, 1835, when another council of the Indians was called by General Thompson, General Clinch, and Lieutenant Harris. There was great difficulty in collecting them. When collected, the chiefs shuffled and made every excuse to avoid the subject of removal, until General Clinch told them that they talked too much and did nothing. He said the time was now come to declare whether they would abide by the treaty they had all agreed to, or not ;—he waited for a final answer. Eight out of the thirteen chiefs present, reluctantly agreed to remove, five utterly refused ; among the latter was Micanopy, who left the council. Those who agreed to remove, begged to remain until they should collect their harvest. This was conceded to them, on condition of the whole nation removing at once, and the 1st of December was appointed as the time of removal.

The chiefs also petitioned the government, to pemit them to live separate from the Creeks, on the opposite side of the Canadian branch, and that they might have an agent to reside with them.* The government agreed to the first request, but decided that one agent must serve the Creeks and Seminoles. From this period a deadly enmity was apparent, between the Indians who agreed to remove, headed by Holate and Charley Emathla, and those who were opposed, headed by Powel and Jumper, who threatened death to the first that should attempt to remove. Had means been used to remove the Seminoles as soon as the deputies returned, there is no reason to believe that any opposition would have been made ; but two years delay opened a wide field for tampering with the ignorant savages. Part of the Creeks were opposed to emigration. Their agents told the Seminoles, that when removed to the west of the Mississippi, they should reclaim the slaves which had been carried from the Creek nation to Florida.

The State of Georgia claimed 250,000 dollars of the Creek Indians, for slaves stolen from them, or for the runaway slaves harbored among them. One hundred thousand of this claim has been allowed, and affords a claim on the Seminoles from which they dread a collision. Great exertions have also been made, to get the Indian negroes away, by other false claims, of individuals ; and under cover of these claims, many negroes have been taken away by force and fraud. There exists a law among the Seminoles, forbidding individuals from selling their negroes to white people ; and any attempt to evade that law, has always raised great commotions among them. In 1835, Gen. Call asked permission of the President, to purchase of the Indians, one hundred and fifty negroes ; Presi-

* The treaty with the Seminoles, promised them a particular portion of the country of the Creeks. But the treaty with the Creeks authorized the location of the Seminoles among them—no separate district of land.

dent Jackson granted this permission. The agent in a letter to the Secretary at War, expostulated in a very strong terms against this traffic, as against the policy and laws of the Seminoles; as unjust to the Creeks, and as having a tendency to set the negroes in opposition to a removal; and it was well known that their influence with the Indians is usually conclusive.

The Seminole negroes, for the most part, live separately from their masters, and manage their stocks and crops as they please, giving such share of the produce to their masters as they like. Being thus supplied, the Indians become idle and absolutely dependant upon their slaves. No one will suppose that negroes, thus situated, would be transferred to the sugar and cotton fields of the white planters, without exerting their influence with their nominal masters, to oppose it. Peace and idleness, had rendered the young warriors restless, their minds were easily excited, and their first efforts at hostilities, were excited by the whites; being successful, and never being brought to punishment, or at most, but a nominal punishment; they also tended to confirm the leading chiefs in their determination to fight, rather than to abandon their homes. To these causes, may be added the counsels of evil minded persons, who took pains to impress upon the heated minds of the savages, that they were cheated by the white people; that they alone had a right to the soil, and ought to resist oppression.

When the Indians had commenced burning houses and murdering the inhabitants, there was no force in Florida, sufficient to control or coerce them. This was the fault of the government. In Jan. 1834, one hundred of the inhabitants of Allachua, sent a respectful petition to the President, representing the hostile appearance of the Indians, and praying for protection against them. In Oct. of the same year, Gen. Thompson, the agent, advised the Secretary at War that the Seminoles utterly refused to remove or adhere to the treaty of Payne's Landing, and urged an immediate reinforcement of troops, at Fort King and at Tampa Bay. In Nov. (same year) Col. Gadsden advised the Secretary at War—" You cannot, therefore, in the opinion of the undersigned, too soon, either re-occupy the Bay of Tampa, or re-inforce Camp King, so that, by a show of military strength, you may demonstrate the ability, promptly to enforce the final resolves of the government." Gen. Clinch also urged the certainty that the Indians " would not go, unless a respectable force be employed, and that it is very probable that such force would have to be actually used, in effecting the object." In Jan. 1835, the agent again informs the Secretary at War, that the troops are utterly insufficient to protect the country and the friendly Indians; that the hostile savages grow bolder by impunity; that a " strong force is required." In Oct., Mr. Harris, the Dispensing Agent, confirms the state of hostile feelings, and tells Secretary Cass, that, "an increase of

INDIANS. 241

military force at Fort King is necessary, say, from two to four companies."
From the above advice, the government were fully aware, that the Seminoles openly refused to leave Florida ; that they determined to make war
on the whites ; that a large military force was necessary to overcome them,
and to protect the inhabitants of Florida and the friendly Indians.

And what did the Government do ? They ordered six additional companies to Florida ; the first of which arrived at Tampa Bay, from Key
West, on the 21st of December 1835, two more companies followed about
the last of the month, and the other three companies arrived about the 9th
February, 1836. Of the seven companies, stationed in the Peninsula, during the year 1835, there was scarcely at one time, two hundred and fifty
men, fit for service.

At the battle of Ouithlacooche, the six companies led into battle by Gen.
Clinch, amounted only to one hundred and ninety-five men, instead of three
hundred and thirty. The other companies sent to make up the fourteen,
were equally deficient. Dade's company, the first that arrived, consisted
of thirty nine men, instead of fifty five. To meet all the deficiencies and
emergencies of removing, against their will, a nation of savages, the government furnished—to the ear—fourteen companies of regular soldiers—or
seven hundred and seventy men ; to the eye, they dwindled down to four
hundred. But these never appeared till the battle was fought and the
question of removal decided against us. Thus much for the causes of the
war. We will now seek for the causes of the failures of the campaign.

And first in the numerous list, was the appointment of a commander, who
had very little, if any, experience in Indian warfare, and was utterly unacquainted with the country. In opposing a civilized enemy, General Scott
would probably have been successful, but among savages he was out of
his latitude.

The campaign was commenced too late in the season. The stores and
munitions of war did not generally arrive until late in the winter. The
season was wet and the roads very bad, as they always are in a new country. All these circumstances tended to delay active operations until the
beginning of Spring. There was a strange want of every useful information. The number of the enemy was not known ; their resources and
means of supporting a contest with the whites, were utterly mistaken.
Their paths through the swamps were wholly unknown ; they could never
be brought to an engagement, except at such time and place as they saw
proper to intrude themselves. Their strong holds, where their ammunition
and their children were secreted, are not known to this day. The numbers of the Florida Indians have usually been rated at three thousand,
when, in fact, they amounted to near five thousand.

31

The inhabitants of several large settlements around the Caximba Inlet, the heads of the Hujelos, St. Mary's, and other southern streams, never appeared at the agency, to draw annuities, but lived by cultivating their fields, hunting, trading at the Spanish ranchos, bartering skins, mocking birds and pet squirrels, for guns, ammunition and clothing, and sometimes assisting in the fisheries. This race of Indians would have remained peaceable to this day, had not an order been issued from the agency requiring them all to remove. They never agreed to remove, either personally, or by their representatives; and they were easily excited to fight, rather than leave the home of their ancestors. Their knowledge of the passes of the country, and their long connection with the Spanish traders and fishermen afforded perfect facilities for supplying the Seminoles with arms and munitions of war, and those facilities are at this time improved to our great injury.

Had General Clinch been at once permitted to assist General Gaines at the Ouithlacooche, it is more than probable that an end would have been put to the war. The enemy would have been beaten, or forced south upon Colonel Lindsey, and they could scarcely have escaped. The excuse is, that there was not provisions at Fort Drane to supply them and to subsist General Scott's army on its arrival. But the provisions actually taken by General Clinch, at last, were principally corn, raised by himself, and cattle belonging to the inhabitants of Allachua. A few barrels of pork, and perhaps a small quantity of bread, was taken from the public stores. But delay had rendered the assistance of General Clinch utterly useless.

General Gaines undoubtedly entered Florida from the best of motives. His troops were actuated by feelings of humanity for the suffering inhabitants of the country; but Powel had the art to render them inefficient, and finally to hoax him with the pretence of a treaty, and thus evaded a second stroke from Clinch.

General Scott's plan of the campaign contemplated a junction of the three columns in the heart of the enemy's country. Each column approached the place of its destination, but no junction was formed. The Indians, instead of being penned up in their towns, had ample time to give each wing of the army a brush in succession, and then quietly waited till the storm passed by them. Had General Eustice, when he reached the Tampa road, proceeded ten miles down the forks of the Ouithlacooche, he would have entered the nest, the strong hold of the savages. Here was corn and beef without going to Fort King and Tampa.

The Seminoles since the commencement of the war, have concentrated about the great cove of Ouithlacooche ; when sought there, they have always been found, until General Jessup's last campaign, when they abandoned it for the everglades. It was there that Clinch, and Gaines, and Scott, and Call, found them. Why then was not the war carried on, at least as long as an enemy could be found? the answer is, that the army had only ten days' provision; but a part could have staid and fought, while the balance should escort the wagons of provisions, either from Tampa, sixty miles, or from Volusia, fifty miles distant. There was corn also at Halliman's Blockhouse, thirty miles distant. Instead of that, the several wings all left the *battle ground*, and marched in succession to Tampa, and there spent one half of the month appropriated for the campaign, comfortably drawing rations. Major Cooper, was indeed left near the scene of active warfare, with a single battalion of men, who found enemies enough to fight during the whole time. What might not one thousand of the force have done, had they been left to scour the country, under the command of General Clinch, or any other active commander.

The order given to General Scott, was to fight the Indians as long as a man of them could be found in Florida. Emboldened by this, the inhabitants of Allachua, and the adjoining country, proceeded again, to the cultivation of their fields. Their cottages were again enlivened, by women and children, "hope told a flattering tale" to the industrious farmer. How were his hopes withered, when, at the end of one month, he sees another order, dismissing the volunteers, and throwing the regulars into summer quarters. Was this pursuing the enemy out of the country? was it not letting them loose upon the country, with tenfold rage? The country was again depopulated, and fire and devastation swept the fields of the suffering Floridians.

About the first of May, Generals Scott and Eustice, took up their quarters at St. Augustine. Four companies were left at Tampa Bay, and ten or twelve were distributed between Fort King, Fort Drane, Fort Defiance, Fort Dobney, and Suwanne Old Town.

About the middle of March, at the commencement of General Scott's campaign, he ordered Major M. Lemore to proceed to the Suwanne River, to procure a quantity of corn, and proceed with it to the Ouithlacooche River, for the use of the army.

Major M. Lemore executed the order, and erected a small blockhouse for its protection, leaving Captain Halliman with a small party to defend it, until the General should send for the corn, and relieve them. But the General appears to have forgotten them. Major M. Lemore died within a few days. On the 12th of April, Captain Halliman was attacked by a large Indian force, at the dawn of day; depending on their overwhelming force, the Indians approached within point blank distance of rifle shot, but the execution done among them, soon taught them to keep at a more respectful distance. The Indians continued to surround, and besiege them for two months, and made more than twenty attacks on the post, but were always repelled. On the 13th of April, Eli Sealy was killed, and on the 3d of May, Captain Halliman was shot, while engaged in strengthening the defence of the post. The command then devolved on Lieutenant Walker, who continued bravely to defend the place. On the 15th of April, the whole body of Indians, from five hundred to one thousand, made an onset upon the post, for two hours and forty-five minutes, but made no impression. On the 24th, they made another severe attack, and set fire to the roof of the blockhouse by lighted arrows, shot by twenty-six Indians, which was finally destroyed ; they also cut loose the flat and let it drift down the river. Four or five men were also wounded. The garrison were twenty-eight days without any thing except corn to eat, and nearly a month without any roof to shelter them. When Major, now General Reed passed the mouth of the Ouithlacooche, at the close of the campaign, he discovered the flat cut in pieces. From this time, it was generally supposed that the Garrison were destroyed, and the excitement through the Territory was very great. General Scott endeavored to cast the blame on Major Reed, but took no measures to look after the garrison. On the the night of the 10th it was determined to attempt sending an account of their situation to Tallahasse. To this end, three men were drawn by lot, from the garrison ; an old canoe was got afloat that had been riddled by rifle balls, they entered it, and pushed down the river as silently as possible, while they heard the Indians running down the banks on both sides to intercept them. Favored by the darkness, they escaped and reached the Gulf before daylight. The Indians fired on them near the mouth of the Suwanne River, but their balls did not take effect.

On their arrival at Tallahasse, a volunteer company was raised, amounting to about eighty men, of which Colonel Reed took command ; they embarked on the steamboat Minerva, on the 22d of May, and arrived off the mouth of the Ouithlacooche the next day. In the evening, they ascended the river in a large barge, and reached the fort about midnight. After taking the little garrison on board, they descended the river again, and reached the steamboat by eight o'clock the next morning. The distance to the Blockhouse, was fifteen miles from the mouth of the river. Since that period, General Reed has published a satisfactory defence against the censures of General Scott, on the above subject.

About the 1st of May, the Indians made an attack on the plantation of Judge Randal, about twenty miles east of Tallahasse, where they took some negroes, and did other damage. On the 8th, they were seen near the fort of St. Mark's. This boldness of the enemy, was a natural consequence of the disbanding of the militia, which left the whole country unprotected. It is true, that the citizens flew to arms and pursued the savages, but they acted on their own responsibility, and could continue in the field no longer than extreme danger rendered it necessary for self-defence.

The month of May was principally occupied by our troops, in conveying provisions and stores, from Black Creek, to forts King, Drane, and Defiance. But as the weather grew warmer, the troops became very sickly, and it was found to be impossible to supply all those stations, with the teams then provided for that service, and an order was sent to abandon Fort King. This was accordingly done on the last of the month. The troops became more sickly as the season advanced. Major Heiliman was appointed to the command of the troops west of the St. John's River, about the first of June ; and General Scott was ordered to Georgia, to take the command of the forces sent to subdue the Creeks.

Major Heiliman proceeded to Micanopy, about the eighth of June, on his way to Fort Drane. There he halted for the day, and sent off an express to Oakland, the plantation of Colonel M'Intosh, to Lieutenant Burke, who was stationed there, to destroy all the stores at that place, and retire to Micanopy with his company. The express had proceeded about half a mile, when he was fired at. Lieutenant Talcot observed it, and being outside the pickets, he took about a dozen men with him, and ran to support the messenger. They directly observed several Indians and negroes, and pursued them ; two other parties of the enemy were seen in different directions. Lieutenants Wheelock, and Humphries, collected their command, and pursued about two miles, but could not overtake the enemy. The express was again sent. He returned with the intelligence, that on the 7th, the Indians, about two hundred in number, had burnt the sugar house of General Clinch, and had attacked Oakland, and burned the sugar house of Colonel M'Intosh. Lieutenant Burke, retired from Oakland to Fort Drane, Major Heiliman concluded to halt at Micanopy, until the post could be reinforced. On the 9th, about nine o'clock in the morning, the Indians fired two rifles, and shortly after two more, about a quarter of a mile from the fort, near the Oakland road, where the express on the day before had been fired on. Major Heiliman considered it a challange, and unwilling to disappoint the savages, he despatched Captain Lee to attack them on the right, and Lieutenant Wheelock with his few Dragoons, on the left. Shortly afterwards, he ordered Lieutenant Humphries to move down, and attack their centre. Captain Lee, some paces in advance, soon found himself close to the enemy, who were watching the movements of Wheelock ; they turned and fired on Lee, and wounded him severely. His men immediately came to his assistance, but he ordered them to push on after the enemy, who were retiring before Humphries and Wheelock, who had opened a brisk fire on them. The Indians continued to retreat, till they entered the hammock on the east side of the Tuscowellar Lake.

Major Heiliman started with a six-pounder after Humphries; but a messenger came from the fort, and stated that the Indians were threatening the fort on the opposite side. He therefore marched back, but found that it was a false alarm; he immediately again sent forward the artillery, in time to prevent the enemy from turning the left flank, which was still at some distance from the hammock. A few rounds of grape sent the red skins out of sight, and the troops retired to the fort. Lieutenant Wheelock, had five men wounded; one mortally. Captain Lee had one wounded. Four horses were killed, and six disabled, in this affair. Seventy-five men were engaged.

When Lieut. Burke arrived at Fort Drane, from Oakland, and informed the commandant that the stores were not destroyed, Lieut. Temple took eighteen horsemen and marched down to that post in the night. On entering the plantation, he discovered the dwelling house on fire, but the store houses, filled with corn, sugar, &c., were standing. He left the main body of his men in the lane, four hundred yards from the house, and proceeded with four men to the ruins, and seizing a brand from the fire, he soon lit up the store houses; while doing this, an Indian dog barked, and Indians were heard to talk. Temple, however, staid till the flames were too far advanced to be extinguished; he then retired to his troop, mounted and rode off at full speed, and barely reached the hammock as the Indians arrived to intercept them.

On the 10th, Wheelock's dragoons were marched to Fort Drane, and returned on the 15th with provisions, attended by Lieut. Burk's company, that were intended to reinforce Fort Defiance. That afternoon Lieutenant Wheelock retired to a room and shot himself. He had complained of illness, and it was supposed that his fatiguing duties had rendered him delirious; he was much regretted by the army, who buried him with the honors of war.

Soon after these events, Major Heiliman died at Micanopy. He had been ill for several weeks, but still pursued his arduous duties, until the cords of life gave way, and the army lost one of her bravest and most efficient officers. May his ashes rest in peace, and justice do honor to his name. He was brevetted a Lieut. Colonel for his meritorious services, but he died before the arrival of his commission.

As the season advanced, sickness continued to increase among the troops at Fort Drane and Fort Defiance. Every escort of wagons from Black Creek disabled from twenty to forty men, until they were so far reduced, that a company of six month's men, stationed at Mandarin, on the east side of the St. Johns, commanded by Captain Curry, were ordered to assist in escorting the wagon train, which being represented to Governor Call, he ordered Fort Drane to be evacuated. About the 19th of July the place was abandoned. Twenty-two wagons loaded with Quarter Master's stores, escorted by sixty-two men, left the place about eight o'clock in the morning. Twenty-six dragoons of the 2d regiment were commanded by Captain Ashley: thirty-six men detached from several artillery companies, and a five and half inch howitzer, under the command of Lieutenant Whitely. On passing the We-li-ka Pond, one mile from Micanopy, several rifles were discharged, which proved fatal to one of the dragoons, named Holmes. Captain Ashley immediately charged into the hammock from which the firing proceeded, but the enemy had fled. The train proceeded unmolested within a quarter of a mile of the fort, when they were again attacked by a strong body of the enemy, supposed to be two hundred and fifty in number. They poured a galling fire in on the front and right of the train, a quarter of a mile in extent. The fire was returned with great promptness, and the battle raged for some time. Captain Ashley was wounded, but refused to leave the ground ; he, however, despatched a dragoon to the fort for a reinforcement. The dragoon was met by two detachments, led by Lieuts. Temple and Talcot, amounting to thirty-one men. Their arrival turned the tide of the contest. Lieutenant Temple charged the point of. hammock from which the heaviest fire proceeded ; he then formed in line, and Captain Ashley then ordered a general charge, which decided the affair. The Indians fled and were seen no more. During the charge Lieutenant Talcot conducted the wagons to the Fort in safety. Captain Ashley sustained the action till loss of blood from his wound rendered it absolutely necessary for him to retire. Lieutenant Whitely rendered excellent service with the howitzer ; several of his men were wounded. Surgeon Weightman was shot through the thigh. Five were dangerously wounded ; four severely and one slightly. The loss of the enemy could not be ascertained. Three horses were killed and several wounded. The worst consequences resulting from the abandonment of these posts, was the loss of ten or twelve thousand bushels of corn fit to harvest, in the fields of Gen. Clinch and Col. M'Intosh, which the extreme sickness of the troops rendered them unable to destroy. This was a clear acquisition to the enemy, and will help to sustain them through another campaign.

All the improvements east of the St. Johns River, and south of St. Augustine and Picolata had, at this time, been destroyed, and the same fate had befallen the settlements on the west side of the St. Johns, south of Garey's Ferry and Newnansville. The green corn dance had been cele-

brated by the Seminoles, and parties of warriors had gone forth to distinguish themselves by some bold exploit.* About thirty warriors passed
between Picolata and St. Augustine on the 16th of July, and proceeded
round the head of Six Mile Creek to New Switzerland, twenty miles within our lines. Col. Hallowes and one other white person resided at the
plantation. Some little negro children ran into the house early in the
morning, and cried that the Indians were in the grove. Col. Hallowes
arose and dressed himself, and sent one of his slaves to the next plantation,
about two miles below, for several of his negroes who were at work ; soon
after, while standing in his hall, he was laid senseless by a ball which passed through his ear and struck his skull. He soon recovered, and he and
the other person, with some of the negroes, ran out of the house, leaped
into a boat and pushed from the shore, amidst a shower of balls. The negroes below had entered their boat and pushed from the shore, when they
discovered an Indian with one of their fellow-servants running down the
shore to intercept them ; they crossed the river and joined their master,
when they discovered the steamboat Essayon, Captain Peck, coming out
of Black Creek ; they entered the boat, and were conveyed to Picolata.
Col. Hallowes' wound proved not to be dangerous.

Lieutenant Taylor, in command at Picolata, despatched an express to
Col. Crane, at St. Augustine, advising that a company should be despatched to New Switzerland, by Six Mile Creek, to cut off the retreat of the
savages ; while he, at the same time, despatched Lieutenant Watson, with
eighteen men, to the landing on Six Mile Creek, to intercept them there.
He proceeded to some distance on the trail towards New Switzerland, that
evening, and lay upon the trail ; the next morning he proceeded, but his
guide led him into a swamp on Trout Creek, and said he had lost the way.
After getting out of the swamp he returned to the landing place for provisions, but the boat was gone. The corporal and four men left in charge
of her, got frightened and returned to Picolata. Major Putnam, on the 17th,
arrived at Picolata with Dummet's mounted volunteers ; they returned the
same day, seven miles to Weedman's, near the head of Six Mile Creek.
On the next morning they proceeded towards New Switzerland, until they
fell in with Lieutenant Watson. They then returned to St. Augustine,
and Watson proceeded to Picolata.

Captain Peck, with the steamboat, returned immediately to the plantation of Col. Hallowes ; the Indians had gone back with their plunder,
about three miles, to a cedar swamp, and left all but one of the negroes behind. To a negro named Harry, they gave a gun, and placed him on the

* They shot Mr. Ridgley, proprietor of the steam saw-mill, about the last of May.

river bank, to keep watch. On the approach of the Essayon, he called to Captain Peck, and informed him that the Indians were near. The Captain, however, ran his boat on shore and took off all the negroes but one, that the Indians had with them. The negroes stated that they first plundered the house and then burned it. They then proceeded to Mr. Colts' and Dr. Simmonds' houses, and plundered and burned them. The amount of plunder obtained at Col. Hallowes' probably amounted to the value of two thousand dollars. How long they were collecting horses and carrying away their booty, no one can tell. The force at Picolata was barely sufficient to protect the place, and Curry's volunteers were on the way to Micanopy, escorting the wagon train.

On the 28th of July in the morning, large fires were seen on the west side of the St. Johns, in the direction of Travers' Plantation. The Essayon started about eight o'clock for Black Creek ; on coming in sight of Col. Travers' plantation, the dwelling-house and kitchen were nearly demolished. Captain Peck ran in shore close to the smoking ruins, but there was not an Indian to be seen ;—they had all gone back to the sugar-works, half a mile distant. Soon after retiring from the shore, the flames of the mill-house arose through the trees, and in half an hour after that, a huge column of flame arose from the boiling-house. Thus sank in flames, the fortunes of a man, who with a most interesting family, deserved a better fate. The volunteers had before destroyed his stock.

As the boat passed the steam mill of the lamented Ridgley, Captain Peck discovered Indians, and fired a volley upon them ; they retired, and the boat proceeded to Garey's Ferry.

Before the Essayon left Picolata, she towed across the river to Bayard, the flats, containing Lieutenant Herbert, and fifteen men, with forty horses, which they were conveying from St. Augustine to Garey's Ferry, by land. Lieutenant Herbert saw the fires, and was assured that the enemy were below ; he however, proceeded unmolested to Black Creek, and returned with his men, to Picolata in the Essayon ; he communicated to Captain Peck, and to his Sergeant, his intention of landing where the enemy had been seen the day before. The boat started at eight in the evening, fell down the creek five miles, and took in wood, and lay there till daylight, when she started and reached the mouth of the creek by six in the morning. One of the hands said that he saw a man come out of the steam mill on the right bank. Capt. Peck ordered the boat to come too, and commenced landing ; the boat's yawl could take but nine persons at a load. Lieutenant Herbert's intention was to march by land to Traver's plantation, a distance of two miles, as soon as the rest of his men could be landed. On reaching the shore he discovered moccasin tracks, thickly upon the

32

sand, and sent off the boat for the remainder of his men.. Three minutes had
not elapsed before he discovered Indians in the hammock, which he engaged immediately. Herbert's men got the first fire, but the Indians were
prepared, and quickly returned the compliment. The first rifle shot wounded one of the men who rushed into the hammock after the Indians. The
wounded man on retiring from the hammock, told the Lieutenant that he
saw about fifteen or twenty Indians drawn up in line, about fifty yards
back, hidden by the woods; they appeared to be waiting for another party.
At this time most of Lieutenant Herbert's men were on the opposite side of
the mill, examining Indian tracks in the road. Lieutenant H. immediately
ordered his men out of the hammock, and directed them to cover themselves behind the pillars of the saw-mill, trees, stumps, or whatever might
shelter them best, and to keep up a warm fire on the enemy, who came
rushing to the edge of the hammock, and firing incessantly. About the
same time that the balance of the men arrived from the boat, the Indians
received a reinforcement of twenty or thirty, who came running and yelling, from a camp up the creek. When they joined their companions, they
raised a horrid yell and rushed towards the mill. Lieutenant H. ordered
his men to reserve their fire, and load with buckshot, eighteen to each
musket. When the enemy emerged from the hammock, at about forty
yards distance, they poured in a destructive fire. The Indians raised a
terrible scream and retreated, frequently calling to carry off the wounded.
They remained back in the hammock eight or ten minutes; they then
cautiously approached again, endeavoring to outflank Herbert's men, by
getting into a hammock in his rear. Twice they attempted it, and were
twice repelled by a steady fire of buckshot; but one Indian reached the
place they sought, and he was shot down just as he entered. They twice
attempted to rush upon our men, but so steadily did the men pour buckshot upon them, that their nerves failed them. The action continued one
hour and twenty minues, when the men informed Lieutenant Herbert, that
their ammunition was nearly exhausted. He then ordered the wounded
to retire towards the boat, while he directed a rapid fire on the enemy, to
mask their retreat; the wounded were on board with the few that assisted
them. Lieutenant H. retreated to the boat with the balance of his little
band. As they came on board, Captain Peck ordered his men to fire on
the Indians with six rifles, which they did till the boat was under way.
The Indians threw about twenty balls into the steamboat, during the engagement. Pollidore, a negro belonging to Mr. Travers, acted as guide to
Lieutenant H., and fought very bravely. The next day, Major Gardner
sent a party of horse to scour the woods down to Ridgley's mill, which the
Indians set on fire on the retreat of Lieutenant Herbert; another party de-

scended the creek by water, and landed at the place of the engagement, where they saw a few Indians at landing, but they immediately disappeared in the swamps. The enemy shortly after retired; their fires were seen for two days in the direction of Rice Creek.

About the middle of this month (August) Lieut. Col. Crane, assumed the command in East Florida, in the place of Gen. Eustice, who removed to Charleston S. C.

On the 15th, Major Pierce arrived at Garey's Ferry on Black Creek, and he took command of an escort, to conduct a train of wagons with provisions to Micanopy. On his arrival, it was reported that the enemy had collected at Fort Drane; he immediately communicated to his officers, his intention to attack them. Notwithstanding the fatigues of a four day's march, they all cheerfully acquiesced. As soon as it was dark, two trusty spies were sent to discover the situation of the enemy, and Major Pierce prepared to move as soon as they should return. At twelve o'clock the spies came in, and reported that the buildings were burnt, and that Indian fires were burning near the pickets of the fort. At two o'clock in the morning Major Pierce marched with one hundred and ten men mounted, one howitzer and a light four horse wagon. They arrived shortly after day light within a quarter of a mile of the pickets, and under cover of a small hammock, arranged the order of attack, in three divisions. The right consisted of fifty men, from companies D 2 and G of the first Artillery, commanded by Lieutenants Irwin and Herbert. The left, forty-five men of Capt. Child's company, commanded by Captain Childs and Lieut. Spalding. The balance, of fifteen men, with the howitzer, was under the command of Lieut. Pickell, who was ordered to move rather slower than the wings, and to operate as a reserve. The troops had scarcely formed, when two rifles were fired near the pickets, as signals. The right and left divisions moved off briskly, each making a circuit so as to arrive on opposite sides of the pickets. The enemy were soon discovered; a large party were running from the pickets, to join their main body at the south part of a cornfield : the whole were rushing towards the small hammock just left by the troops. They were charged by the right division, on horseback, in every direction, until they were wholly driven from the field ; several were killed and rode over, a few extra shots were fired by the men into those who shewed signs of life. The left, commanded by Capt. Childs also rode down and killed one savage, on their way to join the other troops. Two more were killed and rode over by acting Adjutant Betts, while bringing up the reserve, when himself and four of his men were wounded by a volley of rifle shot fired from the edge of the hammock, by the Indians. One of the mounted men stopped to take the rifle from an Indian, which detained him till the division had passed ; he spurred forward and soon found himself among the Indians. He then attempted to retreat, pursued by five savages. He was discovered by Lieut. Herbert, coming over the crest of a hill. He immediately spurred to his relief followed by a few of his men; but before he could reach him, the poor fellow was shot from his horse, and the savages struck a tomahawk into his head, and would have scalped him, had not Lieut. Herbert arrived in time to prevent it. Lieut. Irwin attempted to cut off their retreat, but they were too near the hammock and escaped. Irwin and Herbert carried off their mangled companion, who had six balls through his body. Lieut. Herbert carried off the contested rifle, that had cost the life of a brave soldier.

The enemy being chased into a large hammock, nearly a mile from the place where the attack commenced ; the first division dismounted and formed on the west of a hill, about fifty yards from the enemies' line, which was also re-forming on the edge of the hammock. In a few minutes, Capt. Childs arrived and formed on the right ; in the mean time the wounded were conveyed to the rear, delivered to the care Doct. Triplet. The howitzer was brought to bear on the enemies' line, attended by regular and lively volleys of musketry, until the amunition was nearly expended, that of the howitzer entirely gone. The enemies' fire had slackened and nearly ceased. Major Peirce directed our fire to cease, to mount and retire. The troops retired slowly and in good order, leaving nothing on the field. The wounded had been dressed, they were placed in the wagon and removed to Micanopy by ten o'clock, when the troops were glad to get their breakfast, having since two o'clock marched twenty-five miles, and fought the enemy successfully for more than an hour. The enemy were three hundred strong, commanded by Powel in person, who on gaining the hammock rallied his men, and marshalled them in a line, half a mile in length, and sustained our fire for nearly an hour with perfect steadiness and bravery. On our evacuation of Fort Drane, this chief it seems, had removed his people into regular huts, built in the hammock, close by the extensive corn fields of Gen. Clinch, and were quietly enjoying the fruits of his labors.

Thus far, the summer quarters contemplated by General Scott, have proved more destructive to the health, and more productive of fatigues and death, than the most active campaign. All the posts between Tampa Bay, and Black Creek, could not, in the month of August, muster one hundred and fifty men fit for duty.

On examining the state of the fort at Micanopy, Major Pierce found that there was not sufficient provision, to last until the train of wagons could go to Black Creek and return ; but four days' forage for the horses, that most of the garrison were sick, and the heat of the weather, and want of necessaries, were destroying the troops. Under these circumstances, he, with the unanimous advice of his officers, determined to abandon the place. The wagons were loaded with the sick and the stores, and the whole removed to Garey's Ferry, on Black Creek.

On the 3d of September, Maj. Pierce escorted a train of wagons, with provisions and amunition, to Newnansville, and reinforced the garrison of Fort Gilleland. No Indians were seen, although they had for some time past been prowling around that post in considerable force.

On the 15th, a party of Indians attacked the house of Mr. Higinbotham, seven miles from Jacksonville. They slept in an out-house close by the dwelling, and at day light, as Mr. Thomas was striking a fire, they commenced an attack upon the house. The door was closed, and the fire returned by Messrs Higinbotham and Thomas, with nine guns. The Indians retreated carrying off the saddle and bridle from the out-house. Mr H. left Mr. Thomas and two women, Mrs. H. and T. to defend the house, and a sick man, while he rode to Jacksonville to give the alarm. Major Hart, at the head of twelve men, immediately went in pursuit. On reaching Mr. Higinbotham's, they found Mr. Thomas and the two women guarding the house, with guns in their hands, ready to repel an attack. A young lady in the house had risen early in the morning, and gone to a brook for water; she had passed the Indians without discovering them, when they fired on her. The balls pierced through all her clothes without touching her body. She ran and hid herself, until an opportunity arrived that enabled her to gain the house. Major Hart took the Indian trail which led to the Tallahasse road, and on that rode ten miles, to the house of M. Cormick, occupied by a Mr. Johns. This house was a heap of smoking ruins, in which was the remains of a human being burnt to a cinder; near to the house was a quantity of female hair. The pursuing party finding fresh horse tracks still on the great road, they pushed on expecting to overtake the enemy at Lowder's, seven miles ahead. On reaching this house it was abandoned, but no traces of the savages were seen. They pushed on to Sparkman's, four miles further; it was night. This family was in great distress. Mrs. Johns was there, still alive. Her arm and neck pierced with balls, and her head, as far as her hair extended deliberately skinned. The poor woman had her senses perfectly, and related the circumstances of the assault of their house. Mr. and Mrs. Johns were about twenty yards from the house, at about ten o'clock in the morning, when they perceived the Indians in the corner of a fence very near to them; they fired and shot Mr. Johns in the breast, both fled to the house and closed the door. The Indians followed close, firing on the house, and at length looked in between the logs, and in English told them to come out, and said they would not hurt them.

Johns refused, but begged the Indians to save their lives. An Indian then gave an order to charge the house. They burst in the door and shot Mr. Johns through the head; he fell dead, and his wife fell upon him. An Indian dragged her to the door, and told her to go; she asked where, he pointed towards Black Creek. At that moment, she saw another Indian level his rifle at her; she raised her arm, the Indian fired, the ball cut the flesh of her arm lengthwise, and passed through her neck. They then dragged her into the house, and tearing the string and comb from her hair, with a large butcher knife skinned all her hair off her head, as the butchers would skin an animal. They then plundered the house, and among other things they took a portmanteau that contained one hundred dollars, and other valuable articles. Finally they set fire to the house, one Indian applying a torch to the clothes of the poor bleeding victim. They then raised the war whoop, and hurried off in the direction of Black Creek. Feeling the fire of her clothing burn her leg, the poor woman seized handfuls of her own clotted blood to quench the flames. When the savages were gone, she raised herself up, saw the house in flames, and her husband bleeding on the floor; she crawled from the flames slowly, and frequently fainted with pain and the loss of blood. She reached a swamp, got some water, and laid down to die; but the eye of a kind Providence was upon her, and she was preserved. About two o'clock P. M. Mr. Johns, sen., with two of his neighbors, rode up to the burning house, where lay the roasted body of his son. On further search, Mrs. Johns was discovered in the swamp. They took her on a horse, and conveyed her to Mr. Sparkman's together with Mr. Lowder's family, whose house they passed. It was the trail of Mr Johns and his party, that misled Major Hart thus far from the direction of the savages. Eight Indians, and one negro, were seen at Mr. Johns house, besides those who took charge of the horses, nine of which, they had stolen and taken with them. They tried to catch Mr. Higinbotham's horse, but he was frightened and kept out of their way. Early next morning, Major Hart, with his party, took the woods in the direction of Black Creek, struck the Indian trail early in the day, and pursued it to the head of Black Creek; but the enemy travelled all night, and had six hours the start of them. The chase was given up with great reluctance.

A notice of the attack had been sent to Black Creek, and Major Pierce sent several parties of men to intercept the savages; he also headed one detachment himself, and pursued their trail near to Santaffe, but without effect. The horses they had stolen were the best in the country, and they pushed them to their utmost speed. From the trail they came, and from other discovered signs, they had been a week or ten days in the neighborhood of Ewbanks and Higinbotham's. Mrs. Johns has since been removed into Jacksonville, and placed in a comfortable boarding house, where medical attendance, and the humane attentions of the citizens, have promptly administered to her necessities, and relieved many of her sorrows; she is in a fair way of recovery.

On the 10th of September, a cart attended by three white men and two negroes was sent from Newnansville to gather corn in a field about a mile from the village; they were fired upon by the Indians. The men and negroes escaped to the fort, but left the cart in the hands of the enemy. It was a rainy evening : spies were sent to discover the situation and force of the enemy. They were discovered in the hammock of San Filaseo, four miles distant, about three hundred in number. The next morning (Sabbath) Colonel Warren marched out to attack them at the head of one hundred and fifty men; one hundred mounted volunteers, twenty-five gentleman citizens, and twenty-five U. S. troops. He advanced in three columns, the right led by Colonel Warren, the left by Col. Mills, and the centre by Captain Tompkins with the regulars, and a twenty-four pound howitzer. Within three-fourths of a mile of the hammock they were met by the enemy, and the battle immediately commenced along the right wing and centre, while the enemy attempted to turn the left flank; but they were charged with spirit by Colonel Mills, who drove them into a scrub on the border of the hammock, from which they were routed by the artillery, which played upon them with great effect. Their next attempt was on the right ; but they were soon driven again under range of the howitzer, which did good execution. The Indians twice charged upon the centre, to take the howitzer, but were repelled, and they were at length routed at all points and driven one and half miles into a dense hammock.

This engagement continued one and a half hours ; during a full hour, the firing was heavy along the whole line. The Indians sustained it with desperate obstinacy, and twice charged on the artillery, with a daring beyond any former example ; but they fired very carelessly, as usual; not one of our men were killed, and but five wounded. We know not the loss of the enemy ; many were seen to fall before the artillery, especially on the left ; but no bodies were found on the field ; much blood was seen. A very tall Indian rode on horseback, and gave orders on the right ; a whole platoon directed their fire on him until he fell, but he was immediately carried off.

The leaders of each column distinguished themselves, by great coolness and activity. Adjutant Gilleland and Captains Beckham, Walker and Ward and Lieutenants Breeton and Hindly, displayed great bravery and good conduct as did Doctors Pelot and Turtelot. Private Weyman was wounded at the howitzer, by the first fire of the enemy, but he refused to leave his post, till compelled by loss of blood.

About the middle of September, the Tennessee brigade under Gen. Armstrong, at the solicitation of Gov. Call, left Montgomery in Alabama, and marched for Florida. At Tallahasse they drew provisions and proceeded to the Suwanne River, which they reached on the 26th. At Old Town they found but one small boat, and were three days crossing the river, by which time their provisions and forage were expended. At this post provisions were expected to have been drawn, but all that could be obtained was half rations of pickled pork and spoiled sea biscuit. Forage there was none ; but the troops being anxious to reach the enemy, pushed forward with tolerable spirits. At Old Town, Gov. Call was announced to the army as commander in chief. The Tennesseans remarked, that it would have been well for him to have placed in depôt, some of the provisions and forage that he had promised them in abundance ; especially as they learned that he could command the funds of the United States Treasury, as far as it should be necessary, in conducting the war, and he had the whole previous season, seven or eight months, to prepare for this emergency.

On the 30th an Indian trail was discovered, leading to the right. Four companies, among which were the spies, were detached in pursuit of the Indians, with directions to join the army that night ; but the guide lost his way and the detachment did not join the army until the 3d of October, at Fort Drane. During this march, they lived on beef broiled without salt.

The army, during their march, discovered a party of Indians collecting cattle ; twenty of which they had penned. Four of the Indians were killed, and the cattle driven off and eaten by our troops. On Saturday, the first day of October, the army reached Fort Drane ; expecting to find Oseola and his red skins at that place ; they had marched thirty miles that day, and their mortification was excessive, on their arrival, to find it abandoned. Large smokes indicated the situation of the Seminoles about two miles east of the fort ; but the troops were encamped. In the morning all arose anxious, and expecting to be led in pursuit of the game almost in sight. No order was given for marching ; it was said that we must wait for the spies. Sunday passed, and on Monday evening the four companies joined the army. The Troops were on the alert again to pursue the enemy. A detachment of two hundered men, had been sent out, on Sunday to reconnoitre ; they discovered the Indian camp, recently abandoned. Victuals cooking on the fire ; cooking untensils, pigs and fowls tied, evry thing indicated a sudden flight, and cart tracks pointed out the course of the fugitives. But the commander in chief, said we must wait for provisions to arrive from Black Creek. The provisions did arrive, and the army finally marched on the 8th of Dec. to *follow* the enemy, who had ample time, either to hide, or choose his place of defence, as might best please him. The troops had submitted to live on half rations of weavel eaten biscuit, and ride their favorite horses without forage ; they had strained every vital to reach the enemy's camp ; they did this, expecting to take him by surprise and end the war at once ; and he was permitted to fly from them without an attempt to check him—to take their women and children, and their corn and baggage in carts, and quietly to wend their way to the strong holds of Ouithlacooche.

Major Pierce arrived at Fort Drane with one hundred mounted men to escort the wagons. The army, one thousand eight hundred strong, with a large train of wagons and artillery, marched on the 8th, following the cart road the Indians had made on their retreat. They were five days reaching the forks of the Ouithlacooche. On the evening of the 12th, the advanced guard fell upon a camp of Indians just at the end of Long Swamp. They killed fourteen men, and took four squaws and six or eight children prisoners. One of the squaws offered to pilot the army to Oseola's camp the next morning, which she said contained most of the warriors of the nation, and all the noted chiefs. On the 13th the army traversed the Long Swamp and entered the open pine woods, where the road divided ; one leading to a ford below the forks of the river, and the other across the north branch. Colonel Guild, with three hundred Tennesseans, was ordered to examine the latter, and attack a negro town, which was situate on the south side of the stream ; while Major Gordon, with the spy guard, should reconnoitre the former. Colonel Guild had proceeded about three miles to a stream, when the guide, Seminole Billy, halted to point out the fording place. First one, then a volley of rifle shots were poured upon the troops from the other shore. The guide fell dead. The troops dismounted and treed in the best manner they could, and opened a fire at random against an invisible foe, for an hour ; during which time three were killed including Billy the guide, and nine wounded. The enemy ceased firing, but, without a guide, no one knew where to cross the stream ; they, therefore, returned to camp. Major Gordon approached the main river through a thick swamp; the waters were high and covered the trail. At the bank of the river a fire was opened upon them from the western bank, but the distance being 250 yards, little execution could be done. Major Gordon received a slight wound in the breast from a spent ball. Cudjoe, a negro guide, and the squaw, entered the river and offered to cross, but the troops were recalled.

The army had now been from Fort Drane five days, and their ten day's rations were gone ; so says the report. Orders were given to march to Fort Halliman, near the mouth of the river, to meet General Reed, who was ordered to bring on supplies in steamboats. A detachment was sent forward to make discoveries and report. Early the detachment returned

33

and reported that no provisions had arrived.   A council was called, and a retreat to Fort Drane determined on.

It was afterwards discovered that the detachment never went to Fort Halliman; that General Reed was in the river, but had lost his steamboat; the bow and stern being aground at high water, on the falling of the tide, the centre of the boat settled and broke in two, and became a wreck.   He afterwards built a large barge, and ascended the river; but no depôt of provisions was ever placed there.

The next day, the 16th, an express reached the camp of the Governor from Colonel Lane, who had just crossed the Ouithlacooche at Gaines' Battle Ground.   An escort, under Lieutenant Petway, was sent to him, and he joined the army on the 19th at Fort Drane, with seven hundred friendly Indians.   An express was sent to Black Creek with orders to Major Pierce to join General Call.   The Tennessee brigade was ordered to Black Creek, having lost more than half their horses by fatigue and starvation.   The troops were promised that their horses should be replaced in a short time.   The friendly Creeks were spread over the woods from Fort Drane to Santaffe.

Shortly after the arrival of Col. Lane, he expressed himself well pleased with his tour of service, and appeared in good spirits; said his health was good, except something of a brain fever.   He was invited into the tent of Captain Goff.   On remarking that it was rather warm, Captain Goff stepped out to have the sides of the tent raised; on his return, he found Col. Lane on his knees, with the point of his sword entered above his right eye into the brain : he expired immediately.   This disaster cast a gloom over the whole army.   He stood high in the estimation of all the officers and soldiers of the army.   The act was universally imputed to accident, not design.   Lieut. Col. Brown made a report of the expedition from Camp Brook, Tampa Bay, to Governor Call.

This detatchment consisted of regulars and friendly Creeks.   They embarked at Appalachicola on the 28th of September, and arrived at Tampa Bay the next day.   The forces were landed on the 30th.   Colonel Lane being informed that the Seminoles were committing depredations in the neighborhood, he started the same afternoon with twelve mounted men and one hundred Creeks, to seek the enemy.

After a rapid march of twelve miles the enemy were discovered on the east side of Indian River.   Without waiting for the Creeks, he charged the enemy, two hundred in number, who concentrated themselves in a large hammock lower down the river, where they were kept at bay until Major Watson arrived with the Creeks.   A warm engagement ensued for fifteen minutes, when Major Watson led a charge across the river.   The Seminoles poured in their rifle shots until the Creeks reached the shore; they then began sullenly to retire, still keeping up a running fire for one and a half miles: they then separated and fled in every direction. Colonel Lane and the mounted men pursued them till dark. During the engagement a Mr. Kelly observed an Indian take deliberate aim at Col. Lane; he threw himself before his commander, and received the ball in his body. This act of devotion, shews the enthusiasm of a lofty and generous mind, and deserves a record in the history of these perilous times. May the actor find a balm for his wound in the sympathy of his admiring countrymen. Maj. Watson and Lieut. Linnard are said to have distinguished themselves in this affair. Two only, of our men were wounded.

Col. Lane continued at Tampa until the 10th October, when he crossed the Hillsborough River, and encamped one mile from the fort. In the three succeeding days they had progressed fifty-seven miles without discovering an enemy. On the 14th, having marched about four miles, a hostile Indian appeared on the right flank; he escaped. On arriving at the place where he disappeared, the army were in full view of the Olocklikany, or Spotted Lake, which extended northwardly, as far as the eye could reach. It was sprinkled with islets of heavy timbered land, some of which were detached or insulated; others were connected together by marshes more or less extensive, and usually covered by tall, heavy grass. A fresh trail was soon found, and a village soon after discovered. Horses and baggage were left, and the trail pursued in a north-east direction to the village; it was deserted. They turned southwardly, passed fine hammock land, arrived at a ford two hundred yards wide, dashed in, raised their ammunition on the point of their bayonets, and had to swim part of the way. They found the south shore covered by extensive corn fields, with a few cattle and ponies. Here was another small village. They followed the trail past this settlement, across a marsh, at least a mile in extent. The Creeks plunged into the water and mud, which in places was five or six feet deep. The volunteers followed; the few horses rode this far were abandoned, and the balance of the way crossed on foot, up to their neck in water and soft mud. On reaching terra firma, they found themselves on a beautiful, fertile island, several miles in extent. The trail still continued southerly. In about a mile it led to an extensive village, recently abandoned. Here were cattle, hogs, domestic utensils, and several white men's scalps. The trail then turned westwardly half a mile, and led to another large and flourishing village, with similar improvements. The two villages contained at least one hundred and fifty houses. In another half mile, the trail led to a declivity, at the foot of which was a small pond, skirted on the left by a dense scrub for half a mile; on the right a hammock of thick, heavy timber. Here the enemy made a stand, and saluted their invaders with a shower of rifle balls. The fire was promptly returned for half an hour, when the Indians retreated to the hammock. They were pursued for more than a mile, skirmishing the whole way. At length their path crossed an open field, across which the Indians scampered, our men in full chase. On reaching another hammock the Indians scattered in every direction, and the chase was given up. The loss of the enemy was unknown, as were their numbers. We had one man wounded. The troops drove two hundred head of cattle back on their return to camp, and killed probably one hundred, and as many hogs. During the night the Creeks increased our cattle to four hundred head. On the 16th Col. Lane crossed the Ouithlacooche, and joined the army under Gov. Call.

During the first campaign of General Call, orders were sent to the Quarter Master at Garey's Ferry, to forward to the head of Lake George, a quantity of provision for the use of the army; accordingly, the steamboats Santee, John Stoney, and Charleston were sent, loaded with stores, and having in tow two schooners. These vessels lay a week, or more, at the south end of the lake. On the return of the army at Fort Drane, they were recalled to Black Creek.

Major Pierce was then sent to Savanna and Charleston, to procure more horses and forage. While the Tennessee volunteers were stationed at Black Creek, the Creeks strolled over the woods, between Fort Drane and Santaffe. The Governor's head quarters were at Fort Drane, until the 11th of November, at which time, the army, composed of the Tennessee brigade, one regiment of them on foot, under General Armstrong, 950 strong, 350 regulars, 200 Floridians, and the Creek regiment of six hundred Indians, 2100 in all, marched again to the forks of the Ouithlacooche; the next day they encamped within three miles of that river.

On the 13th, the Tennessee volunteers applied for the honor of forcing a passage across the river; but it being reported that the enemy had retired, they were detached to make an attack on the negro town, on the south side of Spring Creek, where Colonel Guild, with three hundred Tennesseans, had been foiled during the last campaign.

The Creeks under Colonel Pierce, supported by the regulars, crossed the river without opposition. The water was very cold; the stream, more than two hundred yards wide, one fourth of the distance swimming, and quite swift. Many of the troops suffered severely, and four of the regulars were drowned.

The Governor afterwards crossed the river with Colonel Warren's mounted volunteers. The whole region of the cove had been deserted for several days. The freshest trails led towards the Wahoo Swamp, which extends up the south, or main branch of the Ouithlacooche, nearly to the Tampa road.

Colonel Pierce with his Creeks, Warren's mounted volunteers, and part of the regulars, were detached to make a circuit round the south branch of the river, and to unite again with Governor Call, on the Tampa road; while the Governor recrossed and joined the Tennessee troops at the camp, on the east side of the river.

He found General Armstrong at the camp. The Tennesseans succeeded in swimming Spring Creek without opposition; they burnt two negro villages, and took a negro, old and infirm, who told them that all the Indians had removed into the Wahoo Swamp.

The Governor then proceeded with the Tennessee and regular troops, up the east side of the Ouithlacooche, in search of the enemy. They were discovered about four hundred yards from the line of march, on the 17th; they were encamped near a large hammock. Colonel Bradford's regiment was detached to attack them; the enemy fled, leaving many of their packs of provisions behind them. At the edge of the hammock they made a stand, under cover of the forest trees. The volunteers were ordered to dismount; while executing the order, they received the enemies' fire. The fire was quickly returned, and kept up until an order was given to charge the hammock, when the Seminoles fled, leaving behind their horses and baggage. Twenty red skins were found dead in the wood, and numerous bloody trails were followed into the swamp, where our men pursued them waist deep in mud. Our loss was one killed, and ten wounded; one mortally.

The army then retired about four miles to the pine woods, and encamped. On the 18th, the waggon train was placed under a strong guard, and Colonel Trousdale's regiment, part of the first regiment, and the spy companies, were sent under the command of General Armstrong, to penetrate the Wahoo Swamp; they found a large trail which led through some hammocks and across two streams into a large field, covered with bur weeds, with a few houses. The enemy had set fire to these and retreated to the hammocks. Colonel Trousdale's foot regiment were formed in open order, to charge the hammock, while the horse were formed on the right and left to protect the flanks. Before the order was given to charge, a heavy fire was poured upon the whole line. Our troops returned the fire, and slowly approached the hammock for some time, until the order to charge, sent them shouting into the hammock. Immediately the enemy opened their fire on both flanks, and on the rear, where about fifty bolted into the field. The horsemen dismounted, and charged into the woods, where the ground was contested with desperation for more than half an hour, when the Seminoles gave way on all sides. Captain Fletcher, with a small company drawn from the left flank, charged, and dispersed the enemy in the rear. The troops were then recalled to the field, and formed in order. Our loss was three killed, and fifteen wounded. Twenty-five Indians were found dead in the hammock. The force of the enemy was supposed to be seven hundred. They had every advantage of position, and at one time surrounded us. Our open order, and rapid charge saved the army, which was marched back to camp in the night.

On the 19th, the army was marched to Dade's battle ground, where a junction was formed with Col. Pierce.

This division had been detained all the 16th in crossing Cove Creek, which they reached about five miles from their encampment at the Forks. On the 17th they marched about twelve miles in a southern direction, over a pine country ; encamped at four o'clock, and sent out several scouting parties. One of the flanking parties had discovered five Indians, and gave chase ; the Indians dropped their packs, and made their escape.

18th. Left the camp under a guard, and marched east on a plain trail, about six miles to the river. On the way, the advanced guard discovered five Indians, probably the same before discovered, on the edge of a small prairie, painting themselves ; gave chace, but the Indians escaped to the left of the trail. On reaching the river, a canoe was found at the landing ; one of the volunteers got into it, and paddled nearly across the river, but found it too deep to ford. On his return, one of the officers entered the canoe and examined the river ; after which the canoe was ordered to be cut in pieces. As soon as that was begun, a shower of balls from the other shore indicated that the owners put their veto on the act. The fire was returned, and kept up an hour and a half. Some of the enemies' balls struck our men without entering, and the distance was evidently too great to do much execution. The division was marched back to camp. At 4 P. M. the line of march was again resumed, and the troops finally encamped for the night, on the S. W. bank of the river, six miles south of the ford visited in the morning. During this day's march, many Indian settlements were passed ; they were usually situate on the borders of the hammocks, or in the edge of the pine woods.

At the present encampment, the western bank of the river was high, a plain trail led to a ford where a raft was tied ; it had lately been used for ferrying over cattle. The river was deep, about one hundred yards wide, and covered with bonnets, or nymphæ.

19th. Marched S. E. to the Tampa road, which they struck one fourth of a mile south of the south fork of Ouithlacooche. They forded the river, which was only knee deep, and continued five or six miles to the north fork, where they camped.

20th. Proceeded to Dade's battle ground, and joined General Call. Preparations were made for another attack on the Wahoo.

21st. The army marched in three columns. The Tennessee troops formed the right. The regulars with Colonel Warren's volunteers, the centre, led by Colonel Pierce. The flank regiment the left. They reached the scene of action of the 18th, about 10 o'clock A. M. The Seminoles were ready to receive them. The right and centre columns marched directly to the hammock in line of battle, received the enemy's fire, and without discharging a gun, rushed into the hammock, beat up the enemy, and then poured upon them a destructive fire, which immediately routed them. Their route was soon discovered. Colonel Pierce with his division and the Creeks, pursued. Colonel Trousdale, and Colonel Warren followed to support them. Colonel Brown, with a small body of Creeks, followed close upon the heels of the enemy, until they entered a cypress swamp, where they were brought to bay. They were strongly posted behind a deep creek, flanked by two boggy ponds. Major Moniac, an educated Creek warrior, in attempting to force the creek, fell dead, as did some other Creeks who supported him. The Seminoles were elated, and Colonel Brown considering his command in danger, retreated until the Florida militia, and the volunteers of Warren arrived to support him. Several companies of artillery under Colonel Gardener soon arrived, and these were succeeded by Colonel Pierce, with Colonel Trousdale. Some of the regulars and Tennesseans, had unfortunately taken a trail that led into an impassable morass, from which they were with difficulty extricated. When the fire of all our troops opened upon the enemy, his fire slackened, but was partially continued in different parts of the line, till 4 o'clock P. M. During the engagement the hostile chiefs were heard to assure their men that the whites could not cross the creek, and our commander appeared to be of the same opinion ; for he withdrew the troops from the swamp and after forming them in the open field, they were withdrawn four miles to the camp; where they arrived at 10 o'clock in the evening, and where the Seminoles followed them, and cut the throats of twenty of their horses. The next morning the army was marched for Volusia. Seven schooners, and four steamboats, awaited them at the head of Lake George, laden with provisions. Five regulars were killed, one Tennessean, and three friendly Creeks, among whom was Major Moniac. Captains Ross, and Maitland were wounded ; the former since died, the latter recovered. Seven regulars, and eight Tennesseans wounded. Ten Seminoles were found dead, north of the creek. There was no means of ascertaining their loss on the south side.

The army arrived at Volusia on the 24th, where they were joined by

General Jessup, who arrived from Tampa Bay with four hundred mounted Alabama volunteers. Here he received orders from the Secretary at War, to assume the command of the army, and Governor Call of course retired. On his rout, Gen. Jessup had taken thirty-three negro prisoners, and an Indian who was placed as a guard over them. These negroes were the property of Col. Rees, taken at Spring Garden plantation. They stated that they had generally been kept on acorns and such roots as they could dig in the woods.

Thus ended the third campaign against the Seminoles.

For this campaign, Gov. Call had the whole summer to prepare, with power to draw on the treasury of the United States for any amount of funds he might deem necessary, and to employ as many troops as he pleased.

It was a service anxiously sought by him, if we may judge by his letters. That directed to the President, Jan. 9th, 1836, reads thus. " I should be highly gratified to command the army, and believe I could soon bring the war to a close. I fear however, that I cannot do it without injustice to General Clinch. He is a brave and good man, but I fear he is too slow in his movements, to conduct a war against the Indians." His Excellency's letter on the subject of his appointment to the command, instead of Gen. Jessup, indicated a similar desire. We regret that we cannot at this time obtain a copy of it.

The Seminole war has not yet been " brought to a close." So far from driving the Seminoles from Florida, they have driven his excellency from their boundaries.

The army of Gov. Call, consisted of one thousand Tennesseans, four hundred regulars, two hundred Florida volunteers and seven hundred Creeks; in all two thousand and three hundred. With these, he was more than two months in the field. More than ten times the force, commanded by the *slow General Clinch*, and with fifty times his resources. Let us refer to his official report to see what he accomplished.

" All the strong holds of the enemy have been penetrated and explored, and they have been defeated in four several engagements." This is very well if true. But other parts of the report seem to contradict these statements. " Yet the passage was not gained, for all previous attempts to turn or pass it had failed, and its practicability was unascertained. The officers in command of the troops engaged, decided that the attempt should not be made, at so late an hour in the day, *with an entire ignorance of the country behind :* and they accordingly withdrew their men." Withdrew them four miles from the swamp, to a camp in the pine woods, where the Indians followed them, and cut the throats of twenty of their horses before morning. We are informed, that on the 17th and 18th the Seminoles met our troops at the edge of the hammocks, from which, after sustaining sharp·skirmishes, they retired to *one* of "their strong holds," expecting undoubtedly to have been pursued, to a situation where they could defend themselves more advantageously. In this they were disappointed. On the third day, the 21st, they effected their object, and what was the result. Take the words of the official report. "The officers commanding, decided that the attempt (to force the creek) should not be made," and they accordingly withdrew the men. Can this be defeating the enemy? Is this penetrating their strong holds? The strong holds of the Seminoles, are the Wahoo swamp; the islands of the Olocklikany; Tokopalika and the Everglades. Governor Call's army have played around some of these; they have penetrated not one. Col. Lane peeped into one or two of the Olocklikany islands, and drove off seven hundred head of cattle from them; Col. Brown is still living and can point them out, when men can be found seriously disposed to beat up the strong holds of the enemy.

But where are the four several engagements mentioned in the official report? we can find but three hinted at; unless the burning of the negro houses on Spring Creek be called an engagement. Were it not better for the Reporter to leave out the word *defeated* altogether?

" The army having exhausted the last day that could be spared, without incurring actual starvation." They had been absent from Fort Drane ten days. " Encumbered with an immense baggage train."—An immense baggage train! from sixty to eighty five horse wagons, to hunt Indians, and carry only ten days' provisions!!! " The enemy weakened, defeated, dispersed, can offer no effectual resistance to the fine army commanded by Jessup." We have no evidence that the enemy are either weak, low spirited, or fled. Rumor states that they are ordered to concentrate at Tokopalika; this may be true, or it may not; should it prove to be true, General Jessup will, at this late hour, have the bull to take by the horns. Tokopalika is the strong hold of Philip, the most mischievous of all the Seminole chiefs; he who has committed more depredations in Florida, than all the rest of the nation put together; and this Philip has not, during this long Florida war, been even pointed at.

Now we will not say that our governor has done nothing: but we do say that he has done much less than he promised; some think, much less than he ought, with the means and the time he commanded. His eulogizers would have done their chief more honor, and themselves more credit, by acknowledging the injustice he did Clinch; and instead of boasting of victories, to have confessed that his errors in neglecting to prepare for the emergencies of the campaign, subjected him to great disappointments.

We cannot dismiss the official report without one more passing commentary. "This was really a most brilliant affair." "At the point of ground in the centre of the field, occupied by the commanding general and his staff, the balls were *distinctly seen*, and heard to strike and cross each other, from three sides at the moment."

The commanding general and his staff are greatly to be envied. There are few men of taste that would not volunteer one campaign, to behold so brilliant a phenomenon. These Seminoles are the most amusing enemies, and know how to distinguish the aristocracy of the army. The knaves made no bones of plumping the blood-thirsty Ross and Maitland, and Moniac, and the sorry fellows who pursued them to the border of their "strong hold," but fired their rifle balls slowly merely to be seen, *not felt*, by the "commanding general and his staff."

One word respecting DEPÔTS, and we dismiss this campaign. General Reed, early last summer, published at Tallahasse, an opinion on this subject. He being supposed a favorite of the governor, his plan was considered as rather official, and it was universally approved. The plan consisted in establishing depôts of provisions as near the heart of the Indian country as steamboats could ascend. Say on the Suwanne, the Ouithlacooche, and Spanish, or Clear Water River,—on the Gulf side; at Volusia, and Lake Monroe, on the St. Johns River; and if extended to the Atlantic, along the coast. Were this done, a detachment of soldiers, in pursuit of the enemy, would, at no time, be more than two days' march from a depôt of provisions. This would save the expense of "immense baggage trains," with all their train of evils. We happen to know that some of the governor's best friends approved of this, and urged upon him its importance; and what is more, we have been assured that he approved of it, and said that it was perfectly consistent with his own opinion. Let us ask then why was it utterly neglected? A writer in the St. Augustine Herald has stated, since this campaign has gone by, that it were folly to establish depôts; that to defend four depôts would require more troops than the army contained. Yet the small post of Halliman's, was, by thirty men, defended six weeks against the whole Indian nation. General Jessup has declared that he could do nothing successfully, until a cordon of posts was established across the country. Dear-bought experience has taught us, that where military posts and depôts of provisions cannot be maintained, the country must be abandoned to the enemy.

December 13th.—A fourth campaign has commenced under the command of General Jessup. He has left the "immense baggage train," and of the two thousand horses he has taken a few only to pack provisions. In the mean time, the General and his troops have taken packs of food upon their backs, and have sought the enemy in their swamps. We sincerely wish them success, but we know the country, and the resources of the enemy, too well to expect a conclusion of the war this season.

The Tennessee brigade being collected at Volusia, moved with the army under General Jessup, who left about one hundred men under the command of Col. Gardener, to protect the post.

By the middle of December General Jessup was prepared to commence operations; he had sent orders to Tampa Bay for Colonel Foster to meet him, or rather to approach the west side of the Ouithlacooche below the military road, and to scour the hammocks and the cove of Olocklikany, with all the troops that could be spared from Fort Brook; while he, with the troops left by Governor Call, pushed into the "strong holds" of the enemy. He explored the forks of the river, and the heart of the Wahoo Swamp, where he found the habitations of the Indians recently deserted, but not an enemy could be found. Having learned the force of the present commander, they thought it not prudent to meet him on a spot that had become too well known. They had therefore removed their quarters. The two divisions of the army continued simultaneously to scour the country on both sides of the river, until the General was satisfied that the enemy had fled. One solitary native was found and taken prisoner.

The army retired to Tampa Bay, where the Tennessee troops, under General Armstrong, were embarked for New Orleans, on their way home; their time of service having expired.

After the Tennessee troops were disposed of, General Jessup removed his head quarters to Fort Dade, a post that had recently been established at the point where the old military road crosses the south branch of the Ouithlacooche. From this post reconnoitering parties were sent in every direction to scour the country and endeavor to discover the enemy. It was at length discovered that the leading trails all pointed to the south east, towards the Everglades.

On the 22d of January, General Jessup marched in pursuit of the enemy, pursuing their trails to the south east.

On the 23d, Col. Cawfield, accompanied by Lieut. Chambers, was despatched with a battalion of the Alabama volunteers, Captain Harris's company of marines, and Maj. Morris's Indian warriors, to attack Osuche, who was reported to have a large force near the Apopke Lake: they were overtaken, and Osuche and his son were killed; nine women and children, and eight negroes were taken prisoners; the rest of the Indians escaped. One of the friendly Indians was mortally wounded.

As the trails still continued south eastwardly, they were vigorously pursued across the sand hills, that rise very high about the head waters of the Ocklawaha. The ascent of these hills is so great, that large details of men were employed with drag ropes to draw up the artillery and baggage on the 24th.

On the 27th, numerous herds of Indian cattle were discovered feeding about the prairies of Thlapackhatche Creek, and the converging of the trails indicated the collecting of the Indians into one body. A careful reconnoisance was ordered.

Col. Henderson, with Col. Cawfield's battalion, Harris's mounted marines, and Morris's Indians, were detached to scour the country, and, if possible, bring the enemy to battle. The detachment was accompanied by Lieut. Chambers, one of the General's aids. The enemy were discovered on the Hatche Luste Creek, near the Uche-anatho-clucco Swamp. They were attacked with vigor; the Indians hastily fled into the swamp. Lieut. Chambers at the head of Price's Alabama volunteers, made a rapid charge on the horses and baggage of the enemy, and captured them, with twenty-five women, children and negroes. Col. Henderson pursued the fugitives into the swamp, and across the Hatche Luste Creek, where they made a short stand, but finally scattered and disappeared.

The first express sent to the General, was shot by the Indians.

At this period information was brought in, that a large Indian force were lying about two miles to the right of the camp. Major Whiting's battalion being left in reserve, the sixth infantry, with Major Graham's company, and a small body of Creek warriors, were sent to that point, but the enemy had fled, leaving their fires burning and provisions cooking. Night approaching, the detachment returned to the camp, which they reached about nine o'clock. In about an hour afterwards Colonel Henderson also returned. During this day an Indian woman was taken sick on the trail; her husband refused to leave her, and they were both taken to the camp.

On the 28th, the above mentioned Indian was sent out to invite Abraham, the interpreter of Micanopy, to come into the camp. The army then moved on to Tokapalika Lake, and took up a strong position on the west bank, near to where the Big Cypress Swamp joins it. Several hundred head of cattle were taken on the borders of the Lake.

On the 29th, the prisoner returned, and reported that Abraham and Alligator would visit the General. On the 31st, Abraham came in and conversed with the General. On the 3d of February he brought in Jumper, Alligator, Hopatophe and another. They agreed to meet General Jessup at Fort Dade, with all the other chiefs, on the 18th, to make another treaty. In the mean time, it was agreed that hostilities should cease.

The army commenced its return march on the 4th, and reached Fort Dade on the 7th of February.

Early in December, Col. Fanning was despatched to Lake Monroe, to

Drawn by M. Creware's Lith.

FORT MELLON, LAKE MONROE.

(East Florida.)

30. Wall Street, New York.

establish a military post with about four companies of artillery, and a battalion of South Carolina volunteers, under Major Harlee, and thirty friendly Creeks, under Paddy Car, and Captain Piercy. A small picketing, and breastwork were commenced on the south west bank of the lake. On the 8th of February, Philip brought a force of about four hundred Seminoles against them. He commenced his attack about 5 o'clock in the morning, by pouring a volley of rifle shot upon the tents, and raising the war yell. The troops directly turned out and returned the fire, and a smart engagement was kept up for three hours. The Seminoles dashed into the camp of Paddy Car, and ejected the Creeks without ceremony, carrying away their baggage. They at one time got behind one end of the line of pickets. Lieutenant Thomas was sent on board the steamer Santee, that lay at anchor in front of the post, from which he opened the fire of a six pounder, loaded with grape and cannister, and raked a part of the enemie's line. Early in the engagement, Captain Mellon, a veteran offirce of the artillery, was shot through the breast and immediately expired; Lieutenant Langley was also badly wounded. About 8 o'clock, the enemy fled. They were followed by the Creeks, who mocked them and dared them to come back, but they quickly disappeared. We had one killed, and fourteen privates wounded. We have since learned by negroes that have come in, that the Indians had twenty-five killed, and a much greater number wounded. After retreating several miles, the Seminoles met three hundred of their companions coming to join them. They were about to return, but a runner came in from Micanopy, informing them of the Armistice. It is believed that Philip was badly wounded, as he has not been seen abroad since the time of the battle; and the Indians say that he is sick.

Several chiefs of the Seminoles came in according to agreement, and the old treaty of Payne's Landing, was agreed to be fulfilled.

The Chiefs agreed to collect all their people, and have them ready to embark by the 10th of May, and to bring in, and deliver up to General Jessup, all the slaves they had taken during the war. The United States was to pay for all their cattle and ponies, and the annuities and subsistence, according to the former articles. Nearly all the chiefs signed this new treaty except Philip, who never came in; Coe Hajo, however, agreed to answer for all his people, alleging that he, and not Philip, was their lawful chief. On the 10th, very few of the Seminoles had come in, and another day, the 25th of May, was fixed on as the time for embarkation. In the mean time a great number of transports had been collected at Tampa Bay, for the purpose of removing them, the expense of which was enormously great. Before the 25th, a report got in circulation among the Seminoles, that the pale faces were going to get them all embarked on board the transports and then cut their throats; this was made an excuse for all the Indians to run to the woods again. General Jessup directed the chiefs to send out runners, and contradict the report, which they agreed to do, and a new day was set for embarking. In the mean time several murders were committed in Allachua, and Columbia Counties; several whole families were cut off, their houses plundered and burned.

On the 5th of April, the commanding General issued an order, (No. 79 which see in the Appendix B,) in which he forbids all white men, except those employed in the service of the United States, to enter any part of the territory between St. John's River, and the Gulf of Mexico, south of Fort Drane.

This order gave great dissatisfaction to the inhabitants of East Florida. A large meeting was held at St. Augustine, and a spirited remonstrance was got up and published, and copies of it sent to General Jessup, and to the secretary of war. We have never heard any result of this measure, except that General Jessup directed that any slaves taken from the Indians, should be sent to Fort Mellon, instead of St. Mark's.

Large bodies of Seminoles, commanded by Powel, and Coe Hajo, collected near Fort Mellon, about the last of April, where a great ball play was got up, in order, as Powel said, to bring in all the scattering Indians. At the time appointed, the officers of Fort Mellon were invited, and many did attend. But they have never proceeded to Camp Brook to embark. On the contrary, it has been discovered that they have planted extensive fields of corn, and evince a settled determination to remain in Florida. The Seminoles continued in large parties around Fort Mellon, till the middle of June, drawing rations, but the chiefs rarely appearing, Colonel Harney refused to give them provisions. This brought Philip to the Fort. It was his first appearance; he alleged that sickness had prevented him, and his emaciated appearance tended to confirm his statement.

On the 2d of June, however, Powel at the head of two hundred Mickasookies came to Tampa, surrounded the camp of Micanopy, and forced them all to take the woods. The sixteen hostages of General Jessup were thus safely disposed of, with the exception of Abraham, who continued in camp, to keep up the farce. Micanopy sent back word to General Jessup, that " he had a straight tongue." He sent also a sum of money to the suttler, which he owed him, and a horse that he had borrowed at the camp, with a general permission to the officers of the garrison, to *ride over his ground.*

Powel also sent in a message stating that his reason for leaving the fort, was a fear of the small pox; the measles having appeared among the soldiers, he said the Indians were alarmed. When the Seminoles returned to the neighborhood of Fort Mellon, they again visited the post as usual.

Colonel Harney hearing of the flight of the hostages from Tampa, determined to make prisoners of as many of their chiefs as possible. To this end he appointed a day to hold a talk with them, determining to close the gates of the fort on them ; one of the steamboats actually carried to the fort several pairs of handcuffs to secure them. The time arrived for the talk, but only a few of the sub-chiefs attended, and they conducted with much caution. Presently a message arrived from Powel, informing the commandant that he had heard of the compliment that awaited him and therefore thought it best to stay away.

Volusia was abandoned early in June ; the troops were very sickly. On arriving at Picolata, there were very few fit for duty ; they all however, recovered very soon after their removal. About the same time the garrison at Fort Mellon, were greatly afflicted with the cholera morbus ; it was attributed to the rapid falling of the waters in the lake and river. This disease was not fatal, nor did it continue long ; but the fort was ordered to be evacuated, and Colonel Harney drew off the garrison to Picolata, about the middle of the month.

At the time the troops left Fort Mellon, Coa-cou-che, the youngest son of Philip, was at the post. Colonel Harney observed to him, that unless the Seminoles removed according to their treaty, the whites would exterminate them. Coa-cou-che said that Iste chatte did not understand that word. General Thompson had talked that way, he said but he paid for it with his blood. The Great Spirit he knew might exterminate them, but the pale faces could not ; else, why had they not done it before. He did not however, appear to be irritated, and promised that he would not burn the post after it should be abandoned.

Directly after the evacuation of this post, the Seminoles spread themselves over the whole country, and the planters generally, abandoned their crops and retired to the vicinity of the posts for safety.

On the 25th of June, a party of Indians shot Captain John Walton, of the light ship, stationed behind Carysford reef. Captain Walton had left the ship with four of his crew, all unarmed ; had gone to Key Largo, where for some years past he had cultivated a garden. The Indians observing them, laid in wait until they landed ; they then rose and fired on them, killing Captain Walton, and one of his men ; the latter fell in the water. The other three men escaped to the boat, and were saved, although two of them were wounded. The Indians pursued them to their boat, and in so doing wet their rifles, so that they were unable to use them until the men were out of reach. The captains of some of the wreckers with their crews, went to the island, where they found Captain Walton and his man, stripped, scalped, and otherwise mangled. Their bodies were taken to Mattacumbe, and

buried. Mrs. Walton and her family, were taken by Captain Sully, of the
mail boat, and conveyed to Key West. The collector of the port, sent Captain Wellington to take charge of the light ship. This act of savage bar-
barity spread universal alarm among the Florida Keys, and has probably
caused all the planters to retire to Key West, and Indian Key. Even at
those places they are much exposed, there being no troops to protect them.
The fires of the Indians are seen along the whole coast, from Cape Sable to
Jupiter Inlet

About the 4th of June, three Indians were taken near Palatka, and a
chief called Bowlegs, near camp Foster, and all detained as prisoners,
being found out of the lines prescribed to them. Other Seminoles that visited Fort King, about the first of July, were fed and permitted to go at large.
At the same time Captain Gilleland was murdered near the Echatucney
Spring, on his way from the Suwanne to Newnansville.

About this time also, a severe engagement took place in West Florida,
near the head of Black River ; between a party of militia, and a large
body of Indians, supposed to be Creeks. The Indians were routed, but the
Floridians had five men killed, and several wounded.

SEMINOLE CHIEFS.

The following is an account of the chiefs and sub-chiefs of the Seminole
Nation, so far as we have been enabled to collect information on the subject.

Micanopy has ever been considered as the legitimate chief of the Seminoles. He was formerly called Sint Chakke or frequenter of the pond ; but
after the death of his brother, who was hereditary chief, being the eldest, he
took the name of Micanopy or successor of the chief. He is a large man
of sluggish, peaceable habits, and much under the control of others,
more from indolence than want of good sense. He spent his early days on
the Wealuste or Black Creek, below Garey's Ferry ; but after he assumed
the title of chief, he fixed his abode in the heart of his tribe, and for many
years past, resided at Pilaklakaha.

Jumper is a Mickasooke, who left the Creek nation and joined the Seminoles to avoid a treaty with Gen. Jackson. He was second in command of
the Creeks, who committed the massacre of Fort Mims, Weatherby was the
leader. Jumper married the sister of Micanopy, and has usually been
considered his sense keeper, or private counsellor. They have often differed
however, and for some time separated. His residence of late, has been in
the Wahoo Swamp.

Abraham, the principal interpreter, was formerly a slave of Micanopy.
After his return from a mission to Washington City, he gave Abraham his
freedom ; he has since, been one of his principal advisers, and has as much

influence in the nation as any other man. With an appearance of great modesty, he is ambitious, avaricious and withal, very intelligent.

Neamathla, an old Creek chief, like Jumper, voluntarily exiled himself from his nation, to avoid signing the treaty with Gen. Jackson. He took up his residence at the Fowl Towns, as chief of the Mickasookies. He cleared himself a farm, on the township since given to La Fayette, and made himself very comfortable, until he was called upon, at the treaty of Moultrie, to sign it. He being rather obstinate, John Hicks was, by some management constituted principal chief of his tribe, and signed the treaty. Neamathla was however induced to sign the treaty, by being permitted to reside with thirty of his friends on a reserve of two miles square, at the Tuphulga village, and receiving five hundred dollars for his improvements. The money he alleged, he was cheated out of by one of the Indian agents; he left the territory in disgust in 1826, and returned to the Creek nation, where he became the second war chief. The history of his capture in Georgia, during the last Creek war, is well known. He possessed stronger natural abilities, than any native Indian we have been acquainted with.

Col. Blunt, late a principal guide of General Jackson, Tuske Hajo, Mulatto King, Emathloche and Econchatti-micco, also had reserves of land assigned to them, on the west bank of the Chattahooche River, where they resided, till near the commencement of the Seminole war, when some banditti of the neighboring country, broke in upon them, disarmed them, stole their slaves and beat and abused Col. Blunt in such a barbarous manner, as to cause his death ; the remainder abandoned their reserves and emigrated with Black Dirt to Arkansas.

The savage treatment of these friendly Indians, may be assigned as one cause of the Seminole war.

Powel, or Oseola, is a native Red Stick ; who his father was is unkown, but it is said that his mother, who was a half breed, was at one time, connected with an Englishman of the name of Powel. We are informed by a respectable Creek chief, that his name is As-sin Yahole, *singer at the black drink*. He was little known before the difficulties commenced with the Seminoles. His daring savage character has since the war commenced raised him in the estimation of the Mickasookies, and he is at this time, a leader of much influence among them. At a visit lately made to his camp, by some of the officers from Fort Mellon, he was found at the head of four hundred and eighty warriors. Public opinion is greatly divided, respecting his character and influence ; the old chiefs are jealous of this man. He will hereafter be better known,

Fucta Luste Hajo—*Black Ragged Clay*—is an old chief of Chicuchatty; was at one time principal war chief. He is usually called Black Dirt.

He has at all times been friendly to emigration, and finally headed the Indians that removed during the last year.

Charley Emathla resided at Witumpke, a few miles from Fort King. He was quite a farmer, and a good man. He was murdered by Powel for his adherence to the treaty of Payne's Landing.

Holate Emathla was a brother of Charley. He resided at Sitarky. He was, at one time, speaker of the nation.

Although not satisfied with the manner in which our commissioners closed the treaty on them, yet he resolved to emigrate, and did so. Before his departure he joined our troops with his son, and fought the hostile Seminoles.

Catsha Tustenugge—Mad Tiger—lived at Ouithlocko. On the death of John Hicks, he was elected chief of the Mickasookies, through the intrigues of the Agent, Major Phagan, in opposition to Charley Emathla.

Yah-hah-hajo resided sometimes at Oakhumke, and at other times near Lake Eustice. He commanded about eighty warriors. He was shot by General Shelton, a volunteer from South Carolina.

Hulputti-hajo—Mad Alligator—resided at one of the towns on Telack-chopko River. He is a pleasant, merry Indian, and is considered a good warrior. He is a very active enemy.

Chatkwa Owluche—Little Cloud.—This chief commanded the Indians at the battles of Wahoo.

Hopatophe, a young warrior, nephew of Micanopy and heir apparent.

Uche Billy resided sometimes at a village west of the St. John's, and sometimes at Berresford. At the commencement of the war he went into the Creek nation, and induced one hundred, or more, of his tribe to return with him to Florida, professing to be friendly; but on his return he was induced to join Philip. Before the war, he had eight or ten followers. He is an Indian dandy.

Tiger Tail—a small chief with ten followers : a Mickasooke, from the Fowl Towns ; friendly to the whites, until he was insulted and threatened by them ; he then became a hostile and savage enemy.

Moka-is-she-larne—Sleeper—a war chief, who lived at the Wahoo Swamp.

Yaholuche—Great Cloud.

Holate Micco—Blue King—principal war chief. He resided at Ouith-locko.

Erepah.

Semethle.

Mithlake.

Yah-hah Emathla Chupko—Leading Wolf.

Hitchiti—Broken Stick.

Aripuki—Sam Jones—resided at Oakhumke. He has become a popular warrior among the Seminoles.

Osuche—Cooper—killed at Apopke Lake.

Coe Hajo—Mad Partridge—claims to be chief of all the Seminoles east of Tokapolika.

Philip has been the active commander of all the Indians that have operated east of the St. John's. He has done more mischief than all the other chiefs put together. The whole coast, up to the neighborhood of St. Augustine has been laid waste by him. His last exploit was an attack on Fort Mellon, where he was handsomely whipped off with the loss of twenty-five killed and many wounded. As he did not appear abroad for some time, it is supposed that he was wounded: his friends said he was sick.

Wild Cat, the eldest son of Philip, headed the Indians at the battle of Dun Lawton. He also commanded the party that scalped Mrs. Johns, near Jacksonville.

Tokase Emathla—John Hicks—son of the old chief.

Emachilochustern—John Walker—resided on the Chattahooche. He was robbed by the whites of a number of slaves, but got no redress.

SUB-CHIEFS.

Billy John, a free negro; lived at Pilaklakaha; joined our troops and served as a guide. He was shot while conducting a detachment of Tennesseans across Spring Creek.

Albarte Hajo,	Creeping Baby,	Long Swamp.
Tustinuc Hajo,	Half Moon,	Do.
Acata Hajo,		Do.
We flacco Matte,		Oakhumky.
Kasko Ure,	Fire Stick,	Do.
Echu Matte,	Water Serpent,	Do.
Topalange,	Wonder,	Do.
Hathaw Matte,	Sea Shell,	Do.
Chan chan tornusk,	Fallen Tree,	Ouithlocko.
Caso Tustenugge,	Yellow Bull,	Wahoo.
Cheti Haiola,	Rising Star,	Ouithlocko.
Powshaila,	Dwarf,	Do.
Emathloche,		Minotte,
Ta Caso Fiscico,		Chetucsta.

Yaha Fiscico,
Tustenuc Yaha,
Conchatte,
Tustenugge,

Crazy Eagle, (killed near Chicu-chatty,)

Do.
Hitchepucksasse
Do.
Wahoo.

GLOSSARY.

Nuntokay—A man.
Hokte- -A woman.
Iste hatke—A white man.
Iste chatte—A red man, etc.
Iste—A person.
Ulke—A tribe.
Seminole ulke—The Seminole tribe.
Chacteka—Father.
Chatske—Mother.
Chase—Brother.
Ewanmaw—Sister.
Chakpootsi—Son.
Chackshosti—Daughter.
Chepawne—Boy.
Hocktoche—Girl.
Eche—Husband.
Chapiwa—Wife.
Micco—King.
Emathla—Leader.
Yattika—Orator.
Tustenugge—Warrior.
Isneesay—Trader.
Timpana—Council house.
Epola—Dancing house.
Chucco—Square.
Echepuckwa—Pipe.
Casalalki—Drum.
Poko—Ball.
Tokonay—Racket stick.
Itchaysucha—Tobacco pouch.
Putchuswa—Hatchet.
Etchasutakay—Rifle.
Saphka—Knife.

Chaco—House.
Talopha—Town.
Topopeke—Pen.
Pithlo—Boat.
Topa—Bed.
Archeta—Blanket.
Connarwa—Beads.
Chalvecanowow—Armlets.
Tofa—Feathers.
Kuphatuka—Hat.
Tuksayke—Hunting-shirt.
Uphe-tayka—Leggings.
Stillspika—Moccasins.
Chasee—Deer-skin dressed.
Huksayke—Wrapper.
Hasse—Sun.
Nethlehasse—Moon.
Hutte chumba—Stars.
Nethlay—Day.
Nethlee—Night.
Totika—Fire.
Wewa—Water.
Ecunnraw—Ground.
Fucke—Dirt.
Nini—Trail road.
Wekiwa—Spring.
Hatch uche—Branch.
Hutchee—Creek.
Wethlucco—River.
Wetikay—Lake.
Tenetkay—Thunder.
Hulallay—Wind.
Itto—Tree.

Elatus—Wood.
Alaha—Orange.
Yallaha—Sweet Orange.
Yallahattmacks—Sour Orange.
Oketoksu—Magnolia.
Itto Micco—Magnolia Glacia.
Eto Micco—Red Bay.
Alatcha—Oak.
Alatka Chumpa—Live Oak.
Tala—Palm.
Tallaloko—Palmetto.
Chuli—Pine.
Helocoppe—Gum.
Uecheanatho—Cypress.
Achena—Cedar.
Haino—Maple.
Halist-chumpa—Sugar Cane.
Chastalay.—Water Mellon.
Fomischay—Musk Mellon.
Conti-katke—Coonte the bread root.
Hehla—Tannier.
Aha—Wild potato.
Atchee—Corn.
Toklike—Bread.
Pahke—Grass.
Echolocco—Horse.
Echo—Deer.
Wauca—Cow.
Yah-hah—Wolf.
Catsha—Tiger.
Efa—Dog.
Tokale—Mole.
Hulputta—Aillgator.
Kowikay—Gopher.
Lutcha—Turtle.
Saputka—Frog.
Chitta—Snake.
Okeepa—Musquito.
Yahchilane—Eagle.
Pochelane—Paroquet.

Wartola—Sandhill Crane.
Wauco—Heron.
Attolochate—Curliew.
Sochapaka—Pelican.
Soole—Buzzard.
Huppe—Owl.
Sukvulbar—Bat.
Futcho—Duck.
Penwa—Turkey.
Fuschatti—Red Bird.
Fuswahaya—Mockingbird.
Patchechole—Dove.
Petche—Pigeon.
Haintstohe—good.
Hulkwa
Hulwak   } Bad.
Holewagus
Hunela—Hand.
Ulwe—Tall.
Chatkwa—Small.
Kachuckanasis—Short.
Yonnotchay—Dark.
Saputhatke—Light.
Manitche—Young.
Hatke—White.
Chatte—Red.
Sopa—Blue.
Ackola—Green.
Lane—Yellow.
Chumpa—Sweet.
Arowah—I.
Oha—Thou, You, Your.
Iste—He.
Ery—My. Mine.
Mastchay—Increase number or length.
Che—Increases size, as
Echo—Deer ; Echoche—Many deer.
Nithle—Dog ; Nithlemaschay—Many dogs.

By a reference to this glossary, many of the names of rivers, towns, &c., may be better understood. Wealuste, from wewa, water, and luste, black. Pithlachucco, from Pithla, a boat, and Chucco, big, because the lake is shaped like a boat, &c.

Understanding the Seminole language but imperfectly, we have borrowed the above from Smith, Simonds, and others.

APPENDIX.

THE TREATY OF MOULTRIE CREEK.

1824.

JAMES MONROE, PRESIDENT OF THE UNITED STATES OF AMERICA—To all and singular, to whom these presents shall come greeting :—

Whereas a treaty between the United States of America, and the Florida tribes of Indians, was made and concluded on the 18th day of September, one thousand eight hundred and twenty-three, at Camp on Moultrie Creek, in the Territory of Florida, by commissioners on the part of the United States, and certain chiefs and warriors of the said tribes, on the part and in behalf of the said *tribes*, which treaty is in the following words, to wit:

ARTICLE I. The undersigned chiefs and warriors for themselves and their tribes, have appealed to the humanity, and thrown themselves on and have promised to continue under the protection of the United States, and of no other nation power or sovereign, and in consideration of the promises and stipulations hereinafter made, do cede and relinquish all claim or title which they may have to the whole Territory of Florida, with the exception of such district of country, as shall herein be alotted them.

ARTICLE II. The Florida tribes of Indians, will hereafter be concentrated and confined to the following metes and boundaries : commencing five miles north of Okehumke, running in a direct line to a point, five miles west of Setarky's settlement on the waters of Amazura, (or Withlachuche River,) leaving said settlement two miles south of the line, from thence in a direct line to the south end of the Big Hammock, to include Chickuchate, continuing on in the same direction for five miles beyond the said hammock, provided said point does not approach nearer than fifteen miles the sea coast of the Gulf of Mexico, if it does the said line will terminate at that distance from the sea coast, thence south twelve miles, thence in a south 30° east direction, until the same shall strike within five miles of the main branch of the Charlotte River, thence in a due east direction to within twenty miles of the Atlantic coast, thence north fifteen, west for fifty miles, and from this last to the beginning point.

ARTICLE III. The United States will take the Florida Indians under their care and patronage, and will afford them protection against all persons whatsoever, provided, they conform to the laws of the United States, and refrain from making war, or giving any insult to any foreign nation, without having first obtained the permission and consent of the United States : And in consideration of the appeal and cession made in the first article of this treaty, by the aforesaid chiefs and warriors, the United States promise to distribute among the tribes, as soon as concentrated under the direction of their agent, implements of husbandry, and stocks of cattle, and hogs, to the amount of six thousand dollars and an annnal sum of five thousand dollars a year, for twenty successive years, to be distributed as the President of the United States shall direct through the Secretary of War, or his superintendants and agent of Indian affairs.

ARTICLE IV. The United States promise to guarantee to the said tribes, the peaceable possession of the district of country assigned them, reserving the right of opening through it such roads, as may from time to time be deemed necessary, and to restrain and prevent all white persons from hunting, settling, or otherwise intruding upon it. But any citizen of the United States being lawfully authorized for that purpose, shall be permitted to pass and repass through the said district, and to navigate the waters thereof, without any hindrance, toll, or exaction from said tribes.

ARTICLE V. For the purpose of facilitating the removal of the said tribes to the district of country allotted them, and as a compensation for the losses sustained, or the inconveniences to which they may be exposed by said removal, the United States will furnish them with rations of corn, meat, and salt, for twelve months, commencing on the first day of February next. And they further agree, to compensate those individuals who have been compelled to abandon improvements on lands, not embraced within the limits allotted, to the amount of four thousand five hundred dollars, to be distributed among the sufferers, in a ratio to each, proportional to the value of the improvements abandoned. The United States further agree, to furnish a sum not exceeding two thousand dollars, to be expended by their agent, to facilitate the transportation of the different tribes to the point of concentration designated.

ARTICLE VI. An agent, sub-agent and interpreter, shall be appointed to reside within the Indian boundary, aforesaid, to watch over the interests of said tribes ; and the United States further stipulate, as an evidence of their humane policy towards said tribes who have appealed to their liberality, to allow for the establishment of a school at the agency, one thousand dollars per year, for twenty successive years ; and one thousand dollars per year, for the same period, for the support of a gun, and black smith, with the expenses incidental to his shop.

ARTICLE VII. The chiefs and warriors aforesaid, for themselves and tribes, stipulate to be active and vigilant in the preventing the retreating to, or passing through of the district of country assigned them of any absconding slaves or fugitives from justice, and further agree to use all necessary exertions to apprehend and deliver the same to the agent, who shall receive orders to compensate them agreeably to the trouble and expenses incurred.

ARTICLE VIII. A commissioner, or commissioners, with a surveyor, shall be appointed by the President of the United States, to run and mark, (blazing fore and aft the trees) the line as defined in the second article of this treaty; who shall be attended by a chief, or warrior, to be designated by a council of their own tribes, and who shall receive while so employed, a daily compensation of three dollars.

ARTICLE IX. The undersigned chiefs and warriors, for themselves and tribes, having objected to their concentration within the limits described in the second article of this treaty, under the impression that the said limits did not contain a sufficient quantity of good land for them to subsist on, and for other reasons: it is therefore expressly understood between the United States, and the aforesaid chiefs and warriors, that, should the country embraced in said limits, upon examination by the Indian agent and the commissioner, or commissioners, to be appointed under the 8th article of this treaty, be by them considered insufficient for the support of the said Indian tribes, then the north line as defined in the 2d article of this treaty, shall be removed so far north as to embrace a sufficient quantity of good tillable land.

ARTICLE X. The undersigned chiefs and warriors, for themselves and tribes, have expressed to the commissioners their unlimited confidence in their agent, Colonel Gad Humpreys, and their interpreter, Stephen Richards; and, as an evidence of their gratitude for their services and humane treatment, and brotherly attentions to their wants, request that one mile square, embracing the improvements of Ewhe Mathla, at Tallahasse, (said improvements to be considered as the centre) be conveyed in fee simple as a present to Colonel Gad Humphreys: and they further request that one mile square at the Ochesee Bluffs, embracing Stephen Richard's field on said bluffs, be conveyed in fee simple as a present to said Stephen Richards. The commissioners accord in sentiment with the undersigned chiefs and warriors, and recommend a compliance with their wishes to the President and Senate of the United States, but the disapproval on the part of the said authorities of this article, shall in no wise affect the other articles and stipulations concluded on in this treaty.*

In testimony whereof, the commissioners, William P. Duval, James Gadsden, and Bernard Segui, and the undersigned chiefs and warriors have hereunto subscribed their names and affixed their seals. Done at Camp, on Moultrie Creek, in the Territory of Florida, this eighteenth day

*Disapproved by Government.

of September, one thousand eight hundred and twenty-three, and of the Independence of the United States, the Forty-eighth.

Wm. P Duval,	L. S.
James Gadsden,	L. S.
Bernard Segui,	L. S.
Nea Mathla, his ✕ mark,	L. S.
Tokose Mathla, his ✕ mark,	L. S.
Ninnee Homata Tustenuky, his ✕ mark,	L. S.
Micanopy, his ✕ mark,	L. S.
Nocosee Apola, his ✕ mark,	L. S.
John Blunt, his ✕ mark,	L. S.
Ottemata, his ✕ mark,	L. S.
Tuskeneka, his ✕ mark,	L. S.
Tuski Hajo, his ✕ mark,	L. S.
Econchatimico, his ✕ mark,	L. S.
Emoteley, his ✕ mark,	L. S.
Mulato King, his ✕ mark,	L. S.
Chocolohano, his ✕ mark,	L. S.
Ematlochee, his ✕ mark,	L. S.
Wekse Holata, his ✕ mark,	L. S.
Amathla Ho, his ✕ mark,	L. S.
Holatifiscico, his ✕ mark,	L. S.
Chefiscico Hajo, his ✕ mark,	L. S.
Lathlon Mathla, his ✕ mark,	L. S.
Senufky, his ✕ mark,	L. S.
Alak Hajo, his ✕ mark,	L. S.
Fahelusta Hajo, his ✕ mark,	L. S.
Octapamico, his ✕ mark,	L. S.
Tusteneck Hajo, his ✕ mark,	L. S.
Okoske Amathla, his ✕ mark,	L. S.
Ochany Tustenuky, his ✕ mark,	L. S.
Philip, his ✕ mark,	L. S.
Charley Amathla, his ✕ mark,	L. S.
John Hassorey, his ✕ mark,	L. S.
Rat Head, his ✕ mark,	L. S.
Holata Amathla, his ✕ mark,	L. S.
Foschati-mico, his ✕ mark	L. S.

Signed, sealed, and delivered in presence of

George Murray, *Secretary to the Commission.*
G. Humphreys, *Indian Agent.*
Stephen Richards, *Interpreter.*

ISAAC N. COX.
I. ERVING, *Capt. 4th Artillery.*
HARVY BROWN, *Lieut. 4th Artillery.*
C. D'ESPINVELLE, *Lieut. 4th Artillery.*
JNO. B. SCOTT, *Lieut. 4th Artillery.*
WILLIAM TRAVERS.
HORATIO S. DEXTER.

ADDITIONAL ARTICLE.

Whereas Neamathla, John Blunt, Tuske Hajo, Mulatto King, Emathlochee, and Econchatimicco, six of the principal chiefs of the Florida Indians and parties to the treaty, to which this article has been annexed, have warmly appealed to the commissioners, for permission to remain in the district of country, now inhabited by them, and in consideration of their friendly disposition, and past services to the United States, it is therefore stipulated, between the United States and the aforesaid chiefs, that the following reservations shall be surveyed and marked by the commissioner or commisioners, to be appropriated under the eighth article of this treaty : For Neamathla and his connections, two miles square, embracing the Tuphulga village, on the waters of Rocky Comfort Creek.   For Blunt and Tuski Hajo, a reservation, commencing on the Appalachicola, one mile below Tuski Hajo's improvements, running up said river four miles, thence west two miles, thence southwardly to a point, two miles due west the beginning, thence east to the beginning point.   For Mulatto King and Emathlochee, a reservation commencing on the Appalachicola, at a point to include Yellow Hair's improvements, thence up said river for four miles, thence west one mile, thence southwardly to a point one mile west of the beginning, and thence east to the beginning point.   For Econchatimicco, a reservation commencing on the Chatahoochee, one mile below Econchatimicco's house, thence up said river for four miles, thence one mile west, thence southerly to a point one mile west of the beginning, thence east to the beginning point.   The United States promise to guaranty the peaceable possession of the said reservations, as defined to the aforesaid chiefs and their descendants only so long as they shall continue to occupy, improve or cultivate the same, but in the event of the abandonment of all or either of the reservations by the chief or chiefs to whom they have been allotted, the reservation or reservations, so abandoned shall revert to the United States, as included in the cession made in the first article of this treaty.   It is further understood, that the names of the individuals remaining on the reservations aforesaid, shall be furnished by the chiefs in whose favor the reservations have been made to the superintendent or agent of In-

dian affairs in the Territory of Florida, and that no other individuals shall
be received or permitted to remain within said reservations without the previous consent of the superintendant or agent aforesaid ; and as the aforesaid
chiefs are authorized to select the individuals remaining with them, so they
shall each be separately held responsible for the peaceable conduct of their
towns or the individuals residing on the reservations allotted them.   It is further understood between the parties thât this agreement is not intended to pro-
hibit the voluntary removal at any future period, of all or either of the aforesaid chiefs, and their connections to the district of country south, allotted to
the Florida Indians by the second article of this treaty, whenever either or all,
may think proper to make such an election, the United States reserving the
right of ordering, for any outrage or misconduct, the aforesaid chiefs or either
of them with their connections within the district of country south aforesaid.

It is further stipulated by the United States, that of the six thousand
dollars appropriated for implements of husbandry, stock, etc., in the third
article of this treaty, eight hundred dollars shall be distributed in the same
manner among the aforesaid chiefs and their towns, and it is understood
that of the annual sum of five thousand dollars, to be distributed by the
President of the United States, they will receive their proportion.   It is
further stipulated that of the four thousand five hundred dollars, and two
thousand dollars provided for by the fifth article of this treaty, for the payment for improvements and transportation, five hundred dollars shall be
awarded to Neamathla as a compensation for the improvements abandoned
by him, as well as to meet the expenses he will unavoidably be exposed to
by his own removal and that of his connections.

In testimony whereof, the Commissioners, William P. Duval, James
Gadsden, and Bernard Segui, and the undersigned chiefs and warriors have
hereunto subscribed their names, and affixed their seals.   Done at camp
on Moultrie Creek, in the Territory of Florida, this eighteenth day of
September, one thousand eight hundred and twenty-three, and of the Independence of the United States the forty-eighth.

WILLIAM P. DUVAL,	L. S.
JAMES GADSDEN,	L. S.
BERNARD SEGUI,	L. S.
NEAMATHLA, his ⋈ mark,	L. S.
JOHN BLUNT, his ⋈ mark,	L. S.
TUSKI HAJO, his ⋈ mark,	L. S.
MULATTO KING, his ⋈ mark,	L. S.
EMATHLOCHEE, his ⋈ mark,	L. S.
ECONCHATI-MICCO, his ⋈ mark,	L. S.

Signed, sealed, and delivered in presence of

    GEORGE MURRAY, *Secretary to the Commission.*

    JAMES W. RIPLEY,

    G. HUMPHREYS, *Indian Agent.*

    STEPHEN RICHARDS, *Interpreter.*

The following statement shows the number of men retained by the chiefs who have reservations made them at their respective villages :—

	Number of men.
Blount,	43
Cochran,	45
Mulatto King,	30
Emathlochee,	28
Econchati-micco,	38
Neamathla,	30
Total,	214

ORDER NO. LXXIX.

Head Quarters, Army of the South,
Tampa Bay, April 5th, 1837.

I.

The commanding general has reason to believe that the interference of unprincipled white men with the negro property of the Seminole Indians if not immediately checked will prevent their emigration and lead to a renewal of the war. Responsible as he is for the peace and security of the country, he will not permit such interference under any pretence whatsoever, and he therefore orders that no white man, not in the service of the United States, be allowed to enter any part of the Territory below St. Johns River, and the Gulf of Mexico, south of Fort Drane.

II.

The inspector general will cause all merchant or transport vessels arriving in this harbor to be immediately examined and the names of all individuals on board to be registered. No one will be allowed to come ashore except for the transacting of public business. Vessels from whence any individuals shall be landed contrary to this order, or on board of which spirituous liquors may be found, will be immediately sent off, and shall not be employed in the public service.

III.

All negroes now at this place, the property of citizens of the United

States, will be sent to St. Marks.   The inspector general will furnish Lieut.
Vinton a list of them, with their owners' names.   Lieut. Vinton will give
notice to their owners to take charge of them immediately.

By order of Major General Jessup,

(Signed,)

J. A. CHAMBERS,

Lieut. Aid-de-Camp, and Adjt. Gen.

Officio.

J. E. JOHNSTON, *Lieut. and Ass. Adj. Gen.*

LAND TITLES.

The King of Spain granted lands to all the inhabitants of his colonies,
whether natives or naturalized, who desired to occupy and cultivate them.
Fees to the officers who made and registered the title papers, and to the surveyor, were all that were required in payment.

To the council of the Indies was entrusted the power of making laws to
regulate the subject of land claims.

The first step necessary to obtain a grant of land, was to present a petition to the Governor, or sub-delegate.   He referred the petition to the surveyor to learn whether the land applied for was vacant, and royal domain.
It was then submitted to the Fiscal, or Attorney General, to know if there
were any legal objections to making the grant.   If near a military post, the
chief engineer was consulted, to know whether the grant would interfere
with the defence of the place.   When all these officers reported in favor of
the grant, the decree was made in favor of the petitioner, and sent to the Intendant, for confirmation.   The officers of Intendant, sub-delegate and Governor, were very often included in the same person.

The quantity granted, was regulated by the capacity of the petitioner to
improve it, and by the amount of his credit with the sub-delegate..   One
hundred arpents were usually granted to the heads of families ; fifty arpents
to each child, and twenty-five for each slave ; but a favorite could usually
obtain as much land as he asked for.   A complete title was, however, rarely made, until the grantee could prove actual residence on, and occupation,
and cultivation for the term specified in the grant ; usually ten years.   For
pasturage, pine lands were often granted to the amount of ten or fifteen
thousand acres, and for erecting a saw mill, sixteen thousand were given.

SALES.

In purchasing lands, the same qualifications were required of the purcha-
ser, as were required of the grantee, and no one was allowed to purchase
any more than he could pasture or cultivate.   Lands were always sold at

auction, as they might be demanded, a price being first affixed by the fiscal, or by appraisers appointed by him : below that price they could not be sold. Sales were also reported to the intendant, for completing the title. All titles were to be recorded in the office of finances.

COMPROMISE.

When a petitioner stated that he had rendered services to the King, suffered losses in his service, or by his servants, or that debts were due him by the government, lands were often granted him by way of compromise. In that case, it was regular to have his audited account filed on the protocol ; endorsed as discharged, by the indemnity ; and the certificate of conveyance certified the whole transaction.

In point of system, the Spanish land office was very defective. All grants were bound up in large bundles called protocols, and marked with the year in which the grants were made ; but it required much labor and some expense, for a petitioner to ascertain whether the land he applied for had not been already granted. It was the business of the Attorney General to ascertain that fact, but he sometimes made mistakes ; when it did happen that a grant was surveyed on another man's land, the sub-delegate always permitted it to be removed to other vacant lands.

It also often happened that planters obtained grants for lands, that were found on trial to be unfit for tillage ; in that case, the location was removed on showing the facts. In both the above cases, the grantee was required to make a formal recession of his first grant, which was duly filed in the public archives.

St. Augustine and Pensacola, were the seats of goverment for the provinces of East and West Florida. The country about Pensacola is poor, and the good lands of the interior were covered by the Seminole Indians ; for these reasons few grants were made in West Florida. On the contrary, some of the best lands in the Territory lie near the sea-coast of the Atlantic, and on many of the navigable lagoons and rivers. The country was settled at an earlier period, and by a people much more enterprising and industrious, than those who established the military posts at Barrancas, St. Rosa, and Pensacola. Besides, the native Indians of the whole country, were long accustomed to visit the convent of St. Helena, at St. Augustine, as the head of all their religious institutions, and a journey to that place was considered in the light of a holy pilgrimage. Agriculture, as well as commerce was greatly encouraged, for the support of the population. And hence it is, that most of the good lands in East Florida were covered with private grants, while in West Florida, there were very few out of the neighborhood of Pensacola.

At different periods, an extensive farming population spread over the country, between the Atlantic coast, and the St. John's River ; but they were often broken up by the enemies of the province.

Lands were granted for the encouragement of every kind of merit : the mill grants were most numerous, although there were never many mills. For every kind of service in peace and war, and some of them of a very extraordinary kind, grants were liberally made ; and yet there can be no reasonable doubt of their having been confirmed to the possessors, had the Spanish government continued in Florida.

These provinces were far removed from the mother country which was itself distracted by revolutions and totally unable to render her colonies assistance in any emergency. She could not even pay the salaries of her officers. The Provincial Goverments were very often obliged to lay under contribution the resources of their citizens ; when they did so, it was just, as it was politic to remunerate them.   Lands were all they had to give, and when they granted them, we have yet to learn an instance of their being disapproved, either by the King or the council of the Indies.

The United States by the Treaty of St. Ildefonso, have bound themselves to do, what the Spanish Government would have done. Had there been no such clause in the treaty, our Government would have been bound in justice, to confirm the rights of the Floridians ; for by their purchase of the Territory, they deprived the inhabitants of the power, of demanding their rights, of their former Government.

The Congress of the United States, taking into consideration, the situation of those inhabitants, that had occupied and made improvements, on lands of the public domain, before the cession of the country, granted to such settlers as were heads of families, six hundred acres in fee simple.

And they have since that time, by successive acts, granted the right of pre-emption to one hundred and sixty acres, to actual settlers on the public lands. The last of those acts expires by limitation, on the first day of January, 1838.

The titles to lands in West Florida, have been all decided by the government ; many of those in East Florida, are still depending in the superior court of the eastern and southern Judicial Districts.

The largest grants in West Florida, were made to John Forbes and Co. by the Seminole and Tallaposa Indians, in consideration of certain robberies and spoliations committed on the trading establishments of the grantees, by the natives.   Two of these grants were located on the east side of the Appalachicola River.   They are estimated to contain, one million three hundred thousand acres, and cover nearly the whole of Gadsden and part of Leon counties.   A third, but small grant on the west side of the Appalachicola, covers St. Vincent Island and a small tract, below Lake Wimico. The titles to these three tracts are confirmed to the claimants by the United States.

In East Florida, the government have confirmed to the claimants, the title to two hundred ninety-three thousand acres, granted to De la Maza Arredondo, situate in Allachua County. It covers some of the finest lands in the Territory.

The claims of Aronbede for ninety thousand acres situate on the Sandwich Gulf, and that of Mirandy, for about three hundred thousand on Tampa Bay are still pending.

The largest grant was made to the Duke of Allagon and since transferred to Richard S. Hackley, Esq., of New York. It commences at the mouth of the Amasura or Ouithlacoochee River and from thence to its head near fort King, thence by the east side of Myacco Lake, to the head of the river Hujelos, thence down that river to its mouth, thence by the Gulf of Mexico to the place of beginning. These boundaries embrace several millions of acres. The title to this grant has not yet been confirmed. But it has been carefully examined by many of the best jurists of the United States, who have uniformly decided that the title is a good one.

For the purpose of fixing on a situation for a new settlement within the boundaries of lands sold by Mr. Hackely, to a company in New-York, Col. George W. Murray sailed for Key West on the 18th of May, 1832, and arrived there on the 8th of June. Here he purchased a small sloop, in which he embarked, together with W. R. Hackley Esq. ,and Mr. P. B. Prior, on the 27th of June, to explore the coast and rivers of the Gulf.

From the journals of these Gentlemen, I have been permitted to extract the following information, respecting this interesting part of the Territory. They have also kindly favored me with their draughts of the coast, and for which I beg leave to tender them my grateful thanks.

COLOOSAHATCHE.

Col. Murray of New-York, accompanied by W. R. Hackley, Esqr. and Mr Prior, visited Carlos Bay in a small sloop, called the Associate, commanded by Capt. Bunce. After visiting Cayo Pueblo, inhabited by several Spaniards and Indians, they proceeded on the 7th of July, to ascend the bay, and at 1 P. M. anchored opposite a fishing rancho.

8th. Proceeded up the bay, found the channel narrow, crooked and difficult to find, frequently ran aground on oyster shoals, returned to the rancho.

9th. Messrs. Hackley, Prior, and the pilot, took the small boat with several days' provisions, and proceeded to explore the Coloosahatche River.

Above the rancho, the bay was about three miles wide. Its shores covered with pine timber, occasionally broken and diversified by grass savannas, four miles to Curlew Point. Then N. E. by E. four miles to Punta Cayman. Then N. E. eight miles to Rocky Point. Thence N. N. E. eight miles to the mouth of the river, which was fresh water. The bay was two miles wide above Curlew Point, depth two fathoms. The mouth of the river is chequered with mangrove islets, and the water among them shoal with oyster bars, but a channel winds through of seven feet. The banks covered with tall pines and saw palmettoes. The islets sprinkled with live oaks and palms, affording good cotton land.

Above the Cayos or islets, the river opens to four hundred yards in width, and from two to three fathoms deep. The shores on both sides a savanna, covered with high grass as far as the eye could reach, diversified with small hammocks of live oaks and palms. The banks usually four feet above the water, at high tide. After noon the banks appeared to be clothed with a thick forest of very large live oaks, and the shores were lined with mangroves; seven miles from the entrance the river forked, the left branch was ascended. The water shoaled to four feet, proceeded two miles, landed and encamped for the night, shot several wild turkeys, they were numerous and tame.

10th. Proceeded up the creek eight miles, by cutting away the branches that interlocked across the stream, poling the boat, being unable to row. The banks were perpendicular, and from seven to eight feet above the water. The course of this branch is about N. N. E. and appears like an artificial canal, only it is very crooked. The water in some places is very deep, and the land on its borders rich. We now returned to the fork, which we reached about 11 A. M. and proceeded up the main stream, about eighteen miles, and encamped. Both banks of the river are covered with dense forests of live oak and palms, entangled with vines; the land is excellent, varying from four to twelve feet above the water, the hammocks more than half a mile wide, where they penetrated it. The river is very crooked, and the width narrowed to fifty yards. The water falling.

11th. The river now bends to the north for five miles, then N. E. The banks varying from eight to fifteen feet high, showing a stratum of shell limestone six feet below the surface. Live oaks and palms of great height cover the banks. Numerous branches, rivulets, and springs of cool sweet water, enter the river on both sides. One spring in particular, burst from the rocks on the shore. The timber on the borders of the river now becomes intermixed with the peccan tree. Messrs. Hackley and Prior, walked two miles into the country, found a good soil and excellent growth of timber, saw plenty of wild turkeys, but no deer, though their tracks were numerous. At noon had proceeded near fifteen miles, the river thirty yards wide. A deep stratum of marle, lined both shores for several miles. The river in the course of another mile, had narrowed to fifteen yards. Here commenced a rapid which continued two miles ; had to haul up the boat by the painter, then entered a small lake three fourths of a mile long, and three feet deep, its course N. E. it was full of grass, innumerable fish, and alligators ; the banks were clothed with excellent pasturage. The land was explored for six miles, N. W. from the falls. The country at first, showed signs of having been overflowed at some distant time ; further north, the land was diversified with grassy plains, broken by springs of water, surrounded with groves of oak, palm, peccan, &c. Numerous small ponds covered, in places, with cane grass and mallows, but no appearance of marshes. The hammock trees were covered with grape vines loaded with fruit, very pleasant and healthful, in appearance much like the isabella grape. The plains near the rapids, rise gradually from the river, and spread off in some directions as far as the eye can reach. The soil a dark sandy loam, very proper for the production of tropical fruits. An Indian hunter who resides here, informed the party that there was an Indian settlement fifteen miles to the N. E. abounding in cattle, ponies, &c. He had a beautiful poney, for which he asked thirty dollars. He said they usually raised two crops of corn, during each season. About ten miles from the mouth of the river, a creek enters from the N. W. whose waters are deep and sluggish, and the hammocks on its banks thick and heavily timbered, and the soil a dark brown sandy mass of earth ; this hammock extends two or three miles, and is then succeeded by pine timber. A small stream of water from the interior, entered the creek with a rapid and forcable current.

After exploring the coast below the Caximba, among innumerable mangrove islands, in search of the Delaware River for several days, Col. Murray and his party returned to Key West, to refit and lay in a new supply of provisions, &c.

On the 27th of August, they again sailed for Cape Roman, and anchored in Chatham Bay on the 2d of September. After sounding out a channel, they finally anchored at the entrance of the Caximbas, the Indian Keys bearing S. S. W. about two miles distant ; the Delaware and Gallivan bearing N. N. E. distant four miles.

September 3d, 1832. Col. Murray, Mr. Hackley and Mr. Prior left the sloop to explore the Delaware, in their small boat. They at first passed through a bay, studded with mangrove keys, thence to the forks of the Delaware and Gallivan, and entered the former ; it being the right hand fork. It was one hundred feet wide and five feet deep ; the banks low but dry; the banks were both lined with tall mangroves; the course at first N. N. W. winding to N. W. by N. Passed a field of corn on the left hand bank, two miles from the entrance. The river now became so narrow that the boatmen had to lay by their oars and pole the boat through the mangrove bushes, while the gentlemen cut the limbs that opposed their progress. In one half mile they came to a fork and took the right hand branch, which was from six to eight feet deep, but the mangroves were so entangled across the stream, that they soon abandoned it and returned to the fork. The left hand fork was then examined, but like the former, led into an impenetrable thicket of mangroves, and was abandoned.

The Gallivan was then entered; it was one hundred yards wide, and eight feet deep. It soon divided, and the left hand branch was examined; the current was very strong, embracing many small keys, and the course varying from W. N. W. to north, then round to south, back to N. W. and N. E. The channel often so narrow that mangrove limbs had again to be cut through. Rowing and poleing by turns, as the river became more or less narrow. They here found many wasps nests suspended from the limbs near the water. It was difficult to avoid the attacks of these belligerent insects. The current was their only guide among the keys; they however found a channel, varying from six to fifteen feet deep, for about eight miles, when they arrived at an extensive grassy plain, inundated with water. The stream then took a N. E. direction; became very narrow, with from four to six feet water. At length the boats rubbed the shore on both sides at the same time, and the banks became marshy. They stopped and Mr. Hackley and Mr. Prior waded through the marsh to dry land. On their return they stated the land to be excellent, the soil a black mould, the timber live oak, palm and cocoanut. There were indications of many wild animals, bears in particular; there were also many vacant huts. The whole distance from the mouth of the river, they estimated at fourteen miles. An observation taken this day, gave 25° 53′ latitude, the Thermometer range, morning, noon and evening, 78. 90. 82.

On the 4th of September, the company weighed anchor and sailed S. E. for the purpose of exploring the St. Marys River. In nine hours they anchored in the bay, into which that river was supposed to disembogue. They found ten feet water, and a safe harbor. Many sea fowls, such as curlews, coots, &c. were killed. Here an Indian, with his wife, came along side in his canoe, on his way to Indian Key, to sell his deer skins and other trifles; he was supplied with provisions, and he proceeded on his voyage. Thermometer, 79. 90. 84.

September 5th, The Party proceeded in the boat, to explore the river. They proceeded in a N. E. course three miles, up a wide passage through mangrove islands ; a spacious lake then opened before them, which they named Oyster Bay. Three miles in a N. N. E. direction, brought them to the confluence of two rivers ; here they landed at an Indian clearing, where some cane was growing luxuriantly ; the place was deserted, though some huts were standing. The western river was three hundred yards wide at its entrance into the lagoon, the waters six feet deep at half flood. A north west course two miles reduced the width to seventy-five yards. It then branched off east and west. The east branch was thirty yards wide and from eight to ten feet water ; it continued to grow narrower, and became enclosed in mangrove bushes, so that they had to abandon it. The western branch was entered with no better success, they proceeded about a mile and had to abandon it. A branch about half a mile above the Indian field was one hundred yards wide, and had ten feet water, but it fell off like the others, which it probably joined, making the Indian field an island. The mangrove trees rise to thirty feet, without limbs, then spread their foliage in a singular manner ; the ends of the twigs often bend over to the opposite side of a stream or in the stream, and there take root and grow into trees ; these interweaving their branches so thickly, that birds can scarcely penetrate them. Here is also button wood and the cotton shrub.

They next explored the north east river which was two hundred yards wide at the mouth, its water, seven feet deep. Their course among mangrove islands, varied from north to south east, alternately. Sometimes they could row the boat, but often the bushes obliged them to pole and cut their way with their knives. The current was very strong against them. They passed through two beautiful lakes from fifteen to eighteen feet deep. In this way they proceeded about ten miles, when suddenly the stream contracted to a very narrow passage, which terminated in an inundated grassy plain, beyond which live oaks, palms and pine trees were seen at a distance. They backed down the stream, having no room to turn their boat for some distance. At length they reached their sloop, and sailed for Charlotte Harbor.

September 5th. Stood out of the St. Marys harbor, which cannot be entered by large vessels. . During the expedition thus far, the showers and tempests of wind and lightning have been violent, and have occurred almost every day ; very often they rise suddenly and as quickly disappear ; at other times the waters would pour down for two or three hours, without intermission.

September, 6th. The sloop was drifted along the coast, by a current leading N. W. Passed Cape Roman at two o'clock in the morning, distant one fourth of a mile, but repeatedly struck the bottom. The night was very dark and rainy. Towards morning, a violent squall struck the sloop, and raged for two hours, during which all sail was taken in, and they lay at the mercy of the seas. By day light, the storm had passed and a moderate breeze, enabled them to hoist sail and lay their course. At four P. M. made the Rancho flag staff; soon after a canoe came off with several of the inhabitants, who were delighted to see them return. Anchored within the outer bar in nine fathoms water.

7th.—Took in a pilot, a Mexican named Greig, to conduct them through Charlotte Bay. Sailed at 8 A. M. inside of the keys, of which there are five, between which there are three passages, north of Sanybal. The first Bocca Seca, Bocca Capativa, and Bocca Grand. At the distance of twenty-five miles from Punta Raza, they made the island inhabited by the Calde family. The old Spaniard is said to be ninety years old. On the same key resides Mr. Willis, inspector of the customs, who was building a house on the north end of the key. Both of these persons were absent at the time. Passed in the course of the day, many keys that were under cultivation; producing corn, pumpkins, melons, potatoes, various kinds of beans, etc. The lime and cocoa-nut trees on Calde's Island looked flourishing, and produced abundance of fruit. The sloop was supplied with these articles. The island contained from fifty to sixty inhabitants.

8th.—Sailed with a fine S. E. breeze, among many small islands to Bocca Grand, which has fifteen feet water on the bar. The bay is spacious and beautiful. From Bocca Grand they steered N. E. by E.; at two miles distance passed the Corona, an oyster reef two miles long. Thence fifteen miles into the estuary where the Macaco and Talackchopko pour their waters. This estuary is about ten miles wide, the banks low and generally lined with mangroves, but in some places with pine woods. Here an observation was taken, the result 26° 53' north latitude. They anchored in the mouth of Talackchopko, in six feet water, near Rancho Point. Thus far a vessel drawing ten feet water may come with perfect safety. The lands in this vicinity are universally pine barrens. Much of the timber had been cut off, but not recently. No fresh water was found except a well of miserable water. Laid by at this place till the morning of the 10th, exploring the neighboring shores and the pine woods.

Sept. 10th.—Left the sloop and proceeded in the boat at flood tide, to ascend the Macaco River. For two miles the river was one and a half miles wide; passed a range of small keys which lay two miles east of us, and extended about two miles. The river now contracted to half a mile wide. Then a savanna covered with tall grass four miles. Then quite an open country, very wet, with islets of dry land. The river now turns northeast three miles. Then it bends alternately from north to west. The land low in places, covered with water. The timber varying from live oak and palm to water oak and cypress. A thunder gust at 11 A. M. Landed, pitched their tent, and remained two hours, when the storm passed over. Continued their course up the river against a strong current, winding from south-east to north-east, then north for four miles and again varying round sharp points to the west for six or seven miles. The banks still low and wet, and the timber varying with live oak, water oak, hickory, maple, cypress, palm, and pine. A large creek here enters through the left bank round a high, bluff point, covered with pine woods. The other side of the creek was bordered with a forest of oaks. The river again turned north-east for two miles. Then for several miles it made short turns N. W., E., S. E., then round to north. Another deep creek enters the left bank, and there the party encamped.

11th Sept.—Continued their voyage at 6 A. M; the river still more rapid, overflowing the banks for three or four miles, among the oak forests. The river continues very crooked, the banks alternately pine barrens and swamps, then hammocks, sometimes sandy plains destitute of trees, but covered with meagre palmettoes. It was not without much difficulty that they found a spot towards evening, on which they could comfortably encamp for the night. Proceeded this day, by calculation, twenty-four miles.

12th.—This day the course of the river was northward ; it continued equally crooked and equally rapid, but becoming much narrower ; proceeded this day about twenty miles. Encamped at 4 P. M. in a wet hammock of live oaks. The party usually halted for a couple of hours in the middle of each day, for the rowers to rest and refresh themselves. The gentlemen then usually scoured the woods in search of game.

13th.—This day passed a very narrow part of the river. It was also much obstructed by drift wood, and the whole country appeared to be inundated by the water. The timber for a few miles was live oak or willows. At length they arrived at a high piny bank, on which was a log house and several palmetto huts ; two canoes were fastened to the bank, and several domestic utensils were scattered about, but no inhabitants were found. The river grew narrower, the bends shorter, and the current so swift, that the rowers with all their strength could make little progress. As a high piny bank rose, and the weather appeared threatening, the party landed and encamped. The hunters went out for game but returned unsuccessful. The river here was thirty yards wide ; the opposite side a dense oak forest. Rowed this day fifteen miles.

14th.—This morning made another hunting excursion, but saw no animal, although the tracks of deer were plenty. Proceeded up the river four or five miles through thick woods of willow, cypress, peccan, oak and palm ; and at length reached pine woods again, where there was an Indian settlement of three families, among whom there was a woman more than a hundred years old. They cultivated corn, tobacco, upland rice, peas beans, pumpkins, melons, etc. Their land was good and they appeared friendly, offering melons to the party, which were received and tobacco given in return. They stated that the head springs of the river were distant three days' journey, the river very narrow and crooked, and obstructed by timber and vines. That around the head springs there were some hundreds of Indians. This information decided the gentlemen of the party to return, besides their provisions were growing scant, and their hunting had lately been unsuccessful. In three days they reached their sloop at the mouth of the river.

The gentlemen of the party on comparing the two streams, Macaco and Coloosahatche, concluded that the Macaco was much the largest, afforded the best navigation, the greatest quantity of timber for commerce, and the greatest quantity of good land, but being flat and wet, it would probably be unhealthy, and require a negro population to cultivate the soil. The Coloosahatche on the contrary, they thought would be more healthy, and afforded many beautiful situations for sea island cotton and tropical fruits, and the game and fish extremely abundant, with a very safe harbor.

September 17th.—The gentlemen of the expedition, sailed down the western coast about eight miles and entered the mouth of the river. It is about two miles wide, at its mouth ; the country is a flat prairie, slightly covered with grass, and the land poor ; at some distance from the banks scattering pine trees are seen, that increase in size and number as you recede farther from the river. Many small streams cross the prairie and fall into the river at short distances apart. Here, water fowls were abundant, and numerous spoon bills and curlews were shot for the use of the table ; the plumage of the former is very beautiful. Many small keys clothed with palms and cedars, diversify the first entrance of the river, for some distance. At the distance of fifteen miles from the mouth, the banks have scattering palms and pine trees, and soon after live oaks of a small size are seen, but the soil, thus far, is sandy and poor. Landed to examine an enclosure of logs, notched together into a pen. It contained the skeleton of an Indian, the scull and vertebræ were resting against the logs, at the east end of the enclosure, the legs were also drawn up. They landed at five o'clock on the right bank of the river, which had contracted to thirty yards wide. The water had varied from twelve to six feet in depth. They estimated their distance from the mouth, at thirty miles.

18th. Continued their route four miles farther, when the channel became so blocked up with sunken logs and brush, that they were unable to force their way any farther. They went into the interior for some distance, but found only a poor, pine barren country.

19th.—Sailed down the bay, past the Corona Shoal, and anchored in front of Cayo Palao, twenty-four miles below the S. W. branch. On this key, there is quite an extensive settlement, perhaps from sixty to seventy inhabitants, who keep an abundance of hogs, and dogs innumerable. Here they obtained clams, oysters, squashes, melons, &c. in exchange for some trifling articles of merchandize.

From Cayo Palao, they steered for Bocca Grand, and examined Casta Firma (called on the old spanish Charts, Cayo Muspa,) it lies south of the main entrance. It is a mass of shells in a state of partial decomposition, covered with myrtle shrubs, hikok or coco plumb and small palms. Some years ago Calde put some hogs on this island ; they increased prodigiously, and furnished his rancho with abundance of excellent meat.

They next visited Pine Island on the east side of the bay ; it was covered with pine woods and various grasses ; some fields were cultivated in potatoes, pumpkins, squashes, mellons, &c. Corn was said to grow well, but the deer were so numerous on the island, that they destroyed it and prevented its cultivation. They were told that the island was eighteen miles long, and that a passage on the east side, four feet deep, separated it from the main land. A sandy shoal extends across the bay, from Pine Island to Bocca Seca, on which there is not more than three feet water, at low tide.

Of the three islands that extend east of Casta Firma, they examined only Sanybal. It is the easternmost of the group, is eight miles long and two and a half wide, has a fine harbor at the N. E. point, varying from two to four fathoms in depth, with fourteen feet on the bar. On the island there are streams of fresh water. The Island is about eight feet above the highest tides, and is dry and healthy, and almost constantly refreshed with sea breezes ; several buildings were erected here, before the Seminole war commenced : all are now destroyed.

March, 1833. Mr. P. B. Prior made a journey from Tampa Bay, through part of the Seminole country, to the mouth of Sanybal River, to purchase some cattle from the Indians. March 13th, he travelled to Dixon's, six miles. The lands here are generally thin, but there are spots on Mr. Dixon's farm that produce excellent crops of provisions, and there was made this year, fifteen barrels of good sugar. Many parts of this neighborhood has a substratum of rich calcareous marle, a few inches below the surface, it has been found to be excellent manure for the pine lands. The range for cattle is good, the country being intersected with small streams of water.

March 13th. Pursued a course N. E. by E. twenty-five miles. The country is rather poor pine lands, but diversified with small ponds and savannas ; there is also very good grass and plenty of water ; on the whole, it is a good range for stock.

14th. The country is similar to that travelled over yesterday, but rather better. Passed many lakes and ponds, on the banks of which there are many small hammocks. Our general course E. S. E. We crossed Tallahchopka about 3 o'clock P. M., where it passed through a large glade cr savanna, and arrived in the evening at the dwelling of Seweky, my Indian guide. It was situated in the forks of the river, formed by the entrance of a large branch from the east. Travelled this day sixteen miles. This river was explored as far as the lake, by Messrs. Hackley, Murray, &c., 16th September 1832.

15th March. This day spent in assisting Seweky to hunt cattle, assisted by Indians and negroes. The two branches of the river meet in a deep swamp, ten miles long, and about two miles wide ; extensive wet grassy plains stretch to a great distance on both sides of the river, which is forty yards wide. We swam it on horseback, driving the cattle across. The lands here are poor. Two miles from the forks on the east side, there is a small Indian town, called Tobasa or Wahoo. Eight miles below there is another new town just built, without a name. This place, the Indians say, is from twenty-five, to thirty miles from the head springs and lakes, on the highest ridge of the peninsula.

16th. Left Seweky's at 10 A. M. with eight large steers, and two cows with calves. Crossed the east branch, and reached the nameless town at 4 P. M. The pine land is here good, better than any we have before crossed. Our course has been S. S. E. eight miles. Staid here the 17th, all the Indians being drunk.

18th. Started at 6 A. M., at 10 crossed a small creek over a natural bridge, called Con Iwa Creek. It rises again half a mile below its exit. Encamped' at a small Indian settlement, where a sorrel horse was purchased for the Indian drivers ; made this day eighteen miles over poor pine lands.

19th. Travelled nineteen miles, most of the way poor pine land spotted with ponds and glades. In the afternoon crossed two fine streams of water. Continued a S. S. E. course.

20th. Continued the same course this day eighteen miles. Suffered for want of water. There was no stream or pond, a few muddy puddles we did find, and strained the water through our handkerchiefs to quench our thirst. This night the cows and horses strayed back three miles, and delayed us hunting them the next morning.

21st. Got our cattle under way, and travelled till noon over a most dreary country. White sand hills then continued till almost night, when a low pine country succeeds interspersed with innumerable ponds. At 4 P. M. passed a small Indian town in sight of the trail. It is called Tallahpopcha. Three miles beyond it we encamped. One mile from our encampment, two runaway negroes had built a camp where they lived securely. Travelled this day 17 miles, same course, S. S. E.

22nd. Proceeded eight miles over plains, a south course, at which time we crossed a creek running eastward, called by the Indians Tallepopcah, they said that it headed thirty miles north west of us, and emptied itself to the eastward in a grassy lake called Myacco, from which they said several large streams ran into the Atlantic Ocean. From this creek our course was S. S. W. as far as the rapids of Sanybal, which we reached before night, swam our cattle and horses over and encamped for the night. This afternoon the trail through the prairies was very good, but it rained all day. We made twenty miles.

23d. This day our trail ran in a S. W. direction. It rained all the forenoon, so that we staid in our camp till 1 P. M., we then travelled eight miles.

24th. This day it continued to rain, but we started at six o'clock, the thunder and lightning very severe. Crossed several streams, the bottoms of which were rock, two of the creeks were large. The banks of one was a mass of white clay, with about one foot of mould on it; a small hammock of good land extends along both sides of the water. Two miles from this creek came to low flat pine woods, covered with water so that we had great difficulty to find a place to camp. Made this day eighteen miles, the course S. W. by W.

25th. The low flat pine plain continued to the edge of the mangroves, half a mile from the coast. Made Punta Raka at 3 P. M. Course S. S. W. twelve miles. Whole distance one hundred and twenty-eight miles.

In the month of July, 1833, the bays of Tampa and Sarrazota were examined with care : the latter has been particularly described from my own observations in 1827. Since that time several settlements had been made, and the country was rapidly improving until the Seminole war broke out.

Oyster river at the south-east side of Tampa Bay, was explored for twenty miles, where it ends in a small stream from the pine woods. The course of this river is E. N. E. It is one mile wide at its mouth, much of this space is very shoal and spotted with islands, but there is a narrow and deep channel for some miles. The banks are from eight to fifteen feet high, and they are clothed with excellent hammock lands, most of the way quite to the head. There was plenty of good spring water in the hammocks, and the musquitoes much less numerous than on the southern coast. Some valuable planters had settled here before the war.

A stream that enters the bay joining the entrance of Oyster River, on the S. W. was ascended about six miles.   It was forty yards wide, and six feet deep, but full of islands.   At four miles from the mouth, a grass plain rises gradually from the west side to the height of fifteen feet, and skirted on the west with hammock land, that extended north and south as far as the eye could reach.

The point between these two rivers is called Negro Point.   The famous Arbuthnot and Ambrister had at one time a plantation here cultivated by two hundred negroes.   The ruins of their cabins, and domestic untensils are still seen on the old fields.

FINIS.

NOTICE TO EMIGRANTS.

Persons desirous to settle in Florida, may obtain land in any of the northern counties, where the lands have been offered for public sale, at the Government price, one dollar and twenty-five cents, by applying to the Land Offices of St. Augustine and Tallahasse, where may be seen records of the lands sold, and maps of those which are in market.

Besides these, there are numerous grants of all sizes, situate in various parts of the Territory, the titles to which, have been confirmed to the grantees or proprietors, by the United States. Many of these tracts are choice locations, selected by the grantees, on account of the advantages of situation, richness of soil, grazing or timber.

Of these private grants, the large tract, called Forbes' Purchase, extending from the western extremity of St. Vincent Island, to St. Marks, is owned by a joint stock company, and the title is vested in trustees. By the articles of the association, the power to sell these lands is committed to directors, for the time being, who may be seen or addressed, at Tallahasse or Appalachicola, by the style of the " Directors of the Appalachicola Land Company." The greatest part of this valuable tract, is still unsold and in market.

The Allagon Grant, now vested in the Florida Peninsula Land Company, extends from the Amanina, Amasura, or Amaxura River, to the Hujelos and from the Gulf of Mexico, to the St. Johns River, embracing perhaps eight millions of acres. It is designated on the Map of Florida, "Hackley's Lands". Almost all these shares have been cancelled, and now appertain to the Florida Peninsula Land Company.

For the purchase of shares or portions of this grant, application may be made to Mr. Steele, at Tampa Bay, Lot Clark, Esq. at St. Augustine, David Clarkson, Henry Dudley, Joseph D. Beers or Col. R. S. Hackley, of New York.

The Arredondo Grant. The large tract of land, known by this name, is situate around the great Prairie of Allachua, in East Florida. The title is about to be vested in trustees, in behalf of a joint stock company, and when these and other arrangements are made for the sale, due notice will be given to the public.

The Delespine Grant of forty-two thousand acres, on the west bank of Indian River, is owned by Michael Lazares of Charleston.

Flemmings' Grant of twenty thousand acres, on the St. Sebastians, a tributary of Indian River, is owned by the family of Capt. George Flemming, deceased, who reside at Jacksonville, on the St. Johns River.

The Fatio Grant of twenty thousand acres, situate on Nassau River, is represented by Mr. William Robertson of Savanna, and by Capt L. Ergle of Charleston.

Clark's Grant of sixteen thousand acres, situate on the west bank of the St. Johns River, opposite to Picolata, on which the town of Bayard is laid out, is for sale. For commerce or for agricultural pursuits, this tract affords many and great facilities. After crossing the bar, at the mouth of the river, fifteen feet water may be carried thus far. The great road from St. Augustine to Tallahasse and Tampa Bay, passes through it, and opens the shortest and best avenue from the river, to the rich farming lands of Allachua. The situation is peculiarly healthy, the timber excellent and much of the soil of the first quality. This tract is bounded seven miles by the river, and affords many beautiful sites for country seats. Bayard is surveyed on both sides of the great road, and embraces the site of the old Spanish fort San Fernando. For terms of sale, apply to Gen. Duncan L. Clinch, St. Marys, or to J. Lee Williams, at Bayard, or Picolata.

Huertas's Grant of fifteen thousand acres, embracing the old fort of Buenavista, is situate near Palatka, on the east side of the St Johns. Six thousand acres of this tract, owned by Francis J. Avice, Esq., is for sale, apply to the Proprietor at St. Augustine, or to J. Lee Williams, at Bayard or Picolata.

New Smyrna. The site of this old town, that once contained 1800 inhabitants, has been purchased by Col. Andrews and Major Lytle of the army, and we learn that it is their intention to resurvey it in town lots, as soon as the removal of the Seminoles will permit. Vessels drawing nine feet water have often completed their cargoes in Hillsborough and Hallifax rivers. The harbor is safe, and sufficiently capacious. The site is healthy and the water excellent. It is situate four miles south west of the Musquito Bar, on a bank of coquina rock, covered with a fertile sandy loam. The semi tropical fruits are raised here with little attention. The most important staples however, will be sugar and Sea Island Cotton. All the lands for forty miles north and south of Smyrna, lying parallel with, and from two to three miles from the coast, are of an excellent quality. Near the shore they will produce good Cotton and fruits, but are too thin for sugar in their present state. At four and five miles from the coast, the soil becomes poor by constant fires, which destroy all the herbage several times each year.

The lands of East Florida, south of Musquito Inlet, Lake George and Ouithlacooche River, have not been surveyed, and perhaps half of those surveyed have not been offered for sale.

A great number of plantations cultivated before the Seminole war, in provisions, sugar and cotton, have been abandoned, and many of them are for sale. It is very desirable that these should be re-occupied by an industrious and enterprising population. The price of lands and improvements will be much lower here, than the same qualities are held at in the north and west. There can be no doubt that emigrants from the slave holding states, will speedily occupy many of these vacant plantations; but we can see no good reason why the northern farmers, mechanics and merchants should not share in the enterprise.

A southern climate is not necessarily a sickly one. Florida is undoubtedly as healthy as New-York. It is much more congenial to feeble constitutions, while perhaps, to the robust, it is too debilitating. It cannot be denied that there are situations where stagnant waters and a luxuriant vegetation, usually produce fevers; on the contrary some of our small towns have been resorted to, from every part of America, as well as Europe, for the benefit of health. The writer of this article had been, for three years in a very feeble state of health, and was at length reduced to blindness. When he first visited Pensacola, he had no expectations of recovering his health, or of ever being able to transact any business; yet in six months after his arrival, he was as well in every respect, as he was in childhood, and his health has, with few exceptions, continued good to this time, a period of near twenty years. Many other examples, he could point out, who have been equally fortunate, some of them in the city of New-York.

Many Europeans, as well as inhabitants of the northern states, object to live in a slave holding country, and we must grant that slavery is an evil. There is not indeed so great a proportion of slaves here, as in the rest of the southern states; and in general, slaves, with us, are treated with great humanity. But we want industrious and enterprizing men and women to come among us, to set good examples, to prove that white men, although they may not bear the burning rays of the sun as well as negroes, yet that by order, system and economy, they can accomplish more in one day, than a slave will accomplish in a week. We want them to prove that lands may as easily be improved by judicious agriculture, as they are usually destroyed by slovenly planting. We want them to prove that as much good results from the improvement of the mind, as from the cultivation of the soil. And we verily believe, that there are few parts of this continent, where a man can procure more valuable rewards for his industry, than in Florida.

People in our climate should never expose themselves to a noon-day sun. Experience has taught the natives to sleep in the middle of the day. Emigrants should at least be equally cautious. The mornings are always delightfully cool, and the evenings usually pleasant.

We have seen forty white men employed all summer upon a road, where they were every day exposed to labor in water and mud, yet we never saw men more hearty. So far were they from being worn down, that when they left the work, each man could execute double the labor, in any given period of time, that he could do when he began.

Exposures to the night air, should be avoided as carefully as the rays of noon. And intemperance should be avoided with more care than either. The climate is sufficiently debilitating without the assistance of ardent spirits. Bathing has always been successfully practiced, in warm climates. So far as our observations have extended, it has been infinitely more beneficial in Florida, than medicine of any kind. Sea bathing is as regular a habit in Pensacola, among the old inhabitants, as supper in the evening. In East Florida it is not so common, but is equally beneficial to health.

In selecting land in Florida, the Islands and sea coast, produce the best sea island or black seed cotton. The oak ridges of the interior, the best green seed cotton. Hammock and swamp lands produce the best corn and provisions. A clayey or marly soil is best for cane.

Pine lands, on a substratum of clay, are among the most valuable in the Territory. Many of the swamps have the richest and most inexhaustable soils, but the expense of clearing and ditching these is very great. Hammocks usually occupy high and pleasant situations, on the borders of rivers and lakes, delightful sites for country residences. Most of our pine lands change to hammocks when they are preserved from the ravages of fire.

INDEX.

—

I